Before the Armada

THE GROWTH OF ENGLISH FOREIGN POLICY 1485-1588

by

R. B. WERNHAM

Professor of Modern History in
the University of Oxford

JONATHAN CAPE
THIRTY BEDFORD SQUARE
LONDON

FIRST PUBLISHED 1966
REPRINTED 1969

© R. B. WERNHAM 1966

SBN 224 61065 1

PRINTED IN GREAT BRITAIN BY
WILLIAM LEWIS (PRINTERS) LTD, CARDIFF
BOUND BY A. W. BAIN & CO. LTD, LONDON

Contents

CONTENTS

Maps

Acknowledgments

The author is indebted to Her Majesty's Stationery Office for permission to quote passages from *Letters and Papers, Henry VIII*; *Calendars of State Papers, Foreign, Spanish, Venetian, Scottish*; MS. State Papers, Domestic and Holland; and the Historical MSS Commission's *Salisbury MSS* and *Pepys MSS*.

Grateful acknowledgments are also due to the following authors and publishers for permission to quote extracts from the works named: Professor Michael Lewis, *The Spanish Armada* (B. T. Batsford Ltd), and M. St Clare Byrne, *Letters of King Henry VIII* (Cassell & Co. Ltd).

Preface

MANY histories have been written to describe and explain England's political, constitutional and economic evolution, but surprisingly few to describe and explain the growth of her foreign policy. For the nineteenth and twentieth centuries, it is true, such works do exist, but for the centuries before 1815 Sir John Seeley's *Growth of British Policy* (1558–1688), published in 1895, stands almost alone. There are, of course, studies of the policies of particular statesmen and of particular brief epochs. There are a few more extended surveys of special aspects of England's relations with one or other of her neighbours. Nevertheless, since Seeley wrote, strangely few historians have attempted to explain the development of English foreign policy as a whole over any considerable span of years.

This neglect is perhaps especially surprising in the Tudor period, for the later fifteenth and sixteenth centuries, like the eleventh century and the twentieth century, witnessed fundamental changes in England's circumstances. They witnessed accordingly her adoption of new attitudes towards her neighbours, attitudes that were to persist for three hundred years after the last Tudor's death. Moreover, from Henry VIII's reign onwards the state papers of five countries begin to provide a growing volume of information for the study of those changes and those attitudes. And if that information is not yet as abundant as it becomes in later centuries, the amount of it that has been put into print, in full or in calendared form, surpasses anything that is available for any other century before the nineteenth.

It is indeed to the long succession of editors and transcribers of sixteenth-century state papers that a student of Tudor foreign policy must owe his first and largest debt. They cannot all be equally praised or equally trusted. But from the casual Sir Dudley Digges in the seventeenth century to the industrious Thomas Rymer and the careful Patrick Forbes in the eighteenth and on to Brewer and Gairdner, Gachard and Kervyn de Lettenhove,

9

Mattingly and Lefèvre in more recent times, it is they who have made this book possible.

Furthermore, although there has been no single comprehensive history of Tudor foreign policy, the Tudor period has otherwise been remarkably fortunate in its historians. J. A. Froude's *History of England from the Fall of Wolsey to the Defeat of the Armada*, for all its faults, still after the lapse of a hundred years gives one of the best and liveliest accounts of Elizabeth I's policy before 1588. A. F. Pollard's discussions of the policies of Henry VIII and Wolsey and Somerset remain always stimulating, if sometimes arguable. E. H. Harbison has shrewdly interpreted Mary Tudor's unhappy predicaments. For Elizabeth's reign there are, besides Froude, Conyers Read's massive studies of Burghley and Walsingham; A. L. Rowse's richly stored account of the *Expansion of Elizabethan England*; and Garrett Mattingly's splendid *Defeat of the Spanish Armada*, which crowns the work of a galaxy of maritime historians stretching back from J. A. Williamson to Sir Julian Corbett. All these illuminate brilliantly parts of the picture which this book attempts to show as a whole and in perspective. The references in its notes will suggest something of my obligations to these and to many others who have worked parts of the ground before me, though the recent second edition of Conyers Read's *Bibliography of British History: Tudor Period* makes it unnecessary to catalogue them all.

There is, however, one name that cannot be omitted from even the shortest roll of Tudor historians; and to Sir John Neale, kindliest and most stimulating counsellor and friend since my earliest ventures into Tudor history, I owe my deepest obligation.

My gratitude is also due to all those officers of the Public Record Office from whom I have learned so much for so long and in such pleasant ways.

Finally, to my wife this book owes its title, and for her patient endurance and understanding encouragement while it was being written mere words in a brief preface would be but poor thanks.

Worcester College
Oxford   R. B. WERNHAM

Chapter I

Problems and Patterns

In 1453 England lost the last of her French lands, except for Calais. Twenty-four years later the Burgundian ruler of the Netherlands, her ancient ally, yielded finally to France possession of the Somme towns, Picardy, and the ancestral Duchy of Burgundy itself. Fifteen years later still, in 1492, another old ally, the Duchy of Brittany, was annexed to the French crown. Together these events inaugurated a new era in England's relations with the continent. They stripped away the wide belt of possessions and friendly or satellite territories across the Channel that had served her as a land buffer against invasion. They transferred into French hands the entire southern coast of the Channel from Brest to Boulogne and they drew back England's frontier to her own southern shore.

So great an alteration in the country's strategic situation was bound to bring far-reaching changes in her foreign policy and even in her internal constitution and domestic economy. Therein lies a great part of the interest of the Tudor period. For it was under the Tudor sovereigns that this altered situation grew fully apparent and that the changes which it necessitated were worked out and brought near to completion. It was in their time that England reluctantly but finally abandoned her medieval ambition to win and hold dominions upon the continent of Europe, the 'continentalist' policy based upon land power which she had pursued through most of the later Middle Ages. It was under their rule that she felt her way towards an insular policy based upon sea power and regarding herself as an island 'off' rather than 'of' Europe – the foreign policy that was to be characteristic of modern England until the growth of air power enabled continental foes to overleap her 'moat' and moved one Prime Minister to speak of her frontier being no longer on the Channel but on the Rhine.

England had, of course, lost her continental lands more than once before, in the centuries that had passed since in 1066 William the Conqueror first linked the kingdom of England to the

Duchy of Normandy. But in those past centuries loss had always been redeemed by reconquest. Now the loss was final. The French monarchy had grown too strong to be dismembered as of old. It became, indeed, an aggressor rather than an easy victim of aggression. A line of able, or at least fortunate, kings from Charles VII to Francis I restored its authority and revitalized its organization. The conquest of Guienne and Normandy, Picardy and Brittany, whetted their appetites and, if they had listened to some of their counsellors, they might well have added the western Netherlands to their acquisitions. For Flanders and Artois were also nominal fiefs of the French crown; they lay little more than eighty miles eastward of Paris; and their borders presented few natural obstacles to a French invasion. Happily for England, the riches and weakness of Italy tempted Charles VIII southward in 1494 and France missed perhaps her best opportunity of spreading her power eastward from the Channel through the Narrow Seas to the mouth of the Scheldte, even of the Ems. For, while French kings struggled for mastery over Italy, the Netherlands became part of the mighty 'Habsburg aggregate' when their ruler succeeded to the throne of Spain in 1516 and was elected, as Charles V, to the Holy Roman Empire in 1519. So, when at mid-century the French turned their energies again northward, they found themselves faced there, too, by that same Habsburg power that had thwarted them in Italy.

Nevertheless, this 'filling up of political interstices'[1] between the Loire and the Ems, this absorption of a welter of semi-independent fiefs into the two great rival monarchies of Valois and Habsburg, finally ruled out any hope of England recovering her lost possessions or even resuscitating her lost satellites. Most Englishmen recognized this, though some might still dream, like the young Henry VIII, of new Crécys and fresh Agincourts. For Tudor England had neither the men nor the money to repeat those glories against the new Leviathans of the continent. There, the continual wars and the introduction of firearms were making armies at once larger, more permanent, more professional, and vastly more expensive. Even the King of France and the Emperor broke their credit in maintaining them. And, while the Emperor could expect an income of perhaps £1,100,000 a year and the King of France some £800,000, the ordinary revenue of the King of England, before the breach with Rome and exclusive of grants

from Parliament, was seldom much more than £150,000. Tudor
kings could not afford large standing armies. Nor could they
easily have found the men for them. England's population, at a
generous estimate, can hardly have reached four millions – barely
one-half the population of Spain and perhaps less than one-third
of that of France. Moreover, with her southern coast now open
to direct attack along all the three hundred and fifty miles from
Land's End to Dover and beyond, she could spare comparatively
few of her men for offensive operations overseas. Home defence
absorbed most of the levies of the southern and eastern counties,
just as the levies of the northern shires had long been committed
to watching the Scottish Border. Lack of men and lack of money,
and the growth of two great military powers in western Europe,
thus forced the Tudors into policies more insular and more
defensive than those of their Lancastrian and Plantagenet
predecessors.

It was, of course, the almost simultaneous emergence of those
two continental military powers, or rather the growth of an undying jealousy between them, that made such a change in English
policy possible at all. In earlier centuries, when the Anglo-French
conflict was the central feature of European politics, such a reversion to the defensive could hardly have been contemplated. In
the sixteenth century, however, the central conflict was between
Habsburg and Valois, not between England and France. Moreover, from 1494 until almost 1559 the storm centre of that conflict
moved away southwards to Italy. The great continental rivals and
their allies concentrated their ambitions and their energies upon
the Italian Wars and, by doing so, turned their backs upon
England. They were interested in her only so far as they hoped
to secure her assistance or feared to have her stab them in the
back while their faces were turned to Italy. With the ending of
the Italian Wars, the storm centre did move northwards again.
Yet even now domestic troubles and wars of religion frequently
tied the hands of France; while Spain, nervous of French rivalry
and harassed by revolt in the Netherlands, clung desperately for
as long as she could to the fading hope of friendship with England.

Yet during the sixteenth century England could never rely for
her safety merely upon the mutual jealousies of her powerful
continental neighbours. Each of them coveted her support and
feared her hostility and, though their rivalry centred chiefly upon

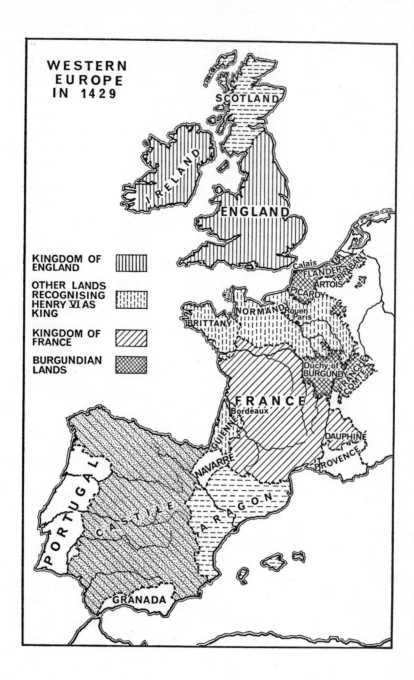

WESTERN
EUROPE
IN 1429

SCOTLAND

IRELAND

ENGLAND

KINGDOM OF
ENGLAND

OTHER LANDS
RECOGNISING
HENRY VI AS
KING

KINGDOM OF
FRANCE

BURGUNDIAN
LANDS

Calais
FLANDERS
BRABANT
ARTOIS
PICARDY
NORMANDY
Rouen
Paris
BRITTANY

Duchy of
BURGUNDY
FRANCHE
COMTÉ

F R A N C E

Bordeaux

DAUPHINÉ

GUIENNE

PROVENCE

NAVARRE

PORTUGAL

C A S T I L E

A R A G O N

GRANADA

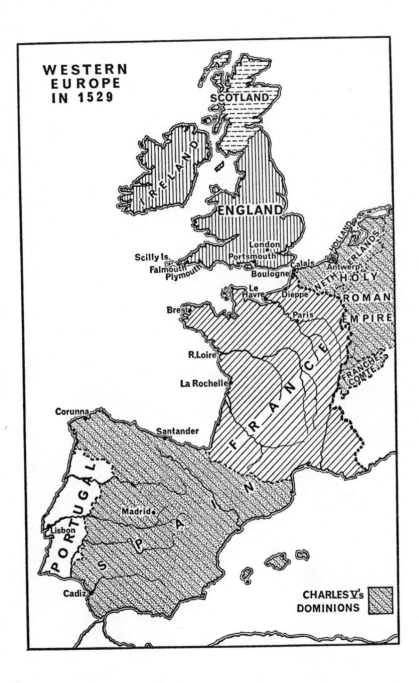

WESTERN
EUROPE
IN 1529

SCOTLAND

IRELAND

ENGLAND

Scilly Is.
Falmouth
Plymouth

London
Portsmouth

Calais
Boulogne

HOLLAND
NETHERLANDS

Antwerp
Brest

Le
Havre
Dieppe

HOLY
ROMAN
EMPIRE

Paris

R. Loire

FRANCE

FRANCHE
COMTE

La Rochelle

Corunna

Santander

PORTUGAL

Madrid

SPAIN

Lisbon

Cadiz

CHARLES V's
DOMINIONS

Italy, the middle Rhine, and the Low Countries, it might at any time shift towards England. To the Habsburgs, an English alliance with France could close the sea route between Spain and the Netherlands; if it also set free French forces to conquer Savoy and Milan, it might in addition snap the Italian link between Spain and the Empire and thus sever the Mediterranean parts of the Habsburg aggregate altogether from the Germanic and Netherlandish parts. To the French, an English alliance with the Habsburgs would certainly expose their northern coasts to invasion and might also enable the Habsburgs to mount an offensive from the Low Countries as well as in Italy. Both sides therefore appreciated the value of English support and either might be tempted to try to secure it by force if ever such an attempt should be made practicable by a temporary loss of power or lapse in vigilance on the part of its rival, or by an evident weakness and lack of unity in England itself. Thus it was that the weakness and divisions of England between 1547 and 1560 made the British Isles, rather than Italy or the Netherlands, for a time the storm centre of Habsburg-Valois rivalry; and that the collapse of the French monarchy in 1585 plunged Elizabethan England finally into the long war with Spain.

Even in more normal times than these, times when the rivalry between French and Habsburgs was more nicely balanced, there was always a danger that one of them might be tempted to use, or at least to threaten to use, force if persuasion seemed to be ineffective. And for such threats, pretexts were seldom lacking in the Tudor period. For in one way the Tudor dynasty's seat upon the English throne was never well assured. Of Henry VII's seven children, only one son and two daughters survived him. The son, Henry VIII, himself left but one weakly son and two daughters; and none of these three had any children at all. This Tudor infertility and 'daughtering out' were serious matters in an age when the sweating sickness, the plague, and other more endemic diseases might extinguish an entire family at any moment, and when men believed that a woman ruler must bring as much woe to the land as a child ruler. It meant that the succession to the throne was seldom fully assured in the Tudor line and was often a cause of most acute anxiety. An uncertain succession kept all possible claimants all too conscious of their pedigrees and was the best possible forcing-ground for faction and domestic dissension.

To make matters worse, the Tudor title to the throne was not itself beyond question. Henry VII was repeatedly challenged by Yorkist pretenders, who at first found ready friends in foreign courts. Henry VIII, when he broke with the Pope, could never forget that Reginald Pole wore the white rose of York as well as the red robe of a Roman cardinal. And that breach with Rome opened the way for new, Catholic, pretenders to take up the role of the dwindling Yorkist stock. It made Mary Tudor a potential rival to her Protestant brother Edward VI and enabled Mary, Queen of Scots, granddaughter of Henry VII's daughter Margaret, to claim the English crown against Henry VIII's daughter Elizabeth I, whom the Papacy first bastardized and then excommunicated. For the continental powers, these Yorkist and Catholic pretenders served as useful levers that could be employed to coerce, perhaps even to overturn, the Tudor monarchy. They made it less than ever possible for England to rely upon her neighbours' jealousies to preserve her own independence. She still had to depend upon her own strength and her own skill – skill as well as strength, for the strength that she could then muster was hardly by itself enough.

The limited military forces of the nation could not be relied upon by themselves to assure England's long coastline against invasion by continental armies superior in experience and equipment and able to choose the place and time for their assault. Land forces could, of course, be supplemented by sea power, for the idea that the encircling sea might serve England 'in the office of a wall or as a moat defensive to a house' was not a Tudor discovery and the use of naval forces to command that moat had been thought out long before the sixteenth century. On the other hand, sea power, even in Elizabethan days, could not yet provide an entirely sure shield. Sixteenth-century ships had only a very limited capacity for sailing to windward and were therefore very much at the mercy of the weather. For England this was a particularly serious handicap, because the prevailing winds in the Channel and Western Approaches blew from between west and south. Southern England was thus for many weeks in the year a lee shore. This meant that French or Spanish fleets coming against her would often sail with the advantage of the weather gauge. They might even find the English fleet penned in its own harbours by the very winds that brought them onward, as the

Armada found Howard and Drake at Plymouth in 1588. More-over, the main bases of the English navy were to the eastward, around the Thames estuary. There the ships lay close at hand to guard the busiest trade routes, those across the Narrow Seas to the Low Countries and over the North Sea to Germany. There, too, they were close to the readiest source of all supplies, London. Henry VII did develop a dockyard at Portsmouth. Under Henry VIII castles were built or strengthened at Sandwich, Walmer, Deal, and Dover to protect the passage from the Thames estuary to the Channel, and that passage was now buoyed and charted by the pilots of Trinity House.[2] Other castles were built to guard the Solent, Falmouth, and even the Scilly Isles. Under Elizabeth I Plymouth was developed and fortified.

Yet Portsmouth, Plymouth, and Falmouth could never in those days replace the Thames ports as main bases. To base the fleet permanently on these Channel ports, even if it had been strategic-ally sound, would have been logistically impracticable. In six weeks at Plymouth in 1589 the Portugal Expedition ate the West Country bare; in the previous year Howard and Drake had been seriously handicapped by the delaying of their supply ships from the east. And the same prevailing winds that held up those supply ships could equally prevent any prompt movement of the fleet from its eastern bases towards the Western Approaches.[3] This inability to sail near the wind also made it impossible to maintain a close blockade of enemy ports to windward. Even at the end of the seventeenth century William III and his Council recognized 'the impossibility of blocking up [the French] fleets for any con-siderable time at Brest in the stormy sea of the Bay of Biscay'.[4] In the sixteenth century it was even less practicable because, until at any rate the latter part of Elizabeth's reign, few ships possessed the endurance for such work. They needed large crews to sail them and before the fifteen eighties few of them could carry enough supplies to keep continuously at sea for more than a few weeks. By the time that they reached their station, their victuals were half gone; and they could stay for only a brief period before running home to replenish their stores. During Tudor times, therefore, the navy, although it developed into a more and more effective first line of defence, could never wholly guarantee England against invasion from the continent.

It was the less able to provide such a guarantee because

England, as Pope Sixtus V remarked, was 'only half an island'[5] and had a land frontier to watch, the northern frontier with Scotland. Ancient enmity still made the Scots look on England's danger as their opportunity and until late in the sixteenth century England had, as it were, one hand tied behind her back by Scotland. Near by, too, there was another island, Ireland, where until the very end of Elizabeth's reign English authority clung precariously to the narrow English Pale along the east coast and where religious differences came to make that hold still more precarious. Both Scotland and Ireland thus made breaks in England's moat. They also might form bridgeheads for a continental invader, for both were liable at any time to ally with England's enemies in Europe. The Scots had in fact been constant allies of France since the early fourteenth century and the Irish were to seek Spanish aid against Elizabeth I.

The turbulence and hostility of their British neighbours was thus an additional reason that prevented the Tudor statesmen from ever becoming indifferent to events on the continent. Even when they abandoned the old ideas of continental conquest, they still had to watch very carefully the actions and attitudes of those who ruled the more likely jumping-off places for an invasion of England. They had to take a special interest in Brittany and the Channel ports, particularly in Calais and Boulogne where England's moat narrowed to a mere score of miles across. They could never be indifferent to the fate of the Netherlands seaboard, of Flanders, Antwerp, Zeeland, and Holland, with their vast wealth and their teeming shipping securely sheltered behind the shoals and sandbanks of the Rhine, Maas, and Scheldte estuaries, not much more than a hundred miles from the Thames estuary and London. The political changes which transformed Brittany in 1492 and the Netherlands after 1567 into garrison areas for the armies and – at least potentially – bases for the fleets of the two great European powers, made everything that occurred there of vital importance to England. She could not stand as a mere spectator on the sidelines of the great contest between French and Habsburgs. She had to join in the play and try to manipulate their rivalry in a manner that would secure her own safety and her own interests.

This was all the more necessary because England's continental interests were not solely strategic. She depended, not indeed for her existence, but certainly for her wealth and prosperity, upon trade with Europe. During the sixteenth century the nature of that dependence altered considerably and in a way that drew English foreign policy farther and farther afield. At first it took the form of an increasing concentration of one great export trade, in woollen cloth, upon one great port, Antwerp. For as woollen cloth became more and more England's largest and richest export, so Antwerp became more and more the distributing centre through which it was dispatched to central and northern Europe, to Italy, and even to eastern lands under Turkish rule. From Antwerp, in return, English merchants brought back the luxuries and the manufactures that were not yet, or could never be, produced at home. This increasing concentration of trade upon Antwerp naturally sharpened England's political interest in the Low Countries and the Narrow Seas.

After the middle of the century, however, Antwerp became less and less satisfactory as a distributive centre. From 1550 the growing volume of English cloth exports periodically glutted its market. In the next decade the beginning of the Netherlands' revolt against Spain impaired its traffic and its prosperity. Thenceforward it grew less reliable and less accessible, until from 1585 onwards the blockade of the Scheldte by the warships of Holland and Zeeland cut off its overseas trade altogether. Elizabethan merchants were thus driven to seek out new markets, or new and more direct ways of trading with old customers whom they had hitherto met at Antwerp. The English government, as its relations with Spain worsened, encouraged these searchings and so helped to bring about a vast expansion in the field, though probably not in the total volume, of England's overseas trade. Direct commercial relations were opened, or reopened, with Germany and the Baltic, with Russia, with the Mediterranean and the Turkish lands, with North Africa and America, and eventually even with India. And where trade went, diplomacy soon had to follow. It followed somewhat reluctantly, and Elizabeth, so far as she could, made the great trading companies themselves provide and pay the agents that their activities made necessary. Thus the Levant Company paid the agent at Constantinople and the Muscovy Company bore much of the cost of embassies to Russia. Nevertheless, the agents went with the Queen's commission; they negotiated in her name; and her policy was compelled to pay some heed to the safety and well-being of her merchants wherever their trade might carry them. Those merchants, too, more especially those belonging to the great chartered companies, Merchant Adventurers, Muscovy, Eastland, and Levant Companies, could not but take a lively interest in the character of royal policy. Some of them sat in the House of Commons, many of them had contacts with Privy Councillors or the friends of Privy Councillors. They could thus do something to ensure that considerations of commerce, as well as considerations of power and national security, were kept alive in the minds of those who shaped or advised upon foreign policy. As a result, trade interests both strengthened and widened the concern of English policy with the affairs of Europe, which still provided and long continued to provide the country's chief markets for her exports and the principal sources of her imports.

This concern was also stimulated by religious sentiment. For England, however eager she might be to work out her own salvation in her own insular fashion, could not remain wholly indifferent to the great conflict between Catholic and Protestant that came to rend sixteenth-century Europe. Many Englishmen found their sympathies deeply engaged on one side or the other. Many went overseas to join in the good fight, as volunteers in the Dutch or Huguenot armies or as exiles for the Roman faith. Their religious activities could never be wholly divorced from politics and inevitably involved their government in international complications from time to time. Further complications resulted from the fevering effect of religious differences upon the ordinary processes of diplomacy.[6] Catholic ambassadors in England soon came to find their friends only among the English Catholics, to rely on them too exclusively for information and to share their hopes and fears. English agents at Catholic courts likewise tended to consort chiefly with Protestant factions. Out of sympathy, indeed often almost out of touch, with the governments to which they were accredited, diplomatic agents on both sides became more and more stridently alarmist in their reports and more quick to counsel or even to attempt desperate remedies of secret plotting or armed intervention. The diplomatic network, so greatly extended during the sixteenth century, was warped from a preservative of peace and harmony into a preparation for war and subversion. It is true that ambassadors, particularly in the latter half of the century, were in general notoriously more bellicose than their governments. Shrewd and calculating politicians like Charles V, Philip II, and Elizabeth I did not easily allow the zeal of a few of their subjects or the impatience of their diplomatic representatives to stampede them into war. Nevertheless, religious enthusiasms could only sharpen English interest in continental affairs, all the more because of the way in which those enthusiasms became entangled with dynastic questions in periods when the succession to the crown was open or unassured.

For all these reasons, then – strategic, dynastic, commercial, religious – Tudor England was never able to cut loose from continental entanglements and relapse into a merely passive insularity. Yet her comparative weakness always made such entanglements dangerous. It called for the highest skill and circumspection in her rulers whenever they had to join in the political rivalries of the continent. And this meant in her kings and queens. For the English state was a monarchy, a monarchy in which the king ruled as well as reigned. The policy of England was therefore the policy of her king. Over foreign affairs in particular, over his relations with fellow-monarchs who likewise ruled as well as reigned, he kept an especially close control and showed an especially close interest. There even Wolsey had to listen to his master's voice and an immense number of Elizabethan state papers bear the trefoils that marked them out for reading by the Queen. In foreign affairs little of importance could be done without the knowledge and consent of the sovereign. Few, except three or four of his 'more inward councillors', usually either knew beforehand what he meant to do or took any active part in its doing. Even these more inward councillors could as a rule only seek to persuade. The sovereign alone could decide and, if he decided contrary to their advice, they had (like Burghley), while bemoaning his choice, to 'make themselves appliable'[7] to his will, wish his policy well, and do their best to bring it to success. The personal inclinations and ambitions of the sovereign, the interests of his family and dynasty, therefore of necessity played an important and usually a decisive part in the shaping of foreign policy.

It was thus fortunate for England that most of the Tudors had a strongly developed sense of the possible and that none of them, except Henry VIII in his younger years, thirsted after military glory. It was perhaps also fortunate that, of the five of them who sat on the throne, the first was a man who had learned in years of precarious exile to abhor needless risks; the third was a mere boy who did not live to manhood; and the last two were women whose sex debarred them from martial exercises. For, as a result, they instinctively pursued policies that for the most part were well suited to their country's needs and resources. They took advantage of the mutual jealousy between the two great continental rivals to secure themselves one powerful ally, at least for a great part of the time and until the balance between Habsburg and Valois was temporarily destroyed by the weakness of France. They played upon the internal stresses that the strain of incessant rivalry eventually produced both in France with the Wars of Religion and in the Spanish monarchy with the revolt of the Netherlands. Also they turned religious divisions to their own profit, not only in France and the Netherlands, but even more notably to wean Scotland from her French dependence and draw her into England's orbit. Yet, except at the beginning of Henry VIII's reign, they did not seriously attempt conquests upon the continent. In general, they relied more upon political skill than upon martial force to secure their safety and to maintain their interests.

This did not mean that martial force was altogether neglected. Henry VIII and Mary did something, Elizabeth I a good deal, to refurbish England's antiquated land forces. Although they could not afford a professional standing army, they did re-enforce the ancient but long-neglected obligation of all able-bodied Englishmen to serve at need in their country's defence. Elizabeth I developed the county trained bands, re-equipped them (though belatedly) with modern firearms, gave them organization and some modicum of training. These bands, the main strength of the nation by land, were essentially 'territorials', a collection of local defence forces, and they had an immensely long front to defend. Nevertheless, the defensive strength of England in 1603 was undoubtedly greater than it had been a hundred years earlier. And if Henry VIII in his later years was unable to find the strength by land to subdue the Scots completely, Elizabeth was able to send out sufficient forces to put her Protestant friends in power at Edinburgh and at the end of her reign, by a mighty effort, to reduce all Ireland to obedience. It was by the exercise of military force, acting within a ring more or less cleared by diplomacy and sea power, that the 'British Problem' was tackled and England's geographical insularity made complete. English military force, sparingly used at critical points and crucial moments, also played a considerable part at the close of the century in holding Spain off from domination over western Europe until the recovery of the French monarchy could again provide an effective continental counterpoise to Spanish power.

It was, however, the remarkable development of English sea power that really made these last achievements possible. For, even though the Tudor navy could never be relied upon to provide a complete insurance against invasion from the continent, its growing strength and ability did appreciably reduce the risk. Moreover, towards the end of the sixteenth century Englishmen began to appreciate its possibilities for offence as well as for defence. They began to realize that it might be used to make England's influence felt among the nations of the continent as well as to secure her own coasts against invasion. The growth of this understanding resulted from the Elizabethan quarrel with Spain and from the peculiar character of the Spanish empire. For Spanish power then, and for another half-century at least, was vitally dependent upon three lines of communication by sea. She had to keep open a route to the Netherlands, where her main field army was engaged from 1567 onwards; and the quickest and best route to the Netherlands lay through the English Channel. Across the Atlantic there was the route by which came the American silver that financed Spanish policy, paid Spanish soldiers and sailors, and subsidized Spain's allies. Through the Channel again – or in the last resort around the north of Scotland – came the masts and cordage from Baltic lands to equip her armadas and much of the corn to feed them. Elizabethan sailors, and Elizabethan statesmen, too, were not slow to see the importance of these Spanish sea communications. The obvious fact that all three routes lay open to attack by naval forces provided the stimulus which transformed English sea power from a coast defence force ancillary to the army into an independent long-range weapon, cheaper and more effective than the great land armies that would have been needed for continental conquests. The technique and the equipment for using this new instrument were far from being perfected or fully understood by 1603. Nor had the Elizabethans imagined the far-reaching effects upon European affairs of its employment in the Mediterranean, which Mansel first demonstrated in James I's reign. Nevertheless, the defeat of the Armada in 1588 had demonstrated its defensive value and the exploits of Drake and his imitators had made clear its offensive possibilities. The more those possibilities were realized, the more England, with Scotland at her side and Ireland under her thumb, was able to detach herself from the affairs of the continent. She had found the answers to the problems posed by the loss of her French lands and continental satellites in the fifteenth century.

She had done so just in time. For the long search after solutions to these external problems had seriously strained the domestic constitution of the English state. Henry VIII's breach with Rome and his later attempts to subjugate Scotland had involved him in defence preparations and wars that had swallowed up his gains from the spoiling of the monasteries. Elizabeth I's long-drawn Spanish war, and more especially the conquest of Ireland at its close, undid all the economy of her earlier years. Moreover, it forced her to resort to most unpopular financial expedients and to impose upon her subjects almost unprecedented burdens of service and taxation. All this, and the long indecisiveness of a war which repeatedly raised high hopes of speedy victory and as frequently dashed them, bred a new temper in the nation. Sixteenth-century Englishmen had been the most king-worshipping people in Europe. Their worship had found its fullest expression in their adulation of Elizabeth, and even old age did not entirely break the spell of the Faery Queen. Few would have so much as thought, let alone dared to say with Essex, that her mind had grown as crooked as her carcase,[8] and even in 1601 her 'golden speech' could bring tears of love and loyalty to angry and critical members of Parliament. Nevertheless, the burdens, frustrations, and grievances of the long Spanish war provoked widespread grumbling and bred a new spirit of criticism. It needed the accession of an alien and less understanding dynasty to the impoverished and indebted crown to turn criticism and grumbling into opposition and eventually rebellion. But the foundations had already been damaged by the strains of war, which had undermined both the monarchy's finances and the popularity of its policies. The great war against Spain had indeed the same kind of effect, though in a lesser degree, upon the Tudor monarchy that the Hundred Years War had had upon the Lancastrian and the Italian wars upon the Valois in France. Unlike the Lancastrians and the Valois, however, the Tudors had largely achieved their aims abroad by the time that the strain of their efforts began to tell at home. England could, for the next half-century or more, almost detach herself from the continent and turn inwards to constitutional experiment and westwards to oceanic and colonial expansion.

Chapter 2

Simnel and Brittany

Of all the Tudor sovereigns Henry VII was probably the least inclined to indulge in an active and spirited foreign policy. We must say 'probably', because his reign is so much more thinly documented than those of his successors that all too often there is little except his actions to suggest what were his motives and purposes. The impression of calm and detached, half amused and half cynical realism that he gives, may itself owe something to this scarcity of personal detail about him. Nevertheless, the most impressive head, sculptured perhaps by Torrigiano, of his effigy in Westminster Abbey certainly suggests a man of cool and powerful intellect, 'a wonder for wise men' as Francis Bacon called him.[1] There are also enough stories to prove his pawky sense of humour and more than enough to testify to his care for money. Yet otherwise he remains a somewhat remote and shadowy figure.

Certain things about him are, however, clear enough. He was twenty-eight when he won the throne of England by defeating and slaying Richard III at Bosworth on August 22nd, 1485, and by then he had already had more than his fill of adventure and excitement. Born in 1457, almost at the beginning of the Wars of the Roses, troubled by ill health in his early years, and forced at the age of fourteen to seek in exile safety from the triumphant Yorkists, he had that suspicious wariness towards men and fortune which seems often to be the legacy of a delicate and insecure boyhood. Once upon the throne, therefore, his main concern, like that of Charles II later – it is perhaps their only resemblance – was not to go upon his travels again. His fourteen years of exile, first in Brittany and latterly in France, may have taught him not to risk his new-won crown by renewing the Lancastrian challenge to the growing strength of the French monarchy. A few months as King of England must certainly have shown a man of his shrewd intelligence that his chief work lay at home. For Richard III's usurpation had reopened the wounds that Edward

27

IV had begun to heal. It had made the monarchy once again the sport of faction and had lowered again respect for the crown which had now been – not inappropriately – picked out of a thorn bush on Bosworth Heath before being placed by Lord Stanley upon Henry's head. Henry's chief tasks must therefore be domestic tasks. He had to bring his subjects back to ordered ways. He had to root out faction, so as to reduce lawlessness from a political to a police problem. He had to enrich the monarchy and enhance its prestige until it was no longer a poor relation among overmighty subjects. He needed to develop the means of making its authority felt through the length and breadth of the land. All this was work enough to occupy his energies to the full and he might well have been content, if it had been possible, to dispense with a foreign policy altogether.

It was, of course, not possible, if only because England still had interests abroad that no king, least of all a new and insecurely seated king, could safely afford to ignore. The ancient quarrel with France was not yet settled and the French might not prove so friendly to Henry now that he was King of England as they had been when he was merely an exiled Lancastrian pretender. For France, having driven the English from Normandy and the Burgundians from Picardy, was now preparing to complete her control of her northern shores by the acquisition of Brittany and perhaps of Artois and Flanders too. Such an extension of French power, so detrimental to England's interests and security, would almost certainly revive the old hostility. In such a quarrel the French could not count at this moment upon much help from their old allies, the Scots. Many Scots, it is true, were eager enough to snatch back Berwick from the English, to whom it had been restored as recently as 1482. But the feeble Scottish King James III, who like the French had encouraged Henry Tudor's bid for the English throne, was too much at loggerheads with his nobles to pick quarrels with anyone else. On the other hand, if there was not much for France to hope from her old Scottish ally, there was equally little for her to fear from her old Burgundian enemy. For the Netherlands since the death of Duke Charles the Bold in 1477 had also been torn by domestic strife. The death of his only child, the Duchess Mary, in 1482 had given faction a new lease of life. Mary's husband, the Austrian Habsburg Archduke Maximilian, found his authority as regent for their infant son, Philip, paralysed by a widespread rebelliousness, particularly among the great cities of Flanders. Moreover Maximilian, thus harassed by his rebellious cities, had no means to spare, and perhaps no great inclination, to curb the Yorkist intrigues of his mother-in-law, the dowager Duchess Margaret. Margaret was a sister of Edward IV of England. Playing Juno to Henry VII's Aeneas, she was a rabid enemy of all Lancastrians and a ready-made godmother for any Yorkist pretender. In her dower lands she had the resources to give their pretences substantial backing and the breakdown of the Netherlands government left her free to act very much as she pleased. The Netherlands therefore could be almost as dangerous to Henry as France or Scotland. It was unlikely that he would be allowed to settle down for long to his tasks at home untroubled by anxieties abroad.

It was true that the Yorkist party had been split in two by Richard III's usurpation and by his notorious[2] connection with the mysterious disappearance of Edward IV's two sons, the boy King Edward V and his little brother Richard, Duke of York. Many Yorkists, forgetting their ancient enmity to Lancaster in their more recent hatred of the usurper, had actively helped Henry to the throne. A number more had come over to him after his victory. Yet there remained an irreconcilable faction, drawn chiefly from those who had stood by Richard to the end. Henry had already defeated them *per verum Dei judicium* in the ordeal by battle at Bosworth – that was indeed his strongest, though not his only, title to the crown. But the god of battles had so often changed his mind during the Wars of the Roses that these irreconcilable men saw little reason to accept Bosworth as his final verdict. It was perhaps unlikely that, if Henry's policies were wise, they would find much support in England. The great majority of Englishmen, even of the great nobles, were weary of civil strife and unwilling to risk life or property in doubtful causes. This very apathy, however, meant that many would stand neutral until the first clash of arms announced which side fortune was likely to favour.[3] An initial military success might thus rally decisive support and amid the widespread apathy comparatively small forces might suffice to win an early victory. This possibility gave hope to the Yorkist cause. For, even if France and Scotland remained cold, there was always help to be had from Margaret of Burgundy. Moreover, in addition to Margaret there was

Ireland. There Henry VII had as yet little control even within the narrow English Pale. Over the Anglo-Irish lords outside, particularly the Fitzgerald Earls of Kildare and Desmond, he had almost none; over the 'Wild Irish' beyond the Pale none at all. The latter could be ignored, but the Anglo-Irish lords (except the Lancastrian Butlers, Earls of Ormond) had long been devoted to the White Rose and their equally strong attachment to home rule made that devotion grow more fervid as the House of York's power to control them passed away. Ireland could provide a base, and the Irish and Margaret the forces, for renewed attempts to re-establish the Yorkist cause. Yorkist plottings, as well as French designs upon Brittany, thus made it unlikely that Henry would be able to relapse into a policy of insular isolation, ignoring the attitudes and activities of his neighbours. The last campaigns of the Wars of the Roses and of the Hundred Years War with France had yet to be fought.

For the first eighteen months of his reign, however, Henry's peace was not seriously troubled. Abroad, the French King Charles VIII, like the Burgundian Duke Philip, was a minor and the French regent, Anne of Beaujeu, was almost as preoccupied at home as Maximilian was in the Netherlands. A combination of rebellious French noblemen, linked to the anti-French party in Brittany, was challenging her authority. Maximilian spasmodically encouraged them, and Anne in revenge lent her support to his Flemish rebels. So neither the Netherlands nor the French governments were eager to provoke an additional quarrel with the peaceable King of England. James III of Scotland, too, harried by his turbulent nobles, listened readily to talk of an Anglo-Scottish alliance and kept in constant communication with the English King. He dared not abandon, nor would Henry VII concede, the Scottish claim to Berwick, and this made a full settlement difficult. But he did agree to a series of truces that preserved England from any serious attacks across her northern borders.[4]

The Yorkists also were temporarily at a stay. If they were to challenge Henry, they must have a Yorkist prince to set up against him. The failure of Lord Lovell's rising early in 1486 showed that. But it was the House of York's misfortune that it could not at this moment provide such a prince. Richard III had murdered both the sons of Edward IV, though a certain mystery still hung about their disappearance. Edward's elder daughter, Elizabeth, became Henry VII's wife in January 1486 and was anyway a woman. His nephew and nearest surviving male kinsman, the Earl of Warwick, was Henry's prisoner and anyway a mere boy. The grown-up John de la Pole, Earl of Lincoln, whom Richard III had named as his heir, had too doubtful a claim and too feeble a following to fill their place. So the Yorkists, with no genuine prince available, had to find and train an impostor. They found one eventually in Lambert Simnel, the twelve-year-old son of an Oxford organ builder; but it took time to train him for his part and it was not until January 1487 that they were able to present him to the Irish lords in a carefully rehearsed impersonation of the young Earl of Warwick. Until 1487, therefore, Henry VII was able to concentrate almost undisturbed upon domestic affairs.

Nor was Simnel's enterprise particularly impressive when it did mature. A twelve-year-old boy, and a fairly obvious impostor to boot, was but a poor challenger to pit against an experienced king in the prime of his manhood. In England only Lincoln, Lord Lovell, and a handful of Richard III's old supporters were ready to risk their necks in so doubtful a venture. Abroad no one except the Irish and Margaret of Burgundy gave any help. Margaret's contribution of 1,500 German mercenaries provided only the bare nucleus of an army and the Irish, who made up the rest, were too ill-equipped to be any match for the royal troops.

Nevertheless, despite the poorness of his claim and the weakness of his forces, Simnel went near to shaking Henry's throne. In the summer of 1487 most of the Anglo-Irish lords rallied to his cause. He was crowned in Dublin as Edward VI and then went over with his Germans and Irish to invade Lancashire. Few Englishmen came to join him and after twelve days his forces were destroyed by Henry at the battle of Stoke on June 16th. Simnel himself was captured, Lincoln was slain, Lovell disappeared (perhaps to an uglier fate at Minster Lovell), and the Yorkist danger was temporarily scotched.

The failure, however, was not of a kind that killed all Yorkist hopes or calmed all Henry's fears. Simnel had achieved a remarkable opening success in Ireland. In England his forces had been crushed only after a stiff three-hour contest. At that battle, too, only half of Henry's forces had come into action. Whether the remainder were genuinely unable to get up in time or were deliberately dragging their feet, the surviving evidence does not make clear. Possibly Henry himself never knew; but even if he did not suspect some of his supporters of getting ready to repeat Sir William Stanley's change of sides at Bosworth, he may well have pondered the hazards of pitched battles. Quite apart from the danger of his vanguard being beaten before his other forces could join it, there was always the chance that a lucky or well-aimed shot might deal him the same fate that had befallen Harold at Hastings. It might still be true, as William Rufus had once told his sailors, that no one had ever heard of a king being drowned in a storm at sea; but in 1487 men did not need to go back to Harold for proof that a King of England could be killed in a battle on land. Clearly, Henry needed to make sure that no Yorkist pretender should ever again compel him to stake his crown upon the uncertain outcome of a pitched battle. He could no longer ignore the attitudes and activities of his neighbours after so small an assistance from abroad had enabled so unpromising a pretender to make so serious a challenge for his throne. The year 1487 is therefore a date as important in the development of his foreign policy as it was in his domestic affairs, where Simnel's defeat was quickly followed by the so-called 'Star Chamber Act' and by the rapid revival of the financial activity of the Chamber.

Henry hardly had time to digest these lessons of Simnel's rising before a crisis in the affairs of Brittany pointed them still more sharply. The Duchy of Brittany, the last great fief of the French crown to preserve its independence, was now ruled by an ageing and ailing widower, Francis II, who had two young daughters but no male heir. For some time Anne of Beaujeu had been intriguing with a faction among the Bretons to annex the Duchy to the royal demesne of France by marrying the elder daughter Anne to the young King Charles VIII. Hitherto Duke Francis and the more patriotic (or more provincially-minded) Bretons had been able to counter these intrigues by allying themselves with the regent's enemies among the French nobility and, in 1486, by arranging that the Breton heiress should marry the Archduke Maximilian, whose prestige (if not his power) had just been enhanced by his election as King of the Romans, as successor-designate to the Holy Roman Emperor, his father Frederick III. By the middle of 1487, however, Anne of Beaujeu had triumphed over her domestic enemies and their leaders, Louis of Orléans and Alain d'Albret, had sought refuge with their confederates in Brittany. There the French army now followed them. Its progress at first was slow. An abortive siege of Nantes held it up for some weeks, discontented its Breton adherents, and gave time for the hostile party in Brittany to rally to their Duke's defence. Maximilian sent him 1,500 men; Ferdinand of Aragon grudgingly allowed d'Albret to recruit another 1,000 in Spain; and Lord Scales brought several hundred volunteers from England. This, however, was to be the sum total of foreign assistance. For in February 1488 Maximilian was made a prisoner by his rebellious Flemish subjects and no one else was prepared to move against the French. The Spanish sovereigns, Ferdinand of Aragon and Isabella of Castile, were now entering upon the final phase in their conquest of Moorish Granada and could spare little. Besides, although they were eager to seize any opportunity to recover from France their lost Pyrenean provinces of Cerdagne and Roussillon, they had no love for the Bretons' ally d'Albret. For, only four years before, d'Albret by marrying his son to the heiress of Navarre had frustrated their designs upon that coveted kingdom. Ferdinand and Isabella, therefore, were not likely to do anything that would further d'Albret's present schemes for his own marriage to Anne of Brittany. Nor was Henry VII in England yet sufficiently alarmed at French progress to turn aside from the work of clearing up after Simnel's rising at home. He did send Christopher Urswick over in May 1488 to attempt mediation. But when the Bretons refused to listen, he renewed his peace treaty with France on July 14th and assured the French ambassador that Scales's adventure had been undertaken without his privity or consent.

For the Bretons' position, though serious, was far from desperate when their army encountered the French forces under la Trémouille at St Aubin-du-Cormier on July 28th, 1488. Indeed, if divided and hesitant counsels had not prevented them from attacking their enemy promptly before he had time to form order of battle, that day might have brought them a notable victory.[5] Instead, it brought their resounding defeat. 'Never within living memory was there so wonderfully complete a rout,' Charles VIII wrote gleefully to his Flemish allies.[6] The Bretons' resistance was broken and on August 20th the Duke capitulated, acknowledging

33

himself the French King's vassal, undertaking that his daughters should not marry without his overlord's consent, promising never again to call foreign forces to his aid, and leaving St Malo, Dinan, Fougères, and St Aubin in French hands as pledges of his sincerity. Three weeks later Duke Francis II died and the French government at once claimed the wardship of the twelve-year-old Anne. With the Bretons themselves divided, Maximilian too weak to save them, and Ferdinand and Isabella still deeply engaged in Granada, the union of Brittany to France seemed on the verge of accomplishment.

Now the acquisition of Brittany by France would bring to England's traditional enemy a considerable increase of power. It would remove a valuable base and asylum for the feudal opponents of the French monarchy. It would give France control of almost the entire southern shore of the Channel and, in addition, add to her dominions a maritime province with a vigorous seafaring population and the best – indeed before the founding of le Havre, almost the only – bases for an invasion of England or for preying upon English trade. It would therefore threaten important and valued English interests, which even so reluctant a warrior as Henry VII could not afford to neglect. If he made no attempt to ward off such a menace, he might ruin his credit at home and his prestige abroad and smooth the path for a more fortunate Simnel. He had to intervene to save 'so great and opulent a Duchy and situate so opportunely to annoy England either for coast or trade'.[7]

Yet a full-scale war with France must grievously strain his still precarious finances and might bring him to that bankruptcy which had ruined his Lancastrian predecessors. Moreover, Anne of Beaujeu would just as readily conspire with his Yorkist enemies as she had with Maximilian's Flemish rebels or with Henry himself against Richard III in 1485. Gratitude for that former favour could not blind a man like Henry to its ulterior purpose, and he was well aware how easily a war with France might bring a new Yorkist rising in its train. Accordingly, he sought to save Breton independence as much by diplomacy as by arms, by rallying the powers of Europe rather than by launching great English armies across the Channel. By making an agreement with Maximilian and by concluding the Treaty of Medina del Campo with Spain in March 1489,[8] he tried to share the burden and limit his own liabilities. By calling a Parliament in January and demanding from it a grant of £100,000 to maintain 10,000 men for one year, he sought to avoid any undue drain upon his ordinary revenues. By the Treaty of Redon in February[9] he obtained the Bretons' promise to pay the cost of the 6,000 men he undertook to send them and he was granted two strong towns as pledges for the payment. Finally, by limiting his Breton expeditionary force to 6,000 men and by confining his military plans and operations strictly to the defence of Brittany, he made clear that he was fighting only to protect England's essential interests, not waging a war of conquest. It is true that his occupation of Morlaix and Concarneau, and perhaps his earlier proposal of marrying Anne of Brittany to his subject, the young Duke of Buckingham, might suggest deeper designs. And the French made the most of this in their propaganda among the Bretons. Nevertheless, the general restraint of his policy does seem to have encouraged Anne of Beaujeu likewise to do her best to limit the Anglo-French quarrel to Brittany and to pursue her ends there as much by intrigue as by force of arms.

However, Henry's attempts to limit his liabilities failed. He was let down both by his subjects and by his allies. His subjects paid only £27,000 of the £100,000 that Parliament had voted[10] and in Yorkshire they rose in rebellion rather than pay anything at all. His allies were equally unsatisfactory. Maximilian, a man who always had too many irons in the fire and too little money in his pocket, was away defending the Austrian Habsburg lands against the Hungarians. So, after sending a few troops in 1489, he let the French King buy him off in July 1489, despite the English help which had saved Dixmude from his rebels and their French allies in June. He returned to the fray next summer and in December 1490 married the Duchess Anne. But he was still too preoccupied by Imperial and Austrian affairs, and by renewed unrest in the Netherlands, to give any effective aid and even his marriage was performed by proxy. The Spanish sovereigns likewise devoted most of their energy to Granada. They did send 2,000 men to Brittany in 1490, but they withdrew them before the year was out. The Bretons themselves grew more than ever divided. One faction, under de Rieu, tried to use the English troops to impose their own views upon the Duchess; d'Albret, despairing of his own suit for her hand, in April 1491 betrayed the fortress of Nantes to the French; and the young Duchess herself came to regard further resistance as hopeless. In December 1491 she threw over Maximilian and married the French King – this time not by proxy. Anne of Beaujeu and Charles VIII had completed the work begun by Joan of Arc and Charles VII. Brittany was theirs and nothing short of a total defeat of the French monarchy was now likely to restore the Duchy's lost independence.

Two courses only were left open to Henry VII. He might attempt to liberate Brittany by conquering France as Henry V had done; or he might sacrifice Brittany, make the best terms that he could with France, and then at leisure try to devise more effective safeguards against another such setback. There could be little doubt what his choice would be. He knew that France had grown too powerful for England to conquer her again single-handed. His allies had proved unreliable and ineffective. His treasury was not yet overflowing with money. He had managed to cover past expenses by getting a fifteenth and tenth from Parliament in 1490 and by collecting a forced loan in 1491. But the Yorkshire rising had warned him that his subjects were more ready to call a martial tune than to pay the piper. In such circumstances to have revived the Lancastrian policy of continental conquest would have been suicidal.

On the other hand, to preserve his credit at home, Henry had to make some show of warlike intention. He could not accept the loss of Brittany without at least an armed protest. Accordingly, in the autumn of 1491, when the ruin of the Breton cause was imminent, he announced his intention of asserting his claim to the crown of France. Thereby he persuaded another Parliament to vote him two more fifteenths and tenths. Yet if Englishmen thought that the days of Agincourt were returning, they were soon sadly deceived. Henry VII's model was not the Lancastrian Henry V but the Yorkist Edward IV. What he sought was another Treaty of Picquigny not another Agincourt victory. All through the spring and summer peace negotiations continued alongside the martial preparations and it was not until the autumn of 1492 that he crossed the Channel with an imposing army of 26,000 men. He did not begin his first operation, the siege of Boulogne, until October 22nd. By then the campaigning season was virtually over and it was clear that he had come to bargain rather than to conquer. He was fortunate to find his adversary of the same mind. Charles VIII was now nearing manhood and eager to set out upon his projected Italian expedition. He was therefore in no mood to haggle over terms, provided he could retain Brittany. So, on November 3rd, 1492, by the treaty of Étaples, he promised to give no aid to Henry's rebels and to pay an indemnity of about £159,000 in half-yearly instalments of £2,500.

Henry VII had salvaged his credit and usefully augmented his income. By his show of force he had won peace – peace, perhaps, without dishonour but no less certainly without victory. For the treaty of Étaples was a major setback to English interests. Brittany's independence was gone. The entire southern shore of the Channel, except for Calais, had become French. The French monarchy had been immensely strengthened by the reduction of this last great independent fief and its power to attack England and harass English trade had been immensely enhanced. For the moment, certainly, the French had been encouraged to turn away towards Italy by Henry's manifest reluctance to revive the Lancastrian tradition of continental conquest. That reluctance was to remain the keynote of his policy throughout his reign and it ensured that he would never provoke a new clash with France. But English goodwill could not by itself guarantee French good behaviour. French ambition might not always find satisfaction beyond the Alps and Anne of Beaujeu's support of the Flemish insurgents against Maximilian had made abundantly clear the direction which its next turn might take. The old feud between France and Burgundy was by no means dead. France might still seek to repeat in Flanders the success she had just achieved in Brittany; and Flanders and Antwerp, the great distributing centres of English cloth, so close to Kent and the Thames estuary, were commercially and strategically of greater importance to England than Brittany had ever been. England's interests and England's security, as well as the security of the Tudor dynasty, required guarantees more reliable than the perhaps temporary change in the objects of French ambition. They needed alliances that would provide adequate deterrents to French aggression against the Low Countries or Calais, or that would at least make it unnecessary for England again to choose between sacrificing a vital interest and dangerously overtaxing her strength in a more or less lone attempt to defend it.

Chapter 3

Perkin Warbeck

SIMNEL'S rising and the crisis over Brittany forced Henry VII out of the somewhat passive attitude towards his neighbours that had characterized the opening months of his reign. Those events had made him realize that he must prevent another Yorkist pretender from obtaining outside England support enough to win the initial military success that might rally to his side the apathetic majority within the kingdom. They had emphasized the importance of the British Problem, of the attitude of Scotland and the Irish. They had made clear how vitally England's strategic position and commercial interests could be affected by changes in the policy or ownership of other lands bordering upon the Channel and Narrow Seas.

For the rest of his reign, therefore, Henry was compelled to pursue a more active and much more elaborate foreign policy than he had at first attempted or perhaps desired. Yet his aims remained essentially defensive, subordinated always to the over-riding domestic purposes of making the monarchy rich and its subjects obedient. As a result, his policy developed piecemeal, as the outcome of a series of defensive reactions to external events, and he would have agreed heartily with a later English foreign minister that 'there is in great affairs so much more as a rule in the minds of the events (if such an expression may be used) than in the minds of the chief actors.'[1] For his policy was never out-lined in any great master document nor ever summarized in any *Testament Politique*. It was not a carefully planned system, foreseen clear and whole from the start. It grew into the likeness of a coherent system because Henry's reactions to external pressures sprang from firm-seated and consistent instincts, or rather from a clear and balanced understanding of the basic interests of the dynasty and the nation. Its aims and its methods were defined gradually, almost reluctantly, as first one factor, then another, came into play and evoked its appropriate response.

The Breton crisis had already pushed Henry the first few steps along this path, but he was still a very long way from the goal when that crisis ended. The treaty of Medina del Campo had given him an alliance with the Spanish kingdoms, recently united by the marriage of Ferdinand of Aragon to Isabella of Castile. Ferdinand, the leading partner so far as Spanish foreign policy was concerned, was the wiliest and most unscrupulous old fox of all Europe's rulers at this time. He took it as an insult to be told that he had cheated the King of France once when he knew that he had cheated him twice. Those who supped with Ferdinand therefore needed a very long spoon and so far the fruits of Medina del Campo had been more satisfying to Spain than to Henry. The Spanish kingdoms were certainly closed to Yorkist pretenders, and Ferdinand and Isabella had promised that their three-year-old youngest daughter Catherine should marry Arthur, the Prince of Wales, when the two children had attained to more marriageable years. This, however, meant some years of waiting and in that age cases of royal breach of promise were by no means uncommon. Meanwhile the meagre help that Spain had given to the Bretons did not augur well for Spanish zeal in any future emergency. Indeed, the Breton crisis had served to emphasize that Spanish interests were centred, even more than the new ambitions of France, upon the Mediterranean.

Moreover, if the Spanish alliance was to serve Henry's purpose, it needed not only to be made less one-sided in its benefits but also to be supplemented by an equally firm and advantageous alliance with the Netherlands, the possible victim of another French aggression. And the unstable English entente with the Netherlands had been completely wrecked by the treaty of Étaples. Maximilian, conveniently forgetting his own past record, chose to regard himself as shamefully deserted by Henry. He was therefore by no means eager to join England in any pact for mutual security. On the contrary, he now began to collaborate with Henry's arch-enemy, Margaret of York, in promoting the designs of a new Yorkist pretender, Perkin Warbeck.

Warbeck, a charming though slightly squint-eyed young man of seventeen, was the son of a Tournai customs official. He had begun his imposture in Ireland. For some time the Yorkist irreconcilables had been looking around for a successor to Simnel and back in 1489 there had been a plot to release Warwick himself. Just when and where they picked upon Perkin, we do not know.

But his arrival in Cork (November 1491), in company with the Yorkist plotter John Taylor[2] though nominally as servant to a Breton merchant, can hardly have been quite so innocent and mercantile as he later pretended. At all events, now or earlier, he was persuaded to impersonate Richard, Duke of York, the younger of Edward IV's murdered sons. The Cork Yorkists and the Earl of Desmond backed him, but Ireland for the most part, once bitten, was twice shy. Warbeck, too, had not yet fully mastered his part – he had, among other things, to learn the English language. So, a tiny force sent from England under James Ormond and Thomas Garth was able at least to contain his rebellion.[3] However, with England and France virtually at war over Brittany, the moment was opportune for this new Yorkist conspiracy and, indeed, the French may well have had something to do with its framing. In 1492 therefore Warbeck left Ireland for the French court. At first he was royally received, but very soon the treaty of Étaples banished him from France. It was then that Maximilian and Margaret took him up and helped him to continue his preparations in the Low Countries. With their help a wide and far-reaching conspiracy developed that involved not only Desmond and the Irish Yorkists but also the new King of Scotland, James IV, and a number of English notables, among them no less a person than Sir William Stanley.

Henry's intelligence service, however, seems to have worked more efficiently than in 1487 and this time he did not under-estimate his danger. He won over Sir Robert Clifford, one of the principal Yorkist agents, and from him and from his own spies learned full details of what was afoot. Then in the autumn of 1494 he struck at those conspirators who were in England. The execution of Lord FitzWalter, Sir Simon Mountford, and several others broke up the Yorkist organization within the kingdom, and in February 1495 the execution of Sir William Stanley demonstrated convincingly that the King had the power, the will, and the knowledge to deal effectively with even the greatest who could be suspected of dabbling in treason. These executions, and the legislation of the 1495 Parliament which followed them, practically removed all danger of a domestic uprising.

About the same time that these events were occurring in England, in October 1494, the mission of Sir Edward Poynings to replace the Anglo-Irish Earl of Kildare as Lord Deputy of

Ireland[4] deprived the Yorkists of that most useful base. Poynings's small forces were insufficient to assert the royal authority effectively over the whole island, but it was among the Anglo-Irish lords and within or around the English Pale that the real danger lay. There Poynings was strong, and skilful, enough to do what was required of him. Kildare was arrested, attainted, and dispatched to England to cool his Yorkist ardour in the Tower of London. English officials were placed in the highest posts of government and justice. The famous Poynings' Laws, passed by the Irish Parliament at Drogheda (1494–5), made all Acts of English Parliaments binding upon Ireland and made it illegal for an Irish Parliament to assemble without the King's assent or to discuss or pass any bills that had not first been approved by the King and his Council in England. Other Acts provided for the resumption of all royal grants made since 1327 and for the establishment of a militia among the English colonists. Yet others forbad private wars, maintenance, and retainers and the special Irish method of supporting them at the expense of the peasantry which was known as coign and livery. It was not to be expected that so ambitious a programme could be fully executed, even within the Pale. But at least Poynings had made it difficult for Warbeck to obtain, as Simnel had obtained, an Irish parliamentary blessing upon his imposture. Above all, the imprisonment of Kildare was a demonstration of Henry's strength that was as convincing to the Irish as Stanley's execution was to the English.

With foreign powers Henry likewise took his precautions or his counter-measures. The treaty of Étaples, and Charles VIII's invasion of Italy two years later, assured him of French quiescence and even goodwill. Continued marriage negotiations with Ferdinand and Isabella kept Spain closed to the Yorkists. The danger zones were thus confined to the Netherlands and Scotland. Against the Netherlands Henry acted with vigour and decision. He answered Maximilian's refusal to abandon Warbeck by prohibiting all English exports to the Low Countries in 1493. The Merchant Adventurers were directed to make Calais instead of Antwerp their staple town and even the German merchants of the Hanseatic Towns had to give a bond of £20,000 as a pledge that they would not carry English cloth into Flanders. There could have been no better demonstration of how seriously Henry regarded the danger from Warbeck than the adoption of this policy of 'economic sanctions' against the customer upon whom the prosperity of the English trading classes and sheepowners chiefly depended.

The immediate effect of Henry's action was to sharpen the quarrel. The Burgundian government placed a counter-embargo on all trade with England and in December 1494 made a formal agreement with Warbeck. Seven months later the pretender launched his attack. The event soon proved that Henry's counter-measures had really broken the enterprise before it started. A brief and very discouraging sojourn off Deal and an abortive attempt, with Desmond's support, to take Waterford soon showed Warbeck how little backing he could look for either in England or in Ireland. Scotland remained and there James IV gave him a more royal welcome and a nobly-born bride. But before the Scots were ready to take the field, Warbeck lost his only other ally, the Netherlands. Maximilian had already begun to forget his anger against Henry in his alarm at Charles VIII's astonishing success in Italy. As early as March 1495 he joined Ferdinand and the Pope in a Holy League to drive the French back over the Alps and his allies had long been urging him to abandon his support of Warbeck in the hope of thereby enticing Henry into their alliance. The Netherlands government, too, had little zest for continuing a dispute that harmed their countries' economy almost as much as it damaged that of England. On February 24th, 1496 they made their peace with Henry. By the treaty, known later as the *Intercursus Magnus*, trade was restored on the old terms and no new duties were to be imposed upon those engaged in it;[5] each government agreed not to countenance the other's rebels; and the Netherlands government promised that the dowager Duchess Margaret should be deprived of her dower lands if she would not conform to this undertaking.

Warbeck could now only hope for Scottish help and even this hope was to prove delusive. For against Scotland, too, Henry had taken his counter-measures. By his policy of friendship with France and now by his agreement with the Netherlands he had deprived James IV of foreign support. The French did indeed send an agent to Edinburgh but he, like the ambassador Ayala sent from Spain in the summer of 1496, had instructions to work for peace. Peace was also urged by the English party among the Scottish nobles, a party that Henry had begun to build up by secret compacts with John Ramsay and Archibald Douglas, Earl of Angus, as long ago as 1491, when the Scots had seemed likely to side actively with France over the Breton question. By now, the growing strength and boldness of this faction was beginning to put a serious restraint upon James's hostility towards England. Moreover, Henry, freed from anxiety about his continental neighbours, was turning his whole attention towards Scotland. A brief and inglorious raid across the Border by James and Warbeck in September 1496 gave him the chance to call upon his subjects once again to open their purses for the defence of their country. The City of London and individual men in the provinces showed only a moderate willingness to lend the King their money, but in January 1497 Parliament responded handsomely. It voted two fifteenths and tenths, and then a subsidy on top of them, to provide 'by sea and land two armies royal for a substantial war to be continued upon the Scots'.[6]

Other work, however, was to be found for one of those armies before it could continue the war upon the Scots. For Henry's new taxes provoked a revolt in the poor and remote county of Cornwall. The Cornishmen were chiefly moved, like the Yorkshiremen in 1489, by a natural dislike of paying taxes at all. They particularly disliked paying towards the punishment of 'a small commotion made of the Scots'[7] at the other end of the kingdom. So, at the end of May some fifteen thousand of them crossed the Tamar and marched towards London to lay their protests before the King. Henry, mindful perhaps of what had happened at Stoke, was careful to concentrate overwhelming forces before he struck at them. But on June 17th – ten years and a day after the defeat of Simnel – he crushed them swiftly and utterly on Blackheath. The Cornishmen were not consciously disloyal to the Tudor dynasty. They seem to have had no Yorkist connections and the only nobleman to join them was a disgruntled Lancastrian, Lord Audley. Their movement was less a rebellion than an armed protest march against what they considered unnecessary and unfair taxation. Nevertheless, that they had been able to march unopposed across the breadth of southern England, indeed that they had marched at all, was another sharp reminder to Henry of the domestic perils that attended upon a too active foreign policy.

Henry little needed the reminder. His purpose had always been to make of Scotland a friend rather than an enemy and as long ago as 1486 he had suggested that the two royal houses should be drawn together by marriage alliances. In 1495 again, he had offered his own elder daughter Margaret as a wife for James IV. Now, as soon as the Cornishmen had been suppressed, he instructed his ambassador, Bishop Fox, to offer peace in return for the surrender of Warbeck and the payment of a reasonable indemnity. At the same time Fox was to suggest a personal meeting between the two kings on English soil. Clearly, Henry's military preparations, like those against France in 1492, were designed to hasten a settlement rather than to prepare a conquest.

James IV, however, was not yet quite ready to make his peace with Henry. At the end of July, indeed, he once more crossed the Border on a raid that proved as useless and inglorious as that of the previous autumn. On the other hand, he did now rid himself of Perkin Warbeck, who had already put to sea with a small band of followers (in a ship called the *Cuckoo*) before Fox could again demand his surrender. Just what Warbeck hoped to achieve, it is not easy to see. He must have known before he sailed that the Cornishmen had been beaten – the news from Blackheath cannot have taken a month to reach Scotland. Anyway, his first landing was at Cork, the scene of his first imposture in 1491. This time he found less support in Ireland than he had done even in 1495. Disappointed there, he soon sailed off to see whether there was still any fire left beneath the ashes of the Cornish revolt. On September 7th, 1497[8] he landed with a few score supporters at Whitesand Bay. A few thousand West Countrymen risked their heads a second time by rallying to him, but they were little better than an unarmed mob. They failed to seize Exeter and, though they eventually advanced as far east as Taunton, Warbeck did not dare with such feeble forces to await the attack of the oncoming royal armies. During the night of September 21st he slipped away and, after failing to break through to the coast, sought sanctuary in Beaulieu Abbey. A few days later he surrendered to Henry and publicly confessed the full story of his imposture.

So, with barely a skirmish on English soil, the second and last really dangerous Yorkist conspiracy flickered out. Henry might still occasionally feel or feign alarm over stirrings among the irreconcilables, as in 1499 when he sent Warbeck and the unfortunate Earl of Warwick to the scaffold. He might still allow his purposes sometimes to be deflected, as with the Hanseatic Towns in 1504, by the bogey of Yorkist pretenders at large in foreign lands. But, with Warbeck's failure, the Yorkist danger ceased to be a dominant concern of his foreign policy.

Nevertheless, although the Yorkists had failed to shake Henry's position at home, they had notably influenced his policy abroad. They had compelled him to complete the development of a balanced and comprehensive policy towards both his continental and his British neighbours. With Warbeck at large, Henry had been kept too busy to be tempted into taking advantage of French entanglements in Italy after 1494. He did in July 1496 join Ferdinand, Maximilian, and the Pope in their Holy League; but he joined only when the League was already seeking an agreement with France and only upon condition that it would not involve him in war. Even in joining the League, therefore, he reaffirmed his renunciation of the ancient enmity.

Besides being encouraged to give this renewed proof of his fixed determination not to provoke French hostility by English aggression, Henry had also been spurred on to create that system of continental alliances which, as the Breton crisis had shown, might still be needed as an insurance against any future French aggression in regions vital to England's security. He had been able both to strengthen and to improve the terms of his alliance with Spain. For Spain, anxious about Italy, had come to covet the support of a strong England no less than England coveted the support of a strong Spain. In 1496 Henry's adhesion to the Holy League was rewarded by an agreement that Catherine should come over to marry Arthur as soon as Arthur was fourteen, that is in 1500. The final defeat of Warbeck, a convincing demonstration that the English monarchy was indeed strong, was followed by the formal betrothal of the pair in August 1497. Two years later they were married by proxy, a ceremony that was repeated in 1500, significantly as a result of Spanish, not of English, insistence. In October 1501 Catherine, and 100,000 crowns of her dowry, arrived in England. On November 14th she and Arthur were married in St Paul's. The Anglo-Spanish alliance, so hardly won in 1489, seemed now firm and assured, on terms almost as beneficial to Henry as to Ferdinand and Isabella.

Five years earlier, in 1496, the *Intercursus Magnus* and his adhesion to the Holy League had given Henry the second ally that he needed on the continent, the Netherlands. Since 1493, too, the accession of Maximilian as Holy Roman Emperor and the transference of the Netherlands government to his son, the Archduke Philip, gave native interests more influence in Netherlands policy and thus strengthened its friendliness towards England. At the same time, Philip's marriage in 1496 to Joanna of Castile, second daughter of Ferdinand and Isabella, linked the Netherlands and Spain much more closely together – within a few years, indeed, much more closely than the Spanish sovereigns had ever intended, for the deaths of their only son Juan (1497), of their eldest daughter Isabella (1498), and of her only son (1500) were by 1500 to leave Joanna heir to both their realms.

These marriages and alliances gave Henry a reasonable hope that he would not again be left to struggle alone, as in 1492. Admittedly, his insurance against the breakdown of his good understanding with France was still the triple alliance of England, Spain, and the Netherlands that had proved so fragile and ineffective in the earlier crisis. But it had now been reconstructed upon much sounder foundations of common interests and dynastic ties. Moreover, the one region on the continent where the French might still threaten vital English interests was the Netherlands themselves. They must assuredly fight in their own defence; and the Spanish sovereigns could hardly ignore altogether an attack upon their own daughter's possessions. Thus Henry could reasonably reckon that, if he were again forced to quarrel with France, he would have on his side an assemblage of strength sufficient to insure against another such setback as he had suffered over Brittany. On the side of the continent he was as secure as diplomacy, matrimony, and the self-interest of other dynasties could make him.

Warbeck's conspiracy, however, had shown the need for security on the British side as well as on the continental side. It had shown again that the precariousness of English rule in Ireland offered an irresistible temptation to the King of England's enemies. It had, in addition, reiterated the old lesson that a hostile Scotland could be a serious nuisance on England's one remaining land frontier, even when her hostility was not encouraged by France. Henry could therefore no more neglect British affairs than he could neglect the affairs of the continent. Yet his Irish and Scottish policies had to be subordinated, just as much as his continental policies, to domestic considerations. He could not there attempt violent and drastic solutions that might overtax his strength and so jeopardize the mounting success of his work at home. The expense of Poynings's administration in Ireland and the Cornish rising against the taxes for a Scottish war made it doubly clear that he could no more think of trying to conquer Ireland and Scotland than of trying to conquer France. In the British Isles, as on the continent, he had to build up a preponder- ance of power on his side by winning over his enemies rather than by bludgeoning them into submission.

Accordingly, in Ireland Poynings was recalled in 1496, as soon as the worst danger from Warbeck was over. The chastened Kildare was then restored to his wonted place as Lord Deputy. According to the well-known story, Henry did this against the advice of some of his counsellors, who warned him that all Ireland could not rule the Earl of Kildare. He replied that, if this was so, then the Earl of Kildare had better rule all Ireland.[9] At a time when the task was beyond the power of anyone else, even of the King, it was the most practical answer and for the remainder of the reign Kildare's loyalty was to justify the risk that Henry had taken. It was obviously a shelving rather than a solution of the real problem, for Kildare's loyalty depended largely upon Henry's willingness not to interfere with his doings. Nevertheless, govern- ment and justice were, however indirectly, exercised in Henry's name and Ireland was no longer either a drain upon his resources or a happy proving ground for Yorkist conspiracy.

Warbeck's failure also enabled Henry to abandon force and to proceed by persuasion with the Scots. James IV, deprived of all foreign encouragement and discouraged by the lukewarmness of his subjects, accepted the generous terms that Henry was ready to offer. So, in September 1497, the truce of Ayton was concluded. Renewed in 1499, in January 1502 it was transformed into a full treaty of peace, the first to be made between the two countries since the breach of 1328. By this treaty James promised to marry Princess Margaret and the actual celebration of that marriage in August 1503 (when Margaret was nearly fourteen) sealed the peace with the firmest guarantee that dynastic diplomacy could provide. This, again, was not an entirely perfect solution, for Scot- land did not abandon her ancient pact with France when she made her novel agreement with England. Peace between Scotland and

47

England was therefore dependent upon the continuance of peace between England and France. Nevertheless, here too, while Henry VII lived, the prospects were good. Indeed, the Anglo-Scottish marriage alliance opened still wider prospects. For by the time it was completed, Margaret's brother Arthur was dead (April 1502) and only the eleven-year-old Prince Henry stood between the new Queen of Scots and the succession to the crown of England. The union of the two crowns was in fact to be deferred for another century by the survival of Prince Henry and the limited fecundity of his numerous wives. But from the marriage of Margaret Tudor to James IV of Scotland there was born the idea of a united realm of Britain, 'with the sea for its frontiers and mutual love for its garrison', that was to haunt statesmen on both sides of the Border until its achievement in 1603.

Perkin Warbeck's six years of adventure between 1491 and 1497 had thus driven Henry VII far along the paths which Simnel's rising and the crisis over Brittany had first forced him to tread. They had compelled him to develop something very like a complete and balanced system of relationships with both his continental and his British neighbours. The core of that system was a good understanding with France. Henry's steady refusal during these years to regard France's involvement in Italy as an opportunity for England to reopen the Breton question showed that, on his side at least, the Étaples settlement (renewed in 1498) was final. He did not abandon the empty style of 'King of France', but, Calais apart, he had clearly abandoned the territorial claims that had gone with it in earlier times. For him that ancient quarrel was over. At the same time the closeness of his alliance with Spain and of his understanding with the Netherlands provided him with reasonable assurance of adequate support if the French on their part should start a new quarrel by pressing claims in the Low Countries that English interests could not tolerate. Within the British Isles, too, he had won over Ireland by loosening the reins that he had once shown himself capable of tightening; and by marrying his daughter to the King of Scots he had planted in Scottish minds new ideas that might in time undermine the old exclusive predominance of French influence. Peace with France and Scotland, reinforced by the reinsurance policy of alliances with Spain and the Netherlands, provided a pattern of relationships behind which England and the Tudor dynasty could prosper unmolested by Yorkist conspiracies or foreign interference. Henry had been moved to sketch the first lines of that pattern by the pressure of Simnel's rising and the Breton succession dispute. Under Warbeck's impulsion he had by 1497 filled in most of its detail. With Arthur's marriage to Catherine in 1501 and Margaret's marriage to James IV in 1503 it became formally complete.

Chapter 4

The Last Years of Henry VII

THE marriage of Prince Arthur to Catherine of Aragon in November 1501 and the treaty of peace with Scotland in January 1502 were the twin peaks of Henry VII's achievement in foreign policy. The formative period in the development of that policy was now over and the remaining years of his reign were occupied chiefly with the care and maintenance of a system whose principles had already been established and whose pattern had already been laid down. This did not mean that the King now took a less vigilant interest in the affairs of his neighbours. On the contrary, his diplomacy became more active than ever and sometimes reached out towards projects that seem, at first sight, to border upon the fantastic. Indeed, many historians have seen in these latter-day projects evidence either of a febrile senility or else of a judgment corrupted by success, a return to Lancastrian megalomania or an anticipation of the futile blusterings of the Wolsey era.

Now it is true that after 1502 Henry's freedom from domestic worries, his abundant wealth, and his high prestige abroad, might well have tempted him towards over-ambitious courses. Yet a more careful scrutiny of his actions suggests that neither the man nor the policies underwent any radical change. The principles governing those policies did not alter and the King, if he became more active, pursued very much the same objects as before. His actions were still defensive reactions to the challenges of external events rather than the outcome of overweening ambitions or deeplaid plans. And if they developed at times a somewhat feverish appearance, in that they only reflected the unstable and swiftchanging political conditions of the continent. For the system of friendships and alliances that Henry had built up, rested upon the shifting sands of continental politics. Whenever the sands moved, the system had to be readjusted and underpinned anew. Care and maintenance therefore called forth no less activity now than building and development had called forth in the fourteen nineties. Indeed, it called forth more, because in the early years of the new century a sudden mortality among princes produced a series of sudden and unforeseen changes that undermined the foundations at several most vital points. Prince Arthur died in April 1502; Elizabeth of York, Henry's Queen, in April 1503; Isabella of Castile in November 1504; and the Archduke Philip of the Netherlands in September 1506. Each of these deaths produced new problems or led to fresh groupings of the powers, and it is those problems and regroupings that explain the extraordinary convolutions of Henry's later policies.

Prince Arthur's death was a grievous blow to his parents, as we know from the touching story of their breaking down and comforting one another by turns.[1] But if Henry grieved as a father, he grieved also as a king. In less than two years, two of his three sons had died – Edmund, the youngest, in June 1500, and now Arthur. The continuance of the Tudor dynasty had suddenly come to depend upon the single life of the one remaining son, Prince Henry; and when Arthur died, Henry was not yet eleven years old. The line of succession to the throne had become dangerously thin and the execution of Sir James Tyrrell for treason in May 1502, along with the arrest of Lord William de la Pole and Lord William Courtenay, suggests that neither Henry VII nor his subjects were blind to this alteration. A royal minority might, and a broken succession almost certainly would, undo all that had been so painstakingly achieved since Bosworth.

Shrewd foreign observers were also conscious of the change in Henry's position. Arthur's death broke the newly forged matrimonial link between England and Spain. The two courts at once set about renewing it by matching the widowed Catherine to her young brother-in-law. But although the Spaniards were no less eager than King Henry to confirm the alliance in this way, they clearly felt that they could now press for better terms. They accordingly tried to include in the new marriage treaty a stipulation that Henry would attack France if the French invaded Spain's new possessions in Italy. Henry would not thus jeopardize his peaceful relations with the new French King, Louis XII, and it was only after much bargaining that a new treaty was at last concluded more or less upon his terms in June 1503. Two days later, the thirteen-year-old Prince Henry was solemnly betrothed to Catherine *per verba de praesenti*. Whether he was of age thus to enter into legally binding contracts was perhaps arguable; but there was still another obstacle more serious than the immaturity of the prospective bridegroom. If the words of the 1503 treaty may be believed,[2] rather than the assertions of Ferdinand and Isabella at the time[3] and of Catherine herself twenty-six years later, Catherine's previous marriage to Prince Arthur had been consummated. At all events, the treaty stated this as a fact and acknowledged that Catherine and Prince Henry therefore stood inside the degrees of consanguinity within which the law of the Church forbad matrimony. Nothing short of a Papal dispensation could enable her to become the lawful wife of her deceased husband's brother. Precedents for such an exercise of the Papal dispensing power were not entirely lacking, but they were few and recent and the new Pope, Julius II, felt, or professed, some doubt about his capacity to grant what Spain and England asked.[4] So it was not until the autumn of 1504 that Henry VII heard from Rome that the dispensation had at length been granted.

The delay had not been due to lack of enthusiasm on either the English or the Spanish side, for relations between the two courts had now grown closer and more friendly than ever. The death of Elizabeth of York in April 1503 had set Henry VII himself looking around the courts of Europe for a second wife by whom he might strengthen the Tudor line, so dangerously attenuated by the deaths of his sons Arthur and Edmund. His choice had turned towards the young Queen Joanna, widow of Ferdinand II of Naples and niece of Ferdinand of Aragon. He therefore needed the good offices, which the Spanish monarchs offered, to further his suit. They in their turn had become more than ever anxious to preserve their English alliance because of the steady worsening of their relations with France. Having failed to stop Louis XII acquiring Milan in 1500, they had incurred his bitter enmity by first agreeing to partition Naples with him in 1501 and then in 1502-3 expelling him from his share of the spoils. Louis had countered by cultivating the Archduke Philip and the Emperor Maximilian. At the time of the partition of Naples he had secured their acquiescence by promising his infant daughter Claude to Philip's small son Charles. In April 1503, after his quarrel with Ferdinand had reopened, he renewed this agreement with Philip and news of this hastened the Spanish sovereigns' acceptance of Henry VII's terms in the new Anglo-Spanish marriage treaty of June. Yet the Franco-Habsburg rapprochement continued and in September

1504 Louis, Philip, and Maximilian entered into an even closer compact. Louis now promised that when Claude and Charles were married and if he himself died without male heirs, Claude should have Milan and Brittany and the French claims in Naples. As Claude was not yet five, Charles not yet four, and Louis no more than forty-two, the provisos were perhaps more significant than the promises. Yet the promises were enough to win Louis at least the neutrality of Philip and Maximilian; and that he was prepared to promise so much, clearly presaged a speedy attempt at vengeance upon Ferdinand. Threatened by the incensed King of France and deprived of their Habsburg allies, Ferdinand and Isabella had greater reason than Henry VII to hasten Catherine's remarriage.

It was at this point, in November 1504, just as Pope Julius's dispensation arrived in Spain, that Isabella died. Thereupon the Spanish kingdoms, first united by her marriage to Ferdinand, began to break apart. For Ferdinand was King only of Aragon. In Castile the lawful ruler was now his and Isabella's eldest surviving daughter Joanna. Moreover, Joanna was devoted to her husband, the Archduke Philip, and Philip, as we have seen, was already drifting rapidly into the camp of Ferdinand's enemies. Isabella had hoped that Joanna might be content to remain in the Netherlands and leave her father to administer Castile as regent in her name. But this hope did not allow for the ambition of Philip or for the spirit of the Castilian nobility. The latter saw an opportunity to regain much of their lost independence by playing off daughter against father; and the Archduke Philip hardly needed his father Maximilian's promptings to grasp at the chance of a crown.

Thus the marriage between the Spanish and Burgundian houses, which in 1496 had seemed to bind Spain and the Netherlands in secure partnership, was now breeding enmity between their rulers. The two allies upon whom Henry depended for his insurance against a possible breakdown of his good relations with France, these two allies were now bitter rivals and one of them, Spain, seemed almost on the verge of disintegrating into its component parts. Here, indeed, was a temptation to the French to turn their ambitions back towards the Netherlands and to present Henry with a repetition in Flanders of the problems that had faced him earlier in Brittany. Here, then, lies the explanation of the tortuous and sometimes sordid shifts of his continental diplomacy during the remaining years of his reign. It explains his urgent, almost exaggerated, gestures of friendliness towards France, his suggestions in 1505 of the possibility of marriage alliances between the English and French royal houses. For, now more than ever, he had to avoid needlessly provoking France.

It explains, too, the increasing closeness of his relations with Philip and his growing estrangement from Ferdinand. Doubtless the growing importance of the Antwerp market to English cloth exporters encouraged and facilitated closer relations with the ruler of the Netherlands. Doubtless, too, Philip acquired a useful diplomatic counter when, in July 1505, he secured the fugitive Edmund de la Pole, Earl of Suffolk, younger brother of the Earl of Lincoln who had fallen at Stoke, and virtually the last of the Yorkist pretenders. But neither the pull of the Antwerp market nor the presence in the Netherlands of the White Rose's last faint hope, can quite explain the rapidity of the Anglo-Burgundian rapprochement in 1505–6 and the extent of Henry's support for Philip against Ferdinand. The explanation of that must be sought in the European situation created by the death of Isabella of Castile and the rivalry between Philip and Ferdinand which followed it.

For, now more than ever, Henry needed continental alliances to insure him against a possible break with France. The first of those alliances must obviously be with the Netherlands, with the potential victim of any French attempt to profit in that region by the rivalry of Philip and Ferdinand. Henry had therefore to side with Philip. But the Netherlands and England alone were not a sufficient counterpoise to the power of France. Henry needed a second ally and he could find one only in the Spanish kingdoms. Yet his necessary friendship with Philip increasingly made friendship with Ferdinand impossible. He was therefore compelled to favour Philip's designs to wrest Castile from Ferdinand, since England and the Netherlands needed the addition of at least Castile to make them any sort of a counterweight to France. In April 1505 he lent Philip £108,000, in September another £30,000,[5] to help him to prepare his and Joanna's expedition to claim the throne of Castile. Throughout most of the year, too, he was discussing the possibility of his own remarriage to Maximilian's daughter Margaret of Savoy.

As his friendship with Philip and Maximilian grew more cordial, his relations with Ferdinand grew more acrimonious. Although the

Papal dispensation came through at last, the negotiations for the remarriage of the widowed Catherine to her young brother-in-law, Prince Henry, made no headway. Henry VII retained the Princess's dowry as a useful bargaining counter and kept her herself upon somewhat short allowance, refusing or evading all her father's requests for the completion of the marriage or her return, with her dowry, to Spain. Moreover, the young prince was persuaded to register a formal protest in June that marriage with his deceased brother's widow was against his will and conscience.[6] This may have been done secretly; but Ferdinand could hardly avoid noticing the growing friendliness of Henry VII and Philip or hearing of the plans for Prince Henry to marry the French princess, Margaret of Angoulême. It was all too clear that he had not only lost his Habsburg allies, but was fast losing his English ally too. Isolated, unable to agree with Philip, and despairing of his ability to hold Castile singlehanded, Ferdinand turned to his old enemy, France. The French, now more afraid of a union of the Netherlands with Spain and Naples under Philip than of Aragon and Naples under Ferdinand, welcomed his advances. Agreement was soon reached and in October 1505 Ferdinand married Germaine de Foix, Louis XII's niece. Moreover, in return for a promised payment of a million crowns, Louis recognized Ferdinand's rights to the kingdom of Naples, so that bone of contention was buried. In the following May, the infant Princess Claude, heiress of Brittany and lately the prospective bride of Charles of the Netherlands, was betrothed to Francis of Angoulême, the heir presumptive of France. Philip's ambitions had driven Ferdinand into the French camp and produced a new and somewhat improbable alignment of the powers of Europe. Louis and Ferdinand were now allied against Philip, Maximilian, and Henry, with Castile as the prize of victory.

But not, perhaps, only Castile. For Louis XII might well think that his best way of aiding his new ally and advantaging himself was to distract Philip from Castile by an attack upon Flanders. If he did, then Henry would be faced with the same dilemma, in still more urgent form, as that which before had baffled him over Brittany. Ferdinand's French alliance made it more than ever necessary to back and hasten Philip's designs. The Archduke needed no goading and in January 1506 he and his wife set out with a large fleet from the Netherlands to take possession of

Joanna's kingdom of Castile. They soon paid the penalty for thus
tempting the Channel winds in midwinter. For, after they had
been two days at sea, a violent storm blew up. The fleet was scattered into various havens along England's southern coast and
Philip and Joanna themselves had to seek refuge in Weymouth.
Henry VII can hardly be blamed if he sought to use this heaven-
sent opportunity to strengthen and formalize his alliance with Burgundy, though it would not be true to say that he took unfair
advantage of Philip's plight. He at once invited Philip and Joanna
to Windsor, where he entertained them royally while their fleet
slowly reassembled and repaired its damage. Philip was installed
as a Knight of the Garter, in return admitting Prince Henry to the
Order of the Golden Fleece. On the same day, February 9th,
Philip and King Henry signed a treaty of alliance by which each
promised to help the other to defend his dominions, present and
future, and to give no aid or countenance to the other's rebels.[7]
The latter provision bore immediate fruit, for in March Philip
handed over the unfortunate Suffolk, whose life Henry promised
to spare. In the treaty Henry also recognized Philip as King of
Castile, though without committing himself to any great efforts to
assist him in asserting his claim. He promised to help only with such
an army as he might be able to spare and as the circumstances
might demand. On March 20th, when Suffolk was already in
Henry's hands, a second treaty was signed, in which Philip and
Joanna promised to secure Henry's marriage to Maximilian's
daughter, Margaret of Savoy, and a dowry of over 300,000 crowns.
Finally, just before his departure in early April, Philip authorized
the opening of commercial negotiations which were to result in an
agreement favourable enough to England to be dubbed the *Intercursus Malus* by the Netherlanders.

In many ways, then, Henry had driven good bargains. He had
secured an alliance promising mutual assistance; he had closed the
Netherlands to English rebels and gained possession of the last
serious Yorkist pretender; he had the promise of a rich wife for
himself and of fresh privileges for his merchants in their principal
foreign market; and he guarded himself against any over-burden-
some military commitments in support of Philip's Castilian design.
Nevertheless, he had aligned himself openly and formally with
Philip's ambitious projects; he had committed himself up to the
hilt politically. That was the price he had to pay in the hope of

preventing Ferdinand from carrying Castile as well as Aragon into the French camp and giving France a preponderance in western Europe that might jeopardize vital English interests.

However, during the next few months it seemed as if Henry's Burgundian investment was paying off handsomely. Philip and Joanna were warmly welcomed in Castile and during the summer established their hold upon the kingdom. France seemed unready to move, except for some underhand encouragement of Duke Charles of Gelderland to reopen his endemic quarrels with the Burgundians. Ferdinand therefore did not dare to resist the taking over of Castile by his own daughter and son-in-law and in fact, by the treaty of Villafavila, recognized Philip as regent there for Joanna. With Philip's success, it seemed that Henry VII had more or less repaired the breach in his foreign arrangements opened by Isabella's death. He was still on good terms with France and Scotland; there was no immediate French threat to Flanders to jeopardize these good relations; and he had the alliance, no longer indeed of the Netherlands and Spain, but still of the Netherlands and Castile to cover him if they should be jeopardized. It was not the best conceivable cover but it was the best available; and he had secured it at no great cost to himself beyond the diplomatic effort involved in negotiating it.

The fateful tale of mortality among princes, however, was not yet complete. In September 1506 the Archduke Philip died and, with him, the union of the Netherlands and Castile. His Netherlands possessions passed to his six-year-old son Charles, whose grandfather, the Emperor Maximilian, reassumed as regent there his now familiar task of Burgundian baby-watching. In Castile Joanna was still Queen, but her highly strung temperament snapped under the shock of her husband's death. Her obvious and morbid insanity – for weeks she carried her husband's coffin with her wherever she went – made her impossible even as a figure-head of Castilian independence and Ferdinand was able to resume the office of regent from which Philip had deposed him.

Once again, therefore, Henry's protective web had been shattered by events over which he could have no control. The government of the Netherlands had passed into the feeble hands of a small boy, guided by the shifty Maximilian; that of Castile into the all-too-capable hands of an unfriendly Ferdinand, already allied to France. In these circumstances it is not altogether surprising that

57

Henry's diplomacy became somewhat feverish during the next couple of years. Taking advantage of Catherine of Aragon's unhappy position in England, he persuaded her and the Spanish ambassador, Dr Puebla, to propose to Ferdinand that he, Henry, should marry the widowed Joanna. In return, possibly some agreement might then be reached about Catherine and her dowry; and possibly Henry might send English archers to join Ferdinand's forces in a crusade against the Moors of North Africa. It is this scheme for his marriage to the mad Joanna that has most aroused the scorn and indignation of the historians of Henry VII's later years. Nevertheless, we should remember that there is some evidence to suggest that Henry, at least at first, was not entirely convinced of the reality of Joanna's madness; that he suspected that the reports of it might be another trick of the wily Ferdinand.[8] Also, if one of Henry's purposes in seeking a second wife was to strengthen the succession by begetting children, we must remember that sixteenth-century ideas about psychology and heredity differed widely from ours; that in fact Joanna's six children all proved quite sane; and that Dr Puebla may not have been merely cynical in suggesting that marriage to so sensible a man as Henry VII might be the best cure for her derangement.[9]

It seems clear, however, that Henry's motive was primarily political. The proposal was an attempt to provide a desperate remedy for the broken pattern of his continental alliances. It seemed the only way now left open to preserve the triple alliance of England, the Netherlands, and Castile, England's insurance against undue trouble with France in Flanders. But the way proved not to be open. For, even if Ferdinand should prove amenable to pressure through Catherine – and he did seem prepared to go some way in order to secure her marriage to Prince Henry – the mounting insanity of Joanna made projects for her remarriage more and more obviously chimerical. Accordingly Henry, while still doing his best to isolate Ferdinand, gradually abandoned hope of rebuilding the broken trinity of England, the Netherlands, and Castile. He turned instead to the policy of establishing a triple entente between England, the Netherlands, and France. It was not altogether easy, for the Netherlands government was by 1507 quarrelling again with the Duke of Gelderland, whose French and Scottish connections gave these quarrels a more than local significance. Moreover, Maximilian's determination to make a journey into Italy, to receive the Imperial crown from the Pope, not only alarmed Venice but also roused French fears for their possession of Milan.

However, Henry's new policy made fair headway. He confirmed his friendship with the Netherlands by abandoning in 1507 the commercial concessions which he had won for English merchants by the *Intercursus Malus*. He mediated a peace between Maximilian and the Duke of Gelderland. Then, in December 1507, he secured Maximilian's agreement to a marriage between the young Arch-duke Charles and Henry's younger daughter Mary. The kingdom of Castile, it was also agreed, was to be their marriage portion, though just how it was to be secured for them was not made clear. Possibly Henry hoped that the growing isolation of Ferdinand might eventually bring these castles in Spain within tangible reach. More likely the provision was a token compensation for his fading hopes of his own marriage to Joanna. Certainly, in 1508 his main energies were directed towards Maximilian and Louis XII rather than against Ferdinand directly. He pressed again his suit for the hand of Margaret of Savoy until, and even after, that lady had made unmistakably clear her conviction that three experi-ences of matrimony were enough for any one lifetime.[10] At the same time, he reiterated his goodwill towards France by reviving his former proposal for Prince Henry to marry Margaret of Angoulême; and when, in that same summer, Maximilian made a truce with Venice and abandoned his proposed Italian journey, the last obvious cause of friction between France and the Habs-burgs seemed to have been smoothed away. Thus, when the congress of Cambrai met at the end of the year, ostensibly to plan a crusade against the Turks, Henry for a time imagined that it would prove the last step in the establishing of a direct understanding be-tween his French and Habsburg allies and the final isolation of Ferdinand.

Things did not fall out quite as he had anticipated. Louis XII, whose chief concern was to safeguard and enlarge his possession of Milan, was not prepared to sacrifice his understanding with Ferdi-nand, his most dangerous Italian rival, for an entente with England and the Netherlands, whose interests and influence in Italy were negligible. In 1505 he had bought Spanish acquiescence in his claims in northern Italy, in Milan, by recognizing Ferdi-nand's rights in the south, in Naples. Now in 1508, under cover of the crusading talks at Cambrai, he was planning to buy off his other Italian rival, the Emperor Maximilian, by inducing him to join in partitioning the mainland territories of the Venetian republic. The Pope was prepared to give the project his blessing, but it was essential that it should also have Ferdinand's support. The offer of the Adriatic towns which Venice had occupied, and the prospect of strengthening his alliance with France and restoring his relations with the Habsburgs, were enough to win his ready agreement. Thus, when the League of Cambrai was formed against Venice in December 1508, its members were the Pope, Louis XII, Maximilian, the Archduke Charles – and Ferdinand. It was Henry VII who was left out, not Ferdinand.

However, although he had been left out, Henry was hardly left isolated. For all the Cambrai powers showed themselves desirous of his goodwill. France cultivated his friendship; Ferdinand was still ready to talk of Catherine's marriage; and Maximilian showed his friendly desire for English subsidies by allowing the marriage of Charles and Mary to be celebrated by proxy within a week of the conclusion of the League. All, moreover, were bent upon despoiling Italy, where England had no interests that they could harm. Indeed, the humbling of Venice might even benefit her reviving trade in the Mediterranean. Actually, this sudden coming together of all the continental powers was for Henry more a gain than a loss. Since 1496, or even earlier, the main purpose of his policy had been to cherish the friendship of the Netherlands and to provide a deterrent to any French aggression there. The Netherlands apart, there was very little direct clash of interest between England and France; and England had good reason to avoid a quarrel which would probably involve a further quarrel with Scotland and so prevent the isolation of the British question from continental politics. It was only because a clash between English and French interests might arise indirectly out of a French attack upon the Netherlands that Henry had been so eager to build up a deterrent system of continental alliances. Now, by the League of Cambrai, that danger was removed. Louis, Maximilian, and Charles were allies and Henry could be friends with all his neighbours. So long as the League lasted, the Netherlands were safe from French attack. The danger, which Henry's alliances had been designed to meet, had ceased. That danger might revive when the League broke up, but its break up must surely provide excellent opportunities to rebuild the alliances which its existence made superfluous.

The truth was that England's vital continental interests were still confined to the regions just across the Channel and the Narrow Seas. Therefore, so long as Italy, where England had few interests and no influence, remained the centre of attraction for the continental powers, there was little danger that any of those powers would seriously threaten England. Henry VII knew this well enough and probably did not worry overmuch about his exclusion from the League of Cambrai. There would be time enough to take up again the complicated threads of his continental policy when the Cambrai allies fell out and their renewed rivalries began again to involve English interests. When that time came, however, Henry VII was dead (April 1509) and the direction of English policy was in more ambitious and less prudent hands.

Chapter 5

Sea Power and Trade, 1485–1509

ONE side of Henry VII's foreign policy remains to be considered. Francis Bacon wrote of him that 'he could not endure to have trade sick' and a modern historian adds that 'he pursued a settled design for capturing trade.'[1] Both perhaps claim a little too much for him. For, here again, although we can see a system of policy developing, a general pattern emerging, it hardly looks as if the system was any more foreseen and foredesigned than the rest of Henry's foreign policy. The pattern seems again to have been gradually built up by a series of coherent responses to external opportunities and challenges. Moreover, Henry repeatedly subordinated, and sometimes even sacrificed, the encouragement of trade and navigation to more pressing dynastic and strategic interests. It was, in fact, seldom more than a subsidiary purpose in his policy.

This is not to say that he did not regard it as important. After all, the more overseas trade flourished, the healthier his customs revenue became and the customs produced something approaching one-third of his total ordinary revenue.[2] Besides, overseas trade meant ships; and the more of those ships were English, the greater would be England's naval power. Fifteenth-century Englishmen were fully aware of the importance of guarding well their 'moat', of maritime supremacy in the Narrow Seas and the Channel. But Henry VII could no more afford a large and permanent royal navy than he could afford a large and standing army. On land he had his small, regular, bodyguard, the Yeomen of the Guard. But for his armies he relied upon the ancient obligation of all able-bodied Englishmen to serve, and of all Englishmen of property to provide weapons, for the defence of their country, supplementing this by the somewhat less ancient device of commissioning nobles and gentlemen to raise companies to serve him under indentures of war.

At sea, in like fashion, he relied upon a small and permanent royal navy, supplemented at need by merchant vessels hired for the occasion. This royal navy was a slightly more substantial nucleus than the Yeomen of the Guard could provide on land. It was also essentially Henry's own creation. He did inherit four 'King's ships' from the Yorkists, but these seem to have been vessels designed rather for trade than for war. The five that he handed on to his son in 1509 included, on the other hand, at least two that were, for their day, powerful and imposing warships. The *Regent*, a four-master of about 600 tons, completed in 1490, carried 225 guns, 180 of them serpentines, the heaviest naval artillery then in use. The *Sovereign*, completed in the same year, carried 141 guns. Now it is true that they also carried bows and arrows as standard equipment and that even the serpentine fired only a quarter-pound ball. They relied upon their artillery, that is to say, only to bring their enemy to a standstill by damaging his rigging and upper works. After that, it was up to the archers to sweep his decks and to the swords-men and billmen to take him by boarding in the traditional man-ner. For this reason, when fully manned they carried almost twice as many soldiers as sailors. They also retained the traditional high poops and forecastles, from which the soldiers could more easily jump down on to the enemy's deck but which made them far from easy for the sailors to handle, least of all to work to windward. And, of course, their sea endurance was very limited, for with all those guns and their powder and shot, all the sailors and all the soldiers, they had scant room for stores for a lengthy voyage.

These last handicaps were somewhat lessened by Henry's de-velopment of a naval base for his ships at Portsmouth, where the royal navy's first dry dock was constructed between 1495 and 1497. This made it much more possible for his warships to operate for considerable periods of time in the Channel without returning to the main bases in the Medway and the Thames estuary. The same vessels could be employed either westwards in the Channel or eastwards in the Narrow Seas. At the same time Henry developed these eastward bases and assembled at Greenwich and Woolwich stores of guns, ammunition, bows and arrows from which hired merchant vessels could be speedily turned into useful fighting units. No other sovereign in western Europe possessed warships of such fire-power, bases that gave their warships such mobility, or organization for reinforcing them so speedily.

Nevertheless, the number of the King's ships was very small, far too small for all the tasks that war might require of them. In war, they would need to be very substantially reinforced with merchant vessels hired and armed for the occasion. Thus, during the crisis over Brittany, Henry hired a considerable number of vessels from the subjects of his new Spanish ally. Now it seems clear that he hired Spanish ships because he wished to avoid interfering with his own subjects' trade. But it may also have been that his subjects were unable as yet to provide the numbers and kinds of ships that he needed. For the quantity of English shipping, and the number of sizable ships suitable as naval auxiliaries and transports, were probably not yet great enough to provide substantial reinforcements to the royal navy without either causing an appreciable hold-up of overseas trade or else allowing a good deal more of that trade to pass into the hands of foreign carriers who would be more easily let in than pushed out again.

Moreover, the continued growth of English merchant shipping was restricted by the fact that foreign carriers had long controlled a considerable part of the country's overseas trade. Indeed, in the fifteenth century there had been a shrinkage in the areas to which English merchants were able to trade direct in English ships. The great commercial league of north German cities, the Hansa, had driven English traders out of the Baltic and Scandinavia and almost out of Iceland. They had shut down English trading establishments at Danzig and Bergen and secured a practical monopoly of English commerce with those regions. By the treaty of Utrecht in 1474 they had promised, in return for the restoration of their former privileges in England and their headquarters, the Steelyard, in London, to give the English a reciprocal freedom in their territories. But they had shown no inclination to perform that promise and the English remained virtually excluded from direct trade with Scandinavia and the Baltic. Meanwhile the Venetians maintained a somewhat similar stranglehold upon England's Mediterranean trade. Their galleys, mistrusting the as yet ill-buoyed and ill-charted passage past the Goodwin Sands and into the Thames estuary, made Southampton their usual port of call. It was they who brought thither the spices and luxuries of the Orient, the malmsey and sweet wines of Greece and Candia (Crete) and the currants of the Levant. It was they who took thence, along with tin and other goods, the wool and woollen cloth of England to be dyed and finished in the workshops of Venice and northern Italy, as the Hansards took some of the cloth from London to the workshops of Antwerp and Flanders. The Venetians, in fact, excluded the English traders from the Mediterranean as effectively as the Hansards excluded them from the Baltic. Even in the wine trade to Bordeaux and Gascony, and the London and West Country cloth exports to Spain, foreign carriers played a part. In the Netherlands, it is true, the English Merchant Adventurers and the wool Staplers increasingly dominated the trade in cloth and wool; yet even there the Hansards and other alien carriers had a considerable share.

Now all this necessarily constricted the growth of England's merchant shipping, of the reserve of shipping upon which the royal navy must chiefly depend in time of war. But there was more to it than that. Bacon may have been right in thinking that Henry VII 'bowed the ancient policy of this estate from consideration of plenty to consideration of power'.[3] Yet Henry was well aware that plenty means prosperity and that his subjects' prosperity was one of the surest guarantees of his own power. And, owing to the peculiar character of fifteenth-century England's economy, overseas trade – though not essential to the nation's survival as it became three centuries later – could make or mar the prosperity of some of the most important sections of English society. For England's one great export had been for centuries the wool of her sheep. In the fifteenth century, as a native clothmaking industry spread more widely over the countryside, woollen cloth was more and more taking the place of wool. But, whether it was wool or woollen cloth, its ability to find markets overseas was a matter of vital concern, not only to the Merchant Adventurers of London and the south-east and east coast ports, or to the clothiers of the West Country, the Midlands, and East Anglia, but also to the landowners and farmers whose sheep provided the wool and to the families, in the country as well as in the towns, who did the spinning and the weaving. A depression in the export trade, or its manipulation by alien merchants for foreign profit, could hit them all. During the Wars of the Roses, the Yorkist inclinations of great cities like London and small clothing centres like Newbury in Berkshire[4] – soon to be the home of one of the most famous of sixteenth-century clothiers, John Winchcombe – were in part at least inspired by hopes that Edward IV would give stronger government and better trade than the feeble Lancastrian. They looked for no less from the first Tudor.

Henry was not slow to answer their expectations. He gave direct encouragement to native shipbuilding by offering a bounty, increasing with tonnage, to any of his subjects who built ships of eighty tons and upwards. But he appreciated that few would build ships, even with the help of his bounty, unless those ships could earn their livings by finding markets to which they could carry their cargoes. His, or his government's, awareness of this was made clear at once, in his first Parliament in 1485. An Act[5] was then passed forbidding the sale throughout his dominions of Gascon wines unless they had been imported in ships owned and predominantly manned by his subjects. In 1489 another Act[6] extended the same prohibition to the import of Toulouse woad. In addition, it forbad the King's subjects – though not alien merchants – to export or import any goods in foreign ships when English ships were available. These were sensible measures, at least in so far as they did not attempt too much. And to judge from the effect upon Spanish shipping and the outcries of the Hansards, they were in Henry VII's time quite effectively enforced.[7]

However, it was obviously of little avail to insist that English ships be used for English trade unless reasonable conditions could be assured to them when they reached their overseas markets. Diplomacy therefore had to be used to supplement legislation. And the interests of trade were, in the end, to involve Henry's diplomacy over a far wider area of Europe even than that into which it was drawn by dynastic and strategic interests. His first care, none the less, was always to confirm and if possible to extend the right of English merchants to trade freely in the Netherlands. For the Netherlands had long been England's principal overseas market, or at least distributing centre; and during Henry's reign and his son's the remarkable growth of Antwerp drew more and more of England's growing cloth production thither.[8] The improvement of access by water up the Scheldte, and the comparative ease and cheapness of overland and river communications with the Rhineland and south Germany, made Antwerp from the mid-fifteenth century onwards a natural meeting place for English exporters and their German customers. It became even more so when the political turbulence of Bruges and Ghent made the Flemish cities less attractive as trading centres. Many of the Italian merchants followed the English and in 1488 Maximilian, during his conflict with the Flemish cities, required all 'nations' of foreign merchants to transfer themselves from Bruges to Antwerp. More and more of them did so. In 1499 the King of Portugal's factor, who had already moved with the rest in 1488 and stayed until 1493, transferred his headquarters permanently to Antwerp. In August 1501 the first consignment of spices from Lisbon arrived there and for the next fifty years Antwerp remained the entrepôt for Portuguese spices for all north-western and central Europe. With this it became the economic Carfax of Europe, the meeting point and exchange centre for the four great international and intercontinental trades. From the Baltic area the Hansards brought the corn, timber, hemp, tar, that the Iberian and Mediterranean countries as well as the Netherlands increasingly needed; from England Merchant Adventurers and Staplers, and Hansards too, brought cloth to be sold, finished, and distributed over northern, central, and even eastern Europe; from Augsburg, Frankfort, and other cities of southern and western Germany came metals, especially copper and silver; while from Spain came fine wool and from Lisbon the Portuguese brought their oriental spices. To assist these operations, banking, credit, and insurance facilities rapidly expanded, while in and around the city cloth finishing and metal working and other industries flourished.

Antwerp during the first half of the sixteenth century was indeed the economic wonder of the age, if not of the ages; and its greatness drew all men and all trades towards it, not least or last the English cloth export. Even at the beginning of Henry VII's reign its attraction was great, although at that stage – before Vasco da Gama had reached India or the Portuguese royal factor had finally deserted Bruges – the English merchants were still able to play off Middelburg, Bergen-op-Zoom, and other towns against it. By maintaining their right to trade to any of those towns, they were able to extort privileges from all without committing themselves exclusively to one. But as the predominance of Antwerp increased and as the power of the Burgundian dukes, always supporters of loyal Antwerp against rebellious Bruges and Ghent, recovered from the long weakness of Philip's minority, so the English merchants' chances of bargaining for themselves in this fashion decreased. More and more they needed the support of the King's diplomacy.

Henry was eventually to give that support abundantly, but during the first ten years of his reign his merchants were more instruments, even victims, than beneficiaries of his foreign policy. In those years trade was certainly manipulated in the interests of state policy rather than state policy being shaped in the interests of trade. Thus, in the late summer of 1493, when Maximilian and the Netherlands refused to curb the activities of the pretender Perkin Warbeck, Henry's retaliation was to forbid the Merchant Adventurers to trade to Antwerp or other Low Country ports and to order them to join the Staplers in using Calais as their staple. He in fact sought to apply economic sanctions by diverting English cloth exports away from the Netherlands. How effective those sanctions were, it is hard to say. They remained in force until the *Intercursus Magnus* was concluded in February 1496 and they were answered by the counter-embargo which the Netherlands government imposed in May 1494. But although the double restraint of trade caused serious loss and distress to the Netherlanders, it may well be that it hit the more backward economy of England at least as hard, especially as something of what English merchants lost the Hansards gained, at least for a time. In the end it was the Netherlands government that gave way, but the reason for this is probably to be found in the exigencies of general policy rather than in the strain of economic pressures. At least, it was the failure of Warbeck and the desire of Maximilian and Philip to secure Henry's support in their negotiations with France, as well as their desire to reopen trade, that led them to conclude a general settlement in February 1496.

The economic provisions of this settlement, which we have come to know as the *Intercursus Magnus*,[9] were indeed the Magna Carta of the English traders' position in the Netherlands. They were allowed to sell their goods wholesale and freely in any part of Philip's dominions except Flanders (in 1502 this was extended to the Emperor Maximilian's dominions as well); they were not to be subjected to new tolls and duties in excess of those prevailing during the past fifty years; they were promised speedy and fair justice in the Archduke's courts; and careful, precise rules were laid down about inspection of cargoes, punishments for fraudulent dealing, recovery of debts, carriage of arms and contraband, and almost all the matters over which disputes might arise. If Henry had sacrificed trade to his dynastic necessities in 1493, he amply repaid the debt in 1496.

But the price of these liberties was eternal vigilance. The Intercourse was hardly ratified before Philip imposed a new import duty on English cloth, which the Merchant Adventurers regarded as a plain breach of its terms. Promptly Henry ordered them back from Antwerp to Calais once more. Hard bargaining followed and in July 1497 a new agreement was concluded by which the new duty was abolished. But now Philip tried to insist that the English should confine their trade to Antwerp and Bergen-op-Zoom as their staple towns. Determined not thus to lessen their opportunities for playing off town against town, they refused to return upon such conditions and remained at Calais until the autumn of 1498. By then a new and more satisfactory settlement was in sight. It was finally agreed at Calais in May 1499.[10] The 1496 Intercourse was confirmed. Henry consented to some reduction in the duty on wool sold to the Netherlanders by the Merchants of the Staple at Calais. Philip, for his part, confirmed the withdrawal of his obnoxious new duty on English cloth and abandoned his attempt to confine the Merchant Adventurers to Antwerp and Bergen-op-Zoom. They were again to be free to sell their cloth wholesale in any part of his dominions except Flanders.

In 1504 there were fresh disputes about duties, Philip perhaps hoping that the presence in his father's dominions of the White Rose of York, the fugitive Earl of Suffolk, might soften Henry's resistance. If so, he deceived himself, for Henry's answer was the usual one of transferring the cloth staple to Calais (January 1505) and then suspending trade altogether. Then, however, came the death of Isabella of Castile and Philip's unintentional visit to England on his way to claim his wife's Castilian inheritance. At his departure he empowered commissioners to settle the commercial disputes between his subjects and Henry's. The result of this was the so-called *Intercursus Malus* of April 1506 whose principal novelty was that it allowed the English to sell their cloth wholesale in any part of Philip's dominions and retail anywhere except in Flanders. The importance of this treaty can, however, easily be exaggerated. Philip died before ratifying it and his death, as we have seen, made Henry too anxious for the Netherlands alliance to insist upon conditions that they could hardly tolerate. When an agreement was finally made and ratified in 1507, it took the form of a straightforward confirmation of the 1496 Intercourse. The permission for the English to sell their cloth retail was left out. Nevertheless, if Henry once again was unable to hold all his gains, he had done a good deal to establish the Merchant Adventurers in a secure position and a wide freedom in the Netherlands market. Moreover, the new charter which he granted to them in 1505 gave them more of a monopoly over this principal 'vent' for England's cloth exports; greater powers to regulate trading practices, restrain cut-throat competition, and to settle disputes among English traders; and better organization to exercise these powers. In a measure this was a limitation of private initiative, a restriction of trade to a favoured Fellowship, though the new £5 entry fee was only a quarter of the fee that the Adventurers were seeking to impose. But probably at this stage the powers of direction and organized bargaining that the new charter confirmed were more likely to expand trade in this vital and challenging market than the competitive and unco-ordinated efforts of private and individual enterprise. Thus organized, the Fellowship of Merchant Adventurers could hold its own at, and with, Antwerp; backed by royal diplomacy, it could hold its own with the Netherlands government. With Antwerp just entering upon the golden age of its greatness, these were achievements of no small significance.

Henry VII, however, was not a man who liked to see all his eggs in one basket. Hence, just as he sought alliances with Burgundy and Spain to insure against any failure of his friendship with France, so also he sought to encourage English merchants into other regions to insure against an excessive dependence upon Antwerp. In 1486 he made a commercial agreement with the Duke of Brittany; and another with the King of France, which removed all the impediments and burdens that had been imposed upon Anglo-French trade since Edward IV's accession. The quarrel over Brittany led to new French impositions upon English merchants, but these again were mitigated by the treaty of Étaples in 1492 and removed altogether in 1495, while a further Anglo-French commercial treaty was concluded in 1497. In 1489 the old treaty of 1378 with Portugal was confirmed and renewed.

In December 1485 Henry confirmed the privileges granted to Spanish merchants by Edward IV in 1466, which exempted them from the duties that other aliens (except the Hansards) paid when exporting English goods, and placed them upon the same footing as English traders. Under shelter of these privileges, they had come to dominate the small but growing Anglo-Spanish trade. They had also gained a share in the Gascon wine trade and a more considerable share in the Toulouse woad traffic. The two 'navigation' Acts of 1485 and 1489 put some check on their activity in these last two fields; and then came the commercial clauses of the treaty of Medina del Campo (1489).[11] These regulated the issue of letters of mark, or reprisal, to subjects of either crown who were injured by subjects of the other; they allowed subjects of either crown to dwell and trade in the dominions of the other on the same footing as its natives; and they fixed customs duties on both sides to the rates prevailing thirty years previously. The Spanish councillors who negotiated these clauses must have been nodding badly. For thirty years ago meant about 1460, well before the concessions granted to the Spanish merchants by Edward IV's treaty of 1466. The nodding councillors were speedily awakened by those merchants' outcries, but protests to Henry availed nothing and, as he grew stronger, their prospects of success grew steadily dimmer. A new treaty in 1499 did not even mention the question, so anxious were Ferdinand and Isabella then to assure Catherine's marriage to Arthur. Now that the Spaniards had lost their privileged position, they lost also much of their former dominance in Anglo-Spanish trade, much more of which was now carried in English ships. Here again, however, Henry was not able to hold all that he had gained. In 1501-2 briefly, and from 1505 more persistently, the Spanish government, or at least that of Castile, began to enforce its own 'navigation' law of 1494, which prohibited the export of goods in foreign ships when Spanish vessels were available. These measures had considerable effect in deterring English ships from visiting Spain and there was a marked decline in the trade in these later years.[12] Nevertheless, by depriving the Spaniards of their privileged position, Henry had broken their dominance in that trade and given English merchants and shipping a firm foothold in it.

But to secure reasonable insurance against possible difficulty or shrinkage in the Netherlands market, it was necessary to look further afield than France and Spain. It was necessary to look to the great markets in Germany and the Baltic, to which the Hanseatic League barred the way, and to those in the Mediterranean and Levant, over which the Venetians stood guard. Against the powerful Hanseatic League, Henry had to move warily, especially in his early years when pretenders were challenging for his throne. In March 1486 he granted the League a charter confirming all their extensive privileges: of paying export duties on English goods slightly lower than those paid even by Englishmen; of importing their own goods at reduced rates; of residing where, and as long as, they pleased; of selling some of their goods retail and of keeping what has been described as 'a sort of jug and bottle section of the Steelyard'[13] for retailing their wines. Gradually, however, he began to sap at these privileges. What he granted by charter, he to some extent took back by Act of Parliament. Thus, an Act of 1486 forbad any aliens, including Hansards, to export undressed cloth; another, of 1489, revived earlier legislation against their taking money or bullion out of England, insisting that they must spend their takings upon the purchase of English goods; above all, the 'navigation' Act of 1489 hit at their carrying trade by insisting that the King's subjects must use English ships whenever they were available. Henry also turned a blind eye to his subjects' harrying of the Hansards, to Hull's refusal to admit them in 1488 and to the Londoners' continual efforts to ignore those privileges which clashed with the City's own charter. When the Hansards' attempt to profit by the suspension of English trade to the Netherlands in 1493 provoked mob attacks upon the Steelyard, he did little to compensate the Germans. Indeed, soon afterwards he made them deposit with him £20,000 as security that they, too, would not trade to the Netherlands while the suspension lasted. Worst of all, he began to interpret their privilege of bringing in 'their goods' (*suae merces*) at preferential rates of duty as applying only to goods produced or grown within their own towns and territories. Against all these harassings they protested repeatedly but in vain. Conferences were held at Antwerp in 1491 and again at Bruges in 1498-9 without the pressure being alleviated or a settlement reached.

Now the ultimate purpose of Henry's measures was not to exclude the Hansards altogether from England's trade – native shipping and resources were not yet ready for that. It was to reduce them as far as possible to the same status as other alien merchants, just as was being done to the Spaniards. Its purpose, above all, was to force the League to allow English merchants and English ships reciprocal freedom of access to the Baltic and north German markets. To this end, Henry also cultivated the King of Denmark. In 1489 he concluded an alliance, amplified in 1490, whereby the Danish King promised freedom of trade on favourable terms to English merchants in Denmark and Norway, the restoration of their depot at Bergen, and the right to fish in Icelandic waters under his safeguard. Of this latter privilege at least English ships took real advantage. Indeed, the treaties, coming on top of all the other pressures, drove the Hansa to agree at the Antwerp conference in 1491 to allow the English to trade direct to Danzig. This concession bore no fruit, for Danzig refused to allow it. A few years later, however, Riga fell out with the League. Henry promptly made a treaty with the town in 1499, allowing English merchants to trade freely there and Riga merchants to enjoy the Hansards' preferential rates upon 'their own' goods (in the restricted sense) imported into England. This, again, bore little fruit. Before any advantage could be taken of it, Riga made up her quarrel with the Hansa and the treaty became a dead letter. Even so, when Riga drew back, the King of Poland began to come forward and negotiations went slowly ahead with him.

At this point there came, to all appearance, a sudden reversal of Henry's policy. The 1504 Parliament passed an Act confirming all the Hansards' privileges, as they had been confirmed in 1486. The reason for this astonishing change of front was, it seems, that the White Rose pretender Suffolk was now a fugitive in Germany and that Henry was anxious that the Hansa should not take up his cause. Perhaps he remembered that it was largely their help that enabled Edward IV to regain the throne in 1471. Suffolk was hardly more an Edward IV than Henry VII was a Henry VI and it is hard to believe that the situation called for so desperate a remedy. Indeed, Henry VII himself recovered rapidly from his panic once Suffolk was safely out of Germany. The 1504 Act, he discovered, had a proviso saving the privileges of the town of London. Taking advantage of this loophole, he began again to exact the higher duties on the ground that the preferential rates were an infringement of the City's privileges. In 1508, too, he declared the Hansards' 1493 pledge of £20,000 forfeit on the ground that they had broken their promise not to trade with the Netherlands during the 1505 stoppage. When he died in April 1509, his total achievement in this sphere was probably not very great. His treaties with Denmark had enabled Englishmen to secure a legal position in the Iceland fisheries, perhaps to regain a small foothold in Denmark and Norway; but he had been unable to do more, at most, than maintain a flicker of English trade into the Baltic. He had pared down the Hansards' privileged position in England and so won a little more elbow room for native traders and shipping. The Hansa was still too powerful to be broken by the English, still too necessary to be altogether dispensed with. To have

73

halted their advance, even turned them back a little, was perhaps as much as a King of England at that time could hope or afford to accomplish.

Against the Venetians Henry was somewhat more successful. From the middle of the fifteenth century a small but growing number of English ships had begun to find their way into the Mediterranean. Now they were starting to go direct to Crete for the wines that the Venetians normally carried to England. At once the Venetians imposed a tax of four ducats a butt upon all wines carried in foreign ships. Against them, Henry thereupon used their rivals, Florence, much as he had sought to use Denmark and Riga against the Hansa. In 1490 he made a treaty by which trade was to flow freely between England and Florence and the Florentine port of Pisa was established as the Italian staple for English wool.[14] The export of wool to Venice was at the same time restricted to six hundred sacks a year and those to be carried in English ships. Venice replied by prohibiting her ships from taking wines to Pisa and offering a bounty to those that carried Levant wines beyond the Straits of Gibraltar. Henry thereupon, in 1492, imposed a new and prohibitive duty of 18s. a butt on the wines brought in Venetian ships. After the beginning of the Italian Wars in 1494, the strife gradually died down and both parties slowly relaxed their tariffs. But that was in effect a victory for the English, who by the end of Henry's reign had established a regular and lucrative trade to Pisa and to Chios. Small as this trade was when set against that with the Netherlands, the opening of the Mediterranean and the Levant to English shipping was an achievement of real substance.

While Henry sought in these various ways to expand England's commerce eastwards and southwards, into and around Europe, he also encouraged it to look westwards across the Atlantic. The idea of undermining Venice was perhaps present here also. Her commercial ascendancy rested upon her virtual monopoly of trade with the Orient and her rivals, particularly Genoa and Portugal, had long been searching for new routes which would circumvent this monopoly. Now it was a Genoese who had become a citizen of Venice, John Cabot, who helped to direct the Atlantic explorations of the Bristol adventurers; and Cabot in his 1497 voyage, like Columbus in 1492, was looking for Cathay when he stumbled on America. In his own thrifty fashion Henry VII encouraged this voyage, a second in 1498 on which John Cabot was lost, and later voyages by John's son Sebastian and others.[15] In return for a fifth of any profit their voyages might produce, he granted the Cabots and their backers in 1496 sole ownership of any heathen lands they might discover and sole enjoyment of any trade they might create. In 1502 a new patent authorized them to occupy and establish settlements in any territories not in the actual and effective occupation of any Christian prince – the first enunciation of the doctrine that was to become the stock English answer to Spanish and Portuguese claims to ownership by right of first discovery. In 1505 he gave Sebastian Cabot a pension, as he had done to John in 1498. 1506 saw the organization of the Bristol company of 'adventurers into the New Found Lands' which backed Sebastian's next voyage, when he apparently found his way into Hudson's Bay and, returning, explored the north American coast southwards almost to the Delaware. By the time he got home, full of hope that another time he would find a clear westward passage to Cathay, Henry VII was dead. Westward enterprise was still a long way from paying dividends, but it already seemed to hold promise of finding a route to the Orient that would circumvent both the Venetians and the Portuguese.

When we come to sum up the total achievement of Henry VII's encouragement of overseas trade and shipping, it is not easy to reach any very precise conclusion. Clearly, his own income did not benefit to any spectacular degree. After a sharp rise at the beginning of his reign, the customs revenue showed no very remarkable increase and such increase as there was probably owed as much to more efficient collection as to the expansion of trade.[16] English shipping perhaps benefited more and by 1509, even from London, Englishmen were shipping more cloth abroad than all the alien merchants put together, while in other ports they now dominated the trade. But we must remember that, the Netherlands apart, that trade was still on a very small scale. Henry's diplomacy had opened doors in Spain, in Scandinavia and the Baltic, and in the Mediterranean; but comparatively few English traders, in the Baltic very few indeed, had as yet pushed their way through. England's commercial development was still too immature for there to be that surplus of capital which was needed to nourish and sustain risky ventures in distant or problematical markets. In the Baltic and the Mediterranean, as well as across the Atlantic, Henry's reach exceeded his subjects' grasp. They could not yet consolidate the claims that he had staked out. Nevertheless, by defining those claims he had done much to stimulate and to mark out the paths for the wider expansion of English commerce which the benefits of his strong government were beginning to make possible. Maritime expansion was to be checked again by the taxation for Henry VIII's wars, by the diversion of capital to land speculation during the Reformation, above all by the irresistible attraction of Antwerp in its golden age. Yet the course which that expansion followed when, under Elizabeth I, it resumed its advance, is perhaps the best justification of the wisdom and foresight of Henry VII's policy. For it was very largely along trails that Henry VII had blazed that the Elizabethans were to move forward.

Chapter 6

Henry VIII's First French War

ON April 21st, 1509, Henry VII died. His crown passed to his only surviving son Henry VIII and a new restless spirit began almost at once to inform English policy. It was not merely that an old king of fifty-two – old at least by sixteenth-century standards – was succeeded by a young king of eighteen. The difference between father and son was more than a difference between crabbed age and eager youth. Henry VII had been the child of adversity, schooled by exile and early dangers into a wary approach to life, more anxious to avoid risks than to seize chances. Henry VIII, born in 1491, was the child of prosperity, who could remember only the affluent and peaceful later years of his father's reign. The crown picked up on the battlefield of Bosworth descended to him in peace, with neither contest nor challenge and richly endowed. To it he himself brought the one thing that the Tudor monarchy so far had lacked, an enthusiastic popularity among its subjects. For to Englishmen, to distinguished foreign visitors, even to foreign ambassadors, the young Henry VIII appeared the very pattern of a king. Handsome and fair, tall and well built – not yet the athlete run to fat of his later years – he was endowed with overflowing physical energy as well as the steady hand, the good eye, the balance that enabled him to excel at all the sports that his subjects most esteemed. In addition he was, for such an athlete, almost indecently well endowed with intellectual and artistic gifts. Whether or not there is truth in the story that, before Arthur's death, his father had intended him for the Church and ultimately for the See of Canterbury,[1] he was certainly to be the only sovereign of his time to write a scholarly theological book in refutation of Martin Luther's heresies. His interest in Erasmus and in other men of the new learning, such as Thomas More, was genuine and informed. He was a musician of merit and some at least of his compositions are still occasionally heard in the twentieth century. Add to all this a bluff, hearty manner and a liberal generosity with money and we have the picture of one who possessed in reality most of the graces and accomplishments that flattery ascribes to all princes in their youth. He seemed, as Thomas More was soon to write in his *Utopia*, 'in all royal virtues a prince most peerless'. Time was to reveal other and darker sides of Henry VIII's character, but it is small wonder that at his accession Erasmus dreamed 'of an age that was really golden and of isles that were happy'.[2]

Even at this early date, however, there were other observers who noted that the young King was 'so made for war that there is no military exercise in which he does not equal (not to say surpass) his soldiers'.[3] Yet others commented upon his contempt and hatred for the French. He was as anxious to win a name for himself by some spectacular exploit as the young Frederick the Great was to be in 1740. And where should he look for his Silesia except in France? How better could a young King of England enhance his popularity and win himself renown than by regaining the French lands, perhaps even the French crown, that his Lancastrian predecessors had lost? That these were with Henry serious ambitions and not just idle day dreams, seems clear enough from the evidence left to us[4] and it was not long before Erasmus's hopes were dashed. It became apparent all too soon that the greatness which Henry sought was, after all, the warlike greatness of a Henry V, that his virtues were not so very different from the usual *virtù* of the Renaissance prince.

In a monarchy where the King ruled as well as reigned, the accession of such a king was bound to have far-reaching effects upon foreign policy. Henry VIII was not likely to trudge for long in the cautious footsteps of his father. It did, however, take him some time to find his feet and to assert his own ambitions against the counsels of his father's old advisers, most of whom seem still to have inculcated Henry VII's principles of peace. Besides that, it was some time before a situation developed abroad in which he could assert himself. When he came to the throne, France was still allied with all the other powers of Europe in the apparent harmony of the League of Cambrai. So long as that League lasted, an English attack upon her was therefore obviously out of the question. Nor would Henry find much opportunity to display his prowess by joining the League so long as it was directed against distant Venice.

However, he had been on the throne only a few weeks when the Venetians begged him to mediate their peace with the Cambrai powers. This gave him an opening that he might exploit in either of two directions, either likely to lead him to the very centre of the European stage. If he could reconcile the Venetians with all their enemies, he might stand forth as the unifier of Christendom, as the King who had brought the League of Cambrai back to its original purpose, the defence of Christendom against the growing menace of the infidel Turks. Much the same idea was soon to occur also to James IV of Scotland in his anxiety to avoid having to choose between his old French ally and his English brother-in-law. It was to recur more than once as a theme to which Henry's policy at least paid lip service during the next twenty years. In addition there is some evidence to suggest that Henry saw himself as an agent not only of peace and unity but also of reform in Christendom – at least, Ferdinand of Aragon twelve months later wrote as if the convocation of a General Council to reform the Papal curia and the Church was an idea that would appeal to him.[5]

The second direction in which Henry might exploit the Venetian appeal was less likely to lead to Christian peace and reform, to the golden age of Erasmus's dreams. He might try to redirect the League of Cambrai not against the Turks but against France, to convert it into an alliance to expel the French from Italy and help him to regain England's lost French possessions, perhaps even the French crown itself. The Venetians were quick to point out this possibility and Henry no less quick to seize upon it. By marrying Catherine of Aragon on June 11th, 1509 he drew close again to the one continental monarch, Ferdinand, with whom Henry VII's relations had grown cold and distant. By pressing for his sister Mary's marriage to the Archduke Charles he sought to secure the Netherlands and Charles's grandfather, the Emperor Maximilian. By sending Archbishop Bainbridge to Rome[6] he sought to reconcile the Pope to the Venetians and build up opposition to France in Italy. All this pointed towards a new league of England, Spain, the Netherlands, the Emperor, the Pope, and the Venetians, while a stiff note warning Louis XII against dismembering Venice showed that the league would be aimed against France. At home, too, Henry began at once to build two sizable new warships for his royal navy; he added to his father's Yeomen of the Guard a new corps of Gentlemen Pensioners to train and retain skilled captains; and he ordered general musters to check the equipment and preparedness of the county forces.

All this showed clearly the direction his thoughts were taking. But he soon found that he was moving too fast. Although his young friends among the nobility, the Duke of Buckingham for example, egged him on, most of his councillors had been trained in his father's school. Their pacific counsels were for the moment reinforced by those of his young Queen. At first sight this seems curious, for Catherine of Aragon was no friend of France. After her unhappy experiences in the previous reign, she was determined to use her influence to bind England and Spain, husband and father, in indissoluble friendship. And what better way of doing this could there now be than by uniting them together with the Pope against their common enemy, France, and so at once securing Ferdinand's hold upon Italy and satisfying Henry's ambition to regain England's lost lands across the Channel? But Ferdinand, although alarmed by the growth of French power, was not ready to challenge Louis XII with only England's support. He meant to 'continue in amity with the French King ... unto the time that the Emperor and he shall be agreed'. [7] He did in December 1509 conclude a treaty with Maximilian settling the succession to Castile upon their mutual grandson, the Archduke Charles. But Maximilian, still bitterly hostile to Venice, would not desert the French. So Ferdinand, using the Queen of England as Aragon's ambassador in what Catherine once called 'these kingdoms of your Highness', [8] laid a restraining hand upon the impetuous young Henry. The war rumours died down and, to the dismay of Bainbridge and the Venetians, in March 1510 Henry renewed his father's peace treaties with France and Scotland.

Over the next two years things did gradually move Henry's way, though only at a pace which must have sorely tried his patience. In February 1510 the Venetians, helped by Bainbridge, were able to make their peace with the Papacy. For by then Pope Julius II's fear of French predominance in northern Italy was beginning to outweigh his enmity towards the republic. In March he made an alliance with the Swiss cantons. In July he assured himself at least of Spain's benevolent neutrality by formally investing Ferdinand as King of Naples. Thereupon with his Italian and Swiss allies, and Ferdinand's secret encouragement, he moved into the attack to clear northern Italy of the foreigner. The Papal galleys assaulted one French client, Genoa; Papal, Swiss, and Venetian troops assailed another, Ferrara. But all these attempts came to nothing and Louis XII replied not only by sending armies to protect his allies but also by challenging the Pope nearer home. Two assemblies of the French clergy formally demanded the summoning of a General Council of the Church. Then, in May 1511, a few French and friendly cardinals, with the backing of Louis, sent out invitations for September to a General Council at Pisa.

Julius II answered by summoning a Lateran Council of his own for April 1512. But whether the cardinals and bishops of the various nations would obey the Papal call to Rome or the schismatical invitation to Pisa, depended largely upon the attitudes of their secular rulers. Moreover, the abortive military operations of the Papal and allied forces in 1510, and their equally unsuccessful efforts in 1511 when Bologna was lost, showed that the task of expelling the French was not something that *Italia farà da se*. For both Council and camp Julius needed more than ever to league the powers of Europe around him against France. Now his chances of doing that were improving, though slowly. As early as June 1510 Ferdinand of Aragon was beginning to have nightmare visions of the French King mastering northern and central Italy, replacing Julius II by a Pope favourable to France, going on to conquer Naples, and becoming monarch of Christendom.[9] Yet still the Emperor Maximilian's hatred of Venice and fondness for France were very slow to evaporate and Ferdinand dared not risk a conflict with both Louis XII and the Emperor. Through Catherine he did draw closer his ties with England and Henry VIII obediently pressed the Netherlands government to urge Maximilian to agree with Venice and break with France. More than that, when France's client, the Duke of Gelders, again fell into a quarrel with the Netherlands government in the summer of 1511, Henry quickly remembered that he had a treaty of mutual defence with the Netherlands and dispatched Poynings with 1,500 men to their assistance. Maximilian, grateful for this English help and somewhat shaken by the schismatical proceedings of the French, now at last began to retreat into something like neutrality. Thereupon, in October 1511 Ferdinand of Aragon joined the Pope, the Swiss, and the Venetians in a Holy League against the schismatical French King and appealed to the young King of England to come over to the continent to help them.

At first sight the position in 1511 was not unlike that in 1496 when another Pope had sought and won Henry VII's adhesion to another Holy League constructed against the French. But there was one essential difference. Henry VII had joined the League in 1496 when, and because, it was about to make peace with France. In 1511 Henry VIII was being invited to join a league that was about to make war upon France. For this reason Bishop Fox, *alter rex* as the Venetian ambassador called him,[10] and most of the more responsible councillors were opposed to his joining. They realized that to join now would be to abandon what Henry VII had established as the cardinal principle of English foreign policy, the principle of not provoking France, of not opposing her actively unless she threatened real English interests.

For it was perfectly clear that no English interests were involved in the struggle for power in northern Italy, while the possibility of the French King becoming monarch of Christendom was a nightmare still very remote from reality. It was equally clear that the French were flatteringly anxious to retain England's friendship. Louis XII paid very punctually the half-yearly instalments of the pension due to the King of England according to the treaty of Étaples, right up to the payment in November 1511. He did not resent English action against the Duke of Gelders. He did his best to smooth over the disputes between his Scottish ally and the English, which arose from the usual Border 'ruptiouns and attemptatis'[11] and from lawlessness at sea. So far his efforts there had been completely successful and James IV still breathed peace even in 1512. Yet experienced English Councillors needed no telling that the surest way to wreck Anglo-Scottish friendship was to start a war against France. And to wreck both Anglo-Scottish and Anglo-French good relations would be to knock away the very foundations of Henry VII's achievement.

Henry VIII, however, was by now obviously spoiling for a fight. Besides the 1,500 men against Gelders, he had already sent this summer another 1,500 under Lord Darcy to help Ferdinand's 'crusade' against the Moors of North Africa, although in the event their services were not required and they came home in some disgrace after misbehaving themselves at Cadiz. In August, too, the King's ships under Lord Edward Howard had fallen upon Andrew Barton, a Scottish privateer who had perhaps pursued his prey without too nice a regard for international relations. Henry had arrogantly refused to listen to James IV's protests about the incident. Moreover, although most of his father's old councillors advised peace, there were others who egged him on to war. Buckingham, Lord Edward Howard, and other of his boon companions among the younger nobles urged it. Archbishop Warham and some of the bishops, to whom 'the enemies of the Church ... be little better than infidels', were apparently not altogether averse to a holy war to defend the Pope.[12] Above all, Queen Catherine, his most intimate and still probably his most influential adviser, was now ardently drawing her husband into a warlike alliance with her father.[13]

By the autumn of 1511, too, Catherine had secured a useful ally among the native councillors. This was Thomas Wolsey, sometime bursar of Magdalen College, Oxford. Wolsey had been employed by Henry VII on various minor diplomatic errands, but at first found little favour with Henry VIII. It was not until November 1509 that he was appointed, apparently on Fox's recommendation, to the minor office of King's Almoner and sworn as one of the King's many Councillors. The office of Almoner, minor though it was, brought him into personal contact with the King and by September 1511 he was upon terms of trust and some intimacy with his royal master. The pacific inclinations of nearly all the older Councillors, Fox not least, gave the ambitious young Almoner a rare opportunity to curry royal favour by encouraging the warlike mood of his King and Queen. Yet, although there is no doubt that he seized his chance with both hands, it was they and not he who now plunged England into a needless and aggressive war. His part was only to aid and abet. Henry, egged on by Catherine and Ferdinand, hardly needed his additional prompting. When war with France ensued, the King did turn more and more to his uniquely capable Almoner for the organizing of victory. But it was the French war that made Wolsey, not Wolsey who made the French war.

The final commitment came in November 1511, when Henry joined the Holy League and concluded a treaty with Ferdinand by which he promised to attack France before the end of April 1512. Ferdinand himself had joined the League only in October and the coincidence of the dates indicates how closely he, through Catherine, kept English and Spanish policy in step. Yet Henry was no mere puppet of his father-in-law. Ferdinand may have dictated the pace, but Henry had chosen the road for himself and he meant it to lead him to conquests in France, if possible to the

French crown. Thus in March 1512 Bainbridge, now a cardinal, persuaded the Pope to draw up a brief transferring Louis XII's realm and titles, including the title of Most Christian King, to Henry VIII.[14] The brief was not handed over to Bainbridge, and it was not to be published or become operative until Louis was defeated; but it helped further to spur Henry's martial ardour. In February 1512 he had called a Parliament which voted him two fifteenths and tenths to assist him in opposing the insatiable ambition of France and the insubordination of the Scots. With this grant added to his father's savings,[15] he did not greatly need to count the cost and by the spring his preparations were well advanced. He hired and purchased ships to reinforce his small royal navy, besides laying down the great *Henry Grace à Dieu* of a thousand tons. In April Lord Edward Howard, now Lord Admiral, with eighteen sail of warships swept the Channel and Western Approaches, preparatory to escorting an English army of 15,000 men to join Ferdinand's forces in northern Spain for an invasion of France from the south.

This was Ferdinand's idea. Henry accepted it because this was the one theatre of the war where his own forces could have substantial support from an ally and he hoped with Spanish help to conquer Guienne. After all, Guienne had once been just as much English as Normandy. Ferdinand encouraged this hope, but his real purpose was somewhat different. His real intention was that the English should contain the French forces by threatening an invasion round the western end of the Pyrenees, while his own troops overran the kingdom of Navarre, further to the eastward. Accordingly, he concentrated his forces, somewhat larger than the English expedition, against Navarre. The English, under the Marquis of Dorset (an old pupil of Wolsey's at Oxford), received no Spanish support and, although too strong for the French to ignore, were not strong enough to undertake an offensive on their own. From June until October 1512 they had to sit idly around Fuenterrabia. Their food supplies were badly organized, beer ran short, and they took to drinking wine as if it were beer. Digestions suffered, discipline decayed and by autumn all were either down with dysentery or up in mutiny. In October, in defiance of their commander's orders, they came home. They had done Ferdinand's work. Navarre was now his. But they had gained Henry not one foot of England's lost province of Guienne and their misconduct had done nothing to revive the ancient glory of English arms. Lord Admiral Howard's success at sea, in driving the French fleet into Brest, was poor compensation for Dorset's failure on land, all the more as the *Regent* had been lost when a French ship that she had grappled blew up. Altogether, 1512 brought a very slender return for Henry's high hopes and very considerable expenditure

Worse was to come. Maximilian, for what he was worth, did join the Holy League in November 1512. In April he and Henry did bind themselves to join the Pope and Ferdinand in an immediate fourfold attack upon France. But only a few days earlier Ferdinand had secretly made a year's truce with Louis XII and it soon became clear that he was unlikely to take any very active part in the year's campaigning. As the Venetians had already made their peace with Louis (March) and Maximilian was not an ally from whom much could be expected, Henry's hopes of success depended – apart from the distant Swiss – upon what he could achieve by his own efforts. And the comings and goings of envoys between France and Scotland made it all too probable that those efforts would have to be divided between two fronts. Nor were the opening naval operations encouraging. Lord Admiral Howard not only failed to destroy the French fleet in Brest, but lost his life in an attempt to cut out the galleys which Louis had brought round from the Mediterranean. Then fear of bad weather, lack of victuals, and an epidemic of measles put an end to an attempt to keep Brest blockaded and the English fleet came home in some disorder.

It was now that Wolsey showed his mettle as an organizer of victory. While Surrey mobilized the north against the possibility of an invasion from Scotland, it was Wolsey who took charge of the reorganization of the fleet and the preparation of a great army of some 25,000 men to invade France under the King's personal leadership. With that army Henry crossed to Calais at the end of June. Early in August Maximilian joined him, but with barely 2,000 men and an offer to serve personally as a volunteer at a lansknecht's pay. However, Henry's own forces were sufficient to win him at least a show of the glory that he was seeking. At Rome the new Pope Leo X 'and all other great men here doth look daily to hear that Your Grace shall utterly exterminate the French King', or so Bainbridge wrote in words that Henry himself was to echo twelve years later.[16] In the upshot, the French King was by no means exterminated but on August 16th, a French attempt to relieve Thérouanne was decisively repulsed at the cavalry skirmish which came to be known as the battle of the Spurs, from the haste with which the would-be relievers spurred their horses off the field. On August 23rd Thérouanne surrendered and a month later the more important town of Tournai (Perkin Warbeck's birthplace) was also taken. A month after these resounding, if hollow, victories, Henry returned home. Just before he left he concluded a new agreement with Maximilian and Ferdinand, providing for a triple invasion of France by June 1514. The pact was strengthened further by a renewal of the old agreement that Charles was to marry Henry's younger sister Mary, this time by May 1514. As the French had been driven out of Milan by the Swiss and Papal forces after the allies' victory at Novara in June 1513 and had lost Dijon to the Swiss in September, Henry had some reason to hope that the 1514 campaigns would put him again in possession of a substantial part of the lost Lancastrian lands in France.

This seemed the more possible because, while Henry was winning his spurs in France, Surrey had ended the danger from Scotland. Henry's invasion of France had at last brought the reluctant King of Scots into the field to assist Scotland's old ally. In August James IV crossed the Border with a large army. Outmanoeuvred by Surrey, the Scots were utterly routed at Flodden on September 9th. James himself was killed and with him perhaps 10,000 of the Scottish host, among them many of the leading nobles of the kingdom. The artillery was lost, the army completely broken, and Scotland left almost defenceless. The crown passed to the dead King's only surviving son, James V, an infant of seventeen months, and the regency into the hands of his English mother, Henry VIII's elder sister Margaret. In 1514 the King of England would have no war to worry about on his northern frontier.

Henry, however, still had much to learn about the realities of European politics. By the end of 1513 Ferdinand was again negotiating secretly with the common enemy and in March 1514 he renewed the Franco-Spanish truce. Maximilian soon followed his example and a new Pope, the Medici Leo X to whom Louis XII had submitted in October 1513, was also working for peace, if in a more open and honourable fashion. No progress could be

86

made towards Charles's marriage to Mary and it became increasingly clear that Henry was being left in the lurch by all his
allies. If he still hoped for conquests in 1514, he must depend upon
his own unaided resources to defeat a France no longer distracted
by continental foes.

But the vanity of any such hope as this was also fairly obvious
by the end of 1513. For Henry's lavish efforts in 1512 and more
especially in 1513, had practically emptied his treasury. The
campaigns and preparations since the spring of 1511 had cost
him, according to Professor Dietz's figures,[17] at least £922,000,
over £650,000 of it in 1513. For a King whose ordinary annual
income, apart from parliamentary grants, was under £150,000,
these were sobering figures. They meant that two years of war
had swallowed up almost all Henry VII's painfully accumulated
savings as well as all that Parliament had granted to Henry VIII –
two fifteenths and tenths in February 1512; a third, as well as a
poll tax, in November; and a subsidy in 1514. Such was the cost
of attempting to compete on level terms with the leading military
powers of the continent. It is difficult to see how the attempt could
have been made at all without the inherited asset of substantial
savings made in the previous reign. Now that asset was dissipated,
Henry VIII must finance his foreign policy out of his own limited
income, supplemented by parliamentary grants. And although
Parliament had voted money readily enough so far, the grants as
voted were relatively small and their yield was even smaller.
The subsidy of £160,000 voted in 1514 brought in no more than
£48,000 (and another vote of £110,000 in February 1515 to
make good the deficiency, was to bring in only another £45,600).
In fact, the three fifteenths and tenths, the poll tax, and the subsidy
voted in 1512 and 1514, between them brought in no more than
£167,000, to which Convocation added £50,000 from the clergy.
These figures make it hardly necessary to add that, what Parliament voted, the taxpayers paid 'unwillingly and with extreme
complaint'. The spirit that Yorkshiremen had shown in 1489 and
Cornishmen in 1497 was far from dead by 1514. Already Henry
was being made aware not only of the fickleness of foreign allies
but also of the serious limitations of his own resources. Lack of
money was already forcing the prodigal son to return to his
father's policies.

His return was no doubt hastened by his desire to outsmart his perfidious father-in-law. The story that he was so angry with Ferdinand that he even considered divorcing Catherine, rests upon very slender evidence and is descredited by his solicitude for her comfort during her pregnancy in 1514.[18] Nevertheless, in the diplomatic field he and Wolsey did countermine Ferdinand and Maximilian with a success that even those old hands might have envied. In the spring of 1514 Henry, too, began secret negotiations with France. In August these resulted in a treaty of peace and mutual defence between the two countries. Henry kept Tournai and Thérouanne, which he had won in 1513, and his French pension was restored and increased. The French also agreed that the Scots might be included in the peace upon Henry's terms. Nor was this all. For in addition to the treaty of peace, there was also a treaty of marriage whereby the gouty fifty-two-year-old Louis XII was to marry Henry's young sister Mary, the Archduke Charles's discarded fiancée. The marriage was completed in October 1514 and Henry found himself with one sister Queen of France and the other Queen Regent of Scotland. It was Ferdinand and Maximilian who were now left in the lurch, not Henry. The English alliance with France was restored and strengthened, with the Pope's benediction; Scotland was no longer a cause for anxiety; and if Henry had only Tournai and Thérouanne to show of his hoped-for conquests, he and Wolsey had at least shown themselves capable of beating such masters as Ferdinand and Maximilian at their own diplomatic game.

Thanks to the desire of Louis XII and the Pope for peace and to Wolsey's skill as a negotiator, Henry had emerged fairly creditably from his first rash adventure into continental politics and war. Yet their achievement, such as it was, rested upon very flimsy foundations both at home and abroad. Louis XII, after all, was as old as Henry VII had been when he died. His death might well bring new revolutions in the affairs of Europe and jeopardize the new Anglo-French entente. Henry VIII had run through his inheritance and must henceforward finance his policy out of income. Whether he had learned the lessons of 1512–14 and was now a wiser as well as a poorer man, yet remained to be seen.

Chapter 7

The Diplomacy of Wolsey

THERE was not long to wait before the new revolutions in the affairs of Europe began. On December 31st, 1514, less than three months after his marriage to Mary Tudor, Louis XII of France died – danced to death, some said, by his young bride, whose brother had promised her that she should choose her next husband for herself.[1] Louis was succeeded by his ambitious young cousin and son-in-law, Francis I, and within a few months the imposing diplomatic edifice that Wolsey had built in 1514 began to crumble. It is true that Francis confirmed his predecessor's treaty with England in April 1515, as he confirmed that with Charles of the Netherlands in March. But before the year was out, the French had again invaded Italy; won the great victory of Marignano over the famous Swiss infantry (September); made themselves masters of Milan; and gained the Pope, Venice, Genoa, and eight of the thirteen Swiss cantons as their allies. At the same time they had restored their influence in Scotland, where Margaret had lost many of her supporters by her marriage to the unpopular Archibald Douglas, Earl of Angus. In May 1515 the Duke of Albany, the infant James V's cousin and next heir, had come back from France. In July he was able to deprive Margaret of her position as regent and in September to drive her out of the kingdom. French influence was thus supreme once more in Scotland as well as in Italy.

These startling events in themselves were enough to put a severe strain upon the Anglo-French entente and they did so the more because they added a strong element of personal rivalry to Henry VIII's native suspicion of the traditional enemy. He manifested, indeed, an almost feminine jealousy towards Francis, cross-examining the Venetian ambassador about his appearance very much as Elizabeth I was later to question Melville about the charms of Mary, Queen of Scots – 'is he as tall as I am? is he as stout? what sort of legs has he?'[2] With Francis triumphant in Italy and Scotland, Henry was hardly in a mood to welcome reminders about the lessons of 1512–14.

Yet at home events occurred in 1515 that made those lessons even more pertinent. This is not the place to discuss at length the uproar over the death of Richard Hunne in the Bishop of London's prison (December 1514); the disputes over the Commons's attempts to renew the 1512 Act limiting benefit of clergy, which the bishops held was contrary to the recent decrees of the Pope's Lateran Council; or the quarrel over Convocation's attack upon Dr Standish for his defence of the Act. Suffice it to say that in the two sessions of the 1515 Parliament (February to April and November to December) these matters provoked 'most dangerous discords between the clergy and the secular power over the liberties of the Church', as the Clerk of Parliaments, who was also Prolocutor of Convocation, put it.[3] The discords seemed to churchmen all the more dangerous because not only did the Commons show a bitter anti-clericalism and a zeal for encroaching upon clerical privileges, but also in Standish's case the King himself showed an alarming readiness to listen to their arguments.

These were matters of considerable significance for English foreign policy as well as of great domestic concern. For the war of 1512–14 and the peace of 1514 had left a proud churchman as the King's most trusted and most successful adviser on foreign affairs and the advance of France in 1515 made Wolsey's services seem more than ever indispensable. Archbishop of York since 1514, created Cardinal in September 1515, a pluralist holding the see of Tournai *in commendam* by papal dispensation, and with an illegitimate son to find preferment for, Wolsey could not stand by while such dangers threatened clerical privileges and Papal decrees. If reforms had to be made, and he was not blind to the need for them however much he personified the abuses complained of, they must be made by the Church itself and not imposed upon it by secular authority. He did not mean again to kneel in public before his King and crave pardon for the clergy, as he had done over the Standish affair. Partly to that end, he was already pressing the Pope to grant him a commission as Papal Legate *a latere*, which would enable him to override even the Primate, Warham, Archbishop of Canterbury, and Convocation and to get something done to remove the laity's worst grievances. But it was equally important for him to stop the voice of criticism. That meant suppressing Parliament and, as soon as the subsidy bill was through, he began to urge the King to end the session. With foreign affairs so pressing, he had his way. On December 22nd, 1515, Parliament was dissolved. On the same day Archbishop Warham, advocate of frequent Parliaments, resigned the Great Seal and Cardinal Wolsey succeeded him as Chancellor of England, the highest office in the state under the crown. During the fourteen years of his Chancellorship Parliament was to be summoned but once, in 1523, and then from dire financial necessity.

Now as we have seen, even with a willing Parliament, the limitations upon an active foreign policy were stringent enough. With no Parliament at all, they were almost prohibitive. It is true that, as Chancellor, Wolsey did assert the royal authority as it had perhaps never been asserted before. During the next few years, the years of his greatest personal activity in the Star Chamber and Chancery, he taught the King's subjects of all ranks his 'new law of the Star Chamber'[4] to such effect that the country had seldom appeared so obedient to the royal will. But he had chosen the way of coercion rather than the way of persuasion and even he could hardly hope within a few brief years to coerce Englishmen into such habits of obedience that the King would be able to command their services and their purses just as he willed. Unless he was to risk outbursts like that in Yorkshire in 1489 and Cornwall in 1497, he must keep his foreign policy inexpensive and rely mainly upon diplomacy unsupported by arms to check the growing ascendancy of France and satisfy his master's desire to cut a figure in Europe.

That Wolsey appreciated this, seems clear enough. In October 1515 he had made a treaty with Ferdinand of Aragon, but it involved this time no commitment to any English campaign on the continent. At the same time, with the second session of Parliament decided upon and the prospect of a subsidy in view, he dispatched Richard Pace to hire troops from the five Swiss cantons that had not gone over to the French. With these he hoped to help Maximilian to reverse the defeat at Marignano and free Milan. Yet, while the subsidy of £110,000 duly voted by Parliament in November was to bring in only £45,000, Pace's enterprise cost £80,000 and that to no effect.[5] For Maximilian and the Swiss proved ineffectual allies. They shied away from an attack upon Milan in March 1516 and did nothing to loosen the French grip upon northern Italy. Nor could other allies be found.

In January Ferdinand of Aragon had died, leaving all his dominions in Spain, Italy, and the New World to his young grandson Charles of Burgundy. Spain and the Netherlands, which Henry VII had tried so long to hold together as a counterweight to France, were now united under a single ruler. But Charles and his Flemish advisers were as eager as ever Henry VII had been to avoid any needless clash with France, at least until Charles had established his authority in his new Spanish kingdoms where some would have preferred his younger brother Ferdinand as their King. In August 1516 therefore, they concluded the treaty of Noyon with France, confirming Charles's undertaking to marry Francis's infant daughter Louise and promising to restore Navarre to France, while Francis was to keep Milan in return for his renunciation of all his claims upon Naples. This was perhaps only a temporary expedient, a device to gain time for Charles to establish himself in Spain; but it ruled out all possibility of his joining England against France for some time to come. Four months later Maximilian also made his peace, accepting the Noyon treaty in return for a payment of 200,000 ducats. England was left isolated in face of a general reconciliation of the continental powers with a France whose influence was dominant in Scotland and Italy.

This isolation was not in itself particularly alarming, for once again all those powers were anxious to gain England's goodwill. Charles needed it to assure his safe and peaceful passage down the Channel to Spain. Francis wanted it because he was alarmed at the growing power of Charles and worried about what might happen when the old Emperor Maximilian should die. Also it was notorious that Charles's councillors regarded the treaty of Noyon as binding only so long as it served his interests and one of Charles's first actions after arriving in Spain was to inform Francis that the return of Navarre to France was quite impracticable. Yet if the situation held no serious dangers for England, it could be dangerous for Wolsey. The retirement first of Warham and then of Fox to their long-neglected ecclesiastical duties, to the sees that they so seldom saw, may possibly indicate opposition among the older Councillors to the vain expense of the subsidies to Maximilian and the Swiss.[6] And if their retirement betokened his victory at home, his hold upon the King's favour, the very basis of all his power, still depended upon his continued success abroad. Henry's sense of his own importance did not make him patient in the role of odd man out.

Besides this, Wolsey needed for his own purposes to get back into the centre of the European stage. He had not yet obtained the coveted commission as Legate *a latere* and it was not easy for him to put pressure upon the Pope unless he was able to play a leading part in European affairs. For England was very thinly represented in the College of Cardinals – in fact by Wolsey alone – and the King of England's arm could not reach over the Alps. England's isolation, or the fact that she was playing only a minor and secondary part in continental politics, was thus a serious obstacle to Wolsey's promotion in the Church.

In the end, the Pope and Francis I came to his rescue. As early as June 1517 Francis recalled Albany from Scotland as a gesture of goodwill. Then in the following summer the Pope sent Cardinal Campeggio as his Legate *a latere* to beg for support and money for a crusade against the now rampant Turks. This was Wolsey's opportunity. He kept Campeggio at Calais from May until July, refusing him admission to England until he had extracted from the Pope a commission as Legate *a latere* for himself jointly with Campeggio. That done, he took up the Papal appeal with an energy and breadth of view that turned it into an English diplomatic triumph as spectacular as that of 1514. In September a special embassy arrived from France. In October a new Anglo-French treaty was concluded. England ceded Tournai back to France and in return Francis promised to pay Henry 600,000 crowns in yearly instalments of £5,000 in addition to the annual £10,000 previously promised by Louis XII. Wolsey, too, had his *pourboire* for Tournai. Furthermore Francis promised to keep Albany out of Scotland and the new pact was reinforced by the promise that Henry's two-year-old daughter Mary should eventually marry the equally youthful Dauphin.

This treaty, though less favourable to England than that of 1514, was still a considerable achievement. But it was only a part of an even more notable achievement. For Wolsey seized the chance of having Campeggio and the French embassy in London, to expand the Anglo-French agreement into a treaty of universal peace and co-operation against the infidel.[7] Maximilian and Charles were induced to join the Pope, Francis, and Henry in pledging themselves to perpetual friendship and to joint action against the Turks, in a league to which the adhesion of all other Christian princes and states was invited. No doubt there was much insincerity in all this. Charles needed peace to settle himself in Spain; he and Francis both wanted to keep their hands free from the coming Imperial election when Maximilian should die; and promises to take part in crusades always sat lightly on sixteenth-century princes. Nevertheless, Wolsey had put himself and England right back into the centre of the stage. The man who had organized victory in France in 1513 and had won peace in 1514, had now made the peace of Europe and organized Christendom for a crusade. He had, as the Venetian ambassador flatteringly pointed out to him,[8] shown himself capable of performing a function that was more peculiarly associated with the Pope and the fact that the pact had been negotiated in London reflected some of his glory on to his King, casting him in an almost Imperial role. It was an achievement even more spectacular than that of 1514 and even Bishop Fox could not forbear to cheer.[9] For it, Wolsey could again justly claim the credit. More had told the Venetian ambassador that during the negotiations 'even the King hardly knows in what state matters are' and a little later the Venetian ambassador was to expand this into the generalization that 'this Cardinal is the person who rules both the King and the entire Kingdom.'[10]

More may well have been right, but the Venetian ambassador was almost certainly wrong. The next ten years were to demonstrate that, although Wolsey might run England's foreign policy, it was the King who decided what it should be. And new decisions were soon called for, for once again Wolsey's diplomatic triumph proved brief and hollow. New revolutions in the affairs of the continent undid what he had done. England was faced with new problems, or perhaps old problems in a new guise, and the answers that were given certainly look as if they originated with Henry rather than with the Cardinal.

In January 1519 the old Emperor Maximilian died and his death undid the achievement of 1518 just as that of Louis XII had ruined the work of 1514. On June 28th, despite all Francis I's intrigues and bribery, Charles of Spain and Burgundy was elected Holy Roman Emperor in succession to his grandfather. The Austrian lands and the Empire were thus added to Spain, Naples, and the Netherlands to form a 'Habsburg aggregate' which threatened to encircle and constrict France on every side. Francis, already wounded in his vanity by the Imperial Electors' rejection of his candidature and offended by Charles's refusal to return Navarre, was not likely to sit quietly under the shadow of so great a menace. Another and even greater European conflict was clearly approaching, a conflict in which sooner or later most of the smaller fry would be compelled to group themselves around one or other of these two Leviathans.

England's position, however, was happier than that of most other states, for neither her interests nor her independence were likely to be involved directly or immediately in the Habsburg-Valois conflict. Of course, if either Charles or Francis achieved a decisive victory, and with it virtual domination of the continent, then there might be danger. But in 1519 they looked too evenly matched for that. Francis ruled a strong, compact, and obedient kingdom and would have the advantage of operating upon interior lines. Charles ruled over a much larger area, but his territories were widely scattered, often loosely held, and peculiarly dependent upon peculiarly vulnerable communications. Already French control of Milan and Genoa cut one of the vital lines linking his new and still precariously held Spanish kingdoms to his even newer Austrian and Imperial dominions and to his ancestral Netherlands. It was not, therefore, easy to foretell who would win and not unreasonable to anticipate a long-drawn and indecisive contest. Moreover, the main battleground must obviously be once again northern Italy, for Francis could not willingly abandon Milan and Charles could not easily tolerate his remaining there. In such a contest no vital English interests would be involved, yet both parties would be, indeed already were, most anxious to secure England's friendship. To Charles, now that Milan and Genoa were French, the one remaining line between Spain and the Netherlands, that through the Channel and Narrow Seas, was of vital importance. If England stayed neutral, that line, too, might be endangered by French ships operating from Breton harbours and perhaps also from the new base at Le Havre (which the English, so confusingly for us, called Newhaven). If England became hostile, this link must be severed altogether, for from Dover and Calais the comparatively powerful English fleet could command the Straits of Dover and Narrow Seas far more easily than French armies in Milan could command north Italy.

Therefore, although Charles's first task must be to drive the French out of northern Italy, he must also bid high for England's friendship. For the opposite reasons, and also to avoid war on yet another front, Francis was prepared to pay well to keep England at least neutral.

Rarely has an English government been offered so favourable an opportunity to play the honest broker so profitably and with so little risk. And for some two years after Charles's election as Emperor, it seemed to outward appearances as if Henry and Wolsey were content to play that part. In May 1520 Charles visited England on his way back from Spain. He arrived late owing to contrary winds and the meeting between him, Henry, and Catherine was therefore somewhat hurried. Nevertheless it laid the foundations of a good understanding and showed the Emperor's anxiety for English help. In June Henry and Francis met outside Calais, amid all the pageantry and splendour of the Field of Cloth of Gold. The gaiety was occasionally a little forced, as when Henry boisterously challenged Francis to a wrestling match and came off a not very sporting loser.[11] Yet Francis showed himself full of anxiety to please and apparently most eager for English friendship. Some of the French even felt that the meeting had gone so well that Henry might be persuaded to restore Calais to France! Next month Henry and Wolsey met Charles again at Gravelines. There they agreed upon the calling of a three-power conference to meet at Calais and meanwhile undertook that neither would make a separate treaty with France during the next two years. There was talk, too, of Charles marrying Henry's daughter Mary.[12] Before the Calais conference could meet, however, news came that the Spanish *comuneros* were in revolt. Until they could be crushed, Charles was naturally anxious to delay his conflict with Francis. So for the next year Wolsey was still able to maintain a show of mediation, even if English diplomacy was mainly concerned to dissuade Francis from exploiting the opportunity which the revolt of the *comuneros* had given him. Even when the Calais conference began in August 1521, Wolsey kept up the pretence of mediation. But by then the *comuneros* had been finally defeated at Villalàr (April) and Charles was preparing to deal vigorously with his French enemy. The Imperial lion was beginning to prowl and Henry and Wolsey prepared to play jackal to him. Late in August Wolsey visited

Charles at Bruges and concluded an agreement that was to be kept secret until November, when another instalment of Henry's French pension would have been paid. By this treaty, confirmed and elaborated by later agreements in June 1522,[13] Henry was to declare war upon France if Francis refused to make peace with Charles within a limited time. He was also to keep the Channel open for Charles. In return Charles promised to compensate Henry and Wolsey for the French pensions which they must then forfeit. He agreed to plans for the conquest and partitioning of France and to this end undertook to invade from Spain in the spring of 1523 while Henry invaded from Calais, each at the head of 40,000 men. He promised to marry Henry's only child, the Princess Mary, when she reached the age of twelve. In addition he agreed to do his best to secure Wolsey the Papacy at the next election. England had definitely abandoned the role of mediator. Henry had chosen his side, the Imperialist side, and committed himself to war on a scale even larger than in 1513.

Chapter 8

'The Whole Monarchy of Christendom'

WHY did the English government thus abandon its professed role of mediator and commit itself to plunge into a continental conflict that concerned it so little? Why, above, all, did it commit itself to military intervention on a scale even greater than that of 1513? Wolsey's most learned biographer found the answer to these questions in Wolsey's Papal ambitions and desire always to stand well at Rome.[1] Now it is true that in August 1521 at Bruges Charles V did promise to further Wolsey's candidature at the next Papal election.[2] It is also true that Leo X, who had continued Wolsey's commission as Legate *a latere* when Campeggio left England in 1519, did extend and considerably amplify that commission in April 1521, just before the Papal alliance with Charles in May. This may well have been intended as payment in advance for English support against France. Yet Francis I, too, had promised, and promised before Charles, to support Wolsey at the next conclave[3] and there are indications that, at least in 1520, Wolsey was by no means convinced that Charles was bound to win. All this apart, the Cardinal-Legate, who had experienced once before the trials of organizing victory against the French, can hardly have relished the task of having to organize and pay for operations on an even grander scale and without Henry VII's savings to help him. Besides, it was hardly possible to commit England to war on that scale without realizing that it must mean sooner or later coming cap in hand to Parliament for money. So, given Wolsey's attitude to parliaments, this hardly looks like his war. After his care to avoid excessive foreign commitments in 1515 and 1516, it does seem strange that in 1521–2 he should have plunged in and plunged so deeply – unless it were that he had to obey his master's voice.

That does indeed seem the most probable answer. For by now a new problem was beginning to worry Henry VIII, one that could provide a motive strong enough to explain the otherwise extraordinary rashness of his offensive alliance with the Emperor. This was the problem of the succession to the English throne. By 1521 Henry and Catherine had been married twelve years. He was thirty, she was thirty-six. Their only living child was the five-year-old Princess Mary, born in 1516. All Catherine's other children had either been stillborn or had not survived the first week or two of infancy, and what was to prove her last pregnancy ended in another stillborn child in 1518. After this Henry's hopes of a legitimate male heir grew dim and it became more and more apparent that the succession in the direct Tudor line depended on the one life of a girl still barely out of infancy.* For Englishmen whose fathers had remembered the Wars of the Roses, this was a most alarming fact. What if Mary were to die like the rest? What if Henry himself should die during the next twelve or fifteen years, before Mary came to the age of discretion? Neither event was altogether unlikely for, as anyone familiar with the annals or correspondence of any sixteenth-century family soon realizes, life and death were in those days very close neighbours. Besides, this was the time of the sweating sickness, an epidemic disease almost peculiar to England and especially deadly to active men in the prime of life. Its outbreaks certainly caused Henry grave personal concern. He had only to look back across the past century of England's history to the reign of Henry VI, or across the Border to Scotland since Flodden, to appreciate the scriptural warning, 'woe to thee, O land, whose king is a child.' The warning was all the more pertinent when the child was a girl; when there was no prince of the blood royal to act as regent, as Bedford had done for Henry VI; and when there was no nobleman of such unchallenged pre-eminence that his elevation to that office would be accepted without question. Moreover, even if Henry VIII survived until Mary came of age, it might still be remembered that England had never had a Queen regnant; that the only woman who had ever attempted to assert such a title – Henry I's daughter Matilda – had brought the country nineteen years of civil war; and that, if women could inherit the crown, then both Henry VII and Henry VIII must have usurped it from Henry VII's own mother, the Lady Margaret. Catherine's

* And in the indirect line, too, the next heirs were women – Henry's sisters Margaret and Mary.

99

inability to produce a male heir to the throne was therefore a matter for more than personal and private disappointment.

Now there seems no doubt that this problem was already worrying Henry VIII. In 1519 he called physicians over from Spain to see Catherine, while he himself made a vow to go on a crusade if Heaven would send him a son.[4] The execution of the Duke of Buckingham in 1521, because his servants talked too indiscreetly about the succession and his possible claims to it, was probably another indication of the King's anxiety. By then, however, it looks as if he had already seen a possible way out. When the infant Mary was pledged to the infant Dauphin of France by the treaty of October 1518, Henry was still hoping for a son by Catherine.[5] Early in 1521, however, he was pointing out to Charles V that if the marriage between Mary and the Dauphin went forward and the Dauphin became King of France and, in her right, of England too, the navies of England and France would shut Charles out of the seas. The Low Countries would then be in manifest danger and the French King on the way to the monarchy of all Christendom.[6] Probably by then Henry did not mean the French marriage to go on and was merely trying to bring the reluctant Charles himself to the proposing point. But the remark suggests how his mind was working. Marry Mary to some sovereign prince who would have the power to assure her peaceful succession and to hold the realm in obedience, even if this meant sinking England's independence in some larger dynastic whole.

And who better than Charles V? James V of Scotland might bring a union of Great Britain, but he was only eight years old in 1521 and not yet able to hold even his own realm in obedience. The Dauphin might bring a union of France and Great Britain, but he was no older than Mary herself and, as a Frenchman, would be vastly unpopular in England. Besides, a union of the crowns of England and France must arouse the Emperor's implacable hostility and the English seem to have decided after Villalàr that Charles might after all be the more likely winner. 'The victory, we think for many reasons, will be with the Emperor,' Pace wrote on June 27th, 1521.[7] If that were so, then Charles V must seem the most suitable husband and protector for Mary. He was a grown man. The Netherlands, still the real centre of his power, were England's best market. His vast dominions should give him the power to assure Mary's inheritance, while their very vastness left some hope that he would have to leave England, as he left the Netherlands, a considerable measure of home rule. He was, too, not just another prince, another king; he was the Holy Roman Emperor, 'Majesty', the secular head of Christendom. If he could subdue the French, he would be its head in very deed; he and Mary and their descendants might be veritable rulers of the Catholic world. As we shall see, Henry was very much alive to these glittering possibilities in 1525 and it is clear from his treaties with Charles that he caught more than a glimpse of them in 1521–2.[8]

Even if the total destruction of the ancient French enemy and the virtual partition of the continent between uncle and nephew were to prove impossible, lesser but still substantial advantages could be hoped for from assisting Charles to victory. Henry, we have seen, was well aware of the importance of England's command of the Channel and Narrow Seas. From the first year of his reign he had been adding ships to his royal navy. He had also welcomed new ideas for making his ships more powerful. Thus, the *Mary Rose* was armed with muzzle-loading guns of improved design and so much heavier that they had to be mounted in batteries on the lower decks and fired through gunports pierced in the ship's sides. With these heavy 'broadsides' they were much more efficient artillery platforms and ship destroyers than Henry VII's warships had been. At the same time Henry VIII had encouraged the Trinity House guild of Thames pilots to chart, buoy, and train pilots for the tricky navigation of the Thames estuary and the waters southwards past the Goodwins to the Channel.[9] This made it easier to move the fleet from its main Thames and Medway bases to the advanced Channel bases that he and his father had developed at Portsmouth and Falmouth. Yet even now, and more especially since the French development of Le Havre, he needed bases on the southern, windward side of the Channel. For even the newer warships were still lofty, tubby, of short sea endurance, and very much at the mercy of the winds. Successful co-operation with Charles might at least bring an extension of the English Pale around Calais to include Boulogne – we shall see how well aware Henry was of its importance – and perhaps the Norman harbours, including Le Havre.

In addition to all these hopes or dreams, there was also the fact that Charles V was Catherine of Aragon's nephew. He was

already almost one of the family and no one could be more attractive as a son-in-law to the Queen of England. And Catherine's
influence must not be forgotten now, any more than in 1511.[10]
Even if Wolsey did monopolize counsel, there were still times
when the King's wife could advise her husband and even the most
intimate of Councillors could not be present. Finally, of course,
Charles V, although twenty-one years old to Mary's five years,
badly needed England's active assistance.

Whether he would pay the price of serving seven years for
Mary, would depend upon how much active assistance England
would give him and how soon. It would be too high a price to
pay for mere neutrality. On the other hand, the rewards for
assisting him handsomely and at once might be enormous, enormous enough to explain Henry's extraordinary decision of August
1521. In short, the explanation of Henry's undertaking to invade
France with an army of 40,000 men is probably to be found in
Charles's promise to marry Mary when she reached the age of
twelve.

The next three years brought very little encouragement to these
grandiose hopes. The Imperialists drove the French from Milan
and Tournai (November 1521) and defeated them in the field at
Bicocca (April 1522) before England came into the war in May
1522. But these preliminary successes encouraged Charles to concentrate his efforts upon northern Italy. His forces therefore gave
no help to the English army of 15,000 men under young Surrey
when it marched into north-eastern France in August. Unaided,
Surrey could achieve little and by October he had to abandon
his campaign, with only a few burned villages to show for it.
Meanwhile Albany had reappeared in Scotland and menaced
England with invasion from the north. The menace came to
nothing, for Flodden was still too fresh in Scottish memories, and
in October Albany went back to France. None the less, his brief
visit had restored the influence of the French party in Scotland
and faced England again with the familiar war on two fronts.
All this had brought Henry not a step nearer to regaining his
French lands. Wolsey, too, had been deceived in any hopes he
may have had of getting the Papacy, for Charles had allowed,
indeed encouraged, the election of his own old tutor, Adrian of
Utrecht, as Leo X's successor. The Imperial alliance had done
nothing so far to justify the dreams that had inspired it.

Autumn did bring a renewal of hope. The Duke of Bourbon, Constable of France and greatest of the French feudal nobles, quarrelled with his King and was meditating rebellion if the Emperor and King of England would assist him. The chance was too good to miss and, as Charles was again lavish in promises, it was quickly arranged that Bourbon should raise a revolt in southern France as soon as Francis I had committed himself and the main French armies to operations in Italy. Thereupon the allies would launch a triple invasion – the English from Calais into Picardy; the Imperialists from the Netherlands into Burgundy; and the Spaniards into Guienne. The victors would then partition France, Bourbon getting the south-east, Charles getting Burgundy, and the rest together with the crown going to Henry.

Once more disillusionment followed. Francis was too quick and Charles too slow or too preoccupied with Italy. Bourbon's intended treason was discovered and he had to flee to the Emperor for refuge before he could even begin to raise a revolt in France. Charles was chronically short of money and found it much harder to perform than to promise. So the Spanish invasion of Guienne never developed after an initial repulse at Bayonne and the Imperialist army from the Netherlands, 10,000 men under the refugee Bourbon, had to be taken into English pay before it could move. Wolsey, too, had some difficulty in raising funds and the English were not ready much earlier than Bourbon's forces. It was September before Suffolk, with what Wolsey boasted was the largest army that had left England's shores for a hundred years, began to march into Picardy. By then Henry had abandoned his larger dreams, which depended too much upon the Emperor's unreliable promises, and had instructed Suffolk to feint southwards as if to link up with Bourbon, but then to swing west and seize Boulogne. Control of the whole southern shore of the Straits would be some solid compensation for Henry's fading hopes of the French throne. The Imperialists objected strongly to Suffolk's instructions, but in vain.

Then suddenly, on September 19th, Wolsey with great difficulty persuaded his master to order Suffolk to continue his march southwards to join Bourbon's forces from Franche-Comté in an advance towards Paris. On September 14th Adrian VI had died and the Papacy was again vacant. Wolsey, it seems, did not actually hear of his death until September 30th. But Adrian had been seriously ill for some time and on September 8th had warned the cardinals in Rome that his end was near. It seems clear that news of his illness turned the thoughts of his would-be successor to the possibility of an early vacancy and the need for Imperialist support at Rome. At all events Henry reluctantly[11] let Wolsey have his way on this occasion. Suffolk marched as far south as Montdidier and Charles renewed his promises to secure the election of Wolsey this time. These promises proved as worthless as the rest. The Emperor did write to support Wolsey's candidature, but was careful to detain the messenger at Barcelona until a more amenable Italian had been elected as Clement VII (November 1523).[12] Failure in France accompanied failure at Rome. By November Wolsey could no longer find the money to keep Suffolk and Bourbon in the field. Bourbon's German mercenaries deserted him and Suffolk, deprived of their expected support, had also to withdraw.

Thus 1523 reiterated the lessons of 1522. Charles's whole energy had been bent upon Italy and he had done almost nothing to assist either England's invasion of France or Wolsey's designs upon the Papacy. Far from making good the lost French pensions, he had left England to pay for almost all the operations against France itself. He had, in short, used the English to distract the French in the same way that the French were wont to use the Scots to distract the English. If Henry had noticed the similarity, he would not have felt flattered. In any case, it was clear that England could hope for little from the war except what she could gain by her own efforts. So far that had not been much.

Yet the efforts of the past two years had already exhausted the King's resources. Close on £400,000 had been spent upon the war in 1522 and 1523. Over £352,000 of this had been raised by forced loans from his subjects.[13] More could hardly now be raised in that way and what had been raised was, at least in name, a loan and therefore due for repayment. To repay it and to find money for campaigns in 1524 was, as even Wolsey recognized, hardly possible except through Parliament. Accordingly, despite his hatred for that anti-clerical assembly, in April 1523 there assembled the only Parliament that met during his chancellorship. From it he demanded at once a grant of £800,000, four shillings in the pound on lands and goods, on the new and more realistic assessments which he had used for the 1522 forced loans. So staggering a demand, which Wolsey brusquely refused to lower, naturally produced long and heated debates. In the Commons the argument rose to quite unwonted heights and began to touch upon those mysteries of state and foreign policy which were normally regarded as too high for any but the King and his expert councillors to understand. One member, probably Thomas Cromwell, prepared (if he did not deliver) a speech[14] in which he ably denounced the whole policy of intervention on the continent, with its attendant neglect of trade and of the closer and more vital problem of Scotland. Nor did the discussions end with the formal debates. Soon the matter was 'blown abroad in every alehouse'.[15]

Wolsey came down in person to expostulate with the Commons and to hasten their grant. He was greeted with 'a marvellous obstinate silence'[16] very similar to that which was to greet Charles I's attempt to arrest the Five Members more than a century later. The Commons were not to be browbeaten even by the Legate in all his splendour and not until August 13th could a grant be extracted from them. Even then the sum voted was barely three-quarters of that for which Wolsey had asked; its collection was to be spread over two years; and was not to begin until February. These last provisions Wolsey promptly ignored when the death of Adrian VI revived his hopes of the Papacy and made him desperate for money to keep Suffolk and Bourbon in the field. In late October and early November 1523 he appointed commissioners to collect the whole at once 'by anticipation' – words, says the chronicler Hall,[17] which had been hitherto unknown to the commons of England. The Londoners seem to have paid fairly readily, but elsewhere the collection was slower and less easy and in fact the grant seems only to have brought in about £150,000 in all.[18] Anyway, as we have seen, Bourbon's army had disbanded and Suffolk's had retired long before money was forthcoming to hold them together.

Further large efforts were now out of the question. So far the King's subjects had made surprisingly little resistance to his exactions – perhaps they *had* learned something of Wolsey's 'new law of the Star Chamber'. Nevertheless it had taken four months to win Parliament's consent even to three-quarters of Wolsey's demand and that only after some very outspoken criticisms had been made of royal policy. And, if Parliament had voted only three-quarters of what was called for, the taxpayers were to pay only a quarter of what Parliament had voted. For Henry to press them further might prove dangerous and without pressing them further he could do little more against France. Accordingly Charles V was told that in 1524 he must expect no great help from England. The most that Henry could do was to contribute £20,000 towards an invasion of Provence by the Imperial army from Italy under Bourbon. That invasion failed even more completely than those which had preceded it. By the autumn Bourbon's army had broken and the French were back in Italy, besieging Pavia. Long before then, even before Bourbon entered Provence, Wolsey had opened secret negotiations with France. War had become impossible, so he had begun to explore the possibilities of a profitable peace.

He could hardly have chosen a more unfortunate time. For on February 24th, 1525 the French army was destroyed and the French King himself taken prisoner by the Imperialists at the Battle of Pavia. Charles V had apparently won decisive victory just when, as he was well aware, England had begun to desert him and so to forfeit any claim to share in the spoils. It was a maddening situation for Henry and he took the obvious way out of it. Within three weeks of receiving the news of Pavia, he sent Tunstal and Wingfield on a special embassy to Charles in Spain. They were to remind the Emperor[19] that 'one of the chief and principal things' intended by the Anglo-Imperial alliance 'hath always been to expel the French King from his usurped occupation of the crown of France'; and that 'the ambition of France shall always be an occasion to bring all Christian princes and countries unto war, hostility, and division.' Charles and Henry should therefore seize the present opportunity 'utterly to extinct the regiment of the French King and his line, or any other Frenchman, from the crown of France'. That crown should then be placed upon Henry's head, where it rightfully belonged 'by just title of inheritance'. The 'noble countries and great dominions the French King hath and keepeth from the Emperor', as well as all French claims upon 'the Duchy of Milan, Asti, Genoa, the realm of Naples, and other great territories in Italy', should likewise be restored to Charles.

All this, of course, could be accomplished only 'by force, violence, and puissance'. But this, with

the said French King now remaining in captivity, his noblemen, captains, and whole army vanquished, slain, destroyed,
or taken prisoners, and consequently the realm of France
remaining without an head, destitute of courage, good
counsel, ability, or power, is more facile to be done at this
time than at any other that ever hath been known or heard
of: and specially if the King's Highness and the Emperor,
according to the conventions and treaties passed between
them, do make their personal invasion into France this
summer.

Leaving fortresses and strongholds by the way, they should march
straight to meet each other at Paris. There, after Henry had been
crowned King of France, he would, if required, hand over Mary
to Charles and then accompany and assist him 'unto Rome there
to see the crown imperial set upon his head.' Of that glorious
voyage, if this programme were accomplished,

> is like to ensue unto the Emperor the whole monarchy of
> Christendom. For of his own inheritance he hath the realm
> of Spain and a great part of Germany, the realms of Sicily
> and Naples, with Flanders, Holland, Zeeland, Brabant, and
> Hainault and other his Low Countries; by election he hath
> the Empire, whereunto appertaineth all the rest of Italy and
> many towns imperial in Germany and elsewhere; by the
> possibility apparent to come by my lady Princess [Mary] he
> should hereafter have England and Ireland, with the title to
> the superiority of Scotland, and in this case all France with
> the dependencies.

'The whole monarchy of Christendom': the means to solve the
English succession problem, to heal the division of Catholic
Europe, to present a united front to infidel and heretic, to give
reality to the paper union of 1518. Here, given its fullest expression, was surely the dream that had inspired Henry's offensive
league with the Emperor in 1521. It may well appear wild and
chimerical to modern eyes, and historians have perhaps too
readily assumed that, because it seems absurdly grandiose to us,
it cannot have been seriously intended by Henry VIII. But
Henry VIII was at heart more a medieval man than a modern
man. He was a strong traditionalist and his steady support of
Papal authority had not been entirely due to Wolsey's influence.

It was Henry, not Wolsey, who had written a book against Luther and earned from the Pope the title of Defender of the Faith. It was More, not Wolsey, who helped him with that book, and if Henry thirsted for popularity, he also coveted the measured approval of the wise and the learned no less than the fickle applause of the populace. The idea of Christian unity still held its appeal for him, at least if that unity could be achieved under the aegis of his own family. Nor did the preliminary to Christian unity, the conquest of France, appear as chimerical in the light of Bourbon's treason and the radiance of Pavia as it does in the cold afterglow of history.

The final proof of his seriousness is that on March 21st, 1525, less than a month after Pavia, commissions went out for the levy of what, with unintentional irony, was described as an Amicable Grant of one-sixth of the value of their lands and goods from the laity and one-third from the clergy. After all the trouble there had been over getting Parliament to vote £600,000 less than two years before, Henry would never have demanded another £500,000 from the laity alone, without counting the clergy's share, unless the need had seemed imperative. Only war with France could demand such a sum and it was clearly war on the grand scale of the 1521 treaty that he was bent upon.

But now at last the limits of Englishmen's obedience began to appear. The Londoners protested their inability to pay any more and a City Councillor quoted to Wolsey's face the statute of Richard III against benevolences.[20] The Cardinal's hectorings moved neither the City authorities nor the individual citizens whom he summoned before him and threatened with the King's wrath if they refused his demands. They had not learned the new law of the Star Chamber that far. Out in the shires Warham, Norfolk, Suffolk, and the other great lords who had been sent down as commissioners to collect the Grant, met with a resistance even more alarming. In Kent men shouted at the Archbishop that the French wars had ruined the whole nation; that anyway France was not worth conquering and could not be held if conquered; and that for all his loans and taxes, Henry VIII 'hath not one foot of land more in France than his most noble father had, which lacked no riches or wisdom to win the Kingdom of France if he had thought it expedient'.[21] In East Anglia twenty thousand men were up and the demonstration was beginning to wear the aspect of a rebellion. Even the local Justices of the Peace and gentry there were so hostile to the Grant that the only action they would take was to order the bridges to be broken down along the line of the rioters' advance. Most sinister of all, while the commons of Kent were comparing Henry VIII so unfavourably with his father, the Dukes of Norfolk and Suffolk wrote[22] to warn him to look carefully to Buckingham's son, lest the commons of East Anglia should remember that Plantagenet blood ran in the Staffords' veins. Throughout April and May 1525 the whole of southern and eastern England – the very regions most devoted to the Tudor monarchy – were in uproar. In the end, the King and Wolsey had to confess themselves beaten. Henry, 'sore moved' Hall tells us,[23] ordered that the Grant should be abandoned and that all who had opposed it should be granted his full pardon. Thereupon the uproar subsided as quickly as it had arisen.

It is small wonder that Henry was sorely moved. During those few weeks the very foundations upon which the Tudor monarchy rested had been laid bare. The tumult had shown once more that, in spite of Wolsey's work, the monarchy was still founded upon an implicit partnership between King and people, that the King's will could be enforced only so far as it did not actively and seriously harm the interests of the dominant classes of the nation, the taxpaying classes. This was a lesson that Henry was to take to heart and by which he was to profit greatly in the future. But for the moment his disappointment was bitter indeed. The universal opposition of his subjects made him quite unable to play his part in the great plan that Tunstal and Wingfield were on their way to expound to the Emperor. Whatever Charles's answer might be, there could be no English campaign to expel the French King 'from his usurped occupation of the crown of France'. The only course was peace. By the first week in June, negotiations were resumed with the French regency. Also, before Tunstal and Wingfield's account of their reception by the Emperor reached England, a letter from Henry was on its way to inform them – as they summarized it in their reply[24] – 'that your Highness is not so furnished in your coffers that you may continue the war, nor cannot be helped by your subjects'. The insubstantial pageant of a journey to Paris and Rome, the dream of Mary Tudor sharing with Charles of Habsburg the whole monarchy of Christendom, had faded into nothing even as the English ambassadors were having their first audiences with the Emperor.

It mattered little, therefore, that at those audiences Charles told the ambassadors firmly that his purpose was peace, not war, and showed no enthusiasm at all for the idea of carving out of a defeated France a new Angevin Empire for his belatedly repentant ally. But Charles did not stop there. He went on to demand that both Mary and her dowry should be sent at once to Spain. His coffers were certainly as empty as Henry's, but a demand so obviously unacceptable could only have been meant to provide an excuse for the breach of yet another and more important promise. And, surely enough, when it was refused, he immediately asked that Henry should release him from his engagement to marry the nine-year-old Mary and consent to his marrying instead the twenty-two-year-old and richly dowered Isabella of Portugal.

This rejection of Mary by Charles did matter, mattered very greatly. For Henry VIII it was the unkindest cut of all. His subjects had shattered his dreams of conquering France. Now his nephew and ally had shattered the one apparently workable scheme which he had been able to devise for securing a peaceable succession to the throne of England. Charles had failed him in 1525 even more disastrously than Ferdinand had failed him in 1514. Now, as then, the immediate result was a sharp revulsion against the Spanish alliance and a turn towards friendship with England's ancient enemy France. But this time Henry's resentment went much deeper and carried him into revolutionary courses whose effects were to prove far more lasting and wide-reaching.

Chapter 9

The Divorce

THE jilting of Princess Mary by Charles V in 1525 marked the great turning point in Henry VIII's reign. Its full consequences took some years to develop, for Henry, even in passion, was slow to move from ancient moorings. Nevertheless, in the summer of 1525 he began to cast off the ties which so long had bound him to Spain and to Catherine. From that he was to go on gradually to cast off those which for even longer had bound England to Rome and to loosen those which drew her towards the continent. Slowly and hesitatingly at first, then with steadily growing assurance and determination, he began to move out into new and deeper waters, upon a course that was to carry England farther and farther from her medieval habits and beliefs.

The first public sign of Henry's reaction to Charles's infidelity pointed significantly towards new and drastic solutions of the succession problem. Immediately after the news reached England that Charles meant to break his engagement to Mary, Henry drew his one and only illegitimate son out of the decent obscurity in which he had hitherto been kept. On June 15th, 1525 the six-year-old boy, borne to him by Elizabeth Blount in 1519, was suddenly paraded before the court and created Duke of Richmond. The title was that by which Henry VII had been known before his accession to the throne and its new holder was now given precedence over all the peers of the realm, even over the Princess Mary herself. A month later he was made Lord Admiral of England and soon Lord Lieutenant of the North and then Lord Lieutenant of Ireland. The intention behind all this was plain to see. Charles's breach of promise had not only revived the King's anxiety about the succession. It had so angered him against all things Spanish that he was prepared to prefer his illegitimate but wholly English son to his legitimate but half-Spanish daughter as the heir to his throne. He was no longer prepared to consider, as he had been (if rather insincerely) in the previous year, even the possibility of finding a solution by matching that daughter with the next heir, the boy James V of Scotland, his sister Margaret's son.[1]

The King was clearly beginning to consider solutions of his greatest problem in which Catherine and Mary would have little or no part. Soon he began to go further. A bastard son was, after all, hardly more satisfactory than a legitimate daughter as successor to the throne, and Catherine's anger at his sudden promotion served only to drive Henry to more drastic remedies. For some weeks King and Queen were barely on speaking terms. By autumn the storm seemed to have blown over. But his wife's resentment, coming on top of her nephew's infidelity, seems to have turned Henry finally against Catherine. She had already lost her attraction as a woman – 'rather ugly than otherwise', a Venetian had found her in 1515; 'old and deformed', the ungallant Francis I said in 1520.[2] Now that, in her fortieth year, she was past the usual age of childbearing,[3] her maternal devotion to her daughter's rights made her an encumbrance as a Queen. A King of Henry VIII's theological attainments – and peculiarly adaptable conscience – was sure in such a mood to remember, or to be reminded, that she was also his deceased brother's widow. And did not Leviticus xx.21 say that 'if a man shall take his brother's wife, it is an unclean thing; he hath uncovered his brother's nakedness; they shall be childless.' Admittedly, Deuteronomy xxv.5 suggested that this applied only while the brother was alive and that the opposite might be true when the brother was dead without children. But the canon law accepted Leviticus as of superior authority and it was only after obtaining a Papal dispensation that Henry and Catherine had been able to marry sixteen years earlier. Henry himself had formally registered a protest against his betrothal to Catherine in his father's time and doubts had been expressed about the Pope's power to dispense with the law of God on this matter.[4] Since then, the mortality among the royal offspring had been so nearly complete as to suggest that nothing indeed could remove the curse of Leviticus. If that were so, then Henry and Catherine had been living unwittingly in sin for the past sixteen years. For the salvation of their souls, as well as for the assurance of the succession to the throne, the sooner they separated the better.

We cannot tell just when Henry began to provide himself with this most convenient reason of conscience to reinforce his reasons of state. Certainly in 1526 he was consulting the Dean of St Paul's about the authority of Deuteronomy.[5] In September 1526, too, Clerk, the ambassador to France, cryptically warned Wolsey of difficulties likely to arise at Rome *circa istud benedictum divortium*[6] and it is not unlikely that the 'blessed divorce' which he had in mind may have been that of Henry from Catherine. The story of English foreign policy points in the same direction. Hitherto, despite his annoyance, Henry had been careful to avoid any open breach with Charles V. He had hastened to make friends with the French before Charles could settle with them. By the treaty of August 1525 peace was made and the French regent promised Henry a pension of £21,000 a year. Again, when Charles and Francis came to terms at Madrid in January 1526, Henry promptly sent an embassy to encourage the French King to break his promises and especially to refuse to marry the Emperor's sister Eleanor or to hand over the Duchy of Burgundy. In August he agreed to join Francis in pressing Charles to pay his debts to England and to release the French King's two sons whom he held as hostages for the performance of the treaty of Madrid. Yet he was clearly unwilling to break completely with Charles and he was still trying to extract the cession of Boulogne as the price of his friendship with France. Even the entreaties of the Pope could not move him to give active support to the league of Cognac, formed in May to resist Imperial designs in Italy. Henry accepted the title of Protector of the League, but he would send it neither men nor money.

In the autumn of 1526, however, a change began to come over English policy. Henry and Wolsey began to press Francis for a closer and more active co-operation. They ceased to speak of the cession of Boulogne; they hinted that Francis might easily find a queen more suitable than Eleanor; and they sent Russell with 30,000 ducats to encourage the Pope and his Italian allies 'to stick to that that is intended by the League'.[7] The beginning of this change followed close upon the sack of the Papal palace by Charles's allies, the Colonnas (September 1526). The coincidence of dates strongly suggests that the motive behind Henry's new course was a desire to prevent the Pope from falling into the power of Catherine's nephew. This would imply that by now Henry had determined to secure the dissolution of his marriage to Catherine. For, to secure that dissolution, he must keep the Pope out of the

Emperor's clutches. The Church had always reserved jurisdiction in matrimonial causes to its own courts, marriage being one of the sacraments. In recent centuries, the matrimonial suits of princes had usually been reserved to the highest Church court of all, the Papal curia. Moreover, Henry's suit involved the validity of a Papal dispensation and could therefore hardly be decided except by the Pope himself. Ordinarily, the Defender of the Faith might have expected at least a favourable hearing. Pope Alexander VI had readily granted Louis XII of France a divorce in order that he might marry Charles VIII's widow and retain her Duchy of Brittany. The Duke of Suffolk had at least one marriage dissolved, and a dispensation declared invalid, to enable him to marry Henry's sister Mary when she was free from Louis XII. And Henry's other sister, Margaret, was even now getting from Clement VII himself a divorce upon transparently flimsy pretexts. But the wife whom the Defender of the Faith wished to divorce was the aunt of the Emperor; and the Emperor's armies, after taking Milan in July, had just given the Pope reason to believe their leader Moncada's boast that they could with impunity attack even God himself.[8] Henry was probably right in guessing that Charles would not risk a war with England to save his aunt's marriage. But Charles was not likely, if he could prevent it, to let the Pope annul that marriage and set Henry free, free perhaps to marry a French princess. A man of Clement VII's nervous and hesitant character would be easily intimidated and it was therefore essential to prevent the Imperial armies from dominating Rome.

That could only be done by stirring the French into action. Accordingly, in December 1526 Fitzwilliam was sent to make a definite proposal for a match between Francis I and the young Princess Mary. Francis, in despair of getting Charles to modify the treaty of Madrid, responded by sending the Bishop of Tarbes to England in February 1527 and on April 30th an Anglo-French offensive alliance against Charles was signed. Francis, or his second son Henry, was to marry Mary and add another 15,000 crowns a year to the King of England's pension. England and France were jointly to require Charles to pay his debts to England, release the two French princes, and accept a reasonable settlement of all other questions. If he refused, the two allies would declare war upon him. Meanwhile Wolsey was to go over to arrange more detailed plans with Francis and his council. Before he went, a definite though very secret step towards the divorce was taken in England. As soon as the French treaty was concluded and the celebrations over, Wolsey and Warham in the utmost secrecy called Henry before them to justify his marriage to his deceased brother's widow. The inquiry began on May 17th. Its original intention was perhaps that the two Archbishops should pronounce the marriage invalid and present the Pope with an accomplished fact which he might the more readily confirm. If so, the plan was changed. On May 31st Wolsey suddenly adjourned the proceedings, saying that the case was so thorny that he must consult some of the bishops and more learned canon lawyers.

Once again it looks as if we must look to Rome for the true explanation. On May 6th the unpaid and mutinous Imperial army in Italy had stormed Rome. Clement again took refuge in his castle of San Angelo while the uncontrollable and sacrilegious soldiery howled around its walls and committed outrages which shocked and surprised even the Romans. Nor did they withdraw after a few days, as Colonna's men had withdrawn in September. They remained in Rome. The Pope was virtually their prisoner and, with the Imperial armies in control of Rome as well as Milan, a French offensive into Italy became an absolute necessity if Henry was to get Papal confirmation for the annulment of his marriage.

For Wolsey this created a desperate dilemma. He could hardly hope to persuade the French to march on Rome unless he also committed England to a war against the Emperor. Yet there was no money to finance a campaign of any size and to call upon the nation to pay for a war against the master of the Netherlands market might well arouse an opposition beside which the troubles of 1525 would look like a friendly demonstration. Already the French alliance had provoked high words from the Duke of Norfolk in the King's presence. Active hostilities against the Emperor might provoke something worse than high words. They might provoke open rebellion. It was far more probable that they would soon inspire a new policy, a policy such as a Legate *a latere* could neither contemplate nor share in. For Wolsey's leading opponents at home had a bitter jealousy of clerical influence and no great love of Papal authority. The Cardinal knew well, and repeatedly warned Clement VII, that they would be far more ready to defy the Pope and the Church than to fight the Emperor and the Netherlands. If they could convert the King to their views, Papal authority and clerical independence might well vanish from England.

In 1515 Wolsey had been able to avert such a catastrophe. But some time during the summer of 1527 he learned something which must have warned him that this time the King's conversion was all too possible. Henry had fallen in love with Anne Boleyn and, what was worse, meant to marry her. Exactly when this happened, we again cannot tell. He must have seen Anne about the court for several years, since her return from France at the age of fourteen in 1521 or 1522. But until recently it had been her elder sister Mary who had taken Elizabeth Blount's place as his mistress. The transference of his affections to Anne, probably in 1526 or early 1527, need not have affected his policy if she had been content to accept the same role as her sister. Anne, however, though 'not one of the handsomest women in the world' (despite her fine eyes),[9] was ambitious and calculating. Besides, the King's growing dissatisfaction with Catherine gave her an opportunity that had not been offered to Mary. Anne saw her chance to become Queen and, it seems, steadily refused to become the King's mistress until she was reasonably well assured of the more legitimate title. It was a dangerous game to play with a man like Henry VIII, but for six years she played it with a nerve and shrewdness worthy of a better cause and not unworthy of the mother of Elizabeth I. The effect of her resistance upon Henry was to turn a passing flirtation into a consuming passion, his 'great folly' as he aptly termed it,[10] and a prime determinant of English policy. It was not merely that the affair dragged the high matter of the succession down to the level of a sordid divorce-court scandal. It made Henry inflexibly resolved to get his marriage to Catherine annulled and ready, if the Pope should prove recalcitrant, to consider policies in which the Pope and his Legate could have no part.

What was worse from Wolsey's point of view was that around Anne all the forces opposed to him naturally rallied. She came of a family of comparatively recent origin, whose fortunes had been founded in trade, augmented in the royal service, and crowned by marriage into the nobility. Her great-grandfather had been Lord Mayor of London in 1479; her grandmother had been a

Butler, daughter to the Earl of Ormonde; her mother was a Howard, sister to the Duke of Norfolk. Anne and her relations had old scores to pay off against the Cardinal. He had baulked her father, Sir Thomas Boleyn, of the treasurership of the household and perhaps delayed for two years his elevation to the viscounty of Rochford. He had, on the King's instructions but with unnecessary roughness, broken Anne's own engagement to young Henry Percy, the Earl of Northumberland's heir. Norfolk had not forgiven being punished, when Earl of Surrey, by the Star Chamber in 1516; and since his appointment as Lord Treasurer in succession to his father in December 1522, he had become the recognized leader of Wolsey's opponents at court. Through Anne these men now had easy access to the King and in this unofficial fashion something like a new 'council at court' began to take shape over which Wolsey had little or no control. Unless he could again conjure from the empty air a miracle like those of 1514 and 1518, his hold upon the King's favour, the only real foundation of his power, would speedily be lost.

Such was the dilemma facing Wolsey when in July 1527 he went over to discuss with Francis I what measures the allies should take to achieve the objects agreed upon in the treaty of April 30th. The expedients that he devised during the three months of his stay in France show very plainly how desperate his problems had become. His first plan was to get Francis I to invite all the 'independent' cardinals to the Papal city of Avignon, an enclave surrounded by French territory and quite outside the Emperor's control. From them, and if possible from the captive Clement VII as well, he hoped to secure his own appointment as Papal Vicar-General with full powers *omnia faciendi et exequendi durante captivitate summi pontificis*. He would then, in effect, be acting Pope and would be able, as he pointed out to Henry, to settle the divorce case by Papal authority 'without informing the Pope of your purpose'.[11] If that could be done, war against the Emperor might no longer be necessary. However, the Pope, and worse still the Emperor, had been informed already. Before Wolsey met Francis at Amiens in August, he learned that Catherine had managed to warn Charles of Henry's intention to divorce her and that Charles had sent Cardinal Quinones to inform the Pope and support her cause at Rome. In December Charles allowed Clement to escape to the comparative freedom of Orvieto and so took away the pretext for Wolsey's proposed vicariate. There were rumours that, despite this, Francis and Wolsey were planning to set up a patriarchate of the French and English Churches, independent of Rome and with Wolsey as its patriarch. But if this was indeed intended, nothing came of it. Nor did Wolsey's assembly of 'independent' cardinals do much to raise his hopes. When it met, at Compiègne instead of Avignon, only one Italian and three French cardinals came to support him.

The ecclesiastical offensives which Wolsey had planned, thus came to nothing. If the Pope was to be prised out of the Emperor's clutches and induced to grant Henry his divorce, the only way left was by war, by French military action in Italy. If Lautrec advanced, Wolsey's agent at Rome told him in December 1527, the Pope would do all Henry wanted; but if not, he would do nothing.[12] But if Lautrec was to advance, the French would expect England's active support in the war. Wolsey in his desperation was ready to pay that price and on his instructions, given without consulting King or Council, the English envoys in Spain joined their French allies in formally declaring war on Charles in January 1528. Henry, who still trusted to the Cardinal's wizardry, allowed the declaration to stand despite the protests of his other councillors. However, it was one thing to declare war, quite another to induce the nation to provide the means to wage it, especially against the Netherlands and in alliance with France. Those who had kicked at war against France in 1523 and 1525 saw even less reason now to acquiesce in war against the Emperor. The Merchant Adventurers ignored orders, which under Henry VII they had several times obeyed, to transfer their trade from Antwerp to Calais. There was dangerous rioting in East Anglia, Wiltshire, and Somerset, cloth-making areas where a stoppage of trade with the Netherlands meant unemployment and distress. In Kent men talked of putting Wolsey to sea in a leaky boat[13] and Londoners heartily agreed with the proposal. Even the French ambassador admitted that Wolsey seemed to be the only Englishman who wanted a war with Flanders.[14] So great indeed was the opposition that he was unable to have his war. In March 1528 an agreement had to be made with the Netherlands for trade to go on as usual and in June this was extended into a full truce. The truce was not to extend to Italy, but it did mean that there was in effect nowhere for England to attack Charles V directly even if Wolsey had been able to find the means to finance such an attack. All that he could do to help the French was to send them £49,000 in cash and a jewel worth £10,000 and to forego the payment of £53,000 of Henry's French pension.[16]

The French, however, were by now already committed. Lautrec's advance had begun and for a time he carried all before him. All the Milanese, except for Milan itself, fell to him. The Genoese joined him. Their fleet under Andrea Doria gave the French command of the western Mediterranean, cutting off the Imperial army in Italy from Spanish help. Thus when Lautrec marched south, he was able to free Rome and to shut up the Imperial forces in Naples by the end of April. The forecast made by Wolsey's agent in December now proved exactly true. Clement VII's actions over Henry VIII's divorce moved like a barometer recording the pressure and fortunes of the French army. As soon as the Imperialists were safely shut up in Naples, the Pope dispatched Cardinal Campeggio – who was, incidentally, absentee Bishop of Salisbury – to join with Wolsey in hearing Henry's suit in England. On June 8th, with Naples in worse straits than ever, he sent Campeggio a secret decretal commission empowering him and Wolsey, if he judged it well, not only to hear but also to settle the cause in England, to pronounce the decree that would grant Henry his divorce.

Campeggio, however, was an old man and wary. He also suffered from gout. He was not therefore a rapid traveller and it was not until October that he at length arrived in England. By then the situation in Italy had changed radically. The French had quarrelled with Genoa and in July Andrea Doria had taken his fleet over to the Imperialists. Supplies and reinforcements flowed into Naples from Sicily and Spain and it was the French army that now found its sea communications cut. Lautrec himself died of a plague that carried off almost two-thirds of his troops within a few weeks and in September the remnant capitulated at Aversa. The French still clung to their holdings in northern Italy and next spring sent new forces over the Alps to reinforce them. But even in the north their days were numbered. On June 21st, 1529 their army was routed at Landriano and they were run out of Italy altogether.

Long before then the Papal barometer had turned against Henry. Campeggio, on various pretexts including the alleged discovery of new evidence about the original dispensation, managed to postpone the opening of the Legatine court in England. By the end of 1528 the Pope had ordered him to destroy the decretal commission and avoid any definite conclusion. It was not until May 31st, 1529, only three weeks before the final French defeat at Landriano, that the two Legates at last opened their court. Catherine at once denied its competence and appealed from the Legates to the Pope at Rome. While her appeal was under leisurely discussion, news came that the Pope, convinced by Landriano, had on June 29th concluded the treaty of Barcelona with Charles V and vowed to live and die an Imperialist. One of the first fruits of his conversion was the revocation of the commission to Campeggio and Wolsey and the evocation of the Divorce case to Rome. On August 5th the French also made their peace with Charles at Cambrai, abandoning all their claims in Italy. The Pope was again in the Emperor's power and there was no hope of any further French efforts to release him.

Henry's great anxiety now was lest Charles, freed from French hostility, should turn his arms against England in defence of his aunt's rights. Fortunately, Charles, too, had worries besides France to distract him. In the spring of 1529 the Lutheran princes and cities in Germany had made their famous protest at the second Diet of Speyer and were beginning to consider a political union to defend their faith. Philip of Hesse, one of their more influential leaders, had even put out feelers to France, Denmark, and other foreign states. Besides this Protestant problem, there were the Turks. Under Soliman the Magnificent, and not without French prompting, they had already conquered the greater part of Hungary and slain its young King Louis at Mohacs in 1526. Charles's brother Ferdinand, his lieutenant and intended successor in the Holy Roman Empire, had inherited Louis's kingdoms of Bohemia and Hungary, though his title to Hungary was being challenged by John Zapolya who was in touch with Philip of Hesse as well as with Soliman. By the summer of 1529 a great Turkish army, led by the Sultan in person, was advancing upon Vienna, the capital of the Austrian lands of the Habsburgs, and Ferdinand desperately needed Charles's aid. To free his brother from Turks and Protestants was for Charles a far more important task than that of keeping his aunt tied to Henry VIII. Once he had come to terms with Francis and ended the French threat to

Italy, he was therefore ready enough to make peace with England too. The peace, concluded in August 1529, gave Henry, by the mere fact that Charles had agreed to it, reasonable assurance that the Emperor would not treat the divorce as a cause for war. With the Earl of Angus and the Douglas faction again dominant in Scotland, and as friendly as ever to England despite Margaret's divorcing of Angus, Henry could now press forward his suit at Rome by whatever other means he could think of, without feeling any undue anxiety about the attitude of neighbouring powers.

There in fact lay the true significance of the peace with Charles. Wolsey had tried to secure the King's divorce by joining in the great and expensive game of continental politics, exploiting the rivalries of the great powers to coerce the Pope. He had failed utterly by August 1529 and the treaty with Charles, which Wolsey was not allowed to negotiate, was a clear indication that the King meant to put on pressure by other means. That could hardly take any other form than pressure through the Church in England, threats against Papal revenues from the Church and Papal jurisdiction over the Church. In a direct struggle of that sort, with its implied threat of schism, the King needed the full and expressed support of the nation to assert his will over the clergy. The events of 1515 had shown how readily that support would be given for any policy whose goal appeared to be the reform of clerical abuses and the curtailment of clerical privileges. The summer of 1529 showed that Henry had understood these things, for in August writs went out for the assembly of a new Parliament. On October 16th Wolsey was dismissed from his Chancellorship and replaced, significantly, by a layman, Sir Thomas More. There was no place for a Cardinal-Legate in the King's new policy and no place for a foreign minister who could not resist the limelight of continental great power politics, who could not resist the temptation of trying to play as an equal with the two Leviathans of Christendom. Under the stimulus of his desire to divorce Catherine and marry Anne, Henry VIII had at last learned the lesson of 1512–14 and of 1522–3. He had at last learned, what his father had understood by instinct, that England neither could nor need meddle deeply in continental affairs as long as the continental powers remained reasonably evenly balanced and sharply divided by their mutual jealousies.

Chapter 10

The Break with Rome

FOR at least ten years after Wolsey's fall, all English history remains focused upon 'the King's great matter'. Everything revolves around Henry VIII's efforts to persuade or coerce the Pope, vainly as it proved, to grant him the annulment of his marriage to Catherine of Aragon. In a sense, therefore, the whole story of the breach with Rome, and almost all English history during these years, can be regarded as part of the history of Tudor foreign policy. But the methods that Henry chose to employ after 1529 to attain his end were domestic and constitutional rather than diplomatic. He was now putting pressure on the Pope in England and at Westminster rather than in Italy and at Rome; by legislation and confiscation at home rather than by military or diplomatic action abroad. We need not therefore repeat here the often told story of the assertion of the royal supremacy over the English clergy, of the use of Parliament, of the attack upon the Pope's English revenues and jurisdictions.

Foreign policy in the stricter sense of course continued, like everything else, to be governed by the demands of 'the King's great matter'. But it was no longer, as it had been in Wolsey's last years, the principal means for answering those demands. Now, as in Henry VII's time, it was once more subordinated to, and an extension of, domestic policy, not an end in itself but a means to furthering abroad the King's purposes at home. Its chief task was to hold the ring and to prevent any interference by foreign powers with the working out of those domestic purposes. Above all, this meant keeping Catherine's nephew Charles V from interfering. This was not unduly difficult, for Charles, as we have seen, already had more than enough other problems upon his hands. The penalty that he paid for the vastness and wide spread of his dominions was that they made him perforce a principal in almost every quarrel in Europe. The Turks were forced to raise their siege of Vienna in October 1529, but they continued to menace the eastern marches of the Empire. John Zapolya became the

Sultan's vassal and it was not until 1533 that some sort of peace was patched up in Hungary. It left the Turks in control of most of that kingdom and within ninety miles of Vienna. Furthermore Turkish power was beginning to threaten Spanish control of the western Mediterranean. Barbarossa, the great corsair chief of Algiers, became Soliman's vassal and in 1534 was to add Tunis to his dominions. Only the year before, Turkish envoys were welcomed at the court of Francis I. No open Franco-Turkish co-operation followed until 1536, after Charles had wrested Tunis from Barbarossa and was again at war with France. But from 1533 the threat to Spain's communications with Italy was apparent and Charles, by leading the Tunis expedition of 1535 in person, showed how sensitive he was to the menace there.

The German Protestants were another serious problem for the Emperor. In December 1530 they had decided to form themselves into the Schmalkaldic League to defend their faith by joint political, and if necessary military, action. By the end of 1531 the League was formed and at the Nürnberg Diet of 1532 Charles felt compelled to yield them a formal toleration until a General Council of the Church could be held to reconcile their differences with Rome. Despite this, they too were beginning to link up with France. The first overtures went back to 1528. They were renewed in 1534 and resulted in a secret treaty between the League and Francis. Here, as with the Turks, it was this linking with France that was the greatest danger. For France could weld all Charles's problems into one insoluble whole. It is true that until 1536 Francis, after his experience in the 1520s, was afraid to strike; but he was willing enough to wound and his continuing jealousy of the Emperor was Henry's surest guarantee against foreign interference during these crucial years.

The principal tasks of English foreign policy after 1529 were therefore to keep alive French jealousy towards the Emperor, to use it to deter Charles from intervening in English affairs, and to exploit it when possible as a lever upon the Pope. So, for example, after Henry had induced the lords spiritual and temporal to write their threatening letters to Clement VII in July 1530, he followed this up by getting Francis to send an embassy to Rome to urge the Pope to leave the decision in the divorce case to the Archbishop of Canterbury and the doctors of the universities. The Pope's public answer was to forbid Henry to re-marry until he himself had pronounced upon the case (January 1531). Yet, although he had not been persuaded to pronounce for Henry, he had still not pronounced against him. Moreover, in secret he had told the French ambassador that he would be content to see Henry go ahead and marry Anne, so long as the Pope did not have to give his public consent and so long as Papal jurisdiction and prerogatives were not encroached upon.[1] The hint, several times given, was broad enough. It was, indeed, clear that Clement was still only a reluctant Imperialist. As a Medici, he feared for the independence of Florence, now that the Spaniards held Milan as well as Naples and dominated in Genoa and Savoy too. As Pope, he feared lest, by becoming too much the Emperor's chaplain, he might drive France and England into schism. He was therefore already considering the possibility of marrying his young cousin, Catherine de Medici, to a French prince as a first step towards rebuilding an Italian party under French patronage to balance the dominance of Spain in the peninsula and to replace the Papacy in a position of independence between the powers of Europe.

Here was a situation that still gave scope for English diplomacy and in 1532 Henry, his patience now growing very thin, set about exploiting it. In June he concluded a new treaty[2] with Francis which gave him considerable assurance against an Imperial attack. For the French King promised to send a fleet into the Channel and 15,000 troops to England if Charles attempted an invasion. Furthermore, he and Henry agreed to meet at Calais in the autumn. In July the French ambassador, no doubt at Henry's prompting, urged that Anne Boleyn should be invited to accompany Henry and that Francis's sister Margaret, the Queen of Navarre, should be there to entertain her.[3] Clearly, Henry was pressing towards a final decision and hoping to carry Francis with him, for if Francis agreed to receive Anne in this warm and public fashion, it would be an unmistakable declaration of his determination to stand by Henry in the matter of his re-marriage. Francis did agree. In October he welcomed Henry at Boulogne and went on with him to meet Anne at Calais.

Just what was agreed at those meetings is not altogether clear, for Henry and Francis were later to disagree about the exact nature of Francis's promises and Francis was reluctant to repeat them in writing. Certainly they agreed that, at least for the time being, there was no need for either of them to send help to the

Emperor against the Turks. It seems not unlikely, too, that Francis advised Henry to go ahead and marry Anne; quite certain that he agreed to meet the Pope as soon as possible and press him to satisfy Henry about the divorce. If fear of the Emperor held the Pope back, Francis was to suggest that he and the Papal court could leave Rome and return to Avignon.[4] It was over what was to happen if Clement refused to consider this new Babylonian Captivity at Avignon, or any other acceptable solution, that the misunderstandings arose. Henry apparently assumed that Francis would then go with him in appealing against the Pope to a General Council and even, if necessary, in carrying France as well as England into schism.[5] At all events, he seems to have gone ahead upon that assumption. Late in January 1533 he secretly married Anne. In February Parliament, asserting that England was 'an empire governed by one supreme head and king', passed the famous Act forbidding appeals to Rome. In May his new Archbishop of Canterbury, Thomas Cranmer, whose appointment the Pope confirmed in March, pronounced the marriage with Catherine null and void. After the Act against Appeals, the verdict of the Archbishop's court was to all intents and purposes final according to English law and on June 1st Anne Boleyn was crowned Queen of England. Finally, in the autumn, Bonner was instructed to inform the Pope formally of Henry's appeal to a General Council. This was in October 1533.

Bonner found the Pope at Marseilles in company with Francis. After much hesitation and many delays Clement had at last come to meet the French King, bringing with him Catherine de Medici for her wedding to Francis's second son Henry, Duke of Orléans. Bonner and his colleague Stephen Gardiner found Francis in no pleasant mood and he angrily told them that they had marred everything.[6] The cause of his anger is not difficult to divine. He was trying to work himself into a position from which he could again challenge Charles V. With the English alliance he had gained the means of closing the Channel and of cutting the Netherlands off from Spain. That in itself was already bearing fruit. It not only made Charles, partly at Catherine of Aragon's prompting but also upon a wider consideration of the possibilities,[7] decide against an attack upon England in his aunt's cause. It also, after he had attempted to stiffen the Pope's resolution by an interview at Bologna in December 1532, led him in 1533 to acquiesce in the proposed marriage of Catherine de Medici to Orléans and to withdraw the troops which had been propping up that unreliable Imperial puppet, Francesco Sforza, in Milan. Yet Francis needed more than England if he was again to put himself on level terms with the Emperor. His reception of the Turkish envoys pointed to his anxiety to command the western Mediterranean and so to isolate Italy from Spain. But, besides that, he needed a party in Italy itself. This he was trying to build around the Pope and Florence at the price of the Orléans-Medici marriage. To win the Pope and keep a close alliance with Henry VIII at the same time was not easy. Yet, remembering Clement's earlier hints, Francis had reason to hope that he might satisfy both of them, that Clement might tacitly acquiesce in Henry's marriage to Anne Boleyn in return for Catherine de Medici's marriage to Orléans and the prospect of a new political combination which might free him from the overshadowing power of the Emperor. Once that Imperial shadow was removed, the Pope might even find it possible to pronounce in Henry VIII's favour over the divorce suit.

Nevertheless, as he claimed to have told Henry at Calais,[8] Francis could hardly hope to bring the Pope to accept the Boleyn marriage unless Henry refrained from doing anything upon his own authority to annul the marriage with Catherine of Aragon or to encroach further upon papal jurisdiction and prerogatives. The Pope's earlier hints had been clear enough upon those points. Henry, however, had not apparently realized this. It may be, as Froude suggests, that at Calais 'Francis had perhaps said more than he meant; Henry supposed him to have meant more than he said.'[9] More probably Henry had little choice. For by the spring of 1533 Anne was obviously pregnant, with – ironically enough – a daughter, the future Elizabeth I, who was to be born on September 7th. Henry, convinced that he was soon to have the long-desired son, had to do everything in his power to assure and demonstrate his child's legitimacy. At all events he rushed in where Francis had intended him to tread most gingerly. He not only married Anne, but also had his Archbishop annul his marriage to Catherine and his Parliament deny absolutely the Pope's appellate jurisdiction. Clement VII, after some hesitation, had replied in July by framing a bull excommunicating him. To that Henry had now retorted by appealing to a General Council, a threat to Papal authority to which early sixteenth-century popes were always peculiarly sensitive. The breach was almost complete. For Francis, who needed both the Pope and England as his allies, Clement VII's procrastination and Henry VIII's impetuous rush into schism might well seem to have marred everything. Worse still, Charles V had promised the German Protestants a General Council only a year ago and Francis could hardly be blamed if he scented the possibility of an Anglo-Imperial rapprochement in Henry's appeal now.

Francis's anger and Henry's impetuosity did not mean the end of the Anglo-French entente, for each still needed the other. Nevertheless they did bring a somewhat new attitude into English policy. Henry had good reason to continue believing that Charles would not attack him unless there was a good prospect of quick success. For the Netherlands, whence such an attack must come, were making it clear that they could not tolerate a long stoppage of their trade with England. Quick success would be impossible without either a large and successful rebellion in England or the hearty co-operation of France. The ease with which Henry was dealing with the Nun of Kent, Elizabeth Barton, and her supporters or dupes, suggested how disjointed and unorganized was English opposition to the King's measures. If Francis could be relied on, at least not to co-operate with the Emperor, England's danger was not likely to be very great.

Henry, however, could not depend absolutely upon Francis's reliability unless he gave him some encouragement. It was true that in September 1533 the French King consented to stand god-father to the infant Elizabeth and that French diplomacy helped to bring about a truce with Scotland in May. Yet during that summer Francis had toyed with ideas of a meeting between himself, the Pope, and the Emperor to discuss the spread of Protestant heresies and the menace of Turkish power, probably also the problem of the English schism. He had, in fact, met the Pope at Marseilles in October-November and married his second son to the Pope's young kinswoman. The hope behind this arrangement was not only to lay the foundation for a French party in Italy but also to secure Milan for the young couple upon the death of the childless Francesco Sforza. Charles V, however, although he had acquiesced in the marriage, showed as yet no clear readiness to yield the Milanese succession to Orléans. The Pope's suggestions of a Franco-Imperial alliance therefore made no headway and Francis still clung to his idea of combining England and the Papacy against the

127

Emperor. Clement so far came to meet his views as to renew his earlier offer to appoint independent legates to sit at Cambrai and decide the English divorce case finally, if Henry would acknowledge Papal authority by pleading in the Cambrai court and would encroach no further upon the Pope's rights in England.[10] Francis passed on these overtures, but Henry refused to listen. He was uncertain as to how definitely the Pope had committed himself about the nature of the sentence to be given at Cambrai and he preferred the certain road of royal supremacy to further hagglings with the procrastinating Pope. He probably realized also that the one sure way of binding the Pope to keep his promises would be to loose him from Imperial influence. But the Pope could only be loosed from Imperial influence by the destruction of Imperial domination in Italy. As northern Italy was so vital a link in Charles V's communications, that could be done only by war and Wolsey's failure had taught Henry how uncertain it was whether even war could achieve it. Besides, to prevent a war with the Emperor was the essential purpose of his present friendship with France.

This meant that Francis must be weaned from his Papal and Italian dreams. Clearly he could not be persuaded to follow Henry into schism – he had, after all, gained from the Papacy all that a King of France needed in authority over the French church by the Concordat of 1516. But Henry's schism from western Christendom was not yet quite absolute. He had appealed to a General Council, even if he had defied the Pope. Might not Francis be induced to follow him there, at least so far as to seek through a Council to heal the divisions of Christendom on terms acceptable to the King of England and the Lutheran princes of Germany? Charles could hardly object, for he had himself promised the Germans a Council. Yet if England, France, and the powers of northern Europe could come to that Council with a common, co-ordinated policy, neither Pope nor Emperor would be able to dictate its decisions and Henry might perhaps get his marriage to Anne and the legitimacy of Elizabeth recognized by a higher authority even than Rome. Moreover, the prospect of an alliance between France, England, and the German Protestant princes would be a very effective means of deterring Charles from an attack on Henry; and, since most of the Hanseatic cities of north Germany were by now Lutheran, it might provide some alternative to Antwerp for English trade if the Emperor should turn nasty.

These were no new ideas. Before Wolsey's fall, the Imperial ambassador in England, Chapuys, had warned Charles that Henry and Francis meant to take up the cause of the German Protestants. In 1531, as soon as the Schmalkaldic League was formed, there were proposals for joint Anglo-French approaches to it and in 1532 Sir William Paget had been sent on a mission to Germany. He was followed in August 1533 by Stephen Vaughan, though the Elector of Saxony barely consented even to see him for fear of jeopardizing the toleration recently granted at the Diet of Nürnberg.[11] Now, early in 1534 Christopher Munt and Nicholas Heath were despatched to seek the co-operation of the princes of southern and western Germany at the proposed Council; Paget was sent for the same purpose to the King of Poland and the north German towns and princes; and there was talk of overtures to John Zapolya in Hungary.[12] Besides this, the Supreme Head also entered into an alliance (August 1534) with the revolutionary Protestant government of Lübeck and abetted its schemes to place its own candidate on the disputed throne of Denmark. The Lübeck connection prospered for a time,[13] but the other negotiations made little headway, at least so far as the German Protestants were concerned. For Henry was not prepared to make any doctrinal concessions that might cast doubt upon his Catholic orthodoxy at the proposed General Council. Indeed, Munt and Heath were accredited to the Catholic Duke of Bavaria and even to the three ecclesiastical Electors of Mainz, Trier, and Cologne, as well as to Protestant Saxony. Luther and his followers were not eager for an alliance on those terms with the King who had written to defend the faith against them in 1521 and of whose divorce most of them heartily disapproved.

Yet if Henry was resolved to preserve his doctrinal orthodoxy, he was no less determined to complete his ecclesiastical supremacy. The spring session of Parliament brought new acts giving statutory form to the submission of the clergy to the King's headship; confirming the prohibition of appeals to Rome; making absolute the conditional Act of 1532 against the payment of annates to the Pope; recognizing that the succession to the throne now rested with Henry's offspring by Anne; and empowering the King to exact from any of his subjects an oath to maintain that succession. At the same time the execution of the Nun of Kent and her accomplices (April 1534), and the fining of Bishop Fisher for listening to her prophecies, demonstrated the King's determination and ability to deal with the few who dared to oppose his measures. Not unnaturally, those measures brought counter-measures from Rome. In March, despite the efforts of Francis to prevent it, the Pope finally pronounced upon the divorce suit and pronounced in favour of Catherine. England's breach with the Papacy was now complete and the reliability of Francis's friendship was put to the test.

The test seemed to prove that Francis could be relied upon, at least against the Emperor, if not altogether against the Pope. In April a French ambassador came over to assure Henry of French support if Charles should attempt an invasion, as his troop concentrations in the Netherlands and elsewhere seemed to suggest he might. The ambassador also proposed another meeting between the two kings at Calais. Henry did not feel able to leave England at this moment, but he was able to assure himself of French naval support in the Channel during the coming summer 'invasion season'.[14] The summer came and seemed only to emphasize Henry's security. There was, indeed, a dangerous rebellion by the Earl of Kildare and his fellow Geraldines in Ireland. Yet if that proved expensive and none too easy to suppress, it was also true that neither Charles nor the Pope made any move to answer the rebels' appeals for help, while in May the Scots had consented to turn the past year's truce into a full peace. Henry, it seemed, had little to fear from any of his neighbours.

None the less, that immunity did depend upon France and the Emperor remaining jealous rivals. And in the autumn fresh reasons appeared for doubting Francis's loyalty. In September Pope Clement VII died and Cardinal Farnese was elected in his stead, as Paul III. The new Pope was friendly to France, believed to be anti-Imperialist, and alleged to have been in favour of Henry over the divorce suit. He was anxious to heal the divisions of Christendom, even ready to summon a General Council for that purpose. At once Francis's old hopes revived. Here was an opportunity for France to bring together the Pope, England, and the German Protestants and virtually dictate terms to the Emperor. With Barbarossa just installed in Tunis, Charles himself took alarm and the overtures which he now made are perhaps the best justification for Francis's revived hopes. For in November 1534 he sent an ambassador to suggest that Francis should co-operate with him in putting pressure on Henry VIII to settle the English succession on Mary and to marry her to Francis's younger son, Charles of Angoulême. The ambassador was to point out that this would be far better for Francis than getting Milan. But he was also empowered, if Francis would not listen to this proposal, to offer Milan on Sforza's death in return for the breaking off of the French alliance with England.[15] Charles, it seemed, was alarmed enough to consider sacrificing his control either of his Channel communications to preserve those through Italy or of his Italian communications to preserve those through the Channel.

The natural effect of such proposals was to encourage the French King's hopes of victory rather than to tempt him to a pacification. In fact, he promptly informed Henry of Charles's suggestion about Mary and Angoulême. But at the same time he himself suggested that if Henry would also abandon his claim to the French crown and co-operate in a General Council, which the Pope now desired, he should have as his reward Gravelines, Nieuport, Dunkirk, maritime Flanders, and even Antwerp itself. Once again Henry could not accept Francis's proposals in their entirety. He knew that the French were discussing whether Mary was not in law legitimate and therefore heir to the English throne. Also to accept Francis's proposals in their entirety must mean that war with the Emperor which it was Henry's chief purpose to avoid. But he did offer to discuss a marriage between the infant Elizabeth and Angoulême and the renunciation of his claims to the French crown. He was not to be tempted by the offer of lands in Flanders and, as for the Papacy, the first move must come from the Pope in the form of the reversal of Clement VII's judgment in the divorce suit and a full acceptance of all the legislation so far passed in England.[16] Once again Francis's hopes of running with the Pope and hunting with the King of England were wrecked upon Henry's determination not to be drawn into war except in self-defence.

It was Pope Paul III, however, who dealt those hopes their death blow. In June 1535 he conferred a cardinal's hat upon Bishop John Fisher, who had always been one of Catherine of Aragon's bravest champions and who had lately been sent to the Tower for refusing the new oath of succession, a refusal which under the Act incurred the penalties of treason. It was difficult to believe – though it may have been true – that the Pope meant this as a goodwill gesture and Henry naturally took it as a deliberate defiance. Fisher was at once condemned and executed and in July the execution of Sir Thomas More followed for the same offence. The execution of two men of such saintly reputation and of European renown was an unmistakable indication that Henry was in deadly earnest and that he had finished for ever with the Papacy.

It soon began to appear also that he no longer cared about the unity of Christendom in any form, but was determined from henceforth to go his own absolute way. For, having thus sharply rejected Francis's efforts to reconcile him to the Pope, he now set his diplomacy to work to counteract the French King's attempts to smooth the way for a General Council. Francis's envoy in Germany was this summer making encouraging progress in persuading the Lutherans to agree to attend a Council if the Pope summoned one and to frame their demands in as conciliatory a form as possible. In August Henry dispatched Munt, and then in September Bishop Fox, with instructions[17] to do their utmost to dissuade the Elector of Saxony and the other Lutheran princes from agreeing to attend any Council called by the Pope where, they were to point out, the combined influence of the Pope, Emperor, and King of France must always carry the day against them. If the princes could not be dissuaded, they should at least be urged to co-ordinate their policy closely with that of England. And the better to encourage them, the envoys might even hold out some hopes of Henry's accepting the Augsburg Confession and suggest the opening of negotiations in London about this.

It was clear from all this that, while Henry was now very near to rejecting the authority of General Councils as well as the authority of the Pope, he was at least a little worried by the possibility that a General Council might leave him isolated in his insular supremacy. There is no doubt that the man who by now was almost filling Wolsey's place in his administration, Thomas Cromwell, was more worried still. Like Walsingham later, Cromwell was inclined to see a Papalist coalition behind every move of the Catholic powers.[18] He lacked Henry's instinctive appreciation of the mutual jealousies that divided his fellow monarchs. He felt certain that sooner or later the Emperor, or Francis, or both of them together, would seek to enforce by arms the bull of deposition against Henry which Paul III had drawn up after Fisher's execution but which Francis had so far restrained him from publishing. If – or in Cromwell's mind, when – war came, Henry would need money and allies. Money Cromwell had already begun to provide.[19]

Parliament had done no more than cancel the King's obligation to repay the forced loans of 1522–3; and to grant him in 1534 a subsidy and two fifteenths and tenths, some £100,000 if it could be fully collected. But the clergy had paid almost £119,000 to secure their release from the penalties of *praemunire* in 1531; the transference of first fruits and tenths from the Pope had added almost £46,000 a year to the King's revenues in 1534; and now, warned by the expense of the Irish rebellion of 1534,* Cromwell was preparing an even larger augmentation of the royal income at the expense of the Church. The compilation of the *Valor Ecclesiasticus* and the visitation of the monasteries in 1535 prepared the way for the dissolution early in 1536 of most of the monastic houses whose annual income fell below £200. During the next two and a half years the sale of some of their confiscated property and the rents from the rest were to bring in over £65,000. By the end of 1535, in short, Cromwell had almost doubled the King's ordinary, non-parliamentary, revenue and had begun to build up a small reserve of treasure for emergencies. However, he felt that England needed allies as well as treasure. He felt, too, that reliable allies could only be found among those who, like Henry, had rejected the Pope's authority. That among these were those north German and Baltic cities which might serve as partial alternatives to Imperial Antwerp, was perhaps for him an additional point in their favour. At all events, there is no doubt that Cromwell was wholeheartedly behind the overtures to the Schmalkaldic League and the treaty of February 1536 with the Lutheran Christian III of Denmark who, although he had been the enemy of Henry's old allies in Lübeck, was now turning to despoil the church in Denmark just as Henry was about to do in England.

By that time, however, a chain of events had begun to unfold which seemed to justify Henry's confidence rather than Cromwell's anxieties and for a season these Protestant approaches made small headway. In October 1535 the childless Francesco Sforza died and a new quarrel between France and the Emperor over the succession to Milan became imminent. By April 1536 French armies had overrun Savoy and Piedmont on their way to Milan and Charles V

---

* It cost the English government £38,000 in addition to what was raised from Ireland. With a decline in the customs, some alienation of crown lands, and the cessation of French pensions in 1534, Henry's English revenues had fallen to little more than £100,000 a year.

and Francis were at war again. Meanwhile events in England itself made it less than ever likely that the Emperor would seek to attack Henry. In January 1536 Catherine of Aragon died and Henry could exclaim 'God be praised! We are free from all suspicion of war.'[20] Of that he could feel even more sure after the execution of Anne Boleyn on May 19th and his own betrothal to Jane Seymour next day and remarriage on May 30th. However indecent the haste with which Henry had married her, Jane was an uncontroversial figure; and with Anne and Catherine both dead, all parties could accept her as lawful Queen. As Anne's daughter Elizabeth was now reduced by her mother's attainder to a common bastardy with Catherine's daughter Mary, there was little left for the Emperor to quarrel about. Indeed he was soon hinting to Cromwell his desire for a restoration of the old Anglo-Imperial amity and that he would do his best to get Pope and General Council to confirm the Seymour marriage and any arrangements Henry might make about the succession if Henry would legitimate Mary. As young Richmond also died in July 1536 and Jane had not yet had time to produce the hoped for legitimate male heir, Henry was not prepared to agree in a hurry.

The fact of the matter was that Henry now felt reasonably secure. Francis and Charles were fighting each other again. Their mutual jealousy would surely not cease when the war ended. And now that Henry's particular causes of quarrel with the Emperor had been removed by the death of both Catherine and Anne, he might hope to be able to play off Charles against Francis as well as Francis against Charles. Besides, there were always the Lutherans as an additional lever upon Charles's good behaviour if one were needed. So Henry no longer cared very much about either Pope or General Council. In July he secured a vote from Convocation refusing to send English representatives to the Council that the Pope had summoned to meet at Mantua in 1537. What was more, Convocation approved the principle that no Council could be legal without the consent of all Christian princes, who must decide the time and place of its meeting, the appointment of its judges, and the nature of its agenda. By this insistence upon unanimity, upon the right of each prince to impose his veto or at least only to be bound with his own consent, Convocation had given a denial of the supremacy of General Councils almost as plain as the denial of Papal supremacy already given. At the same time Convocation approved the Ten Articles drawn up by the King to define the doctrinal position of his Church. There was little actually said in these articles to which Catholics could take serious exception, apart of course from their royal authorship. Yet they mentioned explicitly only those three sacraments (the eucharist, baptism, and penance) considered essential by the Lutherans and said nothing specifically either for or against the other four which were regarded as equally necessary by Catholics. Thus Henry had preserved his freedom to move in either direction, had kept the line open to the Lutherans without denying his own Catholic orthodoxy. But it was he, the King, not the Pope nor a General Council nor even Convocation, that had laid down what beliefs were necessary to an Englishman's salvation. It was the final breach between England and the Universal Church, the final assertion of the royal supremacy over the *ecclesia anglicana*. It had been made possible, almost easy, by the secular jealousies of the Catholic powers and by Henry's instinctive conviction that those secular jealousies would always outweigh and nullify the influence of a common Catholicism upon the princes who still acknowledged their obedience to the Papacy in spiritual affairs.

Chapter 11

The Years of Peril

HENRY's confidence appeared entirely justified as long as the war between Charles and Francis continued. The last months of 1536 did bring, in the Pilgrimage of Grace, the one and only serious domestic challenge that was ever to be made against his Church policy. This started in October in Lincolnshire, spread into Yorkshire, and for a few weeks cast almost all England north of the Trent into uproar. However, the richer and more populous south stood solidly behind the King, conservative nobles like Norfolk and Shrewsbury fought loyally for him, and the 'Pilgrims' were even more easily duped by his promises than they were overawed by his power. By Christmas the real trouble was over and the wild, disjointed efforts of a disappointed minority in the early months of 1537 served only to provide an excuse for Henry to cancel his earlier concessions. Nothing so much strengthens a government as a rebellion that fails and by March 1537 Henry's position at home was probably more secure than it had ever been.

He seemed equally secure abroad, for the attitude of the Catholic powers completely frustrated the Pope's belated efforts to encourage and support the Pilgrims. Just before Christmas 1536 Paul III, a little slow off the mark, made the refugee Englishman Reginald Pole a cardinal and in February 1537 appointed him Legate *a latere* to organize assistance for the rebels. At the same time he sent a sword and cap of maintenance to the young James V of Scotland, hoping to enlist his co-operation. Before Pole reached France in March, however, even the last spurts of rebellion had ceased in England and neither Francis nor Charles was prepared to incur Henry's enmity in so dead a cause. Francis refused to see the Pope's legate and ordered him out of his dominions. Pole fled to Cambrai, only to be similarly ordered off the premises by the Emperor's regent in the Netherlands, Mary of Hungary. He moved on again, to the Bishopric of Liège, where he remained uneasily and impotently until the Pope recalled him to Rome in August. The total and ignominious failure of his mission demonstrated unmistakably how unprepared the Catholic powers were to sink their secular quarrels in a Papalist crusade.

By the summer Henry felt so secure that he allowed the talks with the German Lutherans to die away and in a new doctrinal directive, the so-called Bishops' Book, he 'found again' the four sacraments that had been 'lost' in the Ten Articles of 1536. In June the Emperor sent an ambassador to London to make formal proposals for the renewal of Anglo-Imperial amity and negotiations went forward happily if slowly during the months that followed. The ambassador, Mendoza, did make a tepid suggestion of reconciling Henry to the Pope; but when Henry made it very clear that this was impossible, Charles said no more about it. He was, it seemed, quite ready to accept Henry upon his own terms. Francis, too, remained very friendly and James V of Scotland showed no signs of taking up the Pope's cause single-handed. England, in fact, seemed at peace with all her neighbours. Then, on October 12th, 1537 there came what Henry might well have regarded as the crowning mercy. Jane Seymour bore him a son, the future Edward VI, an incontestably legitimate male heir to the throne. The curse that had seemed to lie upon his marriages had lifted and Bishop Latimer could exult to Thomas Cromwell that God had clearly shown himself 'an English God'.[1] Even Jane's death, twelve days later, could not entirely eclipse the King's pleasure, and the pleasure of his subjects, in her achievement. The Break with Rome was completed at home, accepted abroad, and now approved by Providence itself.

Yet there was a debit side to the account. The first signs were apparent of the beginnings within England of a Romanist opposition that could grow as troublesome to Henry VIII and his successors as the Yorkist pretenders had been to Henry VII. There might as yet be few Englishmen ready to risk the fate of More and Fisher in the Papal cause. Even in the backward and traditionalist north, or in the 'most brute and beastly' county of Lincoln (as Henry had called it),[2] resistance had been half-hearted. The Pilgrimage of Grace in some ways was more akin to a conservative rally than to a full-blooded rebellion. Besides, religion was far from being its only cause. Indeed, one expert in the history of the Tudor north has said that 'even if there had been no Reformation there must have been a rising in the north about this time.'[3] Nevertheless it was religion that focused all the other northern discontents and provided the banner of the Five Wounds beneath which the Pilgrims marched. And as another Tudor historian has remarked, 'the fiction that men fight under often becomes more real than the factors that make them fight.' The old faith could serve to rally all the economic, social, and political discontents that were the growing pains of a rapidly developing national society.

Moreover, a new Romanist faction might well find the leadership that the old Yorkist faction had so conspicuously lacked. The Papacy would provide, as it were, an undying Margaret of Burgundy, a permanent and *ex officio* foreign director. Besides that, in 1537 Pope Paul III chose to send Reginald Pole as his legate *a latere* to urge France, the Emperor, and the Scots to a crusade against the schismatical King of England. Now Pole was not only a man who had just written a book comparing Henry to Nero. He was also the grandson of Edward IV's brother George, Duke of Clarence. His mother, Clarence's daughter, was Countess of Salisbury; his elder brother was Lord Montague; among his cousins was the Marquess of Exeter, grandson of Edward IV and next in line for the throne if the Tudor line failed or were ejected and the Stuart claim through Margaret were ignored. Here was a nucleus of domestic leadership, of possible new pretenders. And there is no doubt that some of the family were dabbling in dangerous thoughts, if not actually in treasonable correspondence with the Cardinal. 'The last remnant of the old Yorkist faction' was linking on to the first elements of a new Romanist faction.[4]

Like the Yorkists, too, the Romanists could hope to find a base and valuable support in Ireland. The Geraldine rebellion there in 1534 had been no more successful in the end than the English Pilgrimage of Grace. But its failure had been due chiefly to the feebleness of its leaders, 'Silken Thomas' and his uncles, and to the loyalty of their rivals, the Earl of Ormonde and his Butlers. Yet Butler loyalty to a schismatical King might not be unbreakable and the greater part of Ireland was under the control, not of England, but of Irish and Anglo-Irish chieftains who had little sympathy with the new-fangled ideas of religion, government, and land tenure that were now being imposed upon them. The Geraldines in 1534 had posed as champions of the old Church and had sent envoys to seek help from the Pope and the Emperor. Now that the English Parliament in 1536 had made all the English anti-Papal legislation equally applicable to Ireland, the old faith might here too rally all the many, divided, opponents of effective English rule. A Romanist Ireland could be no less dangerous to Henry VIII than a Yorkist Ireland had been to Henry VII.

Finally, England's break with Rome introduced new complications into her relations with Scotland. From Flodden until the fall of Wolsey England had been too deeply involved in continental politics to treat either Scottish or Irish affairs as anything more than side issues. After 1529 the quarrel with Rome still kept Henry from concentrating his attention upon them. Occasionally, the faction-ridden weakness of the Scottish government allowed the perennial Border feuds to get so out of hand that some action had to be taken, such as Norfolk's raid early in 1533. But in general England's friendliness with France during the earlier fifteen thirties had its usual effect of damping down enmity with Scotland. As we have seen, a truce in 1533 was expanded into a full peace in 1534. Then, however, a new source of trouble began to appear. James V was by now grown to manhood and was taking the government of Scotland into his own hands. His greatest problem, after his long and disordered minority, was to reassert the royal authority over an independent and turbulent nobility whose factions had for twenty years been struggling with each other for control of the central power. Not the least troublesome, and by James V not the least hated, were those nobles who, like his stepfather Angus and the Earl of Arran, were supporters of a policy of good relations with England and were opposed to a continuance of the close alliance with France that had borne such bitter fruit at Flodden. Had James's mother and Angus's former wife, Henry VIII's sister Margaret, possessed any particle of the usual Tudor acumen in politics, this pro-English faction might perhaps have won and kept control of Scottish policy. But Margaret's hatred of Angus and readiness to use any means to further her own disordered love affairs, ruined that chance. Angus, Arran, and their partisans became only another element in the nation's political disorders, all the more hated because of their connections with the old enemy.

When James V began to take over the management of affairs, he therefore turned elsewhere for support. In particular he turned to the rich and powerful Church. Its leader, David Beaton, soon to succeed his uncle James Beaton as Archbishop of St Andrews, became his most trusted counsellor. Naturally, Beaton and the clerical party were bitter opponents of any connection with schismatical England, strong supporters of the old alliance with Catholic France. They were able to dissuade James from listening to Henry's suggestions in 1535 that he should follow the English example and make himself rich by despoiling the Church. They were able in the next year to prevent a meeting of the two Kings at York, which Henry had proposed. More than that, in September 1536 James sailed off to France to seek a French bride. On January 1st, 1537 he married Francis's youngest daughter Madeleine. That he should do this, without any mention of his intentions to Henry, just when the Pilgrimage of Grace was occurring; that he should be at the French court, tightening his alliance with Francis and pointedly ignoring Henry, just when the Pope was sending him the cap and sword and was dispatching Cardinal Pole to stir up a crusade against England – these actions could hardly make Anglo-Scottish relations easier. James V was moving more and more towards France and towards Rome just when Henry had broken finally and irrevocably with the Papacy and was beginning to pick up again the threads of his old connection with the Emperor.

This must seriously reduce Henry's ability to play off the two great continental powers one against another. For it would be dangerous to weaken the English entente with France lest the Scots should open England's back door, her only land frontier, to the French. Just over that frontier lay the most conservative and least reliable part of Henry's realm, the area of the Pilgrimage of Grace. Besides that, there were always constant comings and goings between the Highlands and Islands of Scotland and the northern parts of Ireland. During and since the Geraldines' rebellion these ties had grown still closer, not without James V's encouragement. If discontent against Henry's policies were to come to a head again in Ireland and the English north, the Scots were admirably placed to link them together and to give them a back to lean upon. With Papal support, France might then be tempted to turn her attention northwards instead of southwards and to make of the British Isles another Milan. It was true that Charles V would be very unwilling to see the British Isles fall under French control. Yet even if he took up arms to prevent it, that would only cause Britain to take northern Italy's place as the cockpit of Europe.

For the moment these were very distant fears. Ireland and the

English north had been repressed too recently to risk further punishment in the immediate future and neither Francis nor Charles would move unless domestic discontent offered a really tempting probability of Henry's overthrow. Moreover, Francis and Charles were still fighting each other and had their forces fully committed in Italy, the Mediterranean, and along the Netherlands frontier. Their failure to show even common courtesy to the Pope's legate, Cardinal Pole, manifested how far both of them were from any desire to quarrel with England. This probably restrained James V also from any open hostility. Yet when the delicate Madeleine succumbed to the harsher climate of Scotland, he waited no longer than decency required before reiterating his determination to follow a French rather than an English course. In June 1538 he married, as his second wife, Mary of Lorraine, the daughter of the Duke of Guise who was now among the leading counsellors of Francis I.

This marriage coincided almost exactly with the conclusion, by the Pope's mediation, of the Truce of Nice between Charles V and Francis I (June 1538). The war had disappointed Francis's hopes. He had occupied most of Savoy and Piedmont, but quite failed to secure Milan or to overrun Artois. For him the conflict, apart from its expense, was daily growing more pointless. Charles was no less weary of it. If he had held Milan and Artois, his invasions of Provence, Languedoc, and Burgundy had been complete failures. Moreover, while he was engrossed in this quarrel with France, his problems elsewhere were growing acute. Barbarossa's fleet was harrying the southern coasts of the kingdom of Naples and in October 1537 Sultan Soliman defeated Ferdinand at Essek in Hungary. In Germany Lutheranism was spreading like fire in stubble. Würtemberg had been wrested by force from Ferdinand in 1534; Brandenburg had half gone over in 1535; the heir to the aged Duke of Saxony was a strong Protestant; and already little except the Austrian lands, Bavaria, the Palatinate, and the three ecclesiastical Electorates remained true to the old religion. Religious considerations apart, the danger of either France or England allying with this growing German Protestantism made some attempt to deal with the problem an urgent necessity for Charles. Finally, his war taxation was undermining the loyalty even of the Netherlands. Ghent refused to pay the levies voted by the States General in 1537 and was near the point of rebellion. Other cities were more than sympathetic to Ghent's resistance and further impositions might well bring a general revolt. Charles needed peace even more than Francis.

In the cirumstances there was perhaps nothing particularly alarming for England in the mere conclusion of the Truce of Nice. It was only a truce, not a final peace and although Charles and Francis were both at Nice, they refused to meet and conducted all their exchanges indirectly through the Pope. Soon, however, more disturbing portents began to appear. In July 1538 Pope, Emperor, and French King did meet, and apparently in very cordial fashion, at Aigues-Mortes, the ancient port of departure for the Crusaders. As the summer wore on, reports began to come in from Rome of correspondence between the Geraldine Earl of Desmond in Ireland and the Papal court. Informers in the west of England, where the Courtenay family was all-powerful, reported whispers of a new, western, Pilgrimage of Grace to put the Marquess of Exeter, Cardinal Pole's cousin and head of the Courtenays, upon the throne.[5] Exeter was already quarrelling with Cromwell in the Privy Council and it would be easy enough for supporters of the old order to find an excuse for an uprising in the government's campaign against Catholic shrines and images. This campaign reached its height in October with the destruction of St Thomas à Becket's tomb at Canterbury. At that moment Sir Geoffrey Pole, the Cardinal's younger brother, driven by panic or treachery, accused Exeter, Lord Montague, and Sir Edward Neville of treasonable correspondence with the Cardinal and a design to raise a new insurrection against Henry. True or false, the accusations chimed only too well with the general posture of affairs. Accordingly Exeter, Montague, and Neville were arrested, tried, and in December executed. Exeter's wife and Pole's mother, the Countess of Salisbury, were both lodged safely in the Tower and any prospect of a new Pilgrimage was blotted out.

Abroad, however, the outlook grew ever more threatening. In November the negotiations that had been going on at Brussels for Henry's marriage to the Emperor's niece, Christina, began to run into difficulties, difficulties raised on the Emperor's side. In December the Pope made David Beaton a Cardinal and at last published the bull deposing Henry which he had prepared three years earlier. In January 1539 he again dispatched Pole as legate to urge Charles V to join with Francis I and James V in executing the bull by force of arms. For a time it seemed that Charles might agree. There were rumours of a great fleet collecting in the Netherlands ports and of a league between the three Catholic monarchs to invade England in the summer. Francis, it was said, had asked James to have his troops ready by May 15th. At the end of February both the Imperial and the French ambassadors were recalled from London, while in the Netherlands all English ships were arrested on the excuse that sailors were needed for the Emperor's fleet and that therefore no ships might leave the ports until that fleet had sailed. A new French ambassador, Marillac, arrived at the end of March, but almost at the same moment a fleet of sixty large ships from the Netherlands (transports, it was thought) came to anchor in the Downs. Early inApril this fleet sailed off down Channel to Spain, possibly as they said to assist the expedition that Charles was meditating against Algiers. The warlike activity in the Netherlands ports ceased. If Charles had ever intended an invasion of England, he had clearly thought better of it. Marillac's arrival suggested that Francis had reached a similar conclusion, while Norfolk's presence with considerable forces at Berwick gave pause to James V.

For the moment the danger had passed. How real it had been, is not altogether easy to say. Probably much had depended upon what happened inside England. 'Ye never heard nor read that England was overcome by outward realms, nor dare any outward prince enterprise to come hither, except they should trust of help within the realm,' said one of Henry's stouter subjects.[6] Shakespeare was to say it better. But it was true enough that the execution of Exeter, Montague, and Neville had left outward princes little hope of help from within the realm.

Obviously, too, the more prepared England appeared to be to defend herself, the smaller the danger would be. And, as Marillac testified,[7] England appeared very well prepared indeed. During the past two or three years a vast defence programme had been put in hand. The royal navy had been steadily augmented to some forty warships and means accumulated for equipping and arming reserves drawn from England's merchant shipping. In this spring of 1539 Henry had almost one hundred and fifty ships of various sorts at sea in his service. This was the first line of defence. Behind it, in second line, there was springing up an elaborate string of coastal fortresses, whose remains remind us to this day of the perils that were incurred by the break with Rome. Batteries were planted or castles were constructed to guard the south and east coast harbours and landing places from the Thames estuary to Sandwich, Deal, Walmer, Dover, and Sandgate; to Sandown in the Isle of Wight; to Portsmouth, Hurst, and Calshot; to Portland, Plymouth, and Dartmouth; on to St Mawes and to Pendennis at Falmouth; to St Michael's Mount; and to 'Harry's Walls' in the remote Isles of Scilly. There was a similar activity at Hull, Scarborough, Newcastle, and Berwick on the north-east coast and across the Narrow Seas at Calais.[8] Finally, in March 1539 the levies of the southern and south-eastern shires were mustered and put under arms to defend against invasion from the continent and the levies of the northern counties were called out under Norfolk to guard the Borders against the Scots. The expense of all this was enormous and makes it easy to understand why the richer monasteries, absolved from dissolution in 1536, now went the way of the smaller and poorer houses. A monk's head carved over the gateway at St Mawes castle still reminds us from whose ruins it was built. It was in part from the stones of Beaulieu Abbey that Hurst castle was constructed. It was from the lands and revenues of the monasteries in general that Henry and Cromwell found the money for the fleet, the castles, and the musters.

If the Church paid much for England's defence, the merchants paid something too. In 1539 the King by proclamation[9] exempted all foreign merchants for seven years from the payment of any customs dues (except on wool) over and above those paid by native Englishmen. The concession perhaps cost him something in customs revenue. But it benefited principally the trading houses of Antwerp and the merchants of the Hanse. It was thus a strong encouragement to the Netherlanders to stand out again for trade and neutrality as they had done in 1528; a useful way of keeping the north German cities friendly and through them another line open to the German Lutherans in general.

On all these measures there was, it would appear, general agreement. But were other measures also needed? Other measures could only mean a more active foreign policy, designed to gain England allies abroad; and the only allies to be gained were the German Lutherans. About such an alliance opinions differed, not only between Cromwell and Norfolk in the Council but also between Cromwell and the King. Henry, with the support of Norfolk,

Southampton, Gardiner, and the other conservative Councillors, was most reluctant to make those concessions to Protestantism at home without which he could not hope for a Lutheran alliance abroad. Thus the doctrinal discussions between German Lutheran theologians and English bishops in London in the summer of 1538 had come to nothing because the King would yield on none of the points which the Germans regarded as essential. In January 1539,[10] when the invasion scare was at its height, he did allow Cromwell to make overtures for an alliance with Duke John of Cleves. Henry, it was suggested, might marry the Duke's daughter Anne. But Duke John, although he was father-in-law to the Lutheran Elector of Saxony and treated his Church rather in Henry's own manner, was neither a Lutheran nor a member of the Protestant Schmalkaldic League. An alliance with him would be a warning hint to Charles V, yet not an act of provocative menace. Nor would it entail doctrinal concessions at home.

In February 1539, however, Duke John died. This caused some delay and then on the English side the passing of the invasion scare lessened the sense of urgency. Moreover back in June 1538 the new Duke William of Cleves had inherited the Duchy of Gelderland, Charles V's old enemy and rival for control of the northern Netherlands. To maintain that inheritance and its pretensions against an Emperor now free from war with France, Duke William needed allies. He turned therefore both to the Lutheran Schmalkaldic League and to England. In July 1539 he gave his formal consent for a marriage between his sister Anne and the King of England. But the same reasons that made Duke William come forward, now made King Henry draw back. Henry's purpose was to warn Charles, not to provoke him, and Charles's sudden revival of the proposal for Henry to marry Christina showed how sensitive he was to the possibility of a triple alliance of Cleves, England, and the German Lutherans. Clearly such an alliance, if persisted in, might all too easily provoke him. Again therefore the Cleves negotiations languished. At the same time Henry cooled towards the Lutherans. In June, Parliament, against the opposition of Cromwell and Cranmer, passed the Act of Six Articles. This insisted upon the real presence, communion in one kind for the laity, the permanent validity of religious vows, celibacy of priests, private masses, and auricular confession. Of these, all except the first were matters over which the 1538 negotiations had broken down; and the protests of Melancthon and the Elector of Saxony showed plainly that the German Lutherans regarded the Six Articles as a direct rebuff to themselves. They were no less a rebuff to Cromwell and they provided him and his supporters with another powerful motive for seeking to commit the King to a German alliance that would be incompatible with the maintenance of the Articles in England.

Suddenly in the autumn of 1539 the Cleves negotiations came to life again and it looked as if Cromwell was to get his own way. Gardiner was dismissed from the Privy Council; the Six Articles ceased to be at all strictly enforced, to the Elector of Saxony's joy; and on October 6th the treaty for Henry's marriage to Anne of Cleves was signed at Hampton Court. At the end of December Anne landed at Deal. Henry met her at Rochester on January 1st, 1540, and on January 6th they were married. Why he allowed himself to be thus entangled, when Cleves had just been united to Gelderland and was moving towards the Lutherans, is not entirely clear. He was certainly trying at this time to revive Francis's jealousy of Charles V. It could be that he was seeking to form an offensive coalition between England, France, the German Protestants, and Cleves-Gelderland to exploit the opportunity for an attack upon Charles offered by the revolt that had now flared out at Ghent. In February 1540 he was to send Norfolk to France to tempt Francis with just such a proposal. Yet the general run of his policy hardly suggests that he would now plan so aggressive a move against the Emperor whom he had been at such pains to warn but not to provoke. It looks more likely, although there is no conclusive proof in the evidence available, that he had already got wind of Charles's coming journey from Spain through France to suppress the rebellion in Ghent. If so, that could well explain the Cleves marriage treaty, while Charles's actual journey through France in December sufficiently explains why Henry went through with the wedding even after he had seen his unprepossessing German bride. For if the friendship between Charles and Francis was so fast that Charles could trust himself to ride with only a small suite right across his great rival's realm, then Henry indeed had need of allies. The possibility of a Franco-Imperial Papalist crusade might be a good deal more real than he had believed. And even if he had no intention of leading a great offensive coalition against the Emperor, he needed the pretence of some such grandiose scheme if he was to offer Francis a temptation great enough to induce him to break his present entente with Charles. That seems the most likely reason for Norfolk's mission in February 1540.

By then, however, the outlook was again changing. Charles had crushed the revolt in Ghent (February) and seemed about to turn on Cleves-Gelderland. Henry, it seemed, might become involved whether he wanted to or not. Gradually that danger also passed, for in April Charles agreed to accept the German princes' mediation between himself and Duke William. But this meant that the Lutherans were no longer inclined to take a stand against the Emperor and that England's alliance with Cleves thus lost any value it had as a bridge to a wider alliance with the Schmalkaldic League. For Henry the Cleves marriage had become a political embarrassment as well as a personal distaste. Only fear of the Franco-Imperial entente had held him to it and now Charles's manifest reluctance to satisfy Francis about Milan was damping down that fear. By June Henry's confidence of finding safety in the mutual jealousies of the Catholic powers had revived sufficiently for him to allow the overthrow of the minister who had so entangled him. The arrest, trial, and execution of Thomas Cromwell were the work of his domestic enemies and occasioned by domestic rivalries.[11] But the King's acquiescence in his downfall opened the way for a new policy abroad. Early in July Convocation annulled the Cleves marriage and Parliament confirmed its decision. Anne, perhaps no less content than Henry, accepted a settlement of £4,000 a year in lands and agreed to remain in England, where she was soon reported to be as joyous as ever and wearing new dresses every day.[12] Henry, remarried within little more than a month to Catherine Howard, was freed from his embarrassing and unprofitable German connections.

The growing breach between Charles and Francis made such connections daily less necessary. Charles would no longer hear of yielding Milan. He did suggest a marriage between his eldest daughter and Francis's young son, offering to give them the Netherlands and Franche-Comté if Francis would cede to them the Duchy of Burgundy and also evacuate Savoy and Piedmont and renounce all claims on Milan. But Francis would not consider thus abandoning Italy and resurrecting the Burgundy of Charles the Bold. He refused the offer and thereupon in October 1540 Charles V invested his own eldest son, Philip, as Duke of Milan.

After this it was only a matter of time before the two great rivals fell out again. While Francis began secretly dealing with the Turk, Charles prepared to secure his Mediterranean communications by attacking Barbarossa in Algiers and to assure himself elsewhere by buying off his possible opponents. At the Diet of Regensburg in 1541 he bought off the German Lutherans by extensive concessions. Towards England he also showed himself increasingly friendly. The fall of Cromwell had reassured him that England would no longer meddle in Cleves-Gelderland, just as in 1529 Wolsey's fall had ended his fears of English intervention in the Milanese question. By 1541 it was clear enough that the old amity with Spain was England's again for the asking. By the spring of 1542 Francis, encouraged by Charles's failure at Algiers (November 1541), the Turks' defeat of Ferdinand in Hungary (September 1541), and the prospect of further Turkish offensives against Austria and in the Mediterranean, was once more at war with the Emperor. Everything was back to normal and England's years of peril were past.

Chapter 12

The British Problem

THE events of the years from 1538 to 1541 had in the end proved rather than disproved the rule that England could usually rely on the inveterate jealousy between Habsburg and Valois to preserve her against attack from the continent. Yet those years had also suggested that there might be times when the continental powers would be strongly tempted to intervene if the domestic situation within the British Isles offered them a good prospect of success. England's security clearly required not only that those powers should be kept in mutual rivalry but also that no doors into Britain should be opened to either of them from the inside. It was to this latter problem, the British Problem as Sir John Seeley has called it, that Henry VIII now turned in the closing years of his reign.

His interest in it was no new thing. It played a part, although there were other and more compelling domestic reasons, in the steady strengthening of the central government's control over England itself. It is evident in the reform of the Council in the North after the Pilgrimage of Grace and in the brief appearance of a Council in the West about 1539. It also played a part in the measures of 1534–6 for incorporating Wales and the Marches into the English judicial and administrative system. It is more clearly seen in the assumption of the title of King of Ireland in 1541 and in the attempts to win the leading Irish nobility by peerages and grants of monastic lands. The effect of these last measures was limited and temporary, for Henry could not spare the effort and the expense required for a proper subjugation of Ireland. Yet they point again to his consciousness of the primary necessity of securing mastery within the British Isles.

The key to that mastery, however, lay with Scotland. For, as we have seen, it was Scotland that could link the discontents of the conservative English north to the turbulence of Ireland. And as long as Scotland remained a client of France, one at least of the great continental powers would always have a back door held open into England. It was to close that back door, and to seize the key to the solution of the British problem by drawing Scotland into England's orbit, that Henry now turned his attention as soon as he felt himself free from serious danger of continental attack. Back in 1540 he had sent Sir Ralph Sadler[1] to invite James V to a meeting at York or elsewhere, tempting him with a hint of the formal recognition of his place in the English succession, which Parliament had just authorized Henry to devise by will. Beaton had frustrated these moves, but in the following summer the negotiations were resumed and in July 1541 Henry made a progress to York in the confident hope that James would visit him there in September. September came but James did not and Henry returned south, to be met in November by the unhappy revelations which were to bring his fifth wife, Catherine Howard, to the scaffold in February 1542. In the summer of 1542 he renewed his overtures to James, but this time more in the form of an ultimatum and with a clear hint of force behind them in Norfolk's mobilization of the northern levies. Again James refused. Forays along the Border grew fiercer. In August Sir Robert Bowes fell into an ambush while chasing some Scottish marauders back into their own country and in October Henry declared war upon Scotland.

His impatience, whether justifiable or not, is understandable. He had come to see in Scotland the key to England's security and was anxious therefore to wean the Scots from France and from Rome. For seven years or more he had tried in vain to entice James V by persuasion, promises, and counsel. Time was slipping away. Henry was already in his fifty-second year, only one year short of the age at which his father had died. His health was not good. He was much too fat and he suffered from an unhealing ulcer in the leg. His only son was delicate and only just five years old; his two daughters had both been declared illegitimate; and next to them in the natural line of succession came James of Scotland. If Henry himself should die before Edward came to manhood and before a settlement had been made with Scotland, James might well throw the whole work of the past ten years into the melting pot and plunge England into a bitter civil and religious war. And just at this moment the renewal of war between Francis and Charles seemed to offer Henry an opportunity too good to be missed for pressing forward to a settlement, if need be by arms.

At first the fortunes of war seemed to justify Henry's loss of patience. A brief invasion of south-eastern Scotland from Berwick

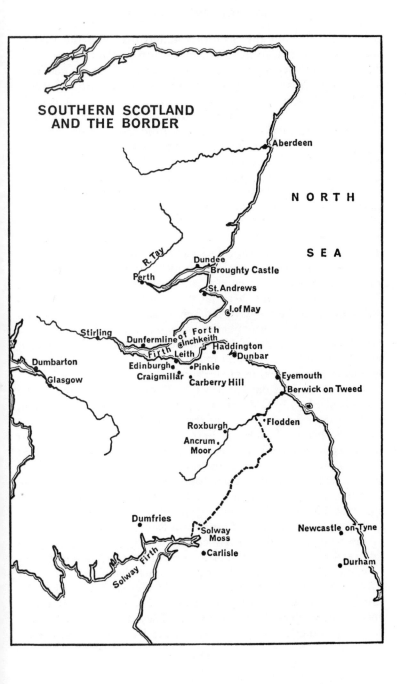

SOUTHERN SCOTLAND
AND THE BORDER

NORTH

SEA

Aberdeen

R. Tay

Dundee
Broughty Castle
Perth
St. Andrews
I. of May

Stirling
Dunfermline
Firth of Forth
Inchkeith
Leith
Haddington
Dunbar
Dumbarton
Edinburgh
Pinkie
Glasgow
Craigmillar
Carberry Hill
Eyemouth
Berwick on Tweed

Roxburgh
Flodden
Ancrum
Moor

Dumfries

Solway
Moss
Newcastle on Tyne

Carlisle

Solway Firth
Durham

achieved little. But the Scottish counterstroke into the western marches towards Carlisle ended in a worse Scottish disaster than Flodden. On November 25th, 1542, at Solway Moss, 10,000 Scots were utterly broken by a bare 3,000 English, who boasted that they had lost only seven men killed. It was a disgrace as well as a disaster and the news of it killed the King of Scots. James V died on December 14th, leaving the Scottish throne to his only surviving child, Mary, Queen of Scots, who had been born only six days earlier. Henry's opportunity looked more golden than ever. Scotland was faced again with a long royal minority and with a struggle for power among the various factions – Beaton and the old Church party backed by the Earls of Huntly and Argyle; the Hamiltons, headed by the Earl of Arran who stood next to Mary in the line of succession; the Douglases, with their exiled head, the Earl of Angus, long in English pay. With careful handling, it should surely be possible to build up an English party from some of these elements, a party strong enough to wean Scotland finally from France. Moreover, the fact that the infant sovereign of Scotland was a girl and the five-year-old heir to England a boy, opened a prospect of a more permanent union of the two crowns, of a united Great Britain secure behind its encircling seas and the ships that guarded them. A happy and final solution to the British Problem looked to be now within Henry's grasp.

The one obvious danger was that France might hasten to the support of Mary of Guise, Beaton, and the Franco-Papal faction, perhaps even get possession of the infant Queen with a view to marrying her to the heir of France. French troops and French money could certainly put Beaton and his friends in the ascendant more easily than English support could establish their rivals. It seemed, too, that French troops and French money would not be long in coming. Francis had already declared his determination to stand by his old allies[2] and in January the Duke of Guise was gathering ships, troops, and supplies at Rouen, though the freezing of the Seine delayed their concentration.[3] Henry therefore now prepared to take direct action to prevent French intervention in Scotland. On February 11th, 1543, he concluded an alliance with Charles V *contra Franciscum cum Turcha confoederatum*.[4] The two rulers swore to each other peace and friendship and the maintenance of the ancient trade agreements. They promised not to harbour each other's rebels. Charles undertook to treat as an enemy any power that invaded or assisted an invasion of England, Ireland, the Channel Islands, the Isle of Wight, the Isle of Man, or Calais and its marches; Henry, any who attacked or assisted to attack Spain or the Netherlands. If the invasions were made by more than 10,000 men, the invaded party then might ask for his ally's aid in men and money up to a limited amount for four months in any one year. Neither was to treat separately for peace when both were involved in a war. As for the objectives of the alliance, the treaty laid down that Charles and Henry should call upon Francis to break off all connections with the Turks; to compensate the Emperor and the Empire for the expenses caused by the recent Turkish attack; to pay the debts he owed to Henry and to cede to him Boulogne, Montreuil, Ardres, and Thérouanne, as security for the regular payment of his pension in the future. If Francis refused, the two allies would declare war upon him. Each would then send armies of 25,000 men to invade him within two years and neither would make peace until he yielded the Duchy of Burgundy to the Emperor and Normandy and Guienne to the King of England.

That final provision rings like an echo of the fifteen twenties. But it was a distant aim and everything else in the treaty has a very different sound. What is indeed so striking about everything except that final clause, is the very careful limitation of Henry's commitments and how relevant those commitments were to the aim of isolating Scotland from France. If he could be called upon for aid against a French invasion of Spain or the Netherlands, the amount of aid was limited and he in turn could call for Imperial help to defend Calais. He was not liable to assist in the defence of Italy. The cession of Boulogne and the Boulonnais would rob France of her nearest port to Scotland and strengthen England's grip on the straits of Dover. It would go far to close the eastward route from France through the North Sea to the Forth and Edinburgh, the nerve centre of Scottish affairs. That would leave the French only the westward route, long and hazardous, from Brittany to the Clyde. Even the undertaking to attack France with 25,000 men committed Henry to no more than would be necessary in any event for the capture of Boulogne; and as there were two years allowed for fulfilling this engagement, he had at least a year in which to achieve a solution in Scotland that would make the capture of Boulogne no longer necessary. Both in its timing and in its terms the treaty was a significant indication of Henry's preoccupation with the Scottish question. It may be that he would have been wiser, as Norfolk wished him, to stick to his former entente with France and to accept the offers that Francis now made of sending no aid to the Scots and of paying his debts to England.[5] But until the news of the treaty with Charles leaked out and the English ambassador was about to leave France, Francis's tone had been very different. He had insisted upon his obligations to the Scots. He was preparing to send aid to them. He made trouble over English privateering. He had arrested English ships in French ports (February). He evaded payment of his debts to Henry. It was therefore very doubtful whether much trust could be placed in these new offers, especially if Henry were to offend the Emperor mortally by repudiating so promptly a treaty that he had only just concluded. Therefore the treaty stood and a war with France was added to the war with Scotland.

In his conduct of this French war during 1543, however, Henry showed that his mind was set upon control of Scotland rather than on conquests in France. When the French invaded the Netherlands in June and the Brussels government appealed for English troops, he did fulfil his treaty obligations by sending 5,000 men under Sir John Wallop. He may have been disappointed that, because Charles had not yet arrived with the large army he was bringing from Spain and Italy through Germany, Wallop and the Netherlands forces were not strong enough to attack Montreuil. He was certainly none too pleased to see the Emperor in August and September using that army to defeat his own late brother-in-law, Duke William of Cleves, and to annex Gelderland. For those operations meant that it was mid-October before Charles arrived on the French frontier, too late in the year for him to be able even to reduce Landrécies, which the French had taken in June. Nevertheless, if Charles had done little for Henry in 1543, Henry had avoided exhausting himself to help Charles and between them they had kept the French pretty busy near home.

Meanwhile, however, Henry badly overplayed his hand in Scotland. On James V's death the Scottish Council at once sent to sue for a truce. They also frustrated Beaton's attempt to secure control of the government and on January 3rd, 1543 they proclaimed Arran regent. Arran was a weak man, but he was Beaton's enemy and he was not ill disposed towards England. Henry might well have given his friendship a trial. But Henry was in a hurry. He wanted to control Scotland now and he preferred to work through his own instruments. At the end of December 1542 he extracted from Angus and the Solway Moss prisoners, as the price of their freedom, a promise to work for a marriage between Edward and Mary; for the handing over of Mary to be educated in England and of Beaton to be imprisoned there; for the admission of English garrisons into Edinburgh, Stirling, and Dumbarton; and for the government of Scotland by a council in which Henry would be represented, instead of by a regent. To ask so much was to risk ruining all. To proclaim in addition, as Henry had done in a printed *Declaration*,[6] 'the true and right title that the King's most royal Majesty hath to the sovereignty of Scotland' – that was to make almost sure of ruining all. It would have been a delicate enough matter to negotiate a marriage between the Scottish Queen and the English heir-apparent, even upon the most generous guarantees for the preservation of Scottish liberties. The Scots knew, as well as Henry VII had known, that the greater would draw the less. It was one thing, moreover, for Scotland to give a King to England; for England to give a King to Scotland was quite another. 'If your lad were a lass and our lass were a lad, would you then be so earnest in this matter and could you be content that our lad should marry your lass and so be King of England?' a Scotsman asked Sadler.[7] By asserting his own present title to the Scottish crown, by demanding custody of the infant Queen and present control of the council, Henry was making a difficult task impossible.

In fact, the 'assured lords' were no sooner back in Scotland than in February 1543 they asked for easier terms.[8] To displace Arran, send the Queen and Beaton to England, and admit English troops to the three garrisons would drive the whole country back into the arms of France. In March the Scottish Parliament confirmed Arran's regency and, although they appointed commissioners to negotiate about the English marriage, refused to send Mary to England. Henry did now come some way to meet them. Mary might remain in Scotland until she was ten and Arran might remain regent provided Henry had a say in the choice of his council. But the Scots must renounce the French alliance and make no foreign treaties without the King of England's consent. This was still too much and again Henry had to moderate his demands. When eventually the treaties of Greenwich were signed on July 1st,

1543,[9] he agreed that Mary should stay in Scotland until her marriage to Edward and he no longer insisted upon the Scots breaking their alliance with France. Neither party was to aid the other's enemies, temporal or spiritual, but all the other demands made of the 'assured lords' in December 1542 were now silently dropped. The pity was that Henry had not been content at the first with what he obtained at the last. For those demands, though dropped, were not forgotten and by making them Henry had undermined the foundations upon which the present agreement rested. He had shown the cloven hoof of English claims to suzerainty too plainly for him to retain more than a small body of supporters among the Scots.

Already Beaton, released from imprisonment at the end of March, was rebuilding his party. By bringing the Earl of Lennox back from France, he provided himself with a useful lever against Arran, for Lennox stood next to the Hamiltons in the succession to the throne and the legitimacy of Arran's descent was not beyond quibble. At the very end of June there also arrived from France sixteen ships with men, money, and munitions. A small English squadron did capture two of them and drive the rest back to France or into the Forth, but not before they had landed their cargoes. Thus strengthened, Beaton and his friends were able to get the infant Queen removed to Stirling at the end of July. In September Arran went over to Beaton's faction and the friends of France were again in control of Scotland. In December Parliament annulled the treaties with England, renewed those with France, passed harsh laws against heresy, and approved Beaton's appointment as Chancellor. Next month Angus and the 'English lords', Lennox now among them since Arran had made his peace with Beaton, were forced to submit and to abandon their support of England, after a vain attempt to seize Edinburgh. Henry's party and his policy in Scotland were both in ruins.

The subjugation of Scotland was obviously going to be a much bigger job than Henry had anticipated. It would now require military operations on a large scale and on two fronts. For Henry could no longer rely upon the dwindling and disheartened band of England's Scottish friends to do his work for him. He must send English troops to rally and reinforce them if he was to prise Scotland from the grip of Beaton's faction. Nor, as the episode of the sixteen ships had shown, could he rely solely upon his naval forces to cut Beaton's faction off from the French aid that might make

their grip unbreakable. If the French aid was to be stopped, it must
be stopped at the dispatching end, by invasions that would keep
France too busy at home to help her friends abroad. These were
prospects that might have daunted a less impatient and imperious
man, but Henry fronted them without a qualm. On December 31st,
1543 he concluded a new agreement with the Emperor. Each was
to invade France by June 20th at the head of 40,000 men. The
English were to go in through Calais, the Imperialists further
south, and the two armies were to converge on Paris. At the same
time Henry resolved to give the Scots a blow that would paralyse
them for the coming campaigning season. In the spring of 1544
he ordered the Earl of Hertford (Jane Seymour's brother) to take
12,000 men into Scotland, to devastate the Lowlands and sack
Edinburgh, Leith, and St Andrews and to put man, woman, and
child to fire and sword without exception where any resistance was
made.[10] Hertford, fearing that such savage measures would drive
the Scots to utter desperation, urged instead the seizure of Leith
and its retention as a rallying point for England's friends.[11] Henry's
other brother-in-law, the Duke of Suffolk, also told him bluntly
that after burning Edinburgh he would have nothing in Scotland
but by the sword and conquest.[12] But the King would not listen
and in May Hertford, though he did not penetrate as far as St
Andrews, carried out the rest of his orders all too faithfully. At
whatever cost to the long-term prospects, Henry thus achieved his
short-term aim. The Scots were paralysed for the 1544 campaigning
season.

Henry was then able to turn his undivided attention to France.
The plans for the French campaign were, however, now somewhat
changed – or was it that Henry now revealed what had been his
real intention all along? A considerable French force was en-
trenched around Montreuil and a considerable French garrison
lay in Boulogne. It would be unwise, Henry now told Charles, for
the English army to rush towards Paris and leave those forces intact
to imperil its communications and supplies. Moreover, two armies
operating separately might be separately defeated. Would it not be
better for the Emperor to make his invasion farther north, in close
concert with the English from Calais?[13] These military arguments
were plausible, but the political purpose of using the Imperial
army for essentially English ends shone through them rather obviously and Charles refused to alter the line of his invasion. But he

could not prevent the English from sitting down before Boulogne and Montreuil at the end of June. By the time Henry himself arrived in mid-July, the English army, now almost 40,000 strong, was fully committed to these two sieges. Charles, whether or not he had ever intended a bold advance upon Paris, also allowed himself to be held up by a seven weeks' siege of St Dizier, so he had perhaps no great reason to grumble. When St Dizier fell late in August, however, he did make a show of dashing upon Paris and he sent an urgent request that Henry would do likewise to sustain the dangerously advanced position into which the Imperial army was placing itself. He had not consulted Henry beforehand about this move and he knew that neither Boulogne nor Montreuil had yet fallen. Perhaps it is not, therefore, entirely ungenerous to suspect that he was advancing in the hope that Henry, by not answering his call, would give him an excuse to listen to the peace overtures with which Francis was bombarding both the allies?

That, at all events, was what happened. Henry took Boulogne on September 14th, 1544. Four days later Charles and Francis made peace at Crépi. The French forces turned northwards and the English, although they just managed to hold on to Boulogne, had to abandon their siege of Montreuil. Worse was yet to come. There was perhaps little danger now of Charles and Francis combining against Henry as they had seemed so likely to do in 1538. Yet while Henry remained at war with France, his relations with Charles were none too good. Apart from the soreness left by the peace of Crépi, there was continual bickering over seizures at sea. Even while Henry and Charles were allies, English privateers, operating under individual letters of marque, had caused trouble by their frequent inability to distinguish Spanish and Netherlands from French shipping. Now, in December 1544, Henry by proclamation[14] gave a general permission for any of his subjects to equip ships to wage private war in the national interest against the French and Scots. At once the Channel, the Narrow Seas, the Bay of Biscay, and even more distant waters began to swarm with English privateers. Moreover, while the Emperor's subjects considered that, now he was at peace with France, they might lawfully resume their French traffic, the privateers acted on the contrary doctrine that a neutral flag did not cover enemy goods. Netherlands and Spanish prizes began to stream in, as well as French and Scots. So serious did the Netherlands complaints become that in January Charles ordered the arrest of all English ships and goods there. It was only after much negotiation and some concessions by Henry, that he lifted the arrest early in April.

By then a similar arrest had been made in Spain as a reprisal for the seizure off Cape St Vincent of a Spanish ship bringing some 20,000 ducats of gold and silver from America. This was the work of a leading Southampton merchant, Robert Reneger.[15] It was a portent of some significance and brought on a new quarrel. Even so, the Emperor did not carry the matter beyond a diplomatic wrangle and the arresting of English ships and goods in Spain. He lacked the sea power to defend his Atlantic coast, as the privateers were quick to realize, and he was not prepared to go to war with England over merchants' quarrels. Certainly not until he had seen how England would stand up to the onslaught that France was preparing against her. His mind was set upon Germany, where the Schmalkaldic League was showing signs of disintegration; upon the Turks, whose fleet at Francis's invitation had just wintered at Toulon; and upon the General Council that was due to meet, on the Pope's summons, at Trent in March, although it did not actually open until December.

Nevertheless, France was now free to concentrate all her resources against England. Twenty-five galleys were brought round from the Mediterranean. Ships were hired in Italy and elsewhere to reinforce the shipping of the northern and western French ports. By the early summer over one hundred and fifty sail, besides the galleys, were assembled at Le Havre and in the Seine estuary, with an army of over 50,000 men behind them. Another land force renewed the siege of Boulogne and 3,000 men under Montgomery were made ready for Scotland. Meanwhile in England preparations were also proceeding on a scale and with a smoothness that is a remarkable tribute to the country's administrative machinery as well as to the people's spirit. A fleet of about eighty sail, half of them at least belonging to the royal navy,[16] gathered at Portsmouth under the Lord Admiral Lisle, while another force of some sixty sail, mostly privateers, watched farther west. Behind the ships, the long line of coastal castles and batteries was manned and provisioned. Behind them the county levies were grouped into four armies – in the north, in East Anglia, in the south, and in the west – ready to concentrate against any landing that the French might make.

It was, however, Lisle's fleet that made the first move, an attempt to break up the French fleet before they could leave the Seine estuary. The attempt failed, for the prizes that Lisle had meant to use as fireships slipped away and bad weather threatened to embay him against a lee shore. He therefore withdrew with little effected. Hardly had he got back to the Solent when the French fleet put to sea. Its purpose was to land its army on the Isle of Wight and at Portsmouth, destroy Lisle's fleet, and then complete the investment of Boulogne and Calais by cutting them off from the aid by sea that made them impregnable. Now the English royal warships were no doubt a good deal more formidable than anything in the improvised navy of France. But until the westward forces came up, Lisle was outnumbered by perhaps as much as two ships to one. Moreover, as an action on July 19th showed, in a flat calm he had little answer to the French galleys, weak though their fire-power was. With the land forces not yet concentrated behind him and the King himself watching from the shore – the challenge in the fleet was 'God save King Henry' and the password 'Long to reign over us'[17] – this was no moment for heroics. Lisle therefore drew back into the Solent, hoping to entice the French in among the shoals and within range of the shore guns. He lost the *Mary Rose*, heeling over to a sudden squall before her lower gunports could be closed, but the French hesitated to swallow the bait he offered. They did land several parties on the Isle of Wight, only to see them cut to pieces by the local levies. Then on July 22nd they gave up the attempt and sailed off up Channel. Lisle followed. He could not prevent another brief landing near Seaford. But as the westward forces came up to join him, the balance of numbers began to swing his way, all the more as disease and plague were now raging among the French who had been crowded together for a month in their ships at sea. There was a brief skirmish off Shoreham late on August 15th, but next morning the French fleet was already stretching away for Le Havre and the Seine estuary. Within another week or two their great armament was broken up and England's danger was over. Lisle was left master of the Channel, free to raid the Norman coast and to pour supplies and reinforcements into Boulogne and Calais. By the end of September the siege of Boulogne was also over.

There had been no great battle, no spectacular engagement,

either by sea or by land. Yet the strength and success of England's resistance, and the national unity behind it, were even more impressive to foreign powers than the preparations of 1538–41 had been. The enormous French effort had failed to break England's control of her home waters and Reneger's escapade showed that, unofficially at any rate, English sea power was beginning to reach out to more distant waters too. The effects were soon to be seen in the attitudes of both Charles V and Francis I. By August 1545 Charles was offering not only his mediation to end the war but also the military help which the 1543 treaty entitled England to ask of him and which previously he had found various pretexts for refusing. By October Francis was seeking peace, even at the price of abandoning the Scots. Henry's determination to keep Boulogne, which Norfolk and Gardiner were willing to give back to France, held up the negotiations through the winter. In the spring fresh preparations were made to continue the war. Hertford was sent over to Calais with an army reinforced to about 30,000 men, while Lisle again made a large fleet ready at Portsmouth. At the same time Charles V renewed his 1543 treaty and confirmed his obligation to send help if England or Calais were attacked. In face of all this, Francis finally yielded and on June 7th, 1546 peace was concluded.[18] England was to keep Boulogne for eight years. At the end of that time France might buy the town back for 800,000 crowns. In addition the French were to pay England a perpetual pension of 50,000 crowns and a further 100,000 to Henry during his lifetime. The Scots might be included in the peace if they would accept the terms of the 1543 treaty of Greenwich.

So Henry had achieved one of his aims. Francis had abandoned the Scots; and the loss of Boulogne would make it difficult for him to take them up again at all effectively. The other aim, however, the winning of Scotland, seemed almost as far off as ever. Henry's bullying had produced a remarkable degree of unity among the Scots and his preoccupation with his French war had given them a breathing space. In August 1544 Lennox (who, with Glencairn, was now almost his only open supporter among the Scottish nobility) had to seek refuge in England. That autumn a brief and unnatural coalition of the Queen Mother, Mary of Guise, with the Douglases failed to shake the power of Beaton and Arran. In February 1545 Arran and Angus, now won back to loyalty, routed a marauding force of 3,000 English at Ancrum

Moor. Then in May, while the English fleet's attention was distracted by the great preparations in Normandy, Montgomery slipped through with money and 3,500 French troops by the westward route across the Irish Sea to the Clyde. His arrival enabled Arran in August to check a little the English harrying of the Borders, even to cross a short way for a short time into England. It was not until September that Henry was able to retaliate in force and then his retaliation did not go beyond a fortnight's raid by Hertford, notable chiefly for the destruction of the great abbeys in the Tweed valley. Attempts by Lennox to seize Dumbarton, so blocking the Clyde, and by Maxwell to hand over his Border castles, both failed in the autumn.

By the end of 1545, then, Scotland's resistance remained still unbroken. Nor could Henry do much to break it in 1546; for, as in 1514 and 1524, his means were almost exhausted. The wars from 1543 to 1545 had cost over £1,300,000. When the cost of the 1538–42 defence preparations and that of holding Boulogne were added, the total extraordinary expenditure during the last nine years of the reign mounted to at least £2,135,000.[19] To meet this, £650,000 had been collected under parliamentary grants and £75,000 or more in clerical subsidies. Parliament had also excused the King the repayment of a forced loan of £112,000 raised in 1542. Another forced loan of £119,000, not yet repaid, was levied in 1545 and a third begun in 1546. About £770,000 had been raised by selling approximately two-thirds of the confiscated monastic lands, whose retention might have given the crown an income that in normal times would free it from all financial dependence upon Parliament. This was still not enough and from May 1544 onwards Henry began to find money by debasing the coinage. He resorted to this vicious expedient to such a degree that within two and a half years it yielded him £363,000, a sum comparable to that brought in during the same period by the sale of monastic property. Even then he had also to borrow heavily at Antwerp, sometimes at as much as fourteen per cent interest, and when he died his debts there amounted to around £75,000. It is hardly surprising that he attempted no large-scale operations against Scotland in 1546.

Yet how was Scotland to be brought within England's orbit without such operations? Lennox was in exile, the English faction broken, Beaton and Arran apparently in full control. A gleam of hope appeared when on May 29th, 1546 a small band of Scottish Protestants, goaded by persecution and the martyrdom of George Wishart, broke into St Andrew's castle, assassinated Beaton, and seized the castle. Scottish Protestants were perforce allies of England and St Andrews could be readily supplied by sea. Yet Protestants in Scotland were still a tiny minority and their obvious dependence upon England would not increase their popularity or their following. They might give the English control of St Andrews, but not yet of Scotland. English control of Scotland seemed, indeed, as far off as ever when Henry VIII died on January 28th, 1547. Pursuing, as A. F. Pollard has said, right aims by wrong methods,[20] he had thrown away the opportunity for an amicable union of Great Britain which James V's death had opened to him five years earlier.

Chapter 13

Failure in Scotland

THE dozen years that followed Henry VIII's death provided ample justification for his anxiety about the succession and about Scotland. His crown passed first to his nine-year-old son Edward VI and then six years later to his elder daughter Mary. Under them the country experienced most of the woes that had been prophesied for a land whose king was a child or a woman. Political and religious faction destroyed national unity; allowed social and economic discontents to break into open rebellion; and tempted the continental powers to make England, instead of Italy, their battleground. Weakened by domestic dissensions, the English were unable to complete Henry's work in Scotland. Such pressure as they were able to exert only drove the Scots into the arms of France and gave the French a position in Britain so commanding that England seemed to have little choice except to become, as under Northumberland, a dependent client of France or, as under Mary, a handmaid of Spain. Loss of unity seemed likely to be followed by loss of independence and the interest of England's foreign relations lay less in what she herself did than in what others might do to her.

At first, however, when Edward VI came to the throne, it looked as if sixty-two years of firm government by grown-up, capable kings might have taught Englishmen habits of unity and obedience that could save them from the evils which royal minorities had brought upon their Scottish neighbours. The sixteen councillors named, with twelve assessors, in Henry's will as his executors and his son's council of regency, hastened to divest themselves of the mantle of supreme authority. Three days after Henry's death they agreed to the appointment of a Lord Protector, the young King's uncle Edward Seymour, Earl of Hertford, now promoted to be Duke of Somerset. Six weeks later they accepted new commissions which converted the council of regency back into a normal Privy Council and left the Lord Protector in possession of virtually full regal powers. Most of the councillors, long accustomed to advise and administer rather than to initiate and decide high policy, welcomed with a sigh of relief this speedy return to government by a single head. Outside the Council, conservatives like Bishop Gardiner or the dismissed Chancellor, Wriothesley, now Earl of Southampton, might regret the Protector's liberal attitude in matters of religion. But none of them were men of Somerset's stature and closeness to the blood royal; and the forces of conservatism had already, just before Henry VIII's death, been thrown into fatal disarray by the fall of the Howards, the one family of an eminence, if not of a capacity, to match the new Protector. The impetuous indiscretion of Henry Howard, Earl of Surrey, had brought him to the block on January 19th, 1547. It had also brought the head of the family, his father Thomas Howard, Duke of Norfolk, to the Tower, where he now lay under sentence of death for treason, alive only because Henry VIII had died before the axe could fall. Thus there was no one as yet willing and able to challenge Somerset's authority. He lacked the name of king, and that was in time to prove a fatal weakness; but for the moment he had most of the power and round him Englishmen closed their ranks and presented a still united front to the outer world.

Nor was the outer world at first much inclined to challenge the new regime in England. The Pope and Cardinal Pole did urge Charles V to intervene at once to place his Catholic cousin, Princess Mary, upon Edward's throne by force of arms. But Charles was deeply committed by now to a struggle with the Schmalkaldic League in Germany. During the autumn of 1546, with the support of the Catholic Duke of Bavaria and by winning over the Lutheran Maurice of Saxony, he had been able to master southern Germany and to force Würtemberg and the Palatinate to quit the League. The decisive trial of strength was, however, still to come and Charles's strength was not overwhelming. His army was superior in quality but inferior in numbers to the army of the League. His brother Ferdinand's forces were tied down in Bohemia by a Protestant revolt there. His new ally Maurice's lands had just been overrun by John Frederick, Elector of Saxony and leader of the League. Charles was thus not yet in a position to dictate a settlement, or even to patch up a truce without sacrificing most of what he had gained by the political manoeuvring and military campaigning of the past year. He could not afford to commit himself to midwinter operations against England which, unless they were immediately decisive, might involve him in another prolonged and dubious contest there. He could the less afford it because it must arouse the hostility of France and therefore might face him in the next campaigning season with a triple alliance of France, England, and the German Lutherans.

Charles was anyway in no mood to listen eagerly to Papal promptings. During the past few months Papal policy had both weakened him militarily and embarrassed him politically. At the end of December 1546 the Pope had recalled the troops which he had sent to assist the Imperial army. He refused to sanction further taxation of ecclesiastical revenues in Spain and Italy to help pay for the war in Germany. He had allowed a General Council of the Church to assemble at Trent, within (though only just within) the borders of Germany, but he had refused or evaded most of the concessions about its procedure that might have induced a significant number of Lutherans to join in its deliberations and perhaps acquiesce in its decisions. Now he was threatening to recall it from Trent to Bologna, though he knew that no Lutherans at all would either attend or recognize a Council held outside Germany. It is, then, hardly surprising that Charles gave the Papal proposals about England a cold welcome and decided to take no action for Mary unless her English supporters made the way so easy that action would be almost superfluous. In fact, of course, this meant his full acceptance of the new English government, for there was never any sign of a movement in England to put Mary upon Edward's throne before her time came. As for the King of France, he must obviously prefer to see the boy-King on the English throne rather than Charles V's half-Spanish cousin Mary Tudor.

Somerset was therefore soon able to turn his attention to Scotland and to seek to exploit such advantages as Henry VIII had won for England there. First, however, he tried to assure himself more fully against continental interference with his designs. In March 1547 he gave Charles V further reason to adopt a benevolent neutrality by refusing an offer of alliance from the German Lutherans. At the same time he succeeded in negotiating a defensive alliance with Francis I.[1] With the Scots, too, he at first tried diplomacy rather than force. There can be no doubt that in so doing he was moved, as in his social and religious

166

policies at home, by genuine and high-minded idealism. More than any other man of his time, he was inspired by the vision of a united Great Britain where Scots and English should dwell together in peace and amity, guarded by the encircling sea 'against the envy of less happier lands'. Lifted above narrow national or class antagonisms by his dream of a Christian commonwealth uncorrupted by 'private profit, self love, money, and such like the Devil's instruments', he was fully prepared to welcome the Scots as equal partners.[2] He said nothing of the old claims to overlordship or sovereignty that Henry VIII had so unwisely revived. He spoke instead of the mutual benefit that a union of the crowns would bring to both realms. He pressed only for the renewal of the broken 1543 engagements. The new Lord Protector, however, had been the chief executor of the old King's ruthless policy in Scotland. It was he who had commanded the invading English armies in 1544 and 1545. To the Scots his government could hardly look other than the old firm under a new name. It could therefore have little chance of making a fresh start upon a new basis of mutual trust and confidence. And the past few years had not made it easier for Scotsmen to see much difference between proposals for a union of Great Britain and designs for an English conquest of Scotland. Somerset's attempt to reach an amicable agreement thus came to nothing and the Scots refused his invitation to send commissioners to Berwick to negotiate a settlement.

Somerset would perhaps have been wise, after this rebuff, to have accepted the advice of Gardiner and Paget that he should 'let the Scots be Scots' at least until Edward VI came of age and could decide for himself.[3] After all, Henry VIII had been trying for the past five years, and without much success, to compel them by force of arms to become, if not English, at least British. The continual Border raiding and the occasional full-scale invasions of those years had only stiffened Scottish resistance. Could the English government's finances, already staggering under the cost of those unavailing efforts, bear the expense of the yet greater and more prolonged pressure that must be exerted to force a decision? And even if they could, where would England, possessing no regular standing army, find the long-service troops to hold the Scots down until at last they ceased to struggle? For merely to crush a Scottish army in another Solway Moss or Flodden, and then to make a few devastating but brief raids into the Lowlands, would clearly not break the will of the Scottish nation. It might perhaps have been wise therefore, particularly during the King's minority and with religious and economic problems growing urgent at home, to have let the Scots be Scots and not to subject England to such a strain as the effort to subjugate them must put upon her.

Somerset, however, had the impatience as well as the idealism of the visionary. Besides, now more than ever, there was the danger that if the Scots were left to be Scots, they might become French long before Edward VI came of age. Henry VIII had indeed forced Francis I to abandon them in 1546 and Francis had concluded the treaty of March 1547 with Somerset. But on March 31st, 1547 Francis I died. His son and successor, Henry II, was less dazzled than he had been by the mirage of conquests in Italy. He was therefore more inclined to listen to the Duke of Guise and the Cardinal of Lorraine and to do all he could through their sister, the Scottish Queen Mother, and their niece, the young Queen of Scots, to restore and extend French influence in Scotland. He was known to be particularly sore over the loss of Boulogne and to have expressed a determination to win it back at the earliest possible opportunity. He was also unlikely to overlook the fact – or, if he did, the Guises would soon call it to his attention – that Mary, Queen of Scots, was a great-granddaughter of Henry VII of England and could claim a place in the English succession next after the schismatical Edward VI, the thirty-one-year-old Princess Mary, and Anne Boleyn's daughter Elizabeth. Married to the Dauphin, she might become a useful agent of French ascendancy, not only over Scotland but perhaps in time over England as well.

Admittedly, Henry II was not yet prepared to provoke an open war with England. He knew that, if he did, Charles V would honour his pledges under the Anglo-Imperial treaty of 1543. For however unwilling the Emperor might be to involve himself in action to replace Edward VI by Mary Tudor, he would certainly not stand by while Henry II replaced both of them by Mary Stuart. And the Emperor, who on April 21st completely routed the army of the Schmalkaldic League at Mühlberg, was not at this moment an adversary to be lightly challenged. Until Charles began to run again into serious difficulties in Germany or elsewhere, Henry II would probably stop short of open war with England. This did not mean that he would do nothing to make Somerset's tasks more difficult. Far from it. After all, neither Scotland nor Boulogne, which had not been English in 1543, was covered by the Anglo-Imperial treaty. Already by the early summer of 1547 'incidents' were occurring along the frontiers of the Boulonnais. There was no general attack, but this continual friction made it necessary to keep garrison and defences at the highest pitch of readiness, a considerable strain on the depleted resources of an already impoverished government.

In Scotland French action had more serious results. The first was the recapture of St Andrews castle from Beaton's assassins. In March 1547 Somerset had sent nearly £1,200 to pay the little garrison of seven score men whom the Scottish regent had been quite unable to suppress. But late in June Leo Strozzi was allowed to sail in from France with twenty-two galleys, a few thousand troops, and some artillery. The English fleet made no serious effort to stop him, for that would have been an act of war which Henry II could hardly have ignored. But, once arrived at St Andrews, Strozzi's guns soon proved too much for the 'castilians'. On July 31st the garrison surrendered and marched out, the gentlemen to imprisonment, the rest (including John Knox) to forced labour as rowers in the French galleys. In six weeks a small reinforcement from France had achieved what the distracted government of Scotland had been unable to accomplish in twelve months. Their success gave the Queen Mother and the friends of France a greater ascendancy than ever. It enabled them to secure the refusal of Somerset's invitation to negotiate at Berwick. It encouraged them to suggest more pressingly that the young heir to the French throne, the Dauphin, would be a more suitable match than the King of England for the little Queen of Scots. With a few more troops and a little more money from Henry II, it looked as if they might before very long reduce Scotland almost to the status of a province of France, to another Brittany. And beyond that prospect lay the shadow of Mary Stuart's claim to a place in the English succession.

To Englishmen brought up, as Somerset had been, under the influence of Henry VIII, it must have seemed indeed that the question was no longer whether or not to let the Scots be Scots but how to prevent them becoming French. If they could not be persuaded, then they must be compelled, despite the cost. And if they were to be compelled, now was the time to do it, while France was still restrained by fear of the victor of Mühlberg. Accordingly, after a month or more of preparation, on September 4th the Protector invaded Scotland at the head of an army of 18,000 men. He marched swiftly up the east coast, the English fleet of sixty sail, thirty-five of them royal ships, guarding his right flank and bringing up his supplies and artillery. Once again, though, an English invasion brought together, if it did not exactly unite, Scotsmen of all factions. So, on September 9th and some six miles east of Edinburgh, at Musselburgh beside the Firth of Forth, the English found their way barred by a Scottish army considerably larger than their own and strongly positioned on a hillside behind the river Esk. Next morning the Scots rashly came down from their strong position, just as their descendants were to come down against Oliver Cromwell at Dunbar one hundred and three years later and with equally disastrous results. Caught in Pinkie Cleuch between Somerset's men and the Esk, their left flank under fire from an English warship lying close inshore, they were broken and put to total rout. Several thousands of them were killed and fifteen hundred taken prisoners, against an English loss of a few hundreds.

Once again a Scottish army had been shattered to pieces and the Scottish capital lay open to the old enemy. Yet although some Scots came over and the Scottish government promised to send envoys to treat of peace, no envoys came and there was no whole-sale defection to the English invader. Once again England faced the problem of how to expand victory into conquest. To this problem a large field army, concentrated in one place, was no solution. Besides, Somerset had brought supplies only for a month and England had neither the supply organization[4] nor the money to keep so large a force much longer in the field. So by the end of September the troops were back at Berwick and the Protector was on his way to London to meet his first Parliament. Before he left, however, he had already sketched the outline of a more intelligent strategy than the mere harrying and raiding of Henry VIII's later years. Raiding and harrying there still was, all autumn and winter, in the western as well as the eastern marches and up the east coast almost to Aberdeen. But in addition, in September 1547 English garrisons were placed on the islands of

Inchholm and Inchkeith in the Firth of Forth, at Broughty castle at the mouth of the Tay, and at Home castle and Roxburgh in the eastern marches. In December Dundee and Arbroath were occupied and in February Dumfries. In April 1548 Lord Grey seized and fortified Haddington, placing in it a garrison of 2,500 men who devastated and levied tribute from Dunbar to the gates of Edinburgh.

The pattern of these garrisons reveals a clear and coherent strategy. From them and from across the Border the Lowlands could be constantly harried and ordinary life there dislocated. By them Scottish troop concentrations could be made difficult and French reinforcements intercepted. Clearly, Somerset meant to follow up his victory in the field with the nearest thing to a permanent occupation that his resources permitted. It is true that even now he did not rely solely upon force. Wherever his troops came, they distributed English Bibles, dissolved monasteries, encouraged preaching against the Roman Church. To some Scots who came over, they provided small pensions; on all who came over, they imposed an oath to work for the marriage of the Scottish Queen to the English King. Nevertheless, these persuasions could at best work but slowly. In the final analysis Somerset, like Henry VIII, had been driven to depend upon military force to hold down the Scots until their spirit as a nation was broken and their faith as Catholics undermined.

Like Henry, too, Somerset was well aware that if he was to hold down the Scots, he must hold off the French. Where, however, Henry had sought to beat off the French by seizing Boulogne, Somerset tried to buy them off by offering to restore the town. He hinted at this to the French ambassador as early as August 1547. In mid-November he made a definite offer to return it if the French would agree to some extension of the Calais Pale and would further the Scottish Queen's marriage to Edward VI. In reply Henry II asked for Calais as well as Boulogne. Calais Somerset had to refuse, but in December he did offer to hand back Boulogne at once in return for the payment stipulated in the 1546 treaty and for French support of the Scottish marriage. The attempt was perhaps worth making. Yet it was hardly to be expected that Henry II, who not unnaturally looked upon the English seizure of Boulogne as flagrant robbery with violence, would regard the cession of that ill-gotten town as a fair exchange for his abandoning the whole kingdom of Scotland to the English. So, although the negotiations went on until April 1548, there was never any great hope of a successful outcome. Henry always meant both to keep Scotland and to win back Boulogne.

Meanwhile in Scotland the English invasion and partial occupation had incensed even those who had favoured the English match. As Huntly put it, 'I hold well with the marriage, but I like not this wooing.'[5] There were many like him, ready to risk losing their independence to the French if thereby they could preserve themselves from the English. And in the person of their young Queen they still held the master card in the game. Immediately after Pinkie she was removed out of English reach, first to an island in Loch Menteith, afterwards to the western fortress of Dumbarton. Then the regent Arran, the Queen Mother, and an assembly of nobles held at Stirling dispatched an appeal to Henry II of France for assistance on a substantial scale.

Somerset answered this by a proclamation[6] to the Scottish people in which he offered them the completest preservation of their own laws and liberties and full freedom of trade with England, if they would agree to Mary Stuart's marriage to Edward VI and the union of the crowns. They knew well enough that the English could defeat them in battle, but let there be no more talk of victor and vanquished, or even of Scots and English. Let the two nations, marked out for union by Providence, language, and geography, come together as equals under 'the old indifferent name of Britons', in one empire of Great Britain. Then the Scots and the English, 'being made one by amity, ... having the sea for a wall, mutual love for garrison, and God for defence, should make so noble and well-agreeing a monarchy that neither in peace we may be ashamed nor in war afraid of any worldly or foreign power.'

All this no doubt was genuinely meant and no doubt it sounded very fine and magnanimous in London, as it has often sounded to later English historians. But the Scots, taught by experience to suspect cloven hooves in any English gift horses, were not impressed. They knew well enough that a united Great Britain was not likely to make Edinburgh its capital, particularly when England provided its King and Scotland only its Queen Consort. They could hardly miss the connection between the timing of Somerset's generosity and their own appeal to France. And while they were little tempted by his offers, they soon received more substantial encouragement from Henry II. For Henry had welcomed their appeal and fully accepted the Guises' counsel to exploit its possibilities as much as he dared. He had sent money in December 1547. In June 1548 a force of 6,000 French troops, escorted by twenty-two galleys, under the Sieur d'Essé, arrived at Leith. Early in July the French ambassador, d'Oyssel, gave Henry's answer to an assembly of the Scottish Estates that met, under the protection of d'Essé's troops and 8,000 Scots that Arran had collected, at the abbey of Haddington, in sight of the English garrison which Grey had planted in that town. The choice of that meeting place was itself a gesture of defiance to England and the upshot of the meeting was a serious, practically a fatal, repulse for English policy. For the upshot was the substitution of a union of the French and Scottish crowns for a union of the English and Scottish crowns. Henry II had asked that the young Queen of Scots should be sent for safety to France, where in due time she should be married to the Dauphin, the heir to the French crown. Thereafter, although Scotland might preserve its own laws and liberties, the two crowns were to be formally and indissolubly united. If the Scots would agree to this, then Henry would defend them to the utmost of his power as if they were part of his own realm.

Agree they did – with one voice, the official record says, though it seems clear there were considerable murmurings against it which the official record was too insensitive or too sensible to register.[7] Arran, who had hoped to strengthen the Hamiltons' position in the Scottish succession by marrying Mary Stuart to his own son, was bought off with the French dukedom of Châtelherault and a pension. Other nobles also fingered French silver and none could forget that d'Essé's troops had alone made their meeting at such a place possible. So, while d'Essé and Châtelherault settled down to a regular siege of Haddington, most of the French warships sailed off round the Orkneys and the Western Isles to Dumbarton. There they took aboard the young Queen of Scots and, sailing round 'the back of Ireland' to avoid the English warships and privateers, carried her safely to Brest. Her arrival, on August 13th, 1548, was greeted by Henry II with the jubilant boast that 'France and Scotland are now one country.'[8]

Somerset's Scottish policy had thus precipitated the very danger that it was designed to avert. The Scots had been thrown into the arms of Henry II; their Queen was in France, destined to be married to the Dauphin; and English military pressure, which had not cowed them when they stood alone, was even less likely to cow them now that they could look for substantial French aid. Moreover, the increasing hostility of France soon began to impose new burdens upon England that made it less easy to keep up the pressure on Scotland. The skirmishings around Boulogne grew more frequent and severe. Privateering by both sides made the Channel and Western Approaches dangerous for peaceful shipping and began to interrupt normal trade. In Ireland French intrigues encouraged O'Donnell to rise and 1,500 Scots came across to assist his rebellion. England was again drifting rapidly into the familiar war on two fronts (indeed, on three fronts with rebellion starting in Ireland) that had so often distracted her during her quarrels with Scotland.

For a few months longer the positions were held. At the end of July 1548 a small force got supplies into the besieged garrison of Haddington. Then the Earl of Shrewsbury marched up with an army of 15,000 men, supported by the fleet on its right flank. The siege of Haddington was raised, its stores replenished, and its garrison reinforced. Shrewsbury had thereupon to return, like Somerset the year before; but the autumn found all the English posts intact, while October brought not only the severe repulse of a French attempt to surprise Haddington by night but also a bloody clash between them and the citizens of Edinburgh.[9] It was a first indication that French troops might become no more popular than English with their Scottish hosts.

Nevertheless Somerset soon found himself in the worst of all positions, one which he could afford neither to hold nor to abandon. Most of the English garrisons still held out and in 1549 Somerset began to gather troops and supplies and to hire German and Italian mercenaries for yet another invasion. But as the spring of 1549 wore into summer the general tide of affairs at home and abroad swept away all hope of another large effort to drive home the pressure upon Scotland. At home the jealous plottings and eventual execution (March 1549) of the Protector's irresponsible brother Thomas Seymour, the Lord Admiral, damaged his prestige. Then the fruits of his own religious and social policies ripened into widespread popular rebellion and disturbance. The new Book of Common Prayer in English, imposed by the Act of Uniformity which Parliament passed in January 1549, provoked sporadic resistance in many parishes. In June it led to a full-scale popular rebellion in Devon and Cornwall. Had the rebels, like their forebears in 1497, marched straight towards London, they might easily have focused the unorganized protest riots of Wiltshire and Dorset, Hampshire and Surrey, Oxfordshire and Buckinghamshire, Sussex and Kent, into a truly formidable reactionary movement. As it was the resistance of Exeter held them up until the Privy Council was able to reassert its authority. Before then, another rebellion of a different kind had swept that authority aside in East Anglia. Ket's rebellion there was social and economic rather than religious in character. It was provoked by the hopes raised among the commons by Somerset's enclosure commissions of 1548, dashed by Parliament in the following winter, and then raised again more desperately by his new proclamation of May 1549. With another rising in Yorkshire and disturbances of a more scattered sort in many other counties, pretty well half of England broke out of control in July and August 1549.

Somerset was not only responsible for the policies that had provoked these troubles. He was also to blame for allowing the troubles to rise to such a pitch of rebellion. Unable to believe in the seriousness of the Western rising and half-sympathizing with Ket, he had shown a fatal reluctance to take prompt measures against the disorders in their beginnings. Paget reminded him how[10] a similar reluctance had allowed the Peasants' Revolt in Germany to swell to such formidable proportions twenty years ago, but the Protector had 'grown in great choleric fashions' towards unpalatable advice and would not listen.[11] In the end the Privy Council, in particular Warwick, Northampton, and Russell, had to take repressive action without and in spite of him. But by then the task of restoring order required all the forces they could scrape together. Unable to rely upon the county levies against these popular uprisings, they had to reinforce their own retinues and those of other nobles and gentlemen by the Italian and German mercenaries that should have formed the backbone of a new invasion of Scotland. It was the Italians under Russell who bore the brunt of relieving Exeter and crushing the Western rebels at Sampford Courtenay on August 17th. It was the Germans under Warwick who were chiefly responsible for the recovery of Norwich and the final defeat of Ket at Dussindale on August 27th. The new invasion of Scotland that Somerset had intended had therefore to be abandoned. Instead, orders were sent to Rutland at Berwick to take such forces as he could muster there, march with them to Haddington, raze its defences, and evacuate its garrison. Broughty castle and Home castle held out for some months longer[12]; but with Inchcolm, Inchkeith, and Dundee already lost in the previous year, the abandonment of Haddington virtually ended effective English occupation of the Lowlands. By the autumn of 1549 both the Queen of Scots and her realm had slipped out of England's weakening grasp.

It seemed very unlikely that either would be grasped again. For the effects of these disasters upon England's relations with the continental powers ruled out any possibility of new enterprises against Scotland. In June 1549 Somerset had sent Paget to persuade Charles V to include Boulogne in the guarantee that he had given to the King of England's other dominions in 1543.[13] If he agreed, Paget was to suggest a Portuguese match for the Princess Elizabeth and a joint Anglo-Imperial invasion of France. At first Charles listened not altogether unsympathetically. He was finding the fruits of Mühlberg hard to garner and the Pope ever more difficult to keep in line. Even before Mühlberg, the Italian and French cardinals had left Trent for Bologna with the Pope's approval. By the Emperor's orders the Spaniards remained at Trent, but the already faint hope of an agreed settlement of the Lutheran schism was now, if not finally doomed, gravely compromised. Reluctant to abandon that hope, Charles in May 1548 granted the Lutherans a renewed, if limited, temporary, and ambiguous toleration by the Interim of Augsburg. This only helped to revive their cause without winning their confidence. Magdeburg, Constance, Strasbourg, and other Protestant cities rejected the Interim. A number of the lesser Lutheran princes began to contemplate a new league and to make approaches to France. The Duke of Bavaria's Catholicism began to wilt before his jealousy of his great Habsburg neighbour. Above all, there was reason to doubt the continued good faith of Maurice of Saxony now that he had gained John Frederick's Electorate as the price of his earlier defection. Charles therefore still had much to do in Germany and was ready enough to see England again tying France's hands as she had done in 1544–6. But he had no use for an alliance whose principal purpose would be to commit him to propping up a tottering English power in Scotland and the Boulonnais, to a war against France on his own part. Thus as soon as the first news of the Western and East Anglian risings came through, his attitude changed.[14] Paget's proposals for a new alliance now found a cold welcome; his requests for Boulogne met with plain refusal.

The news that discouraged Charles V, encouraged Henry II. On August 8th, 1549 he declared war and in person invaded the Boulonnais. Within a few weeks he took all the outlying forts and shut the garrison up in the town of Boulogne itself. There it put on so bold a front that, with winter approaching, he decided to blockade it rather than sit down to a siege in form. Nor did he dare yet to attack Calais, which of course was, unlike Boulogne, covered by the Imperial guarantee of 1543. Nevertheless, if he still stayed his hand from a direct attack upon Edward VI's old dominions, he had effectively checkmated English policy at every point. He had possession of the young Queen of Scots; his friends and servants were becoming every day more complete masters of Scotland; his agents were stirring up the O'Donnells and the O'Neills in Ireland.

So by the autumn of 1549 all Somerset's policies were falling in ruin around him. A statesman who could have survived such an avalanche of disasters would never have allowed them to happen and the natural sequel to this troubled summer was the overthrow of the Protector. Men of all opinions had lost faith in his capacity to govern the country and in October 1549 the conservatively-minded Southampton, Shrewsbury, and Arundel supported Warwick, Russell, and their friends in bringing him to the Tower. The Protectorate was ended and authority reverted to the Privy Council in which Warwick was now the dominant personality.

Warwick's first serious move in foreign policy was to end the war with France and Scotland. Negotiations began in January 1550 and peace was signed in March. Boulogne, which by the 1546 treaty might have been bought back by France for 800,000 crowns in 1554, was now surrendered to her for 400,000. The English troops were to leave Scotland and nothing was said about Mary Stuart's marriage. It was 'the most ignominious treaty signed by England during the century'.[15]

It would, however, be unfair to blame Warwick too severely

for this ignominious peace. It was Henry VIII and Somerset who, by trying to bully the Scots into accepting a union of the Scottish and English crowns, had brought the government to the edge of bankruptcy, the economy to crisis, and social order to the verge of dissolution. If that was what came of trying to coerce the Scots, how could England even consider trying to coerce the French as well? Yet, once Scotland had been driven back into dependency upon France and once Mary Stuart was safely on French soil, the union of the Scottish and English crowns could only be achieved in that way. The war had thus already become pointless when the 1549 risings made it desperate. Peace at almost any price was the only policy that Somerset's failures left open to his successor and in the circumstances the price that Warwick paid for it was no higher than had to be expected. Besides, for that price he did buy an interval of peace which he might have used to rebuild England's strength and to tackle the problems that were imperilling her unity and her independence.

Chapter 14

The Mid-Century Crisis

BEFORE we go on to see how Northumberland used or misused his opportunity, we must pause to take account of the changed conditions to which English foreign policy had to adapt itself from the middle of the sixteenth century onwards. For Somerset's fall marked the end of an era of affluence, when easy money from Henry VII's savings, the spoliation of the Church, and the debasement of the coinage had enabled governments to indulge, periodically at least, in grandiose projects without too minutely counting the cost beforehand. From now onwards ends had to be adapted to means and policies shaped more to the interests and sentiments of the nation that had to pay for them. 'The whole monarchy of Christendom', the crown of France, even a forcible union with Scotland were things now beyond the realm of dreams.

Most Englishmen, indeed, had already long ceased to dream about them. For one of the most strongly marked features of these years was the growth of a conscious sentiment of insular separateness, of contentment with that separateness and pride in it. English contempt and dislike for foreigners, particularly for Frenchmen, had of course long been notorious. Foreign ambassadors regularly commented upon it. It appeared in the common English contrasting of 'the ancient and godly yeomanry of England' with the 'peasantry and slavery of France',[1] and in the jealous hostility towards the privileged Hanseatic merchants. It had showed at its most violent in the London Evil May Day riots of 1517. But during the past twenty years this instinctive and negative xenophobia had developed into a more positive and conscious national feeling. The steady and spreading pressure of Tudor government perhaps had some part in this development. So, too, had the quickening of trade and its growing concentration upon London. So, probably, had the coming together at Westminster of members of Parliament from all over the country in the more frequent and prolonged sessions after 1529.[2]

But undoubtedly the break with Rome was the chief agent in

this change. During and after the break, Henry VIII explicitly taught his people to think of England as an empire to itself, owing allegiance to no other earthly power, temporal or spiritual, neither to Emperor nor to Pope nor even to General Councils. This idea of England's independence, England's separateness, was drummed home from press and pulpit, in Acts of Parliament and royal proclamations. Moreover, while Henry VIII had separated England from Rome and from Catholic Christendom, he had also kept her separate from Wittenberg, Zurich, and Geneva, from the new Protestant Christendom of the continent. For a generation Englishmen had thus lived in an atmosphere which emphasized their insularity, which made them peculiarly conscious that they were a peculiar people, though most of them were equally sure that it was the rest of the world that was out of step. In addition they had the exhilarating and unifying experience of being threatened, though not in fact assaulted, by 'the three corners of the world in arms' in 1538–40 and of beating off an actual double assault by French and Scots in 1545, when the Emperor deserted them. 1545, too, provided an object lesson in the protective value of sea power to an island nation; and with Somerset the idea of rounding off this insularity by making Britain, and not just England, an empire to itself became a conscious purpose. The idea of turning away still further from continental involvements to a still wider empire across the oceans had hardly yet appeared, though the attempts that were to be made under Northumberland to lessen England's dependence upon Antwerp and the European markets would be a first step that way. But the British empire had to begin at home, in Britain; and when Somerset fell, many Englishmen, and some Scotsmen too, were already thinking of the British Isles as a world apart, whose destiny was to go its own way more and more independently of continental Europe.

This more conscious and widespread care for national independence was something that governments had henceforward to take note of. For one thing, it meant that very few Englishmen were prepared to undo what Henry VIII had done. The influential and propertied families who had profited by the spoiling of the Church, of course were particularly reluctant to see England return to Papal obedience for fear that it might mean restoring the monasteries and chantries and giving them back their lands. Parliament was to show this fear very strongly in Mary's reign.

Her first Parliament, for example, met in October 1553, after elections unusually free from government interference. It met at a moment when Northumberland's misrule had heavily discredited the more advanced reformers and when the notoriously Catholic Mary had not yet thrown away the popularity which had swept her to the throne only three months before. It repealed all Edward VI's ecclesiastical legislation, restored the Mass and clerical celibacy, with unexpected willingness. But it would not impose penalties upon those who refused to go to the Mass. It showed a complete unwillingness to abolish the royal supremacy over the Church and return to Papal obedience; an absolute determination not to give back the monastic lands; and a firm resolution to maintain the lawful succession rights of Anne Boleyn's daughter Elizabeth, whose very birth was a denial of all things Roman. Here, in this more than usually free Parliament, we can probably hear the real voice of at least the better-to-do classes. And in these matters it seems as if they were speaking for the nation as a whole. For even the Western rebels in 1549, though they rose in arms against Somerset's mild Act of Uniformity and his ambiguously phrased Prayer Book, though they demanded a pardon for Cardinal Pole and his admission to the King's Council, did not call for the restoration of Papal authority in their manifesto.[3]

The break with Rome had thus both stimulated English national consciousness and been confirmed by it. Yet the consequences of the break did, for a time at least, in many ways blur that consciousness and bring disunity and weakness to the nation. The most obvious cause of disunity was religion itself. It was hardly possible to take away the Pope's authority, the monasteries, and the chantries, and leave it at that. Too many other reforms were needed, of which too many people had been conscious for too long. Besides, the Church itself could hardly rest indefinitely in the curious halfway house where Henry VIII had left it. If it was to be anything more than a collection of sacred buildings in which by the state's command parishioners answered their weekly roll call, if it was to be a distinctive and living Church, it had to define its position more sharply, just as the Roman Church was doing in the Council at Trent and the various continental Protestant Churches were doing under the leadership of Melancthon, Calvin, and others. And that definition must almost inevitably carry it further from the Roman communion. Henry VIII himself, Cranmer said, in his last days realized this. And, if we are not prepared to take Cranmer's word for it, there remain the facts that Henry gave his son and heir tutors of advanced opinions and left men inclined to those opinions preponderant among his executors and in his son's council of regency. The zeal of a minority of ardent reformers and the inner needs of the Church itself were both driving it further from its ancient Roman moorings, to which almost no one wished it to return.

Yet, while almost no one wanted to go back to Rome, the great mass of the people seem to have been equally reluctant to go much further towards Protestantism. Somerset, by repealing Henry VIII's treason laws and letting debate run free, gave the reformers their chance to persuade the nation. Hooper, Ridley, and their supporters, reinforced by Bucer, Peter Martyr, John à Lasco and other Protestant refugees from the continent, made the most of the chance. The commotion that they caused showed how strong a hold old habits still had. Far more than when Henry VIII complained of it to his last Parliament,[4] religion became the subject of alehouse controversy and churchyard brawls, even in remote country parishes. The debate spread so wide and rose so high that even the liberal Protector had to impose an Act of Uniformity and a Book of Common Prayer. Both were mild enough, ambiguous enough. Yet they provoked the Western rising which, but for the hold-up at Exeter, could have gathered substantial reinforcements from the discontented in the southern and midland counties. Possibly sixteenth-century Englishmen were not much interested in theological questions. The character of the printing presses' output would suggest that they were not,[5] though to judge them by that is perhaps a little too like judging twentieth-century Englishmen by what the British Broadcasting Corporation offers them on its Third Programme. But this did not mean that they cared nothing about religion. It is very often true that the more conventional a man's beliefs are, the more quickly he is moved to anger and protest by any attempt to change the traditional modes of their expression. Men who cared little and knew less whether salvation came through faith or works, who had no strong convictions about the number and nature of the sacraments, could easily be outraged by the introduction of new forms of words into the Sunday services, simpler vestments for the parson, communion tables in the place of altars, or the taking away of church bells.

Religion in this sense was still a powerful force, as 1549 showed. It was, moreover, one of the dwindling number of forces that might still counteract the growing national spirit and tempt some Englishmen to join with foreigners of their own faith rather than submit to their countrymen of a different creed. Unless some middle way could be found, along which the great majority were willing to walk together in unity, religious dissension might offer to England's continental neighbours domestic allies a good deal more useful than the irreconcilable Yorkists had been in Henry VII's time. It would not be easy to find the *via media* which would meet the Church's inner need; which would damp down, if not satisfy, the reformers' ardour; and which would still touch outward forms and observances so lightly that the habits and instincts of the mass of the nation would not be outraged. Yet, unless all three of these requirements were met, religious dissension must become a new complication for English foreign policy, a serious threat to national unity and to national independence.

Nor did the consequences, direct and indirect, of the break with Rome end there. There was the 1538–40 alarm lest Charles V and Francis I might join together to restore the Pope's authority over England. That alarm stimulated Henry VIII to force a solution of the problem of his worsening relations with Scotland and so to precipitate the Scottish and French wars of his later years. The alarm and the wars made manifest the need to modernize and reorganize the nation's defences. Henry VIII greatly strengthened the royal navy, improved – indeed, largely created – its administrative organization and the mobilization of its reserves from the country's merchant shipping. He also built the string of modern castles and bulwarks to defend vulnerable parts of the coast. But, besides this, he and his ministers, and more still the ministers of his successors, could no longer ignore the need to modernize the equipment of the country's land forces. In continental armies firearms and pikes had for many years replaced bows and bills as the standard infantry weapons and, though a plausible theoretical case for the long bow could still be made out – was to be made out even in the fifteen nineties[6] – in practice England could not much longer trust her defence entirely to that famous but outmoded weapon. In fact, Henry VIII and Somerset both felt impelled to hire German and Italian 'shot' even for their Scottish campaigns; and these foreign mercenaries played a notable part at Pinkie in 1547, a decisive part against the Western rebels and Ket in 1549.

The new weapons, moreover, or at least the firearms, were very much more costly and more complicated than the old. They were the products of a skilled industry, of which England as yet had only the beginnings. To equip the entire *levée en masse* of the county forces with them was impossible and perhaps undesirable. They could be the weapons only of a selected number. The modernizing of the land forces' equipment, therefore, would mean modernizing their organization as well. Neither task had been really attempted by 1549, which partly explains the hiring of foreign mercenaries. Yet, even so, the demand for cannon for the ships and the castles, of small arms for the footmen, and of gunpowder and balls for them all, had forced Henry and Somerset to look abroad for war materials as well as for men-at-arms. They had to buy heavily in Antwerp to provide the weapons and munitions needed for the wars and for national defence. Here, then, was another tie that was binding England more closely than before to the continent. Until the military forces were rearmed and reorganized, and a native armaments industry sufficiently developed to supply them, England must become more dependent upon the continent in a way that must directly circumscribe her foreign policy.

The wars, and the defence preparations that preceded them, created another problem which made immediate and large-scale modernizing of the land forces almost impossible and which still further increased the government's dependence upon Antwerp. They cost so much that Henry and Somerset could not pay for them completely even by selling off the monastic and chantry lands and debasing the coinage, on top of heavy grants from Parliament. They had to borrow, by 1549 to the extent of £250,000, and they could raise only half of this sum at home.[7] The other half came from the Antwerp bankers. Here was another circumscribing condition for English foreign policy. With the new weapons and the general rise in prices, wars had become so costly that English governments could no longer afford to fight except upon a limited and local scale or for a very brief period. If they did have to fight, they must depend for their war finance upon the willingness of Parliament to make very substantial grants and of the moneylenders to make very substantial loans. And until England's own capital resources and banking facilities should mature, a very considerable proportion of those loans must be sought from foreign bankers, particularly from the bankers of Antwerp.

We have still to see the gravest effects of the wars of Henry VIII and Somerset upon England's unity and independence. A considerable part of the cost of those wars had been met by repeated debasements of the English currency during the fifteen forties. One direct effect of these debasements was to stimulate, temporarily but enormously, England's export trade, especially her cloth exports.[8] Cloth exports had been growing steadily all through the first half-century of Tudor rule, chiefly because the spectacular development of Antwerp assured them better and easier distribution to ever-widening markets. For example, kerseys woven at Newbury in Berkshire and distributed by an Italian firm at Antwerp, have been traced in the fifteen forties as far afield as Hungary and the Turkish Levant.[9] At Antwerp, too, English merchants could buy from the proceeds of their cloth sales almost all the goods that England, with her still backward economy, neither made nor grew at home. A hundred miles or less across the Narrow Seas from London, the trade could be carried in quite small ships. Most of it, indeed, went in vessels of under eighty tons that were comparatively inexpensive to build and to run. On these short voyages they did not have to use up much of their cargo space for their crews' victuals and water or for guns and munitions for their own defence. With capital outlay and running costs low and profits high, it is small wonder that Antwerp as it rose drew to itself an overwhelming proportion of England's overseas trade or that fewer and fewer merchants, particularly of London and the eastern half of England, felt any interest in other and less lucrative trades to remoter places.

In the fifteen forties this quickening trade to Antwerp was spurred to a headlong gallop by the debasement of the English coinage. The exchange value of the pound sterling, which had stood at 27 Flemish shillings in 1542, dropped to 21s. by 1547 and to 15s. by 1551. The same number of Flemish shillings would now buy a good deal more English cloth, for although prices (and therefore production costs) did also rise in England there was a time-lag between the falls in the foreign exchange rates and the rises in the domestic price-levels. Besides this, the English now had to sell more of their cloth to buy the same quantity of return cargoes as before. So, by 1547 the number of cloths exported from London – and probably four-fifths of England's cloth exports now went through London – was twice as great as it had been at the beginning of the century, half as large again as it had been only ten years before in 1537. By 1550 it had risen still higher, to the record figure of 132,000 short cloths. Naturally this accelerated expansion, like the steadier expansion of earlier years, was directed almost entirely to Antwerp. Commercially, England became more than ever dependent on Antwerp. It would be less easy, even than Wolsey had found it in 1528, to play off the French against Antwerp's Habsburg ruler. For, in the vast and complicated network of Antwerp's traffic, the English cloth trade did not now possess quite the commanding position that it had held in earlier years. In matters of commerce, as well as for war materials and loans, England had become a good deal more dependent upon Antwerp than Antwerp was upon England.

Nor was this all. These expanded exports meant expanded production on a scale and at a pace that unbalanced large areas of the national economy and strained the cohesion of society. Such rapid expansion of output was not possible, or not easy, within the ancient gild framework of the old-established clothing towns. Much of the cloth industry accordingly moved out of those towns into the country and into unincorporated towns where there were no gilds to restrict its practices. It was in the as yet unincorporated and gildless Newbury, not in the ancient borough of Reading, that the Winchcombes manufactured those kerseys which we have seen travelling through Antwerp to customers in Hungary and the Levant. Such developments brought dislocation, discontentment, and (at least relatively) decay to the older boroughs. At the same time they brought unsettlement and tensions to the new and growing industrial centres. Agricultural villages could not then, any more than now, grow suddenly into thriving industrial towns without upsetting old habits and unsettling old attitudes to work and to life.

Moreover, these changes affected the agricultural countryside as well as the towns. The demand for cloth meant a demand for wool and for the sheep that grew the wool. Sheep became the most profitable farming proposition. This, too, coincided with a period of rising prices. The acceleration and expansion of trade and of credit facilities, the increased European output of silver, and from the fifteen forties the more spectacular inflow of silver from the mines of America were driving prices up all over western Europe. On top of this, in England during the fifteen forties there were the repeated debasements of the coinage. There prices almost doubled between 1547 and 1551. Now this inflation, while beneficial to the merchants, hit hard the landowners who drew most of their income from rents fixed by custom or by long leases and which they could not quickly increase. To them, the chance to profit largely by investing in sheep offered a way out of their difficulties. The more substantial leaseholders and freeholders also saw their chance. In addition, the Tudor attainders and forfeit-ures, and from the later fifteen thirties the sale of monastic property, threw great quantities of land on to the market just at this moment and so gave townsmen, lawyers, and officials ample opportunity to join in the game. Typically, the second Winch-combe of Newbury now purchased from the crown the near-by manor of Bucklebury, lately part of the estates of Reading abbey. Prospering townsmen, lawyers, and officials had of course been moving into country estates, and the more socially respectable status of landowner, for generations. But these 'new men' had never before come out quite so thick and fast. And their advent, with the new attitude of the older landowning families towards sheep, brought unsettlement and tensions to the countryside as the expansion of the cloth manufacture was doing to the towns. The new families, 'foreigners' among their new neighbours, could not for a generation or two command the old respect and obedi-ence; the older families by their new practices often lost something of the respect that they had formerly commanded.

But besides loosening the bonds of society in these ways, the growing demand for cloth burst the rural economic framework as it was bursting the urban structure. The balance of the farming economy was upset by the disproportionate emphasis placed upon its sheep. Its common pastures could not accommodate their numbers nor its agrarian routines adapt quickly to their needs. So, enterprising landlords took larger parts of their estates into their own hands and threw together into large hedged or fenced pastures more, not only of the waste and grassland, but of the arable as well. By stocking these sheep runs themselves, or by leasing them to substantial tenants, they materially improved their own incomes and met the growing demand for more wool. Wherever these changes were made upon a considerable scale, they were bound to unsettle old habits, remove old landmarks, alter the local landscape. They could change the look and feel of things out in the fields much as Protestant practices could change the look and feel of things inside the parish church. And, for the less fortunate, they could do much worse than that. A single shepherd could watch the sheep in pastures that it had needed many men to till. Enclosure of arable land for conversion to pasture therefore often meant depopulation. Even enclosure of common pasture, where the villager's cow had grazed, or of the waste, where his pigs had rooted, could destroy many families' narrow margin of independence.

No doubt many of these families were able to make up in part for the loss of their cow or pigs by spinning wool, or even weaving cloth, 'put out' to them at piece rates in their cottages by the neighbouring clothiers. Others moved into the new clothing towns and found work with the clothiers there. Enclosures, in fact, probably helped to provide not only the additional wool but also, when added to the steady rise in the total population, the additional labour force that was needed. The outcries at Antwerp and from the Merchant Adventurers in the late fifteen forties and fifteen fifties about the shoddy quality of much of the cloth produced, certainly suggest a labour force that was being considerably diluted by semi-skilled or unskilled workmen. However, even those who thus found new employment in the cloth industry lost something of their former small independence when their employment and livelihood came to depend upon the fluctuations of international trade. And not all the displaced people were absorbed into the cloth manufacture. A good many became workless as well as homeless and had to take to the road to swell the already considerable numbers of unemployed or work-shy vagrants put on the march by earlier social and economic changes and by the growth of population. The succession of poor laws passed by Parliament from 1531 onwards is proof enough that these 'sturdy beggars', 'loose and masterless men', formed another and even more dangerous element of social instability.

The extent of these evils can, it is true, easily be exaggerated.

Enclosure and sheep farming were not innovations in the English countryside. The mid-sixteenth century outcry against them certainly owed a lot to remarkable publicists such as Latimer, Hales, and Crowley, and to unwontedly articulate yeomen like Ket. It may have been as much an indication of an awakening social conscience as a proof of a growing social evil. And, as the eighteenth century enclosures were to show, an enormous acreage of England's land still remained arable and unenclosed, pleasant perhaps but not for most of the year green. Nevertheless, after all these allowances have been made, the amount of smoke that was put up does suggest the existence of a fairly considerable fire and of a fire that blazed up more hotly in the middle years of the sixteenth century. The widespread rebellions and disorders of 1549 were not provoked merely by Somerset's unwise policies or by popular anxiety about his very mild religious measures.

We have seen already how directly and sharply those disorders reacted upon England's foreign policy. News of them encouraged the French to declare war in August 1549 and the effort of repressing them helped to drive the English government to make an ignominious peace in March 1550. They also revealed another danger. Not a few of the men drafted from the counties to serve in Scotland or at Boulogne in 1549 had turned aside to help Ket or the Western rebels. Because of the loosening of social bonds, because of the enmity between prospering landlords and less fortunate peasantry, because of religious antagonisms the old military forces of the counties could no longer be fully relied upon for foreign service, for national defence, or to crush rebellion. The inadequacy of their equipment was already recognized. Now their loyalty, too, had to be doubted. It was the gentlemen and nobles with their retinues and foreign mercenaries who had to crush the 1549 rebellions and to hold down the country afterwards. A government that could not rely upon the county forces and could afford to hire only a limited number of mercenaries – if indeed it could long afford to hire any – could not pursue a strong or independent foreign policy. It could not even feel secure against rebellion and invasion. The turmoil of 1549 made it very clear that the religious tensions resulting from the break with Rome, and the economic and social tensions resulting from the boom in the cloth trade, were together destroying England's unity to a degree that could well destroy her independence.

And just then the economic bubble burst. Boom turned rapidly to slump. In 1550 Antwerp for the first time found difficulty in disposing of all the English cloth that was poured into it. The market was glutted. Foreign buyers could pick and choose. They could and did reject the poorer quality and shoddier cloths. The Merchant Adventurers had to reduce their prices and still had some cloth left on their hands. Things became worse in 1551 and 1552. In the summer of 1551 Warwick's government devalued the currency by fifty per cent, calling down the coins to a half of their nominal value. Now that the pound sterling was worth only 15 Flemish shillings, some such realistic adjustment was almost unavoidable. But Warwick's action was sudden and drastic and it had sudden and drastic effects on the sales of English cloth abroad. In 1550 London had exported 132,000 short cloths. In 1551 the number was down to 112,000 and in 1552 it was only 85,000 or about what it had been in the earlier years of Henry VIII's reign. The repercussions cannoned back all along the line from the Antwerp warehouses to the English sheep pastures. The Merchant Adventurers bought less cloth from the clothiers and paid lower prices for what they did buy. The clothiers gave their spinners, weavers, and other workpeople less employment at lower rates and bought less wool at lower prices from the sheep-owners. The economy, strained already by an over-rapid expansion, shuddered and creaked as the whole movement went suddenly into reverse. The tensions that had been created in society by the boom were now intensified by the slump that followed it.

This happened just at a moment when political developments abroad made weakness and disunity at home especially dangerous. For both the French and the Habsburgs were beginning to turn their eyes away from Italy and towards the British Isles as their future battleground. We have seen how Henry II's ambitions were stimulated in this direction by the counsels of the Guise family and by the opportunity of marrying Mary, Queen of Scots, to the Dauphin. He had already spoken of Scotland and France as being now one realm. He was beginning to hope for England and Ireland as well. Hitherto, fear of Charles V had restrained him to attacking only the outworks not covered by the Anglo-Imperial treaty of 1543. That fear continued to hold him off as long as Charles's affairs continued to prosper in Germany. And when in 1551 Charles began to get into serious difficulties, these difficulties offered opportunities for undermining Habsburg power in Germany that France could hardly ignore, even if to seize them meant neglecting opportunities in the British Isles. So, until a decision was reached in Germany, Charles was too busy and Henry too wary of him for either to threaten England very seriously.

But in 1552 a decision was reached in Germany. Maurice of Saxony, after quietly building up a new Lutheran alliance and buying Henry II's support by the promise of the Three Bishoprics – Metz, Toul, and Verdun – which dominated Lorraine, suddenly turned upon the Emperor. In April 1552 Charles had to flee hurriedly over the Alps. In August he had to acquiesce in the treaty of Passau, which virtually left the princes and cities of the Empire political and religious independence upon the *cujus regio ejus religio* principle that was to be confirmed by the final settlement of Augsburg three years later. He had already had to abandon his hopes of getting his eldest son, Philip of Spain, accepted for his successor as Holy Roman Emperor. Now he had to leave his brother Ferdinand to salvage what he could from the wreckage of Imperial authority. Charles V was still nominally Emperor but his control, indeed Habsburg control, over Germany was gone. He did make a final effort to recover the Three Bishoprics, but after vainly besieging Metz for over two months, he had in December 1552 to raise his siege and retire baffled to the Netherlands.

With Germany lost, England became of supreme importance to him. If the French should master it as they had already mastered Scotland, they might soon master the Netherlands too. For Ferdinand could spare no help there; none could come by sea if England as well as France was hostile; and the French from Lorraine, with their Protestant allies in the Rhineland and northern Germany, could cut off help that came overland. Against a France that controlled the British Isles and the Netherlands and was linked to the German princes, it would not be easy to hold Italy. And English privateers were already beginning to reinforce the French off Spain's Atlantic coasts, off the ports into which the silver from the American mines flowed. French control of England could, in short, be the ruin of Habsburg power. England's independence of France was therefore the foundation stone of the new western European empire that Charles was to devote his last years to consolidating as a bulwark against France and an inheritance for Philip of Spain. From the moment that Charles accepted his failure in Germany, he had to take up the French challenge for England. Hence by the end of 1552 both the great continental powers were poised ready to seize any really favourable opportunity to assert their influence in English affairs.

By then the 1550 peace with France had given Northumberland (as Warwick had now become) three years in which to rebuild England's strength and to heal the tensions that might provide her neighbours with the opportunity for which they were waiting. How he used those years was therefore of vital importance not only for the nation's domestic well-being but also for its continued independence.

Chapter 15

The Policy of Northumberland

It cannot be said that Warwick used well the three years' breathing space that he had bought by the peace of March 1550. He did a few praiseworthy things and his difficulties were formidable. In sum, however, his fault was that he not merely failed to restore England's strength but actually increased her weakness. He was the ablest of the group of politicians, of various shades of opinion, who had come together to restore order and remedy the ill effects of Somerset's well intentioned policies. That gave him the opportunity to become, if not truly the leader of the nation, at least the leader of its propertied classes. He chose instead to become the leader of a faction, to throw in his lot with the more advanced religious reformers, and to push the nation towards a Protestantism for which it was not yet ready. Why he chose thus is not altogether clear. It seems almost as if there was some fatal taint of crooked self-seeking in the Dudley blood that drove them all towards unpopular and desperate courses. They were all men of great abilities and all used their abilities in unpopular and generally disastrous ways. Warwick's father had been one of Henry VII's two most unpopular ministers and had expiated his offences on the scaffold. Warwick and one of his sons were soon to suffer the same fate and if his youngest son, Robert Dudley, Earl of Leicester, Elizabeth I's favourite, had met a similar end, few of her subjects would have grieved for him. Indeed, he even exasperated Elizabeth herself on one occasion into exclaiming that the Dudleys had been traitors for three generations.

Certainly with Warwick lust for power was a stronger motive than zeal for reform. To go back to the old Catholic ways of Henry VIII would mean restoring Gardiner to office, bringing Southampton and Shrewsbury and Arundel back into the King's counsels, perhaps releasing the Duke of Norfolk from the Tower. It would mean sharing power with dangerous rivals and families whose social prestige would make an upstart Dudley seem very small beer. On the other hand, with Somerset discredited, there was no one to challenge Warwick as secular champion of the reforming party. Besides, Edward VI was now twelve. In a few years he would begin to take a part in the government; in a few years more, to take over the government. Now Edward VI had been educated by tutors of distinctly advanced religious opinions and he already showed a precocious child's partisan enthusiasm for their views. Warwick probably hoped, by fanning that enthusiasm, to secure for himself in future years a position as Edward VI's Thomas Cromwell. At all events, he studiously avoided the tainted title of Protector and from the first worked on and through the boy-King, claiming for himself no more than the position of a specially trusted royal councillor.

He was, however, careful to mould the Council as well as the King. The knights and nobles, who had opened their purses to put down the 1549 rebellions, were promptly and very adequately reimbursed at the state's expense. Also, in the New Year Paget became a baron, Russell Earl of Bedford, and Paulet Earl of Wiltshire. But before that, Southampton had learned that he was not to share the power that he had helped Warwick to win. Arundel and several others were disgraced and fined for alleged peculation. The Duke of Norfolk remained in the Tower. And if Somerset was released from it in February 1550 and restored to the Council in April, he seemed now too discredited to be a serious rival, while generosity towards him might please the reformers and perhaps a little appease the people. All this showed fairly clearly the direction in which Warwick was moving. His other actions made it clearer still. During the winter of 1549–50 Parliament passed an Act for the destruction of images in churches and of all service books except the new Book of Common Prayer. It also authorized a new Ordinal of a very un-Catholic character. Then the reformer Ridley was thrust into Bonner's lost bishopric of London, the see was united with that of Westminster, and both were despoiled of a substantial part of their lands. In November 1550 the Council ordered all altars to be removed and replaced by communion tables situated in the body of the church. The next year saw the disciplining and deprivation of Gardiner and several others of the old bishops; further spoliation of episcopal property; and attempts to bully Princess Mary into stopping the celebration of Mass in her household.

The attempts to make Princess Mary conform started a sharp

dispute with her cousin, the Emperor Charles V. Immediately after Somerset's overthrow, Charles had hinted broadly to the English ambassador that his attitude to the new government would depend very much upon the course it took in religious affairs.[1] In April 1550, when the course it was taking had become reasonably clear, his ambassador formally required the Privy Council to leave Mary free to worship in her own Catholic way. The Council refused to promise this but took no immediate action. Nevertheless, in the summer it heard that the Brussels government was laying plans for Mary to escape to the Netherlands, 'so to begin an outward war and an inward conspiracy'.[2] Nothing came of this, but the English government, or at any rate its new Principal Secretary, William Cecil, was considerably alarmed. The greater part of the nation, Cecil believed, and most of its leaders – nobles, judges, justices of the peace, clergy – were opposed to the present course in religion. They might not dislike it enough to rise spontaneously against it in peacetime; but in war they would be quite likely to go over to an invader who came in the cause of Mary Tudor and the Catholic faith.[3]

Cecil may well have been right. Certainly England could not yet face another war, least of all a war of that sort. As the Council's clerk, William Thomas, put it to Edward VI,[4] the country needed 'either friendship to help us or time to make ourselves strong'. Since 'neither is our force so ordered that we may trust thereby to win our time, nor our treasure such as we may purchase it, therefore our extremest shift is to work by policy' to secure friendship. So far the natural balance of forces on the continent had assured England, not of friendship, but of a general disapproval too lukewarm to be dangerous. In the early months of 1551, however, when Warwick began to increase the pressure on Mary, Charles's disapproval changed to a threatening hostility. He flatly refused to allow the English ambassadors at his court and at Brussels, or anywhere else in his dominions, to use the new English communion service. At the same time, he insisted that his own ambassador in England, as well as Princess Mary, should be permitted to have their Mass freely. If not, diplomatic relations would at once be broken off – indeed, the Imperial ambassador in March 1551 threatened that war would follow, though he was perhaps outrunning his instructions. For the moment Warwick climbed down and allowed Mary and the ambassador their Mass without further interference.[5] It was, however, not easy nor particularly safe to let the heir presumptive so openly defy the religious policy to which everyone else was supposed to conform and to which so many conformed so reluctantly. Nor would these particular concessions put an end to the Emperor's enmity. Nothing short of a general reversal of the government's entire policy in religion would do that.

Warwick was by now too deeply committed to his course to contemplate a complete reversal. Anyway, it would have looked so much like capitulation to Charles V that it would have aroused a corresponding hostility in the French. And as it was, England's relations with France were none too reassuring. There was trouble over the settlement of the claims of Frenchmen whose ships and goods had been seized during the war. There were bickerings on the frontiers of Calais, ominously reminiscent of what had happened before around Boulogne. There was friction over the arrest of some Scotsmen on their way through England. In December 1550 Sir John Mason, the ambassador in France, told alarming tales about the Duke of Guise urging Henry II to exploit the weakness of England rather than the difficulties which Charles V was beginning to encounter in Germany and Italy.[6] These tales, however, were perhaps spread by the French for Mason's special benefit, to counteract the threats of Charles V and to bring England to heel before Henry II committed himself to a new quarrel with the Habsburgs. At all events, Henry was also dropping broad hints that everything could still be happily arranged if England would be reasonably accommodating.

To these hints Warwick quickly responded. He did not mean to modify his domestic policies to appease Charles V. Therefore, since England's 'power without some friendship is of small substance'[7] he felt that he needed a foreign alliance impressive enough to keep the Emperor's hostility within bounds. He could not turn, as Cromwell had done, to the German Lutherans, for at the moment their power, too, seemed of small substance and their goodwill was impaired by his harsh treatment of the Hansards in England. There remained only France. So, early in 1551 when Charles's threats grew really menacing, Warwick secretly began to follow up the hints that Henry II had let fall. When the Imperial ambassador gave his warlike warning in March, an envoy was at once dispatched to open negotiations in France. By

April it was clear that an understanding had been arrived at. For Henry II was openly supporting Charles's enemies in Parma, sending money to the defenders of Magdeburg, and threatening to stop French ecclesiastics from attending the new session of the Council of Trent unless Lutheran representatives were also admitted to it. At the same time Warwick sent the Garter to Henry II and dispatched Dr Wootton to inform the Emperor that Mary must conform and that the Imperial ambassador would be allowed his Mass only if the English ambassadors were allowed their communion. Charles, with difficulties thickening around him in Germany, gave Wootton a fairly restrained answer but abated none of his demands.[8] Warwick therefore proceeded no further against Mary or the Imperial ambassador until he had clinched his deal with France. The formal negotiations were leisurely, but eventually in July 1551 the final treaty was signed at Angers. Warwick had gained his powerful foreign ally and bought himself a little more time.

The price, however, was high. The English agreed to the annulment of their 1543 treaty with the Scots and abandoned all claim to Mary Stuart as a bride for Edward VI. They also agreed that in due time Edward should marry Henry II's daughter, Elisabeth of Valois. Thus the 'strait league with a notable knot', which Mason had thought England needed to keep up her reputation abroad,[9] was achieved. But it was France whose reputation was enhanced; England that was straitened and bound. Indeed, at first it seemed that worse might follow, that England might be dragged into war at the coat-tails of her new ally. For, while Henry II began secretly to knit closer his relations with the German Lutherans and Maurice of Saxony, Warwick's first use of his new alliance was to defy the Emperor by putting fresh pressure upon Princess Mary and denying the Imperial ambassador his Mass.

Somerset tried vainly to dissuade his fellow Councillors from these actions. Having failed, he plunged into intrigues which, had they succeeded, might have brought Warwick down as he had brought Somerset down two years before. For Warwick's religious measures, his treatment of Mary, his imprisoning of Gardiner and other bishops, his debasement of the coinage in this very summer, coming on top of the great slump in cloth exports, had created great unrest throughout the nation.[10] That unrest was already at the flash point and needed only leadership to touch it off into revolution. Somerset could well provide that leadership. To the people he was still 'the good Duke'. Among men of moderate religious views and among the less extreme Protestants, he still had a considerable following. He was himself perhaps now more tolerant than Protestant: certainly the zealots were commenting upon his growing religious indifference. But this made it the easier for him to link up with moderate Catholics like Arundel and *politiques* like Paget. Above all, despite his faults, there was no doubt that he was deeply and genuinely concerned for the welfare and independence of England. He represented, too, the old tradition of mistrust towards France and goodwill to the Habsburgs. On such a platform he could hope to rally overwhelming support if Parliament reassembled when it was due, in October.

But if Somerset might thus hope eventually to rally support, Warwick could depend upon the present backing of an armed faction. He had encouraged his supporters out in the counties to entertain armed bands of horsemen, paid by the government, to maintain order and to deal with the widespread disturbances that had continued ever since the great risings of 1549 had been suppressed. To the same end, he made permanent many of the temporary commissions of lieutenancy that had been issued to reliable nobles and gentlemen during those risings. A few trustworthy Lords Lieutenant thus took over from the sheriffs control of the armed forces of many counties. The bands of horse naturally fell also under their command. Here, then, was the nucleus, if not quite of a standing army, at least of a military organization that could be relied on to keep order much better than the old county levies hastily summoned from the plough for brief periods of service when need arose. It undoubtedly had some stabilizing effect upon a disturbed countryside and was capable of being developed into a useful weapon of national defence. But it had other uses too. Its leaders had not yet forgotten that it was chiefly Warwick who had saved them from social anarchy in 1549. They lived in constant awareness of the continuing afterswell of those disorders. Naturally, therefore, they tended to be Warwick's henchmen and through them he controlled an organized force such as his opponents could not command. In addition, since February 1551 the royal guards had been increased to 1,000 men, a useful force at the centre of affairs.

198

In the Privy Council, too, Warwick's power was great. During the past two years twelve new Councillors had been added and all of these were his supporters. His hold over them was further strengthened in October 1551, when he persuaded the young King to make Dorset Duke of Suffolk, Paulet Marquis of Winchester, Herbert Earl of Pembroke, and to distribute knighthoods to various others. Warwick himself at the same time became Duke of Northumberland. Backed by armed faction, controlling the Council, and possessing a remarkable influence over the boy-King, he was now able to get Parliament deferred, to bring Somerset to trial, and in January (on the day before Parliament met) to have him executed.

That left Northumberland the undoubted master of England. He controlled King and Council. The new Lords Lieutenant, with their provosts-marshal and backed by the horsebands of his henchmen, were slowly bringing order back to the countryside. These, and the foreign mercenaries that he began to hire in December 1551 to provide a standing force of infantry, also somewhat strengthened England's ability to defend herself against foreign enemies. They therefore somewhat lessened his dependence upon French goodwill. Nor did he let the French drag him into war after all. In October 1551 he ignored appeals from Maurice of Saxony and the German Lutherans to join them and Henry II in their impending conflict with the Emperor.

To this extent Northumberland might argue that his 1551 French treaty was justified by its fruits. It had won him more time to rebuild England's strength. The obvious flaw in that argument was, of course, that he would not have needed to buy time at all if he had followed more moderate policies in religious matters and towards the Emperor. The heightening tension between Charles, the Lutherans, and the French would have given it him free of cost. That, in essence, had been Somerset's case against him. Somerset was gone and there was no one else who could hope to succeed where he had failed. Nevertheless, his case still stood and very many Englishmen accepted it, the great majority of Englishmen if Cecil's earlier estimate still held true. Northumberland could not convert them. He therefore had to hold them down. For that he had to rely upon the faction of more ardent Protestants and the clientele of Councillors, officials, and swordsmen that had enabled him to triumph over Somerset. His power depended more than ever on their loyalty; their loyalty depended upon his ability and readiness to satisfy their demands; and the satisfying of their demands made any real rebuilding of England's strength impossible. Northumberland had bought time when he might have had it free and he had bought it in such a way that he could not use it to any good purpose.

To satisfy his Protestant supporters, he got Parliament early in 1552 to pass a new Act of Uniformity. This penalized those who failed to attend the services of the established Church on Sundays and festivals, as well as – like the 1549 Act – those who held or attended other forms of worship. Parliament also authorized, for use in the official services, the revised English Prayer Book that Archbishop Cranmer was preparing. When that Book appeared, towards the end of 1552, it proved to be strongly Protestant in content and tone. Even more Protestant in tone were the Forty-Two Articles, drawn up by Cranmer and the King's chaplains and published in June 1553 without either Parliament or Convocation being consulted. Thus England was driven much farther and faster towards Protestantism than most of her people yet wanted to go. Many Protestants themselves were disturbed at the way it was done, at the ignoring of bishops and Convocation, at the general treatment of the Church as a mere department of state to be ordered – and plundered – as the government saw fit. Far from settling religion in some way that would draw Englishmen together, Northumberland made it more than ever a dividing force and a major obstacle to national unity.

This meant that he was more than ever dependent upon his henchmen in the central government and in the counties and upon his swordsmen and mercenaries. But these, too, had their price. To pay it, and at the same time to restore the government's finances, was an impossible task. To restore the finances was not easy anyway. The ending of the war had relieved them of their most insupportable burden, but it still left behind it a debt at home and abroad of about £250,000. Moreover, the rising prices were sending up the everyday costs of government just when revenue had fallen to a low level. The expenses of the royal household, £25,000 in 1538–9, rose to £56,000 in 1551–2. The customs revenue, £40,000 a year in the last years of Henry VIII, fell to £25,900 in 1550–51. The crown's clear ordinary income for 1550–51, Michaelmas to Michaelmas, was estimated at £168,150; its

ordinary expenditure at £131,600 with another £80,000 for the
navy, the Ordnance Office, the defence establishments on the Scottish Border and in Ireland and Calais[11] – and this was before
Northumberland hired his foreign mercenaries.

To meet this annual deficit and build up a sorely needed reserve,
the government could look for no more windfalls like the monastic
lands. Even the chantry lands had almost gone. Court of Aug-
mentations' land sales were down below £8,000 in 1551. In 1551–2
confiscated church plate and ornaments, no longer needed under
Protestant austerity, brought in less than £11,000. The bishops'
lands were being plundered, but as much for the benefit of the
crown's servants as for the good of the crown. The 1551 debasement of the coinage yielded £114,500, but that was a final fling
and could not be repeated. Nor could the £133,000 that France
paid for Boulogne. And, at least until 1553, Northumberland
dared not ask a Parliament for money. He did try to improve the
efficiency of the financial administration. Winchester, Petre, Cecil,
and others spent a lot of time in 1551–2 examining the situation; a
number of those who had handled crown revenues were fined for
peculation, especially if (like Paget) they happened to be opponents of the government; and nearly £17,000 of debts due to the
crown were called in during 1552. Thomas Gresham, a London
Merchant Adventurer who was appointed royal agent at Antwerp
in 1551, saw that the government's foreign loans were punctually
renewed or paid off out of new loans. He could not greatly reduce
the total owing at Antwerp, which still stood at some £132,000 at
the end of 1552 when another £109,000 was also owing at home.
But he did keep the Antwerp interest rate steady at fourteen per
cent when Charles V was paying sixteen per cent there.[12]

Any good these efforts might have produced was more than offset
by Northumberland's need to reward his adherents. In the financial year 1550–51 alone, £20,000 was given away in pensions and
annuities, £12,000 in grants of lands for life. During the whole of
Edward VI's reign more crown land was given away than was
sold – the sales covered lands worth £21,000 a year and brought in
£435,000; the gifts covered lands worth £27,000 a year or, at the
same rate of a little over twenty years' purchase, a capital value of
about £550,000, and on them the crown reserved to itself no more
than £3,260 a year in rents.[13] Not all of this was Northumberland's doing, but he was in control for half of the reign and it was

in his time that the evil reached its peak. It was then the price that he – and England – paid for his faction's loyalty.

By the end of 1552 that price had risen too high for even Northumberland to pay. That autumn he had to borrow £40,000 from the Merchant Adventurers and the Staplers to secure the renewal of the Antwerp loans; the navy was reduced in strength; the foreign mercenaries had to be disbanded; the garrisons in Ireland and at Berwick and Guisnes were cut down; and some of the coastal defences abandoned. Northumberland's anxiety was also shown by the appointment of nine different commissions to scrape up money and by a plan for an audit of all officials' accounts as far back as 1532. Most significant of all, in March 1553, he had to assemble a Parliament and ask it for a subsidy and two fifteenths and tenths. These were granted, but only after long debate. An Act was also passed empowering the crown to reorganize in some more economical form the multitude of financial courts that had grown up from Cromwell's time onwards. But, although considerable care had been taken over the elections, the Commons showed a very critical temper and a very unwelcome readiness to pry into accounts and policies.

This may explain why Northumberland did not even introduce another bill which had been drafted and which might have made a considerable step forwards towards a new commercial policy. From the first, as Gresham's appointment at Antwerp showed, the Duke had been very ready to listen to the great merchants of London. They, it will be remembered, had come to his rescue over the renewal of the Antwerp loans in 1552. They had welcomed his efforts in 1551 to provide a more honest currency. Those efforts had not been very successful, for the debased coins were not called in when new and more honest ones were minted and so the bad old money soon drove the good new money out of circulation. The fifty per cent devaluation, which brought nominal and intrinsic values into line, had also been too drastic and too sudden. As we saw, its effects upon the cloth export trade were catastrophic. Nevertheless, it sharply pointed the lesson of the 1550 glut of cloth at Antwerp, the lesson that supply was ultimately governed by demand. Hitherto governments had tried, and tried in vain, to mitigate the domestic effects of the boom in cloth exports by controlling supply, by direct action to cut down the output of cloth and the enclosure of arable land for sheep pastures. Let them now,

Gresham urged,[14] regulate the outward flow of cloth to Antwerp and the domestic economy would right itself in correspondence.

They could do it partly by taxation, though an increase in the present very light customs duties on cloth would be better than Hales's direct tax on sheep and wool. The customs rates could be revised by the crown without going through Parliaments dominated by landowners and sheepmasters. But more direct regulation was also needed. The cloth exports should all be channelled through London, as four-fifths of them were already. This, incidentally, would bring the collection of the customs more within the limited capacity of sixteenth-century administration. At London control should be concentrated in the Fellowship of Merchant Adventurers. They already exercised it to a considerable extent. An Act of 1497 had implicitly recognized the Netherlands markets as their special preserve by allowing them to exact a fee from all others who traded there in cloth. Henry VII's charter of 1505 had given them a governor and a court of twenty-four assistants to regulate that trade. In February 1552 Northumberland himself removed the chief foreign obstacle to their monopoly by rescinding the charters of the Hanseatic merchants, reducing them to the same status as other alien merchants and forcing them to pay the higher aliens' customs rates instead of their old preferential dues which had been lower even than those exacted from Englishmen.[15]

The Merchant Adventurers' control, however, was far from complete. The 1497 Act had fixed the entrance fee so low that few were excluded from it and the regulation remained effective to only a very limited degree. Gresham complained that many retailers and others unskilled in overseas trade had been tempted by the boom to rush in and spoil the market by undercutting prices and selling shoddily-made cloth. What was needed, in his view, was to give the Merchant Adventurers a legal monopoly, with effective authority to regulate shipments, prices, and so forth and to suppress unauthorized trading. They should, in short, control the export of cloth as the Staplers controlled the export of wool. The 1553 bill would have given them that power and concentrated it in the hands of a small governing body of their leading members. Such a measure, however, would not be popular in an already critical Parliament, whose country and 'outport' members were bitterly jealous of London and of the Adventurers. So the bill was not even brought in. Northumberland may have appreciated the theory that the economy could be stabilized more effectively by regulating exports than by trying to restrict production directly. But he dared not apply it as a remedy.

The 1550–52 commercial crisis, however, taught other lessons too. It taught London merchants that, if they wanted to stay in business, some of them must find other outlets besides Antwerp for some of their trade. It brought home to the government how dangerous it could be to have cloth exports so exclusively tied to Antwerp. Fluctuations in that market could upset a great part of the nation's economy and seriously heighten social unrest. They could also have dangerous political consequences for a government that owed so much to Antwerp financiers and depended so much upon Antwerp for the firearms and munitions that were not yet produced in sufficient quantities at home. Also, the quarrel with the Hanse, a by-product of the Antwerp slump, made it difficult to obtain the masts, cordage, pitch, and other naval stores needed to keep the navy efficient. Nor was Northumberland likely to forget that Antwerp belonged to Charles V, with whom his relations were steadily worsening. What had happened in 1550–52 for reasons of commerce could happen again for reasons of state – had indeed so happened for a few months in 1545.

It was fortunate for those merchants who did look farther afield, that the government's interest was thus aroused. For they had to look far indeed. France was not a very attractive market; the Hansards' hostility barred Germany and the Baltic; the Turks and Barbary corsairs made the Mediterranean too risky; and trade to Spain had become so difficult since England's break with Rome that many West Country traders – even noblemen like Russell – were putting their money into privateering.[16] The privateers soon found Spanish and Portuguese prizes easier and more rewarding than French and Scottish. The bolder of them – Reneger, Russell's captain Thomas Wyndham, William Hawkins of Plymouth – therefore moved out into the Atlantic, down the coasts of Spain and Portugal. Just at this time, old Sebastian Cabot, who had left England in 1512 and had since been Pilot-Major of Spain, was invited back by some of the Privy Council and in January 1548 given a life pension of £166 a year. His knowledge and the London merchants' capital enabled Wyndham to push still further south and in 1551 and 1552 to establish a regular trade with Morocco. In

1553 Wyndham, with the loan of two royal warships, was preparing to move on from Morocco to the Gold Coast.

Morocco and the Gold Coast were, of course, no sort of a substitute for Antwerp and the real hopes of Cabot, the London merchants, and the government lay elsewhere. They hoped to get a footing in the rich trade with the Orient that had made the fortunes of Portugal. English seamen had not yet the experience and knowledge to challege the Portuguese monopoly of the Cape route, nor were English ships yet large enough to carry a worthwhile pay load, in addition to their own essential supplies, on so long a voyage. But Cabot had once tried to find, and still believed in, a much shorter North-West Passage around America, while the learned young tutor of Northumberland's sons, Dr John Dee, believed there was an equally short North-East Passage around Asia. Dee also believed that along the North-East route there were large and shivering populations who would avidly buy warm English cloth. That was a most seductive hope at this juncture and so in the winter of 1552–3 a new company was formed to exploit it.[17] Cabot was the company's governor and it included Wyndham's backers and other City merchants and also Privy Councillors like Winchester, Bedford, Pembroke, and Cecil. Its novel basis, a joint stock made up of £25 shares, spread the risks and letters patent from the crown assured it a monopoly of all discovery and trade both to the north-east and the north-west. In May 1553 its first three ships set sail north-eastwards under Sir Hugh Willoughby and Richard Chancellor.

Thus Northumberland did show a lively and forward-looking concern about the volume, regulation, and direction of overseas trade. Such considerations had played but a small part in shaping England's foreign policy since Henry VII's reign. So long as Antwerp had been able to absorb all that English merchants had to offer, their affairs had called for little attention from the government. Now, with Antwerp failing them, Northumberland began to resume the work that Henry VII had started and that Mary and Elizabeth were to elaborate, thereby adding a new dimension to English foreign policy.

Nevertheless, in matters of commerce as in matters of finance, Northumberland's actual achievements were small and limited. His broader schemes of 1552–3 have an air of desperation about them and they were, indeed, inspired by the knowledge that the time so dearly bought was fast running out. Abroad, things were no longer going England's way. In the spring of 1552 Maurice of Saxony had driven Charles V ignominiously over the Alps and Henry II had seized the Three Bishoprics. In August the treaty of Passau recognized the final failure of Charles's designs in Germany. Henry II seemed thereupon to be turning his attention back towards the British Isles and in September the English government got wind of plans for French attacks upon the Channel Isles, Dartmouth, Falmouth, and from Scotland. Henry, of course denied it; but Northumberland was sufficiently alarmed to appeal to Charles V for support. He could hardly expect a warm response, for only a few months earlier, when the French invaded the Three Bishoprics, he had refused an appeal from Charles for English help on the ground, among other excuses, that Edward VI was not bound by his father's 1543 treaty.[18] Nevertheless, Charles's siege of Metz in October 1552 did probably save England from French invasion that autumn. By the end of the year, however, Charles had again to acknowledge defeat and raise his siege. He now hardly could help Northumberland even if he would, and when spring came the field seemed free for Henry II. England faced the prospect of another 1545 with her fleet run down, her coastal defences and garrisons undermanned, her foreign mercenaries disbanded, her finances still precarious, her economy in disarray, and her people sharply divided over religion.

By then, however, another crisis was at hand. Edward VI, whose health had caused concern for a year or more, was now plainly dying. Northumberland could expect no favour from the lawful heir, Mary Tudor. He therefore embarked upon a conspiracy to alter the succession. He married one of his sons, Lord Guildford Dudley, to Dorset's daughter Lady Jane Grey, the granddaughter of Henry VIII's younger sister Mary. Then he persuaded the dying Edward VI to will the crown to Jane and her heirs male. Whether Edward had the power to will the crown away at all was legally very doubtful; to will it away not only from Mary Tudor but also from Elizabeth, from Mary Stuart, and even from Jane's own mother (who was still living) was politically absurd. It was a desperate design and it destroyed Northumberland; but it did perhaps save England again from French invasion. For Henry II could well have stepped in to prevent Mary Tudor's accession and, if he had, Charles V despaired of stopping him. Northumberland's plot, however, seemed to make immediate French action unnecessary. He was doing Henry's work for him by keeping Mary Tudor out. Having done it, his position at home would be precarious in the extreme and there could be no question of his calling for Habsburg help. He would be at Henry's mercy, to be left as a dependent viceroy for the King of France or pushed aside when the time seemed ripe to assert Mary Stuart's claim.

Henry II therefore contented himself with listening to Northumberland's overtures and assuring him of support for his designs. Both he and Charles, however, had failed to allow for one thing. When Edward VI died (July 6th, 1553) and Northumberland proclaimed Queen Jane (July 10th), almost the whole country rose to maintain Mary Tudor's rights. In less than a fortnight the people of England swept aside Northumberland's conspiracy and deceived Henry II's calculations. By July 20th Mary Tudor was Queen and Northumberland on his way to the Tower.

Chapter 16

The Spanish Marriage and Wyatt's Rebellion

In July 1553 Mary was swept on to the throne by 'the greatest mass demonstration of loyalty ever accorded to a Tudor'.[1] Yet six months later she barely survived the most dangerous rebellion that any Tudor ever faced. And when she died, less than five years after that, 'all the churches in London did ring and at night [the people] did make bonfires and set tables in the street and did eat and drink and make merry for the new Queen' who succeeded her.[2]

For this swift and lasting loss of popularity Mary's foreign policy was largely to blame. Later generations of Protestant Englishmen, brought up on Foxe's 'Book of Martyrs', might think of her chiefly as the Bloody Mary who burned for their faith nor far short of three hundred of her subjects in not much more than three years. Yet even they remembered that she also lost Calais to the French. And it was her Spanish marriage and the losing of Calais, even more than the fires of Smithfield, that lost her the hearts of her subjects. However, her foreign policy was in truth only a manifestation and a consequence of her religious purposes. It hardly existed apart from them. Half Spanish by birth, her life had given her little cause to put her realm before her religion. All through the painful years after her mother's divorce, the old faith had been her stay and comfort. Closer contact with the reformers during her brother's reign had done nothing to enamour her of the new ideas. Now the seeming miracle of her accession convinced her of her mission to bring England back into the Roman Church. Within three weeks of her accession she was secretly corresponding with the Pope. By early August, when the Pope again appointed Cardinal Pole Legate for the reconciliation of England, a Papal envoy was already in London, dealing secretly with the Queen.

Yet Mary appears to have had few illusions about the dangers and difficulty of her task. Unlike some foreign observers, she was not deceived by the willingness of most Englishmen to put the clock back to her father's time; by the fact that the Mass was restored, even in London, 'not by commandment but of the people's devotion'.³ She knew that, although most of her subjects were still Catholics at heart, few of them were Romanists. Most of them, she told the Pope's envoy, mortally hated the Holy See and even the lords of her Council loved their abbey lands too dearly to have any liking for the restoration of Papal authority.⁴ Opposition to her purposes was therefore certain and it would be strong. Moreover, so many favoured her heretical half-sister Elizabeth that the opposition might easily swell into revolution.

For these reasons Mary felt, as her father had felt in the 1520's, that a queen regnant needed a king consort to support her in the man's world of sixteenth-century politics. But there was more to it than that. She was already thirty-seven and, if she died childless, her successor by law and nature would be that heretical half-sister Elizabeth, Anne Boleyn's daughter, who would surely undo all her work. So she must marry, have a child, and that speedily. However, at her age and in that age, childbearing would be a hazardous and perhaps a fatal undertaking. Therefore her husband must be someone who could not only lend her present support but who could also protect her child and preserve her work if the undertaking did prove fatal to her. No subject, no Englishman, could satisfy these requirements. Certainly those suggested were not in themselves very attractive. Cardinal Pole was fifty-three, unwilling, and still by English law a traitor. Edward Courtenay, Earl of Devonshire, Exeter's son, was making up for fifteen youthful years in the Tower in ways that did not at all amuse the rather strait-laced Queen. But chiefly they were ruled out because Mary needed as a husband a prince with princely power. And for what she had in mind, his power must indeed be princely. Even such otherwise eligible foreign candidates as Don Luis of Portugal, Duke Emmanuel Philibert of Savoy, and the young Archduke Ferdinand of Austria would hardly qualify. It was therefore to her cousin and old-time fiancé, the Emperor Charles V, that Mary's thoughts first turned.

Charles V was by now too old and decrepit to make honourable amends himself for his jilting of Mary in 1525. He was, in fact, already contemplating abdication. But his eldest son, Philip of Spain, who was to succeed him in all his dominions outside the Holy Roman Empire, was only twenty-seven and happily a widower. To assure his inheritance, now that Germany was lost and the Netherlands were menaced by France, Philip would need to be sure of England. And how better be sure than by marrying England's Queen? Charles had, it is true, doubts about how Englishmen would welcome such a prospect and it was not until September 11th that he knew Philip was free from any obligations towards the Infanta Maria of Portugal for whose hand he had been negotiating.[5] But by then the Imperial ambassador, Renard, in a series of private and almost clandestine interviews with Mary, had steered the Queen's thoughts so much towards Philip that on September 20th Charles authorized him to make a formal proposal if it could be done 'without bringing about a commotion'.[6] Accordingly, on October 10th Renard at last made his proposal to Mary on Philip's behalf. Three weeks later, on October 29th, after the Queen with a single lady-in-waiting had knelt with the ambassador before the sacrament and chanted with him a *Veni Creator*, Mary gave her solemn promise to marry Philip.[7] On November 8th Queen and ambassador together broke the news of his offer and her decision officially to the Privy Council.

By then the commotion that Charles V had feared was well under way. Rumours of what was afoot had started early in September and had spurred Courtenay's supporters to rally their friends in the Council and to warn the nation by pamphlets of the perils of a foreign marriage. They failed to convince Paget and a few others, but many of the Councillors sided with Bishop Gardiner against the match and in October, when Parliament met, Gardiner and his friends found little difficulty in rallying both Houses to their cause. It was this that had forced Renard to declare his hand on October 10th. For if he could not commit the Queen before Gardiner mobilized Council and Parliament against the match, he might well forfeit the game. As it was, on the day that Mary gave Renard her promise, the Commons began drafting a petition begging her to marry an Englishman. That leading Privy Councillors should be thus organizing opposition in Parliament to the declared policy of their sovereign, was a new and significant portent for the Tudor monarchy and for the future shaping of English foreign policy.

What was more immediately significant was the nature and extent of the support that gathered round the agitation. Of course all those of Protestant leanings in religion naturally supported it.

But they neither organized it nor led it. Its figurehead, Courtenay, came from a family whose reactionary religious tendencies had cost his relations their lives and had left him in the Tower since 1538. Its real leader was that Bishop Gardiner, now Chancellor of England, whom the reformers had long regarded as their arch-enemy. Nor was it merely an alliance of extremes. The great central mass of English opinion was clearly of the same way of thinking or the Commons' petition would hardly have gone through with so little opposition.

The agitation, in short, was essentially nationalist in character and religion played little part in it. It grew out of Englishmen's fears for their country's independence. Paget might argue that England needed a close alliance with the Habsburgs to shield her against the threatening Franco-Scottish power. He might suggest that Mary Tudor's marriage to Philip of Spain would bring a general pacification by forcing the French to peace with the Habs-burgs just as Mary Stuart's betrothal to the Dauphin had forced England to peace with the Scots.[8] But there his analogy came all too close home. Some of his fellow Councillors might remember the Scots' question during the 1543 negotiations: 'If your lad were a lass and our lass were a lad ... could you be content that our lad should marry your lass and so be King of England?'

For Englishmen that was no longer a hypothetical question. What they most feared about the Spanish match was precisely what Paget's analogy suggested, that it would subject them to Spain as the Scots were being subjected to France. They feared that a Spanish king-consort must soon become a king-regnant. For if in defiance of Council and Parliament a mere ambassador was able to do all that Renard had done, what might not a king-consort encompass? Moreover, Mary Tudor was hardly now a 'lass'. If childbearing proved impossible or fatal to her, then Philip, already in control of the government, would be left absolute mas-ter of the realm. Elizabeth would be thrust aside as Northumber-land had tried to thrust aside Mary. England, merged in the vast 'Habsburg aggregate' of territories, would then become another Milan or Naples where (or so an anonymous pamphlet warned)[9] every office of importance was filled by Spaniards. Parliament's petition suggested that, in addition to this, the country might be dragged into crippling wars contrary to its true interests. How prescient these fears were, the history of the Netherlands under

Philip II, as well as that of England under Mary, would soon show.

Mary, however, cared for none of these things. On November 16th, when the Speaker presented the Commons' petition, she brusquely interrupted him. Parliaments, she told him sharply, were not wont to use such language to kings of England. If she were forced to marry against her will, she would die within three months and would have no children. Therefore she would marry as God should direct her choice.[10] On December 6th she followed this up by dissolving Parliament. With Renard's help she also browbeat Gardiner and the Privy Council into sullen acquiescence. Having yielded, they then, on Paget's advice, made the best of a bad job by trying to negotiate a marriage treaty that would provide all possible safeguards for England's independence. This, Paget hoped, would draw the teeth of the opposition. Fortunately Charles V was very willing to meet them more than halfway – after all, he too felt that what Renard had done as ambassador, Philip could do still better as king-consort, whatever the terms of the marriage contract. He would not listen to Paget's plan to marry Elizabeth to Courtenay and recognize her in the marriage treaty as Mary's successor if Mary died childless. But the draft treaties which he did approve and which Renard presented to the Privy Council on December 7th, required only minor alterations before they were finally signed on January 12th.[11]

On paper the treaties yielded almost all that the English could ask. The country's laws, privileges, and customs were guaranteed. Offices in Church and state were to be filled only by Englishmen and Philip was to have no say in their filling, though he was to find places in his household for a 'convenient number 'of Englishmen. He must not take Mary out of the realm without her consent, nor any jewels, ships, or guns; neither must he directly or indirectly involve her in his present war with France. He should enjoy the title of King during Mary's lifetime and might assist her in government, but if she should die childless all his rights in England would die with her. If, however, they had children, their eldest son was to inherit England, the Netherlands, and Franche-Comté; and if Philip's present son Don Carlos had no children, then Spain and its dependencies as well.

On paper this was all very satisfactory. It was, indeed, almost too satisfactory. How would Philip and his Spanish subjects welcome the partial disinheriting of Don Carlos and several other provisions equally wounding to Spanish pride? In fact, when Philip first learned what the terms were, he did register a secret protest that he would not consider himself absolutely bound by them.[12] This, of course, was known only to two or three of his inmost Councillors, but it needed no great perspicacity to guess that his father might be more ready to promise than he would be to perform. When the terms of the treaties were announced to an assembly of English notables, even the notoriously slow-witted Lord Windsor asked what would happen if Philip failed to keep all these promises? Many sharper wits than his were agitated by the same question, some of them to the point of action.

Action, however, could only take the form of open rebellion now that the dissolution of Parliament and the submission of the Privy Council had closed the normal constitutional channels of opposition. For that most of the leading opponents of the marriage were not prepared. Gardiner and the Catholics feared that rebellion might put the Protestants back into power. The lay peers, even those of Protestant leanings, feared that it might open the way for social disorders like those of 1549.

There were, however, some lesser but still substantial men who were more ready to step outside legality.[13] Some of them had been talking about the likelihood of a popular rising to forbid the banns even before Mary so brusquely rejected the Commons' petition. After she rejected it, they began to lay plans to ensure that such a rising would occur and by the New Year the pattern of their plot was fairly well defined. The ringleader in this enterprise seems to have been Sir James Croft who, after a distinguished military career in the wars of Henry VIII and Somerset, had been Lord-Deputy of Ireland in 1551–2. Around him gathered other knights who had made war their trade during the 1540s and who had held office under Northumberland. There were Sir Peter Carew from Devon; Sir Thomas Wyatt, an ambassador's son, from Kent; Sir William Pickering, himself ambassador in France 1550–53; Sir William Winter, surveyor of the navy; and Sir Edward Warner, Northumberland's lieutenant of the Tower of London.

To these we must add some of the more zealous and less responsible Protestants – William Thomas whom we have met already as clerk of Edward VI's Council; Sir Edward Rogers; Sir Nicholas Throckmorton, treasurer of the mint in Northumberland's time.

But Protestantism was neither the prime motive nor the avowed purpose of the plot, which in origin and essence was simply a continuation by forcible means of an opposition that could no longer find effective expression through lawful channels. It began as a plot to force Mary to marry Courtenay instead of Philip, or simply to stop her marrying Philip, and these remained its avowed purposes all through. Also the first plans for the rising centred upon the still Catholic West Country, where Courtenay's estates lay and where his influence was strongest.

Nevertheless as the movement developed, the Protestant elements in it did come to play a larger part. Croft and one or two of the others had connections, if not with the Princess Elizabeth herself, at any rate with her household. They began to think of marrying Courtenay to her instead of to Mary and of putting her upon Mary's throne. Some of them certainly hoped thereby to put England back again upon a Protestant course. Moreover, as the conspirators elaborated their plans, they came to appreciate more keenly the importance of closing, not only the south-western ports against Philip's coming from Spain, but also the south-eastern ports against Imperial intervention from the Netherlands. So while Croft approached de Noailles to secure French naval help in the Channel against the Spaniards, Wyatt was brought in to raise Kent and secure the south-east against help coming to Mary from Flanders. The more Protestant Kent thus became a rival storm centre to Courtenay's lands in the West Country. At the same time the Duke of Suffolk joined the plot. The adhesion of this right-hand man of Northumberland, 'Queen Jane's' father, also somewhat counterbalanced the Courtenay connection. In addition, it made action possible in the Midlands, all the more as Croft had useful connections with the Welsh Marches.

Eventually, therefore, a fourfold rising was planned instead of just a western rising based upon the Courtenay lands. It was timed for Palm Sunday, March 18th, just before Philip was expected to start for England. On that day Carew, with Courtenay if he could slip away from court, was to call out the West Country. Croft was to raise the Welsh Marches and Suffolk the Midlands. Wyatt was to bring out Kent. Then, supported by French naval cover and by ships of their own in the Western Approaches, and supplied with French money and munitions, all four would march upon London.

In the event the rebellion had a rather different pattern, largely because the conspirators were forced into the open two months before their time. Early in January the Council grew suspicious of Carew's activities in Devon and summoned him to London for questioning. This put the conspirators in a quandary. Carew dared not obey the Council's summons, yet he could not ignore it. If he took flight, the vital south-western sector of the enterprise would collapse. If he rose now, he could not be left to rise alone and the whole affair would explode two months too soon. It would go off when the preparations were still incomplete and in midwinter when men were least easily stirred from their own firesides and when foul ways made swift movement most difficult. Yet to wait until March 18th would be to invite disaster. If the Council already knew about Carew, they would soon know about the others and Courtenay, in particular, was not a man to keep a secret. Indeed, on January 21st Gardiner did worm out of him a good deal about what was afoot – just how much is hard to say, for Gardiner was still anxious to protect the young man and only revealed what he felt he could not conceal.

By then, however, Croft and his friends had already decided that boldness was their safest course. They knew that many in the Council and among the nobility sympathized at least with their avowed purpose and were as much afraid of strengthening the hands of their headstrong Queen as they were of encouraging rebellion. As a result the government was hopelessly divided in purpose and militarily quite unprepared. Moreover, it would be little easier for the Queen to levy and concentrate forces in midwinter than it would be for the rebels, especially as she could not entirely rely upon the Londoners' loyalty. And the weather that slowed movement by land, might altogether inhibit movement by sea from Spain or the Low Countries. So, even before Courtenay confessed to Gardiner, most of the rebel leaders were already moving to their action stations.

That was as far as most of them were to get. Carew could not rouse Devon and fled first to Weymouth, then to France. Suffolk and his brothers failed to stir Leicester or Coventry and were rounded up by January 30th – the Duke after spending a chilly night in a hollow tree from which (according to Renard) he was ferreted out by a loyal, or merely inquisitive, small dog.[14] Croft fared little better on the Welsh Border.

So what had been designed as a fourfold rising, with the West Country playing a leading part, became a purely Kentish affair. For only Wyatt made any headway. The headway he made, however, was almost enough to make up for all the rest. On January 25th he seized Rochester and some of the Queen's ships with their cannon as well. In a day or two he had gathered enough men to move on London. Estimates of their number varied from Lord Cobham's 'not above 2,000 men and yet not 500 of them able and good armed' to Renard's 3,000 and the hopeful de Noailles's 12 or 15,000.[15] But to a government as unarmed and as unpopular as Mary's the real danger lay less in Wyatt's strength than in the attitude of London. And on January 29th some 600 Londoners, sent out under the aged Duke of Norfolk, went over as a body to the rebels with shouts of 'we are all Englishmen'.[16] Had Wyatt pushed on at once, the capital might have opened its gates to welcome him. But he dallied and when he reached Southwark on February 3rd he found London Bridge, the only crossing over the Thames below Kingston, closed to him. Two days earlier Mary had gone to the Guildhall and thrown herself upon the wavering loyalty of the City. She would, she promised none too honestly, call a Parliament and be ruled by its advice about her marriage to Philip.[17] Also she revealed that Wyatt, in answer to her offer of a conference to hear his reasons against the match, had demanded custody of the Tower and of her own person and, or so she alleged, restoration of religion as in her brother's time.

The Queen's appeal and Wyatt's procrastination between them just turned the scales. For three days the rebels stayed irresolute in Southwark, while across the river judges, shopkeepers, and even the Queen's chaplain went about their business in armour. Then on February 6th Wyatt, with a force dwindled to under 1,500 men, moved off to Kingston. There he forced a crossing and during the night came slowly back towards London. Too slowly, for next morning when he reached Knightsbridge the alarm had long been given – Mary herself had been roused from her bed at two – and the City was in arms. After a skirmish or two with Pembroke's retinue and the royal guards, he pushed on along the Strand and Fleet Street until, with numbers down to a bare 300, he found Ludgate closed against him. Pembroke was on his heels, his remaining men melted away, and he had to surrender.

He had come nearer than any other rebel to shaking a Tudor

off the throne. How close run a thing it was, even on that last day, the remarkable story of his march from Knightsbridge to Ludgate reveals. On the way he passed close by, sometimes even through, the ranks of London's embattled citizens. None of them joined him as the 600 had joined him the week before. Mary's appeal had stirred their loyalty, and his indecision had sapped their confidence, just enough to prevent that. Yet few of them barred his way and some of them even drew back to let him pass. The vast majority of them stood, in short, as uncommitted spectators while his dwindling band fought it out with the royal guards and the retinues of Pembroke, Clinton, and Lord Admiral Howard.[18]

It was to these former henchmen of Northumberland that, next to herself, Mary owed her throne, to the men who were prepared to acquiesce in a mild Catholic regime but were most opposed to any restoration of Papal authority, clerical power, or church lands. Gardiner and those Catholic Councillors, who might be least unwilling to accept the Pope and to root out heresy, had counselled little but flight – to Windsor, even to Calais. Moreover, their manifest dislike of the Spanish match, and Gardiner's attempts to cover up for Courtenay, had brought their loyalty as well as their courage under suspicion. The faction that would acquiesce in the Spanish marriage was known to be most unwilling to allow a return of the Pope. Now the faction that might let the Pope come back had shown itself ready to go almost to the edge of treason to stop Philip coming in. Wyatt's rebellion had made manifest the fissure at the very foundation of Mary's policies.

It had also manifested how little support those policies would find in the nation. London of course was not England. Nevertheless, its non-committal attitude towards Wyatt had not been so very different from the attitude of Leicester and Coventry towards Suffolk or of Devon towards Carew. And it was, of course, from London and the south-eastern half of England that the Tudors always drew their main strength. Those were the richest, most populous, most influential, and most politically conscious parts of the nation and the monarchy alienated them at its peril. Mary, it was clear, had forfeited their confidence, even if Wyatt had not been able to win it.

There was also something here of wider significance. Tudor Englishmen, despite their insularity, were often surprisingly knowledgeable about foreign affairs. We have seen how shrewdly the men of Kent judged Henry VIII's French wars in 1525. Thanks to the ramifications of the woollen trade, some of the knowledge of men like Gresham seeped down to the market places and the countryside. But hitherto this had only produced protests against the results of particular policies, against the burdens those policies imposed upon the people. Wyatt's revolt was different. It was not a protest against war taxation, as the risings of 1489, 1497, and 1525 had been. It was a protest designed to prevent the adoption of a particular policy, a protest made in advance. It was an attempt to join in the debate about what foreign policy should be. This was something new in English affairs. It points forward to the House of Commons' protestation of 1621, which was to claim for the nation's representatives a voice in the determination of foreign policy. We must not, of course, equate Wyatt and his followers with the nation – whatever we may mean by 'the nation'. But his protest and the Londoners' attitude towards it, taken together, do mark the point at which public opinion, outside as well as inside Parliament, began to claim a positive part in the shaping of English foreign policy instead of merely protesting at its results. The nation was beginning to step on to the stage alongside the dynasts, the nobles, and the ecclesiastics.

Finally, and unfortunately for Mary's purposes, Wyatt's rebellion helped considerably to confuse Protestantism with patriotism in her people's minds. The actual course of events, as we have seen, lent the rising a somewhat more Protestant colouring than the conspirators had intended. Mary, too, anxious to divert attention from the real grievance, did her best to accentuate this by proclamations denouncing the rebels as heretics who had no real national grounds for their subversive action. She only succeeded in strengthening the impression that they were Protestants without weakening the impression that they were patriots, even if overzealous and misguided patriots. Thus some of the discredit that Northumberland had brought upon the Protestant cause was wiped away. Men forgot or overlooked the fact that the conspirators had, like him, sought French help for their undertaking and that those who escaped found new bases for their plotting at the French court and in French ports. After all, no Frenchman actually appeared upon English soil, whereas within a few months Philip of Spain not only appeared but became King of England too. Englishmen therefore came to remember rather the goodness of Wyatt's cause than the wickedness of his rebellion.*

This attitude also had an immediate effect. It halted the royal vengeance and probably saved the life of the heir presumptive. In February and early March between one hundred and fifty and two hundred of Wyatt's followers were summarily executed, along with Suffolk and his brothers, Jane Grey, and her husband. Wyatt and some other leading conspirators were closely examined in the hope that they might be brought to incriminate Elizabeth. The Princess herself was summoned to London and on March 18th, the day originally intended for the rebellion, she was committed prisoner to the Tower. For some weeks she was in great danger. Egmont, who came over from the Emperor bearing the Pope's marriage dispensation, joined Renard in pressing for her execution. It was, they urged, an essential measure to ensure Philip's safety – almost, they made it sound, a condition of his coming. If they had their way, Mary's marriage, like her mother's, would be 'made in blood' and Elizabeth would be sacrificed to Spanish fears as Warwick had been sacrificed in 1499. It looked all the more possible because Gardiner, convinced now that Catholicism without the Pope was impracticable, was also anxious to exclude Anne Boleyn's daughter from the succession.

Happily, most of the Councillors had other views. Back in November Paget had warned Renard that Mary's own life would be in danger if she sent Elizabeth to the Tower.[19] He and his friends were now able to make the Queen see that she could not risk executing her half-sister without at least a proper trial and upon plausible evidence. That evidence was not forthcoming. Elizabeth had covered her tracks too well – if, indeed, she had any tracks to cover. What little Wyatt gave away under examination in private, he retracted publicly on the scaffold. Thereupon the judges confirmed that there was no case against Elizabeth. Further, on April 17th, as if to reinforce Paget's warnings, a London jury acquitted Throckmorton in defiance of the evidence and to the cheers of the spectators. The acquittal of the accused in a Tudor treason trial was an almost unheard-of occurrence and it made proceedings

* A. F. Pollard (*Political History of England*, VI. 112), like J. A. Froude (*Hist. of England*, V. 318–19, 354), believed that Wyatt did as much harm to the national cause as Northumberland had done to the Protestant. Almost all the evidence seems to me to support the contrary interpretation – and see E. H. Harbison, *Rival Ambassadors at the Court of Queen Mary*, pp. 137–8.

against Elizabeth more than ever impossible. A month later she was released from the Tower, still under surveillance but reasonably assured of her life.

Meanwhile, Parliament, under Paget's guidance, had done much to assure her also of her continued place in the succession to the throne. Few men believed that Mary was likely to have a child and even fewer wanted to be left at her death with only Philip of Spain and the French Queen of Scots to choose between. Accordingly proposals, sponsored by Gardiner, to exclude Elizabeth from the throne or to empower Mary to prescribe the succession as her father had done, proved too unpopular even to be framed into bills. A bill that was introduced, to give Philip the protection of the treason laws as if he were King of England, was so debated and amended that it was dropped. This second Parliament, in fact, showed itself as determined as the first to prevent any encroachment upon Elizabeth's birthright.

It also showed itself as unwilling as its predecessor to allow any restoration of clerical power or of Church lands. Gardiner, apparently in defiance of an agreement previously made in the Privy Council, did try to bring back the Six Articles and the old fifteenth-century statutes *de heretico comburendo*, and to revive the bishops' coercive jurisdiction. But, again at Paget's inspiration, these bills were either thrown out or had to be dropped and in their place the Commons passed a bill to safeguard the titles of lay holders of confiscated church lands. Parliament was clearly no more prepared to restore the Church to its former power and possessions than it was to put Philip of Spain above Elizabeth in the order of the succession.

It did without much demur approve the Spanish marriage treaties, for after Wyatt's failure there was no real hope left of forbidding the banns. So on July 25th Mary and Philip were married by Gardiner in his cathedral church at Winchester. Yet if Mary had thus accomplished the first of her purposes, the proceedings in Parliament had shown how difficult and dangerous it would be to press too vigorously towards her other goal – the restoration of Papal authority, clerical power, and the Church's lands. In addition, Council and Parliament and the London jurymen had done their best to ensure that the continued likelihood of Elizabeth's eventual accession would stand like a question-mark against all Mary's work.

Chapter 17

Rome and Calais

MARY TUDOR's marriage to Philip of Spain was to deceive her hopes almost as cruelly as it had destroyed her popularity. For she and Philip entered upon matrimony from very different reasons. She wanted a husband to support her and a son to succeed her, so that she might bring England back to Rome and make that return secure and permanent. Philip on the other hand wanted a wife through whom he could bring England under Habsburg control and, by adding England's resources to the ebbing Habsburg strength, turn the scales of war decisively against France.[1] Of course, Philip also wanted to see England reconciled to the Pope. His own Catholic orthodoxy was deep and sincere. Besides, he could hardly remain king-consort of a schismatical Queen of England when he became, as he would become upon Charles V's impending abdication, Most Catholic King of Spain. But whereas Mary aimed to bring England back to the old ways as quickly as possible and in the fullest possible measure, Philip would be content, for some time at any rate, with a reconciliation superficial enough to raise the least possible resentment in the country.

This difference became apparent almost from the outset. Within a month of his wedding Philip was in close touch with Paget, who had lost Mary's favour because of his opposition to Gardiner's ecclesiastical measures in the recent Parliament. Together they worked to drive a bargain with the Pope that would leave the least possible excuse for opposition. It was Philip's father, the Emperor, who persuaded the Pope in the autumn of 1554 that he must offer a general and unconditional guarantee to the lay holders of the Church's lost lands. It was Philip himself who sent Renard over to the Netherlands to persuade the Pope's impatient Legate, Cardinal Pole, that this sweeping concession was essential.[2] Philip and Renard also played their part in persuading Pole and Mary to let the Papal dispensation embodying this concession be incorporated in the Act of Parliament repealing all the anti-Papal legislation passed since 1528. That Act provided further that no suit concerning those lands should be brought anywhere except in the courts of the Common Law and that anyone who tried to bring such suits before any ecclesiastical court was to be in danger of *praemunire*. The suspension of the mortmain laws for twenty years did allow voluntary surrender of lands to the Church, but few except the Queen were likely to find their consciences tender enough for that and the Act made very sure that those who were not moved by conscience should not be troubled by the law. So the formal reconciliation of England to the Church of Rome on November 30th, 1554, was made upon conditions that satisfied Philip's political caution and disappointed Mary's religious zeal.

Besides thus helping to frustrate Mary's hopes of restoring the Church to its former wealth, Philip also attempted, at least at first, to restrain her zeal in the persecution of heresy. In December 1554 Parliament, with some dissent in the Lords, at last agreed to re-enact the old statutes *de heretico comburendo* and in February 1555 the burnings began. The popular reaction to them at once stirred Philip to put up his Spanish chaplain to preach to Queen and court upon the wisdom and virtue of gentler methods.[3] For a few weeks the burnings ceased. But not even Philip could hold back Mary, Pole, and the more violent of the bishops once they had tasted heretic blood. Soon the persecution went forward again, with rare pauses, on a scale unprecedented in English experience. In the last seven years of Henry VIII's reign, when the Six Articles had reinforced the old heresy laws, barely a couple of dozen heretics had gone to the stake. Now, in the last three and a half years of Mary's reign, close on three hundred were to die in the flames for their religious opinions.

Philip could not stop it. Probably he did not very seriously try after that first gesture in February 1555. Yet he did consider it untimely and impolitic and he realized that it must bring upon Spain a share of the unpopularity that it brought upon Rome. For too many Englishmen knew what was happening in the Netherlands, where under Charles V's fierce placarts against heresy more martyrs perished in a single year than were burned in England during the whole of Mary's reign. Too many merchants and sailors, who still tried to trade to Spain, were equally aware of the fate of heretics there. To convince them that Spain was not, just as much as Rome, encouraging Mary's burning zeal would have required an intervention far more spectacular and far more effective than anything Philip ever attempted. His tepid protests only irritated his wife without gaining him any credit with her subjects.

Nor did experience of the secular results of the Spanish marriage do much to commend it to Englishmen. Philip did try, in his rather stiff way, to make himself popular. He tried to adapt himself to English manners. He drank English beer, if not with relish, at least without making too sour a face over it. He punished sharply any of his suite who fell into affrays with their hosts. He distributed pensions to the nobility and Councillors,[4] whilst several cartloads of silver, that his father had lent to Mary, were paraded through London at the time of his arrival. Yet he made no attempt to learn the English language. Notes of Privy Council proceedings had to be made for him in Latin or Spanish.[5] And he manifested an alarming anxiety to be crowned King of England as soon as possible.

On that, at least, he and Mary were in complete agreement. For Mary now believed herself to be with child. Indeed, in the excitement of receiving the Pope's Legate on November 24th, she was sure that she felt the babe leap in her womb.[6] News of her condition no doubt helped considerably to smooth the path back to Rome, but it also raised the urgent question of what should happen if she were to die in childbed. To both Mary and Philip the ideal solution appeared to be that Philip should be crowned King of England as soon as possible so that he might carry on the government in his own right if Mary should die. This would assure Mary that her subjects would continue in the Roman fold; Philip, that the realm would remain in the Habsburg camp.

It was, however, a solution that Parliament would not hear of.[7] In the upper House the lay lords headed by Paget and the clericalist faction led by Gardiner each wanted so to arrange matters that it would itself dominate the government if Mary died. Neither group wanted to become merely the servants and councillors of King Philip. So the Lords produced a colourless measure that did no more than grant Philip the protection of the treason laws which the previous Parliament had refused him. The Commons, however, were prepared to go a little further. They, too, had no desire to see Philip crowned, for they feared that as crowned King of England he would drag the country into war and they had already rejected more than one suggestion for helping him to assist his father in his French quarrel. Yet they also did not relish the prospect of a revival of the noble and conciliar factions that had torn the realm during Edward VI's minority. Philip therefore, though he could not be trusted as King, might be useful as regent. Accordingly, and perhaps not without Gardiner's encouragement, the Commons rejected the Lords' bill and put forward one of their own. By this Philip was to have, besides the protection of the treason laws, the guardianship of Mary's child. Yet in committee doubts arose whether even this might not be yielding too much and amendments were added denying him the power to call Parliament or to declare war or to arrange his child's marriage without the consent of a selected English Council. In the end, after delicate negotiations between Renard and a committee of both Houses, these amendments were dropped and Philip was left with the protection of the treason laws and the prospective guardianship of Mary's child, but subject still to the terms of the marriage treaty.

The complicated cross-currents that produced this small result are difficult to chart, yet some things stand out clear. The continuing division among Mary's English Councillors, the fissure at the foundation of her government, had again allowed the nation's representatives in the Commons to make their voices heard. And their voices, though discordant on many things, were in unison against giving Philip the power to drag England into an undesired and unnecessary war. On that, their unanimity could not be ignored and Philip had to recognize that the chief purposes for which he had married Mary were still unattainable. He could neither secure full control of England's government nor throw England's resources into the scale against France. For Mary, too, it was a grievous rebuff. By refusing to grant Philip a status that must have blotted out Princess Elizabeth's rights in the succession, Lords and Commons had refused to erase the question-mark that those rights placed against all Mary's work. As the months passed and it became obvious even to Mary that her pregnancy was an illusion, that great question-mark grew larger and bolder. With the abbey lands still in lay ownership and with the growing likelihood of Elizabeth's eventual accession, the future of Papal supremacy over the English Church and the future of Habsburg control over the English state would alike grow darker.

For Mary there was to be no escape from that slow disillusionment. Philip, however, could turn from the narrow and uncongenial English stage to the broader realms that Charles V was waiting to pass on to him. And soon he did turn to them. The constant bickerings between his Spaniards and the English, the refusal of Privy Council and Parliament to agree to his coronation or to help him and his father in their French war, and finally the falsifying of Mary's hopes of a child – all these things wearied him of his position in England. Across in the Netherlands he might win his spurs in the war against the French and take some of the burden off his ageing father. England was fast ceasing to hold his interest or his attention[8] and Englishmen must have sensed this change in Philip's attitude when late in August 1555 he said good-bye to his tearful Queen and sailed off to join Charles V in the Low Countries, threatening (as the Venetian ambassador soon learned[9]) never to return unless he were allowed a full and effective share in the government. It looked as if the propaganda against the Spanish match, with its warnings that Philip would treat England as another Milan or Naples, had shot all too close to the mark.

That impression was strengthened by Philip's attitude to England's economic and commercial interests. Direct trade to Spain, and even to the Canaries, did become a little easier now that the English were at least nominally Roman Catholics. But there was no opening of Spanish America to Philip's English subjects. The 'Castilianization' of the Spanish empire was now spreading more widely into the economic field as Seville and Cadiz were encouraged to tighten their monopoly of Atlantic trade. Thus, although Englishmen might trade to America, and even live and do business there (as some of them lived and did business in Spain), they were not allowed to trade thither direct from English ports. They had to carry on their trade in Spanish ships and through Seville. Spanish America was becoming more than ever forbidden country to English sailors and English ships, as Field and Tomson found to their cost in 1556.[10]

Nor was Philip content merely to maintain Spain's monopoly in America. He was equally prompt to uphold his Portuguese neighbours' monopoly in Africa. The highly successful voyages to the Gold Coast by Wyndham in 1553 and John Lok in 1554–5, publicized at once by Richard Eden's *Decades of the New World*, brought a strong protest from Portugal just before Philip left England for the Netherlands. Philip gave the protest his full support and browbeat the Privy Council into prohibiting any further voyages for the next six months. But the Council's obedient bark had no bite to it and a third voyage went forward that autumn little hampered, as did others in all the remaining years of Mary's reign. Indeed, Lord William Howard, the Lord Admiral and himself a Privy Councillor, allowed the merchants to hire vessels from the royal navy for their ventures. Philip had only increased his unpopularity without being able to stop the traffic. This was of some importance, for although the Gold Coast trade, exchanging cheap cloth, metal goods, and firearms for gold dust, ivory, and pepper, was a tiny fraction of England's total commerce, it was lucrative and promising and it was largely run by London merchants. Philip's opposition to it therefore helped to spread the West Country's growing grievances against Spain to the Londoners who, because of their great trade to the Netherlands, had tended to look upon Spain as a necessary friend, if not as a natural ally.

In another and more serious way, too, Philip weakened any Spanish leanings that the London and east-coast merchants might still have had. For he supported the Hanseatic League against them just as he was supporting the Portuguese. Back in September 1553 Mary had restored to the Hanse merchants their ancient privileges that Northumberland had taken away. The resulting renewal of their competition in the Antwerp trade was a severe blow to the Merchant Adventurers, hard hit already by the slump of the fifteen fifties. It was no less of a blow to English shipping. Further, since the Hanse now exported increasing quantities of unfinished cloth to Germany, it was also a blow to those engaged in the finishing processes of the cloth industry. The outcry that all this provoked compelled the English government in 1555 to return to something like Northumberland's policy. The Hanse merchants were reduced again to the unprivileged status of other foreigners so far as the Netherlands trade was concerned and they were forbidden to export to any other areas more than one unfinished cloth for every three finished pieces at their old advantageous rates. The Hanse, like the Portuguese, promptly and strongly protested and Philip supported their protests too. In deference to his pressure, the new restrictions were temporarily suspended in 1556 and the Hanse were left to enjoy their old privileges for another year while the question was discussed. The League, however, refused to negotiate, so at the beginning of 1557 their privileges were again annulled. They retaliated in August by closing their ports to all

English ships and merchants and the quarrel was still unsettled when Mary died.

Philip, no doubt, had supported the Hanse because his Netherlands subjects welcomed any weakening of the Merchant Adventurers' monopoly which might improve their own bargaining position. But this tenderness for Netherlands interests and indifference to the interests of what was by far England's greatest export trade, did him little good with his English subjects. Coming on top of his refusal to admit them into the American trade and of his support for Portuguese protests at their African enterprises, it made him seem ready to act in any interests except those of England. In commercial as well as in political matters, it seemed as if he indeed regarded England as no better than another Naples or Milan.

Only in one direction were English maritime enterprises not barred by his prohibition or hampered by his support of their rivals. He made no demur at the new charter, granted in his and Mary's joint names in 1555, to the company formed in Northumberland's time for the discovery of a North-Eastern or North-Western Passage to Cathay. In its 1553 voyage north-eastwards, two ships and their crews under Willoughby had perished in the search for such a passage, but Chancellor and the third ship had found their way into the White Sea, to Archangel, and from there Chancellor had gone overland to Moscow. The Tsar Ivan the Terrible had welcomed him and during the rest of Mary's reign the company gradually laid the foundations of a useful trade to Russia by this White Sea route. Philip's explicit recognition of these Englishmen's right to navigate, trade, and settle in north-eastern and north-western latitudes established a useful precedent for the enterprises of the next reign and held out prospects of some immediate profit. Yet it was poor compensation for the denial of tropical America and Africa and the lack of support against the Hanse. It is not therefore surprising that the effect of Philip's commercial policies upon English opinion was to line up London and the east behind the western ports in growing hostility to Spain.

Indeed, the whole effort to meet the economic problems of the fifteen fifties by more modern methods, which Northumberland had haltingly inaugurated, was slowed down by this Spanish opposition. Except towards Russia, the search for alternative outlets to Antwerp for England's exports was blocked or impeded.

Also, at least until the definite rescinding of the Hanseatic privileges in 1557, Gresham's ideas of controlling the flow of overseas
trade through the Merchant Adventurers could hardly be considered. The government still had to rely, as in the 1555 Weavers'
Act, chiefly on the old-fashioned methods of direct industrial
regulation, which it lacked the machinery to enforce. Hence,
although efforts were still made to put new and firmer foundations
under the economy, Spanish influence over England's government
helped to keep those efforts tentative and limited.

Nevertheless, if in matters of religion and matters of trade the
fruits of the Spanish marriage set Englishmen's teeth on edge, what
chiefly stirred their fears was Philip's known desire to be crowned
and to draw the country into the war with France. Back in 1550
Paget had seen the wars as the root of all England's ills[11] and, if he
had now somewhat shifted his ground, his original opinion
had gained a wider support than ever. Caught between her subjects' desire for peace and her husband's pressure for war, Mary
had tried to escape from her dilemma by mediating a settlement of
the Habsburg-Valois conflict. After long and tortuous negotiations
through the French and Imperial ambassadors in London, she
succeeded in May 1555 in bringing the two sides to a formal conference at Marcq, in the Calais Pale. Granvelle led the Imperial
delegation, Montmorency and the Cardinal of Lorraine the
French, while the presence of Pole, Gardiner, and Paget as the
chief English representatives made obvious how heavily Mary was
staking her prestige upon the success of this mediation. The complete failure of the conference in June was therefore a serious
diplomatic setback for England, all the more since attempts to
continue the mediation at ambassadorial level in London also
withered upon Philip's departure to the Netherlands.

Moreover, now that Mary had failed to mediate a peace, Philip
redoubled his pressure for his coronation and for English aid in
his war. News of this soon leaked out. Secrecy was never a strong
point in Mary's swollen and divided Privy Council and even a
London bricklayer got hold of a not-too-garbled version of the
Queen's efforts to persuade the Earl of Shrewsbury to agree to
Philip's crowning.[12] There were rumours, too, of designs to ship
Elizabeth off to Spain or the Low Countries. All this goes far to
account for the intransigence of Mary's fourth Parliament when it
met in October 1555. Whether or not the elections 'witnessed the

earliest concerted attempt of an opposition group to capture control of Parliament in Tudor history', certainly there were in the Commons a hundred or more members who 'formed a remarkably well disciplined and suspiciously well organized parliamentary faction, possessed of unusually shrewd leadership'.[13] They made war impossible by forcing the Queen to content herself with one subsidy and to forgo the two fifteenths and tenths for which she had also hoped. They amended a bill to free the clergy from the payment of First Fruits and to allow the crown to surrender to the Church its clerical tenths. Then, in its amended form they passed it by 193 to 126 only after 'the doors of the House were locked as on a recalcitrant jury'.[14] Finally, they threw out a bill to confiscate the property of Protestants and others who had taken refuge overseas without royal licence. And this time it was one of the opposition leaders, Sir Anthony Kingston, who secured the keys to the chamber and stood guard at the door against another enforced closure. With the House in such a mood, Mary dared not even suggest her husband's coronation.

But Parliament could only obstruct policy, not construct it. So in this winter of 1555–6, as in the winter of 1553–4, the limitations of parliamentary opposition drove some of the more determined critics on to treasonable plotting. Their ringleader was Sir Henry Dudley, a distant cousin of Northumberland's, and they found plenty of sympathy among the growing numbers in southern England who longed for the day when Mary and Philip would be replaced by 'our sweet Lady Elizabeth ... a jolly liberal dame and nothing so unthankful as her sister is'.[15] Yet however patriotic their motives and their appeal, the plotters needed money to mount their assault and a base to launch it from. For both they looked to France, with such encouragement from the French ambassador de Noailles that early in February 1556 Dudley and several others slipped across the Channel to make their final preparations, after arranging with Richard Uvedale, governor of Yarmouth castle in the Isle of Wight, to assist their landing at Portsmouth.

Unfortunately for their hopes, Dudley's arrival in France coincided with the conclusion of the Truce of Vaucelles. That after the failure of the Marcq conference, only seven months earlier, French and Spaniards should now settle their differences by direct negotiations from which the English were pointedly excluded, was a fresh humiliation for Mary. But it probably saved her from another rebellion at least as dangerous as that of Wyatt. For it meant that Henry II was no longer prepared to back Dudley's enterprise effectively. Possibly it was this disappointment that forced the plotters in England back upon the alternative project of securing funds by robbing the Exchequer. Certainly that desperate scheme was their undoing, for it was betrayed to the Council by one of those who had helped to hire a ship to carry the money across to France. On March 18th – a curiously ill-starred date for Marian plotters – the arrests began and the plot was foiled.

It was not entirely without effect, for the uncovering of its widespread ramifications powerfully reinforced the arguments for peace. War with France must clearly bring with it the probability of very dangerous rebellion at home and the English government's appreciation of that double danger was manifest in its reluctance to protest about Noailles's intrigues or the continued harbouring of English rebels in France or the depredations of the Killigrews and other rebel privateers operating from French ports.

It was manifest, too, in the obstinacy with which the Privy Council strove to keep England neutral when the Truce of Vaucelles began to break down. Philip could not be blamed for that breakdown. It was the fault of the new anti-Spanish Pope Paul IV and his French ally that by the autumn of 1556 French and Spanish armies were again facing one another on the frontiers of Naples. Broken in Italy, the truce could not last much longer on the frontiers of the Netherlands and in November Philip, to whom by now Charles V had abdicated all his dominions except the Empire, sent urgently for English help. He wanted not only men and money, but also a formal renewal of the 1543 treaty of mutual defence and a public declaration that England would resist any French attack upon the Netherlands. In spite of Mary's efforts, the Privy Council stoutly refused to promise anything except some money and a few ships. The French attack upon Douai and the resulting declaration of war between Spain and France in January 1557, did a little weaken the resolution at least of the more soldierly knights and nobles of Paget's faction, who began to scent opportunities for personal gain and glory. Yet the Council still refused to do more than prepare the 6,600 troops which the 1543 treaty bound them to provide in such a case.

Even when Philip himself came back to England, late in March, he and Mary could still not persuade the Council to declare war on

France. All through April the debate went on. Mary interviewed her Councillors individually and threatened publicly to dismiss most of them; Philip offered, sincerely or not, to open Spanish America to English trade and to help against Scotland where a small French force was just landing. Under all this pressure, the Privy Council gave way a little, first to offer money as well as the 6,600 men, then to add another 4,000 men and twenty ships. Yet still they baulked at an open declaration of war. Then suddenly, at the end of April, a handful of exiles from France, under Thomas Stafford, landed at Scarborough and seized the castle there. It was a wildcat enterprise that was easily and promptly defeated. But the rebels had come from a French port, in two ships and with arms provided by the King of France. Such flagrant provocation was too much even for the Council's patience and by June 1557 England and France were at war.

Seldom, if ever, has England gone to war so unwilling and so unprepared. It had taken six months' unremitting pressure, crowned by the French King's folly, to persuade even the Privy Council to consent to it. The nation at large could see no sense in it at all, for the war was indeed the *reductio ad absurdum* of Mary's policy. She had married Philip, against the wishes of her people, the better to assure England's return to the Roman fold. Now her Spanish husband, and she at his side, was openly at war with a Pope who had excommunicated him. Her Archbishop of Canterbury, too, Cardinal Pole, the Legate who had reconciled her realm to the Papacy, was now deprived of his legacy, summoned to Rome, and even threatened with charges of heresy. Small wonder Englishmen saw little reason to open their purses or risk their lives in so confused a quarrel. Mary's last Parliament (January–March 1558) voted her only a single subsidy and fifteenth; forty Worcestershire gentlemen were brought before the Council in a single day for refusing to pay a forced loan; troops and sailors deserted or mutinied; the populace were apathetic or worse; and the government itself seemed to lack energy or purpose. Moreover, since Mary's accession nothing had been done to reform or re-equip the country's land forces and only a limited amount to remedy the decay into which Northumberland had allowed the navy to fall. The quarrel with the Hanse meant a shortage of naval stores, while shortage of money crippled action in all directions.

As a result the war, an absurdity from the first, soon became a tragedy as well. In August 1557, 5,000 English troops did help Philip to win a notable victory at St Quentin, though he lacked the money to exploit his success. Yet England got no help from Spain in return. Philip, more than ever careful now of the Netherlands' commercial interests, refused to declare war upon their useful Scottish customers, though the Scots obediently followed their French ally into war against England. Worse still, Philip diverted to his own armies in France 3,000 German mercenaries hired by Mary to defend her northern borders. Later he impounded for his own use arms and munitions bought in Antwerp for the defence of England.

Worst of all, he did nothing effective to defend Calais against the attack upon it that the Duke of Guise was preparing in the winter of 1557–8. The English government itself, however, was guilty of criminal carelessness. When the blow fell on January 1st, the garrison had not been reinforced and the English fleet was still laid up for the winter. In a week Calais was French, though Guisnes held out until January 20th. And during the ten months that remained of Mary's reign, no serious effort was to be made to regain it. Philip did propose joint operations for its recovery, but not unnaturally his offer was conditional upon substantial English help. That Mary could not provide, for throughout the spring and summer fear of French invasion tied down to home defence such forces as she could afford to mobilize. In July a few English ships helped a Spanish force to crush at Gravelines a French contingent from Calais as it returned along the coast from a raid upon Dunkirk. But the Spaniards were not strong enough single-handed to follow up their victory by a rush upon Calais; there were no English troops immediately available to reinforce them; and the considerable naval forces that Mary had at last managed to mobilize under her new Lord Admiral, Clinton, were in the Solent, too far away to help in time. In August Clinton sailed westwards in the hope of seizing Brest, as a counter to bargain against Calais in the peace negotiations that were about to open at Lille. That enterprise, however, was as ill-starred as Mary's other undertakings and England's representatives at the peace talks, transferred in October to Cercamp and later to Câteau-Cambrésis, were left to bargain as best they could empty-handed for the return of Calais. Their task looked, and indeed was to prove, impossible; but Mary was spared the knowledge of this final failure. On

November 17th, 1558, she died, her last days of semi-consciousness troubled, or perhaps we may hope soothed, by dreams in which she saw 'many little children like angels play before her, singing pleasing notes'.[16]

Chapter 18

Elizabeth I

THE accession of Elizabeth I on November 17th, 1558, was greeted, at least in London and the home counties, by a burst of popular enthusiasm almost as great as that which had swept Mary to the throne five years earlier. Yet many Englishmen must have remembered how rapidly the enthusiasm for Mary had burned itself out, like a stubble fire. Had their new Queen, England's second Queen regnant, the qualities to command a more enduring loyalty? First appearances were at least reassuring. Elizabeth, now a mature young woman of twenty-five, was certainly a more impressive figure than her half-sister. She was fairly tall, slim, and shapely. The long oval face, tapering from a broad brow to a rather pointed chin, that her portraits show was recognizably that of Anne Boleyn's daughter. It was a face passably handsome and strikingly intelligent, with coolly calculating eyes and cleanly moulded features that help us to understand why Henry III of France was to call her 'la plus fine femme du monde'.[1] But if in looks Elizabeth featured her mother, in personality she was very much her father's daughter. She had, besides old King Harry's reddish hair, his bluff and loud-voiced geniality, his sudden bursts of kindliness or terrifying rage, that touch of the unpredictable, almost the eccentric, which etches a character unforgettably. 'When she smiled it was pure sunshine that everyone did choose to bask in if they could; but anon came a storm from a sudden gathering of clouds and the thunder fell in wondrous manner on all alike.'[2] She had, too, Henry's popular touch and her first public appearances – her entry into London, her coronation, the opening of Parliament – were masterpieces in the art of winning popularity. From the first, indeed, she went out of her way to show that she was 'very much wedded to the people and thinks as they do – and therefore treats foreigners slightingly'.[3] For, above all, as she was quick to boast, she was by birth 'mere English', with no taint of the foreign blood that had gone so disastrously to the head of the half-Spanish Mary.[4] Altogether, a formidable yet fascinating young woman and, as we might expect from the daughter of such parents, not one to submit easily to other people's domination. Indeed, within a few weeks of her accession the new Spanish ambassador, the Count de Feria, was writing that 'she gives her orders and has her way as absolutely as her father did.'[5] It was all very different from poor Mary sighing tearfully for her Spanish husband to come back and lift from her shoulders the intolerable burden of government.

Elizabeth, too, was at times to find that burden almost intolerable, but she never showed any sign of wanting to shift it on to other shoulders, least of all in matters of foreign policy. For foreign policy was not only vitally concerned with England's independence and security; it was also of vital concern to Elizabeth personally. She was the unmarried Queen of a realm whose fate could decisively affect the destinies of all Europe. Her choice of a husband might, as Mary had so recently proved, ruin her popularity at home and by tempting foreign interventions make the British Isles the battleground of Europe. Equally it could upset the delicate balance between Habsburg and Valois and tilt the scales decisively between Catholicism and Protestantism abroad. Hence she was hardly on the throne before she was besieged by envoys from suitors all over the continent. Her personal attitude to these suitors and to marriage itself, we may discuss more conveniently in a later chapter. But clearly courtship would now become one of the most useful gambits in the game of diplomacy, and marriage could be either the supreme masterstroke or the most fatal blunder of statesmanship. Almost every question of foreign policy was likely to become involved sooner or later with the question of marriage and that was a question which concerned Elizabeth too closely and too personally for her to allow anyone but herself to decide it. And to keep its decision in her own hands, she needed to keep a firm personal control over foreign policy as a whole.

This did not mean that she spent all her days reading, annotating, and answering the routine diplomatic correspondence. That she left to her Principal Secretaries, the ministers chiefly concerned with foreign policy. To them she usually left the drafting, and to them and their clerks the fair-copying, even of the letters that did go out over her signature. Yet the amount of correcting and amending that so many drafts underwent shows how close a watch she kept over them. In the same way the trefoils endorsed on so many state papers indicate how significant a proportion of the incoming correspondence she either read or had read to her. The Secretaries therefore could hardly send out any instructions of importance without her knowledge and there was little that her ambassadors and agents could do without her getting wind of it. Secretaries did sometimes get ambassadors to slant reports to suit their own particular views. Yet even then the Queen's know-ledge was usually too extensive for her to be very much deceived. Moreover, she was not wholly dependent upon her Secretaries for her information. Her fluency in Latin, French, Spanish, and Italian enabled her to talk long and freely with foreign ambassadors and to glean much from them – more than most of them ever gleaned from her, for few of them could match her in the arts of deception and evasion, or indeed of downright lying.

All this is not to say that her Secretaries had little or no influence upon her policy. Like her father and grandfather, she was not afraid of able ministers and her Principal Secretaries were gener-ally among the ablest of them all. Certainly this was true of Sir William Cecil (created Baron of Burghley, 1571), Principal Secretary during the first fourteen years of her reign and then, as Lord Treasurer, still her most trusted and influential Councillor until his death in 1598. Cecil was one of those 'new men' who played so great a part in shaping Tudor England. His grandfather, of a Herefordshire yeoman family, had carved out for himself a substantial position at Stamford in Lincolnshire. His father, of a less thrusting character, had risen imperceptibly from being a page at Henry VIII's court to the not very much more distin-guished position of yeoman of the royal wardrobe.[6] William in-herited both his grandfather's thrustful energy and his father's gift for playing safe. He was ready to strike hard when occasion offered, but he knew the difference between a risk and an oppor-tunity. His capacity for work rivalled that of Wolsey and his appetite for detail was insatiable. Even in the hectic month of the 1588 Armada's arrival he found time to scribble in the margin of a request for supplies: 'nota, how small beer is to be known'[7]; and only Philip II of Spain can have annotated more state papers than he did. Educated at that seminary of Elizabethan scholars, statesmen, and divines, St John's College, Cambridge – in later life 'he would always carry Tully's *Offices* about him, either in his bosom or his pocket'[8] – he had served Somerset as a personal secretary and had filled the office of Principal Secretary under Northumberland. A convinced Protestant, he was yet (like old Lord Treasurer Winchester[9]) enough of a conformer to 'the King religion' to bow in the house of Rimmon under Mary and even to serve her in various minor offices.

Elizabeth had known Cecil at least since 1548 and he had been her surveyor (her estate agent, as it were) since 1550. When appointing him a Privy Councillor and Principal Secretary, immediately after her accession, she had declared: 'this judgment I have of you, that you will be faithful to the state and that, without respect of my private will, you will give me that counsel which you think best.'[10] Throughout their long partnership he fully justified her expectation. At first, like her other Councillors, he was inclined to treat her with a certain masculine condescension. He once reprimanded the bearer of an ambassador's letter for discussing with her 'a matter of such weight, being too much for a woman's knowledge'.[11] Once or twice also, in the early years, he pressed his counsel to the point of threatening resignation if it were not accepted. Gradually, however, he came to respect the Queen's judgment and towards the end of his life he was to tell his son Robert:

> I do hold this course in such matters as I differ in opinion from Her Majesty. As long as I may be allowed to give advice, I will not change my opinion by affirming the contrary, for that were to offend God to whom I am sworn first. But as a servant I will obey Her Majesty's commandments and no wise contrary the same ..., after that I have performed my duty as counsellor; and shall in my heart wish her commandments to have such good successes as I am sure she intendeth.[12]

This was undoubtedly also the attitude of most of Cecil's fellow-Councillors. For of the eighteen men who made up the Privy Council by the spring of 1559, no less than ten had been Privy Councillors to Mary, and eight of these to Edward VI as well. Another four or five had held offices of some importance through all the changes of the past ten or fifteen years. And even the new-comers, added by Elizabeth, were men of very much the same stamp. There were some among the twenty who held strong views, particularly about religion – the Earls of Arundel and

Derby on the Catholic side; the Marquis of Northampton, the Earl of Bedford, and Sir Francis Knollys on the Protestant. But for the most part the Councillors regarded themselves rather as 'civil servants' than as politicians. Most of them had their own jobs to do, their own departmental duties. Cecil apart, only a few of them, and those few only intermittently, were concerned with the day-to-day conduct of foreign affairs, which were primarily the department of the Principal Secretary. Sir John Mason, now approaching the end of his long career, was occasionally consulted until his retirement in 1565. But although 'none seeth further off than Sir John Mason',[13] he was more of a diplomatist than a maker of policies. On occasion, too, Sir William Petre's long experience of the Secretary's office came in useful; but he likewise was growing old and, besides, he had a genius for being unwell or otherwise out of the way whenever grave decisions were to be made. Neither man had the personality to impose policies upon the Queen. Neither took a regular enough part to challenge the control of Secretary Cecil over the diplomatic machinery. Nor did the Council as a whole play a very leading role in foreign affairs. Elizabeth did not often consult it as a body. It was, as a rule, only at moments of crisis, particularly when issues of peace and war hung in the balance, that she risked facing it in full and formal session. And then, while benefiting from its members' long experience, she could usually reckon that its serried ranks of male superiority would be divided enough on the question at issue to leave her free to make the final choice.

Thus in matters of foreign policy at least, the character of the Councillors and Elizabeth's habits in consulting them ensured that the final decisions lay with her. She was as a rule well enough aware of their opinions but she was in no sense bound to follow their advice. She could, and did, listen to other views also, to Wyatt's acquitted accomplice, Sir Nicholas Throckmorton, whose advice she welcomed though not enough to admit him to her Council; to Northumberland's youngest son, Lord Robert Dudley, who won her favour on more personal grounds; to trusted old servants of the monarchy like that expert upon Scottish affairs Sir Ralph Sadler. But it was Elizabeth and Cecil who, day in, day out, conducted England's foreign policy. And, in the last analysis, it was Elizabeth rather than Cecil who decided what that policy was to be.

The decisions immediately demanded of her were not easy ones. For Tudor England was in 1558 at its lowest ebb of weakness and demoralization. Its time of greatness seemed over and there was little hint of 'the spacious days' that were to come. Indeed, if we want to understand Elizabeth's policies aright, we shall do well to begin, not by looking forward to those spacious days ahead, but by looking back at the constricting years just past. For it was in those years since Henry VIII's death that the new Queen, and most of the men who for the next three decades were chiefly to counsel her, had come of age or served their political apprenticeships. It was their experience of England's plight under Edward VI and Mary that shaped their approach and conditioned their thinking about their country's foreign relations under Elizabeth. That chastening experience had given them a more realistic appreciation, than had been possible in the years of affluence, of England's small stature alongside the Leviathans of the continent. They now knew that they had neither the men nor the money to compete on land with Habsburg and Valois in the way that Henry VIII and Wolsey had tried to compete. Their means would not stretch to conquer Scotland, let alone to conquer France. The loss of Calais, and their inability even to attempt its recovery, dramatically emphasized the lesson that the days of continental adventure were over. They had learned, too, that they must not look to foreign alliances to make good their own weakness. Henry VIII had discovered how little foreign allies were prepared to do for England's benefit. Northumberland and Mary had shown how easily the friendly embraces of either of the great continental monarchies could develop into bear-hugs almost as dangerous to England's independence as their hostile assaults.

Yet England's situation in 1558, although dangerous and difficult, was less desperate than elderly pessimists like Paget occasionally imagined. England was not yet a mere 'bone between two dogs'.[14] Mary's Spanish marriage had enabled the country to slip out of the noose which Northumberland had nearly allowed the French to cast around its neck. Mary's death, by breaking that matrimonial link with Philip II, afforded a chance to slip from under the Spanish yoke as well. Of course the breaking of that link made Spanish support against France a little less assured. This was perhaps unfortunate, coming just at the moment when the French King was 'bestriding the realm, having one foot in Calais and the other in Scotland'.[15] Moreover, the French King's daughter-in-law Mary, Queen of Scots, granddaughter of Henry VIII's elder sister Margaret, stood by birth next in line for the succession to the English throne if Elizabeth were to die childless. More than that, Mary would in Roman Catholic eyes be rightful Queen of England now in Elizabeth's lifetime if Elizabeth denied the Pope's authority and allowed him to brand her a heretic. And how could Anne Boleyn's daughter not deny Papal authority? For to admit it would be to confess her own illegitimacy and to admit herself Queen by grace of the Pope. Mary's claims must therefore provide a standing temptation to the French to exploit the advantages which possession of Calais and Scotland now gave them.

Nevertheless, although that temptation was strong, it was not without its pitfalls. The French (and indeed the Spaniards too) still respected England's defensive potentialities, especially by sea. In the dark days of 1557 a shrewd Venetian ambassador could still consider the English well able 'to resist any invasion from abroad, provided there be union within the kingdom'.[16] Admittedly, much did depend upon union within the kingdom; much, too, upon the efficiency of the kingdom's naval forces; and something upon the soundness of its finances and the healthiness of its economy. Yet even in the disunited and inefficient summer of 1558 the French had not seriously considered following up their capture of Calais by an invasion of England. Of course, they had the Spaniards upon their hands as well. Nevertheless, if the pressure of Spain gave them pause, so too did the memory of 1545.

Moreover, this French caution was a manifestation of a subtle psychological change that was coming over most European governments at this time. The expansive confidence of the first half of the century was ebbing fast away and for the next twenty or twenty-five years the states of Europe were to be ruled by men and women who, while still willing enough to wound, were mortally afraid to strike. For, on the continent as in England, the age of affluence was over. The strains and burdens of half a century of great and continual conflict had brought exhaustion both of means and of spirit. Particularly this was true of the two greatest powers, Spain and France. The last great conflict between Habsburg and Valois had by the autumn of 1558 been fought to a standstill. Peace negotiations had begun, military operations had ceased, and both sides were anxious above everything to avoid a renewal of the war. Henry II of France, with his finances in chaos and religious strife beginning to link up with factions among his nobility, knew that another great war might well ruin the French monarchy. Philip II of Spain, on the edge of bankruptcy, with Germany lost, the Netherlands restless, the Moriscos in Spain unreliable, and the Turks threatening in North Africa and the western Mediterranean, was in no better shape than Henry II of France. Moreover, both knew that if the rivalry between Habsburg and Valois were to break out again into open war, that war would most likely take the form of a struggle for mastery over the British Isles. And a new struggle for mastery over the British Isles would be fully as burdensome and exhausting as the old struggle which their fathers had waged for mastery over Italy. Their common reluctance to renew the war and the acute jealousy that each felt of the other stealing a march in England were some considerable guarantees for Elizabeth's safety and freedom of manoeuvre.

There was, however, another change of mood in western Europe about this time that was working less in England's favour. This was the growing influence of dogmatic religion over popular, and even over official, opinion. In central Europe religious strife was now dying down. There Lutheranism was the most widespread form of Protestantism and at Passau (1552) and Augsburg (1555) Lutheranism had, as it were, achieved respectability. Even in Roman Catholic eyes it was recognized as a faith fit, if not quite for Emperors, at least for princes. Within the state it had shown itself a bulwark of princely authority. Between states, its acceptance of the *cujus regio ejus religio* principle promised security to Catholic princes against Protestant princes' encroachments just as much as freedom for Lutherans from Catholic intrusions. In western Europe, on the other hand, Protestant movements were becoming more and more linked with or assimilated to Calvinism. Now, in the eyes of most princes, Lutheran as well as Catholic, Calvinism with its theocratic pretensions and Presbyterian church organization, agreed – as James I was later to put it – as well with monarchy as God with the Devil. Catholic rulers, determined anyway to apply the *cujus regio ejus religio* principle in a Catholic sense within their own dominions, saw in the spread of Calvinistic opinions among their subjects not only an affront to their faith but also a threat to their princely power. And, indeed, wherever in the Netherlands, in Scotland, in France, political and constitutional opposition to princely power was now developing, there the Calvinists were taking station as the extreme revolutionary wing of the opposition movement.

Moreover, Calvinism had an international character such as Lutheranism had never quite acquired. Calvin had made Geneva the seminary, power-house, and general headquarters of militant Protestantism. From there he kept in touch with the faithful all over Europe. At the same time congregations in one country kept in touch across the state frontiers with their brethren and well-wishers in other lands. All this gave them, in the eyes of nervous Catholic governments, the appearance of international conspiracy dangerous to both Church and state. Accordingly, in the councils of both Spain and France there were usually some who, from religious zeal or political panic, urged an immediate joint assault upon the enemies of their common creed. With the kings themselves secular jealousy continued as a rule to outweigh common creed. Nevertheless, they did sometimes talk of joint measures to help each other repress heresy inside their own dominions. Now and then they might even take such joint action on a limited and local scale. This, distorted and magnified by rumour, was enough to make Protestants suspect an international conspiracy against *their* faith. Scared by nightmares of Catholic leagues and Catholic crusades, Protestants of different lands huddled yet closer together and thereby stimulated still further Catholic fears of an international Protestant conspiracy. Even Cecil was not altogether immune from those Protestant nightmares, at least in the earlier years. And, indeed, any English statesman, in his anxiety to avoid being trampled underfoot by either the French or the Spanish colossus, must be tempted to keep those great powers busy at home by encouraging the opposition groups in France, Scotland, and the Netherlands. Yet for a country still halting, as England was, between the old religion and the new, such action might breed a double danger if carried too far. It might so identify England with the Protestant side that some at least of the English Catholics would in their turn look abroad for support. It might so provoke the King of France or the King of Spain that one of them, or even both, would actively take up the English Catholics' cause, to the destruction of the national unity which was the mainstay of England's independence.

Much, therefore, depended upon whether Elizabeth and her advisers had the skill and boldness to make the most of the opportunities offered by the general war-weariness and the strains that half a century of foreign wars and religious debate were now producing in lands under Habsburg or Valois rule. Much depended upon whether they were well enough informed to know just how far they could exploit those opportunities without giving intolerable provocation to their war-weary but acutely nervous neighbours. Much depended upon whether they had the sure judgment and the cool self-restraint to exploit their opportunities without turning them into risks. During the first two years of Elizabeth's reign these very questions were posed urgently and inescapably, some of them by the peace negotiations at Câteau-Cambrésis in late 1558 and the early part of 1559, all of them by events in Scotland in 1559 and 1560.

Chapter 19

Success in Scotland

THE moment that Elizabeth I came to the throne she was faced by two urgent and difficult problems. She must as soon as possible settle religion at home and make peace abroad. The two problems were not made easier by being closely linked together. For Elizabeth could hardly settle religion without denying the Pope; nor could she happily make peace without regaining Calais. Yet to deny the Pope must offend her only foreign ally, the Most Catholic King of Spain. The Spaniards had already all but settled their own differences with the French and Philip II's recent conduct did not suggest that he would in any event be eager to renew the war simply to win back Calais for England. He would be even less eager to help an England that had rejected the Pope. And if Spain would not help, England certainly had not the strength to win Calais back single-handed from the French King, who made no secret of his determination to retain it at all costs.

Yet how could Elizabeth, with all her boasted care for England's prestige and England's interests, begin her reign by ceding Calais to the ancient enemy? It is true that the place was, in one way, a relic of a bygone age. The last sally port for aggressive continental operations and the last bastion of the old cross-Channel land buffer against French invasions, it was the symbol of an attitude and a foreign policy that had become outmoded with the rise of the great continental monarchies. Very soon Cecil was to argue that it was anyway not worth the cost of its upkeep.[1] Nevertheless, its loss was a grievous blow to English pride. Even Mary Tudor, so the story went, had said that the word Calais would be found graven upon her heart.[2] Its loss was also something of a blow to England's power. Havens on the southern, windward, shore of the Channel still had their value and Calais was one of the twin keys to the Straits of Dover, to the Narrow Seas through which passed Spain's best communications with the Netherlands and France's best communications with Scotland. With Calais as well as Boulogne in French hands, England's control of those narrow waters, and so her ability to assert herself against the two great continental powers, was necessarily a little weakened. And to lose Calais just when the French were dominating Scotland was doubly unfortunate.

In the peace negotiations at Câteau-Cambrésis, therefore, Elizabeth had to stand out as long as she dared against the cession of Calais. In the end, of course, she had to yield. But she did not yield until, by playing upon the mutual jealousies of Habsburg and Valois, she had managed herself to slip out of dependence upon either. It was Henry II who gave her the first opening. Through an Italian merchant, Guido Cavalcanti, he secretly suggested that if she would make a separate peace, break with Spain, and marry someone of whose friendship France could feel assured, then even over Calais some expedient 'honourable to both their Majesties' might be found.[3] This was too dark a horse to be changed to in midstream, but it could be used as a pacemaker. So Elizabeth, while listening politely to Cavalcanti, was careful to tell Philip II of his offers. She thus kept the French King talking and made the Spaniards more than ever solicitous for her welfare.

One result of this was that Spanish influence was exerted at Rome to thwart French efforts to get the Pope to declare the English Queen illegitimate and excommunicate. Another result was that, when Cavalcanti's overtures bore no fruit and Henry II, turning to threats, allowed Mary Stuart and the Dauphin to flaunt the arms and style of Queen and King of England, Philip countered by offering to marry Elizabeth himself. He bowed his head most reluctantly towards another English matrimonial yoke, as his instructions to Feria showed[4] – and Feria unwisely showed his instructions to some of Elizabeth's court ladies. Yet the fact that Philip made this formal offer bore public witness to his concern for Elizabeth's welfare and it enabled her to prolong the peace negotiations until the French at last agreed to a face-saving formula. By the final treaty of Câteau-Cambrésis (April 2nd, 1559)[5] Calais was ceded to France, but the French promised to restore it to England after eight years or forfeit 500,000 crowns. It was not a glorious conclusion, for there could be few illusions about what the French would do in eight years' time. Nevertheless, the new Queen had avoided falling into dependence upon either France or Spain and she had yielded Calais only when it had become obvious to all her people that her only alternative was to sacrifice the peace that they needed most of all.

While she had thus avoided falling into dependence upon France or Spain, she had also decisively asserted her independence of the Pope. At first most of her advisers had agreed that only the minimum of religious change would be safe, perhaps no more than the repeal of the old heresy laws that had been re-enacted in Mary's reign. By the time Parliament met on January 25th, 1559, however, the confidence born of playing through Cavalcanti on Henry II's hopes and Philip II's fears encouraged her to go somewhat further. She now contemplated legislation that would assert her independence of Rome by restoring the royal supremacy over the Church. At the same time, though, the excitement of the anti-clerical reaction from the Marian burnings enabled a vigorous and vocal group of members to carry the House of Commons with them in pressing for still more radical measures.[6] They created an additional problem. To yield nothing to their demands might bring on a clash between crown and Commons that Elizabeth could not afford so early in her reign. To yield much might not only make relations with Spain even less easy but also again divide the nation, whose normal mood was undoubtedly more conservative than that of the excited House. With the Commons, therefore, as over Calais, Elizabeth resisted as long as she could and by any means short of an open breach. But once the peace was concluded at Câteau-Cambrésis, she could reasonably assume that Henry II would not immediately risk a new conflict with Spain by attacking England, and that Philip II would not suddenly forget that the most likely alternative to an independent Elizabeth was a French Mary Stuart. Also thanks to Philip, the Pope remained silent and the English Catholics heard no call to resistance.

So, with the conclusion of peace, the time had come for Elizabeth to yield what she must to the Commons as well as to France. Accordingly, when the final Acts of Supremacy and Uniformity were passed towards the end of April 1559, they restored not only the royal supremacy but also, with one or two conservative modifications, the second, 1552, Prayer Book of Edward VI. They therefore not only asserted unequivocally England's independence of Rome but also aligned her fairly firmly on the side of the Reformation. Even so, the settlement fell far short of what the more advanced Protestants, the Puritans, had hoped for. To outward appearance the new Church was still very much like the old and 'the whole tone of its devotion was widely different from the Reformed [i.e. Calvinist] continental worship' – so different that 'it may be doubted whether ... the average Englishman was conscious at first of any marked change in the ministration of religion beyond, perhaps, the use of English in the service in the place of Latin.'[7] In other words, despite all the pressures put upon the Queen, the 1559 settlement was still moderate enough to provide that broad *via media* along which the great central mass of the nation could walk together in unity. With peace restored abroad and a sound foundation laid for religious unity at home, the restoration of the nation's health and strength, the true security for its independence, could begin.

Almost at once, however, a storm blew up that threatened to end England's badly needed period of convalescence before it had really started. In May 1559 a rebellion broke out in Scotland against the Queen Mother, Mary of Lorraine. Ever since she had eased Arran (now Duke of Châtelherault) out of the regency in April 1554, Mary had been steadily riveting French control upon Scotland. The French ambassador, d'Oyssel, became virtually her chief minister; another Frenchman, de Roubay, was given the great seal; and French troops garrisoned all the principal fortresses. Discontent, especially among the native nobility, grew rapidly and by 1559 little more was needed to produce a nation-wide explosion. The regent herself now provided that little more by her adoption of a repressive policy towards the Protestants. Hitherto she had shown them considerable tolerance. Knox had been able to spend a year preaching in Scotland in 1555–6 and English Protestants fleeing from the wrath of Mary Tudor had found asylum there unmolested. As a result the reformers had grown into a formidable party. Gentry and lesser nobility, even some of the greater nobles, joined them and in December 1557 these 'Lords of the Congregation' bound themselves by a covenant to work for the establishment of a reformed Church in Scotland. In 1558 they presented to the regent articles demanding a reform of clerical abuses and exactions, together with the introduction of services in English and communion in both kinds. Even now Mary's attitude was not openly hostile. Early in 1559 she referred the articles to a council of the Scottish Church, under Archbishop

247

John Hamilton of St Andrews, which did promulgate some minor reforms.

By then, however, the discontent against the Catholic Church and the discontent against French rule were linking up in a way that threatened the whole regime. Elizabeth's accession to the English throne, and the anti-Papal nature of her religious settlement, no doubt encouraged the Scottish opposition. So, perhaps, did the secret discussions that Cecil had in March with William Maitland of Lethington, under cover of the Anglo-Scottish peace negotiations.[8] Possibly, too, the French government now pressed the regent to assert herself before her power was too gravely undermined. At Câteau-Cambrésis they had come to an understanding with the Spaniards about joint measures to repress heresy in their own realms and this could give them some hope that Spain might not regard repressive action in Scotland as a threat to the political status quo. At all events, at the end of March the regent forbad all unauthorized preaching. The Protestant preachers took no notice and early in May the chief of them, including John Knox (now back again from exile), were summoned to Stirling to answer for their disobedience.

Thereupon the Protestants rose in arms, supported by James V's illegitimate son Lord James Stewart, by the Earls of Argyle, Glencairn, and Morton, and by a considerable number of lesser lords. They speedily won Perth, Dundee, Stirling, and St Andrews and by the end of June were masters of Edinburgh. Next month Mary, with her French troops and a few loyal Scots, did briefly regain the capital, but by the end of September they were again shut up in Leith. Thereupon the heads of the house of Hamilton, the Duke of Châtelherault and his son the Earl of Arran (newly escaped from France), openly joined with the rebels. With the next heirs to the Scottish throne on their side, the Lords of the Congregation in October declared the regent deposed and the government transferred to Châtelherault and themselves. They would exercise it, Knox wrote, in the names of Mary Stuart and Francis II 'till they deny our most just requests'.[9]

For England these developments were of crucial importance. They offered an opportunity to achieve by goodwill all that Henry VIII and Somerset had failed to achieve by force. For a Scottish government hostile to both France and Rome must of necessity lean heavily towards friendship with England, even towards union with England. The Scottish leaders were fully alive to this. Before the end of May 1559 they were in touch with some English officers on the Border and rumours reached the new Spanish ambassador in London, de Quadra, of a plan to marry Arran to Elizabeth. By July they were writing to Elizabeth herself to beg for support and to Secretary Cecil praying that they might be the instruments of 'a joyful conjunction' of the realms.[10] Elizabeth was no less keenly aware of her opportunity. She allowed Cecil, and Sir James Croft at Berwick, to send secret messages of warm encouragement to the Lords of the Congregation. Cecil, too, organized Arran's escape from France and his secret homecoming by way of Geneva, Emden, and London, while de Quadra heard that the Queen herself had spoken of taking 'a husband who would give the King of France some trouble and do him more harm than he expected'.[11] After seeing the mentally unstable Arran on August 29th, she thought better of that, but she did smuggle £2,000 to the Scots. This money, with the return of Arran, very materially assisted to restore their fortunes in late September.

By then, however, it was becoming apparent that something more substantial than kind words and secret subsidies was needed. For if these Scottish developments were of crucial importance to England, they were no less important to France. The Câteau-Cambrésis settlement had left France ringed round by Habsburg territories and Habsburg client states. Apart from the Lorraine gap, which her possession of the Three Bishoprics held open, the British Isles seemed the only weak link in this encircling chain. With England, for all her new display of independence, still leaning towards the Habsburg camp, the French would find themselves hemmed in on all sides if they let go of Scotland. On the other hand, with Scotland under their control, they might always hope that some day the chance would come to assert the claims of the Queen of Scotland and France to be Queen of England too. Then the tables might be completely turned. France would be in a position to dominate western Europe and the Habsburgs, with Germany already lost, would be hard put to it to hold the Netherlands and Italy.[12] Such a revolution was certainly a long-term hope rather than an immediate aim of French policy. This remained true (though Cecil and others could not believe it) even when Henry II died after a jousting accident in July 1559 and, under the fifteen-year-old Francis II, husband of Mary, Queen of Scots, power passed to Mary's uncles the Duke of Guise and the Cardinal of Lorraine. They were just as nervous as Henry II had been of provoking a new conflict with Spain by a direct attack upon Elizabeth. Their attitude to her therefore remained outwardly correct. Nevertheless, they did allow Mary, as Queen of Scotland, to flaunt the style and arms of Queen of England and they made it quite clear that they would not stand idly by while their sister was deposed from the Scottish regency. By August they had 1,500 French troops ready to embark for Scotland and made no secret of their intention to send their brother Elbœuf with another eight or ten thousand if necessary. If those forces once reached Scotland, the days of the Lords of the Congregation would be very briefly numbered.

If, therefore, the prospect of 'a joyful conjunction' of Scotland and England was not to become very remote indeed, Elbœuf must be prevented from reaching Scotland and Mary of Lorraine from holding the port of Leith open for him. The Scots could do neither of those things. They lacked the warships to deal with Elbœuf. They were quite unable to prevent 1,000 troops coming in from France in mid-August and another 800 early in December. They equally lacked the cannon to batter Leith into quick surrender. Their funds, too, were running low. Another £1,000, sent secretly from Elizabeth, was intercepted on the Borders by the pro-French (or merely needy) Earl of Bothwell. Worst of all, their voluntary forces were beginning to melt away homewards with the onset of winter and skirmishes along the Edinburgh road in November showed that they could not even contain Mary's 3,000 Frenchmen in Leith. Elizabeth did then direct Sadler and Croft at Berwick to smuggle to the Scots another £3,000, with munitions, powder, and perhaps a few of the Berwick cannon 'changed or molten' to disguise their origin.[13] But the Scots now needed much more than this and by December Maitland was in London asking for full and open aid.

Close on his heels came reports that French troops had landed at Eyemouth, just north of Berwick, and on December 13th that Elbœuf had put to sea with forty ships. The first report was soon found to be false and the second much exaggerated, but at the moment it did look as if the crisis was at hand, as if England must decide at once either to preserve the peace by abandoning the

Scots or risk almost certain war by prompt and open action against the French. Cecil was all for the bolder course. He persuaded the Queen on December 13th to instruct Sadler and Croft to expel the French from Eyemouth if they began to refortify the place contrary to the 1559 treaty, though Sadler and Croft should pretend to act of their own initiative and not 'by public authority'.[14] Next day the situation was explained to the Spanish ambassador and Spanish support asked for. Then on December 16th Sir William Winter was given instructions to sail north next day with fourteen of the Queen's ships, not only to escort artillery and supplies to Berwick but also 'to do some effectual enterprise upon the French navy' at sea or in the Firth of Forth. He, again, was to do this 'as of your own courage', upon some pretext that would not commit the Queen.[15] Finally, orders went out for 4,000 infantry to be levied and sent up to Berwick, while Cecil asked Sadler and Croft whether these 4,000 would be sufficient, with 2,000 horse, half a dozen siege guns, and the Scots' help, to expel the French from Leith.

These measures were, of course, too serious to be kept any longer a secret between the Queen, Cecil, and a few trusted officials on the Border. Elizabeth had to inform the rest of her Council and it soon appeared that not all were as bold as Cecil. Some, or so both de Noailles and de Quadra heard, were even displeased to learn that money had already been sent to the Scots. Some could not believe that, if Winter were to sink Elbœuf, the French government would be prepared to regard the matter as merely a sailors' brawl. But it was over intervention by land that the debate was fiercest. Secret subsidies could be denied; strange things did happen at sea (were to go on happening until Navarino in 1827 or the Dogger Bank in 1904); but to send an English army into Scotland to besiege Leith would be an act of open, official, unprovoked hostility beyond all possibility of denial.

Hence it was that young Norfolk, England's only Duke and hereditarily the first soldier-noble of the realm, at first flatly refused to lead an army over the Border.[16] Let Elizabeth, he advised, marry the Archduke Charles, the younger son of the Emperor whose ambassador had been urging his suit for months. Then Spanish support would be assured and the French, though they might master Scotland, would not dare to attack England. And then, incidentally, the Duke no doubt hoped, there would be an end also to the Queen's growing infatuation for Lord Robert Dudley, which was breeding such jealousy and alarm among her nobles and Councillors.

The strongly Protestant Lord Keeper, Cecil's brother-in-law Sir Nicholas Bacon, likewise judged the risks too great. The greater part of the realm did not wish for a 'war of invasion' and the Catholic part could not be trusted in such a war. Nor could the country be ready to fight before the summer of 1561. The Queen still owed £60,000 more than she had the means to pay. She could not afford to supply the lack of efficient English troops by hiring substantial numbers of foreign mercenaries. Yet she would have to 'stand post alone'. For in a war on behalf of rebel Protestants she could expect even less help from the Most Catholic King of Spain than over Calais. The German princes were mostly France's friends and the Hanse Towns were still sore over the loss of their privileges in England. So, the only allies would be the Scots, who lacked the power and spirit to expel a mere 3,000 Frenchmen from their land. It would, all the same, take the French at least a year to conquer them and by then England might be more ready and more united.[17]

These were weighty arguments and as late as December 20th, according to de Noailles, the Council was still inclined to leave the Scots to their fate. By then, however, news was coming in that, although 800 of Elbœuf's advance party had reached Leith, the other 1,000 had been wrecked on the Zeeland sandbanks, while Elbœuf himself had left Calais to consult his government at Blois. There was perhaps yet time to strike before the French in Scotland grew too powerful. At all events, on December 24th the Council advised Elizabeth not only to hasten away Winter and his ships but also to make ready 4,000 foot and six or seven hundred horse to help the Scots by land if she found them (as seemed likely) incapable of expelling the French by their own efforts.[18] Moreover, they advised that these things should be done at once, because if the French were suffered until the spring they were likely both to vanquish the Scots and to grow strong enough to invade England too. In accordance with this advice, Cecil on Christmas Day drafted instructions for Norfolk,[19] who was now on his way to take command as the Queen's lieutenant-general in the north.

It is improbable that these instructions ever went beyond a

draft. For, although Cecil may have convinced most of his fellow Councillors, he had not yet convinced the Queen. She was willing to send out commissions for the levying of the troops and she let Winter sail off northwards as soon as the weather permitted, on December 27th. But on December 28th she rejected the Council's recommendation for prompt intervention in Scotland by land. Two days later she had fresh instructions for Norfolk drafted, and this time sent.[20] He could hardly, she pointed out, attempt any serious operations in Scotland without horsemen and his horsemen, whose levy was only just being ordered, could not possibly be ready before the very end of January. He should therefore avoid any open act of hostility for a month or two and meanwhile find out whether the Scots might not be able after all to manage with only the help of Winter's ships and a few smuggled cannon and 'volunteers'.

Her bolder Councillors were in despair and Cecil even drafted a letter offering her his resignation.[21] But Elizabeth was not to be moved. She was well aware of the desirability of destroying French influence in Scotland, but she had no love for rebels. Nor did the fact that these particular rebels were Protestants endear them to her, for their Protestantism was too much after the Genevan pattern to be a healthy example to her own Puritans. 'God save us', her new Archbishop Parker wrote, 'from such a visitation as Knox hath attempted in Scotland, the people to be the orderers of things.'[22] Knox himself was another stumbling-block. His *Trumpet Blast against the Monstrous Regiment of Women*, published not long before Elizabeth's accession, had been sadly 'blown out of season'[23] and with a prophet-author's arrogance he lacked the worldly wisdom and good manners to explain away his offence convincingly to the proud Queen.

Moreover, Elizabeth had to consider how Spain would react. Philip II was just about to seal his peace with France by marrying the French King's sister. His ambassador in England, de Quadra, and his lieutenants in the Netherlands were so afraid that through Elizabeth's rashness England would become French that they were urging him to step in first and make it Spanish. Three or four thousand Spanish veterans, left over from the late war, were still in the Netherlands, provoking opposition there much as Mary of Lorraine's Frenchmen provoked it in Scotland. Land those Spaniards in East Anglia and surely all good Catholics

would join them – Spanish memories of Mary Tudor were surprisingly short and Spanish ambassadors could never quite
understand that Englishmen could be Catholics without being
Roman Catholics. Philip, short of money, still suspicious of France,
and busy with the Turks in North Africa, seemed not yet to be
listening to such projects. But would he remain deaf to them if
Elizabeth intervened openly to help Scottish Protestants in
flagrant rebellion against their lawful Queen?

Anyway, what was the hurry? Norfolk could not do much by
land for another month or more. Elbœuf's return to Blois and the
talk in France of Aumale, another of the Guise clan, taking
10,000 men to Scotland in the spring suggested that the French
were not anxious to risk their troops a second time in the North
Sea's winter gales. Even if they did, Winter could deal with those
whom winds and waves spared. His action might take a lot of
explaining, but need it inevitably mean war? Why, then, not
wait to see what Winter and the Scots could achieve before taking
irrevocable steps on land?

As it turned out, events ran the Queen's way. Over Christmas
d'Oyssel had marched out of Leith with most of the French troops,
chased the Scots from Edinburgh and Stirling, and pushed along
the northern shore of the Firth of Forth towards St Andrews.
There, although he was better placed to welcome Elbœuf, he
was also much more vulnerable to Winter. And it was Winter,
not Elbœuf, who came. Elbœuf had put to sea with his main force
a few days ahead of Winter, only to be overwhelmed by worse
storms than those that had shattered his vanguard a month
earlier. This happened early in January, when he was almost in
sight of Scotland. Indeed one of his captains actually landed eight
score men before the storm blew him from his anchors and away
to shipwreck on the distant sandbanks of Holland.[24] The disaster
was total and it would be months before another force could be
made ready, for there was 'not a *denier*' in the French treasury.[25]
Moreover, according to Arran and to Throckmorton, now English
ambassador in France, by the spring the Guises would have too
much work cut out for them at home, by their rivals among the
nobility and by the Huguenots, to have anything to spare for
Scotland. The conciliatory tone of a new French envoy, la Marque,
who had just reached London, seemed to confirm these encouraging forecasts.

Winter meanwhile had been delayed at Harwich and in the Humber by the gales that shattered Elbœuf. It was January 22nd before he arrived in the Firth of Forth. But once there, he made his presence felt. After provoking the French into firing the first shot, he destroyed their forts on Burntisland and Inchkeith and sank the two ships and the small craft that were keeping d'Oyssel's forces in Fife supplied across the water from Leith. As barely six hundred French troops had been left in Leith, the whole French position in Scotland might have become suddenly desperate if the Scots could have shown on land the same energy that Winter displayed at sea. But they failed to stop d'Oyssel getting back to his base by an arduous roundabout march through Stirling and they failed to storm Leith from the sea before he got there. Once his forces returned, Leith was again too hard a nut for them to crack without English military assistance.

Until now Elizabeth had always clung to the hope that the Scots might expel the French without her open aid by land. This final demonstration of their weakness compelled her to yield at last to Cecil's arguments and to Norfolk's plea 'a God's name let that which with honour cannot be left, with efficacy be followed.'[26] By mid-February Norfolk's forces were assembled; from Philip of Spain, to whom Elizabeth had sent Montague and Chamberlain to explain her purposes, there still came no positive move; and a new French envoy, de Seurre, brought a despairing offer to withdraw all but four hundred of the French troops from Scotland if England would cease to meddle there. Clearly the time was ripe and on February 15th the Queen, albeit still regretfully, gave Norfolk authority to conclude with the Scots. Norfolk wasted no time. On February 27th by the treaty of Berwick[27] the Scots were taken into Elizabeth's protection 'only for the preservation of the same in their old freedoms and liberties from conquest* during the time that the marriage shall continue betwixt the Queen of Scots and the French King and one year after'. To help them to expel the French already there, she would send an English army to join them when they were ready to take the field on March 25th. In return the Scots were to send forces to aid her if the French invaded England.

Barely a week later the Guises' control of France's government

---

* The draft here contained the words 'as a Christian realm in the profession of Christ's true religion', but these words were left out of the treaty as signed.

was rudely shaken by the conspiracy which Throckmorton had predicted (and possibly encouraged). The Tumult of Amboise failed, but it revealed dangers in France that compelled the Guises to cut their losses in Scotland. They at once sent a new envoy, Monluc, to make the best terms he could with Elizabeth. The Queen, fortified by a memorandum from Cecil and another round robin from the Council, managed to resist Monluc's blandishments and on March 28th Lord Grey crossed the Border into Scotland. Because of the disappointing weakness of the Scots, he took with him some 8,000, instead of 4,000, English infantry. On April 4th they joined the small Scottish army and moved forward against Leith. Next day there arrived in London an envoy from Philip II, de Glasion, to ask the Queen to cease all warlike moves and allow the Spanish troops from the Netherlands to hold the ring in Scotland while the King of Spain mediated a settlement. But de Glasion, a Netherlander well disposed to England, delivered his message so gently that he robbed it of all menace. Privately, too, he urged Cecil and Lord Admiral Clinton to press forward. A few weeks later, in Spain, the Duke of Alba himself was to quote to Chamberlain the Spanish saying that if you found your enemy in the water up to his waist, you should help him out; but if he were in it to the neck, you should push him under.[28]

Even Elizabeth could now hardly doubt that the French were in up to their necks and that there was no real danger from Spain. She hated the whole business; she had no confidence in the Scots; she resented the mounting expense. Nevertheless, as things were, she could hardly do other than press forward the siege of Leith. For the English soldiers, who bore the brunt of that operation, it was also a wearisome stumbling affair. An assault on May 7th failed, partly because the scaling ladders were six feet too short, and they had to turn to the more tedious method of blockade. This caused Elizabeth 'to renew the opinion of Cassandra' and Cecil 'had such a torment herein with the Queen's Majesty as an ague hath not in five fits so much abated'.[29] Yet the outcome was never in real doubt. The garrison could look for no relief from France; their supplies would not last for ever; and the death of Mary of Lorraine on June 10th took the heart out of their resistance. Six days later Cecil, who had been sent up with Dr Wootton to conclude matters, began negotiations with the French plenipotentiaries and on July 6th the treaty of Edinburgh was signed.[30] By it both French and English troops were at once with-drawn from Scotland and Mary abandoned her pretensions to the English arms and title. The Scots were not a party to the treaty, for the French would not capitulate with their Queen's rebels nor admit the right of her subjects to form alliance with the Queen of England. But after much haggling a vague clause was added whereby Mary and Francis promised Elizabeth that they would fulfil the promises made to the Scots in a separate 'concession'. By this they agreed to the destruction of the fortifications of Leith, Dunbar, and Eyemouth. They promised never again to send French troops to Scotland or appoint aliens to office there. They consented, so long as Mary was Queen of France, to leave the government of Scotland in the hands of a council of twelve chosen, seven by Mary and five by the Lords, from a list of twenty-four submitted by Parliament. They undertook also to listen to Parliament's representations about the settlement of religion – though in the event Parliament in August 1560 made not representations but laws, laws abolishing papal jurisdiction in Scotland, making hearing or celebrating Mass a penal offence, and authorizing a Protestant confession of faith framed by Knox and his brethren.

How much of the credit for this satisfactory outcome should go to Elizabeth and how much to her Councillors, particularly Cecil, it is not easy to say. It was no doubt chiefly the Queen's distaste for aiding rebels which made her put off open intervention as long as possible – that and the same deep-rooted reluctance to commit herself irrevocably which was to keep her the Virgin Queen, *l'éternelle fiancée*.[31] Yet she had reason too and there was something fevered about her Councillors' midwinter impatience. Assuming that Winter could deal with Elbœuf, there was much to be said for delaying military action until March. January and February were surely the worst possible months for a Scottish campaign, while Arran and Throckmorton's reports about the state of France pointed to a much more auspicious conjunction of political circumstances in the spring, when Spain's reaction would also be clearer. We can hardly guess whether in the final stages the Queen's ill temper was merely the irritation of one who hated doing what she knew she had to do or whether she might really have drawn back had it not been for the persistence of her Councillors.

At all events, the importance of the success for England needs no emphasizing. The French King no longer bestrode the realm nor had the Spanish King now a foot inside it. With the Scots freed from their French dependence and drawn into English friendship, Great Britain could become politically as well as geographically an island. England's postern gate was closed and the continental powers could invade her only by sea, where her naval strength must make them think twice before risking the attempt. And while they were thinking, there was time to heal the domestic divisions and repair the military and economic weaknesses that had brought the country so low in the past ten years. To have accomplished so much in so short a time, and to have accomplished it from a position of so little strength, was a remarkable achievement. It provided, indeed, the base from which Elizabethan England could launch out into its more spacious days.

Chapter 20

The Succession and Mary Stuart

DURING most of the 1560s the question of the succession to the throne was again one of the dominant issues in both English foreign policy and English domestic politics. It was now more than ever a question of vital importance. For Elizabeth was the last of the Tudors and, if she were to die childless, there was no generally acceptable successor in sight. By birth the next in line was Mary, Queen of Scots. But the Scottish line was excluded from the English succession by Henry VIII's will. Besides, no Protestant Englishman was ready to accept a Catholic as Queen and even the Catholics, after their experience of the half-Spanish Mary Tudor, were not eager to become subject to the half-French Mary Stuart. By Henry VIII's will the next heir was Lady Catherine Grey, younger sister of the unfortunate Lady Jane Grey and granddaughter of Henry's younger sister Mary. But Catherine Grey was little known and the discovery in August 1560 of her clandestine marriage to the Earl of Hertford, Protector Somerset's son, hardly suggested that she was such stuff as queens were made of. Beyond her stretched a shadowy line of claimants with still more remote royal ancestry, chief among them the Protestant Earl of Huntingdon and the more Catholic Lord Darnley, the Earl of Lennox's son. Of all these, none could look for an uncontested succession and so, at any moment, Elizabeth's death could plunge the nation into civil war and anarchy.

Elizabeth was, as the Earl of Sussex said, *ultimum refugium*. It was therefore his hope and the hope of all her subjects that she would soon marry and have a son, 'bring us a blessed prince to redeem us out of thraldom'.[1] This, however, she was never to do – it is the one fact about her that every schoolboy does indeed know. The reasons why she chose to remain the Virgin Queen are not quite so obvious. We can ignore the gossip about her suffering from some physical defect that made marriage impossible or unrewarding.[2] If there had been any truth in it, Cecil and other close advisers must have known of it too and would not have kept pestering her

to marry in order to settle the succession. And certainly her conduct towards Lord Robert Dudley, the Master of the Horse, during
the year or two after the summer of 1559 bears out her own
confession that 'she was but human and not insensible to human
emotions and impulses.'[3] Her behaviour then bore all the marks of
a woman genuinely in love and anxious to marry. But Lord
Robert was politically impossible as her husband. Hated by conservatively-minded men as Northumberland's son, scorned by the
nobility as an upstart Dudley, he had the additional handicap of
being already married. His wife, Amy Robsart, did in September
1560 fall down stairs and break her neck at her house at Cumnor.
It was in all probability an accident, for the signs are that she
suffered from a form of cancer that made a fall likely to have just
such a fatal result.[4] But the accident, occurring when all the servants were out at Abingdon fair, was too timely not to arouse the
darkest suspicions and Amy Robsart dead became a greater
obstacle than Amy Robsart alive. It was bad enough that, in
Mary Stuart's gibing phrase, Elizabeth should think of marrying
her horsekeeper.[5] To marry him when so many suspected him
of clearing the way by murdering his wife, might well cost her
her throne. Sadly Elizabeth faced the facts and in November
1560 assured Cecil that she did not intend to marry Lord
Robert.

Probably she meant it, but it was not yet the end of the affair.
Just at this time preparations were being made at Rome for the
re-assembly of the General Council at Trent and the Pope was
about to send a nuncio, Martinengo, to invite Elizabeth to send
English representatives to it.[6] What we may call Elizabeth's
official policy on this question, the policy pursued through her
Secretary Cecil, was to seek to unite the German Lutherans and, if
possible, the new government of Catherine de Medici in France, in
demanding a truly free and general Council where Protestants
might sit on equal terms. At the same time, however, she was still
anxious not to provoke the open hostility of the Pope and the
Habsburgs. So, early in 1561 she allowed Lord Robert to suggest to
the Spanish ambassador, de Quadra, that if Spain would support
his marriage to the Queen, they would take the opportunity of the
General Council to bring England back into the Roman Church.
How seriously Lord Robert meant this we cannot guess, but it
certainly looks as if in Elizabeth's eyes it was little more than a

political manoeuvre to lull the Catholic powers. Certainly she would never really commit herself with de Quadra. On the contrary in April 1561 she let Cecil pounce upon some leading English Catholics for alleged conspiracy with the Spanish ambassador. Then, in May, on her Privy Council's unanimous advice, she refused to admit Martinengo or to be represented at a General Council such as that at Trent, 'which was already sworn to the maintenance of the Pope's authority'.[7] After this, even Lord Robert himself practically abandoned hope.

So the one man whom Elizabeth might have married for love was ruled out. If she were to marry now, it would be for political convenience and she felt, it seems reasonably clear, that any husband would bring political inconveniences which must outweigh all but the direst political necessities. As the Scot Melville told her (or says in his memoirs that he told her), 'your Majesty thinks if you were married, you would be but Queen of England and now you are King and Queen both: you may not suffer a commander.' Or as she herself once told a presuming nobleman, 'I will have only a mistress here and no master.'[8] A husband, just because he was a man and she a woman, must in the man's world of the sixteenth century become her rival for power. Courtship was still possible; indeed it was too valuable a diplomatic asset to be unused and no doubt Elizabeth often found it fun. But the object was no longer marriage and it was easy enough to find some insuperable impediment whenever the courtship became too pressing or lost its political usefulness. Philip of Spain had already been politely rejected and Henry II's hints of a French match turned down. The Duke of Holstein and King Eric of Sweden, whose persistence was more certain than his sanity, had been more firmly refused. Either must have drawn England needlessly into Baltic quarrels. The various German and Italian princelings who offered themselves had too little else to offer. The Earl of Arran, for whom the Scottish Parliament made a formal proposal in December 1560, was likewise refused. Apart from doubts about his sanity, marriage to him would have given intolerable offence to Mary Stuart and to France. The Emperor's younger son, the Archduke Charles, held the field longer, for most Englishmen would have welcomed him and his hopes helped to keep Spain friendly. But he wanted to be allowed to hear Mass privately and would not come to be looked over. He was said to be of an amenable disposition, but Elizabeth would marry no man unseen – especially, perhaps, one whose head was reported to be as big as the Earl of Bedford's.[9] So in the end Charles, too, lost interest. He was by no means the last of her suitors, but already men at home and abroad were beginning to doubt whether she would ever marry.

Meanwhile the question of the succession remained wide open and with the death of Mary Stuart's husband, Francis II of France, in December 1560 it took on a new significance. Mary, at just nineteen, ceased to be Queen of France. The Guises lost their hold on that country's government and the Queen Mother Catherine de Medici, backed by moderates and Huguenots, seized control as regent for the ten-year-old Charles IX. Mary could be of little use to her uncles in the ensuing French struggle for power. But she was still Queen of Scotland and there, if she played her cards wisely, she might yet salvage something from the wreck of the old Church and the old alliance. Moreover, with Elizabeth unmarried, she could press her claims as heir presumptive of England. So, under her uncles' guidance she came to terms with the Protestant Lords and in August 1561 returned to Scotland on the at least tacit understanding that, if she left them in control of the government and did not upset their religious settlement, they would allow her and her attendants to hear Mass privately and would use their influence in England to secure her recognition as Elizabeth's heir if Elizabeth should have no children.

For some time, at least, Mary kept her side of the bargain. She insisted upon her own Mass but made no overt attempt to upset their 1560 church settlement. She even rode with Lord James Stewart, the Protestant Lords' leader, to crush the Earl of Huntly and his Catholic Gordons in October 1562, afterwards making Lord James Earl of Moray. Yet inevitably her presence acted as a political solvent. The old clergy and Catholic nobles took heart again now that standing up for Rome no longer meant bowing down to France. Men halting between the two religions rallied to their Queen now that she seemed bent upon moderate courses. Most of all, her return widened a split that had already shown itself in the dominant Protestant party. Parliament's rejection in January 1561 of the Book of Discipline, framed by Knox and his fellow ministers, and of the new Kirk's claim to all the old Church's property, had shown that the lay leaders did not intend 'new presbyter' to be 'but old priest writ large'. Now Mary's return deepened the rift, for Knox and the ministers would never have allowed her to come back as a Catholic and they regarded her private Mass as a defiling abomination. This split, by weakening the Protestant Lords' hold upon the nation, made their hold upon the Queen more than ever dependent upon their success in persuading their English friends to recognize her claims as Elizabeth's heir. For the next few years, therefore, Anglo-Scottish relations centred upon this question.

Elizabeth was not unsympathetic to Mary's claims. She would prefer someone truly royal to succeed her and she had no love at all for Catherine Grey. Mary's recognition, moreover, would settle the succession question without involving Elizabeth herself in matrimony. It might make a friend of her most dangerous rival, of the potential leader of a Catholic reaction against her. It would crown the work of 1560 by gaining for it the assent of the Scottish Queen as well as of the Scottish nation and it would bring the long-desired union of Great Britain to the edge of accomplishment. But the obstacles in the way were great and the negotiations that ensued upon Mary's return to Scotland were as difficult and slow as any twentieth-century disarmament conference. They were perhaps not made easier by Secretary Cecil's lack of enthusiasm, for much as he wanted a union of Great Britain, he did not wish to see it come under the Catholic Mary Stuart. 'I mean never to be an author thereof,' he told Throckmorton. He somewhat changed his view later, but Mary's Secretary Maitland repeatedly complained of his writing in parables and 'brief and dark sentences'.[10]

So the negotiations moved slowly forward. They began with Mary asking for recognition as Elizabeth's heir presumptive and Elizabeth countering with a demand for ratification of the treaty of Edinburgh which Mary had so far steadfastly refused. Mary came back with a request for the amendment of the clause in the treaty renouncing her claim to the arms and style of England, since its wording could be interpreted as denying her a place in the succession as well as renouncing her present title to the English crown. She would ratify the treaty, thus amended, in return for formal recognition as heir to England if Elizabeth should have no children. Elizabeth was ready to re-word the offending clause but was not prepared to acknowledge Mary as her heir presumptive without adequate guarantees for her own safety. Otherwise, in her own words, she would 'in mine own life ... set my winding sheet before my eyes'.[11] She knew, from personal experience during her sister's reign, how easily conspiracies gathered around an heir presumptive, even one who did not presume too much and had not a neighbouring kingdom at her back. Yet what sure guarantees could Mary give that some uncontrollably impatient supporter would not seek to hasten the coming of her English kingdom by assassinating Elizabeth, especially when religion might be used to hallow the deed?

In May 1562, however, the two Queens did tentatively agree to meet at York later in the summer. Each was so much a prima donna that the outcome of their meeting was more than usually unpredictable. Yet there was perhaps a chance that it might lead, if not to personal friendship, at least to mutual understanding and trust. Perhaps to something more decisive still, for Moray and Maitland professed to expect that Elizabeth would then easily win Mary over to Protestantism and even Cecil listed among the possible advantages of a meeting 'the religion of the Scottish Queen to be amended'. Nor were these merely Protestant daydreams. If the Queens met, the ambassador Randolph wrote from Edinburgh, 'the Papists think themselves quite overthrown: they say plainly that she [Mary] cannot then return a true Christian woman.'[12]

These promising vistas were, unhappily, soon clouded over by events on the continent. Even before the York meeting was arranged, the not wholly unprovoked massacre of a Huguenot congregation at Vassy (March 1562) by Mary's uncle, the Duke of Guise, had touched off the first of the French Wars of Religion. For a few months this worked in Mary's favour, since Elizabeth's first reaction was to attempt to mediate between the French factions. She had already considerable influence with the Huguenots and she might hope to influence the Guises too by the prospect of concessions to their niece over the English succession. Indeed this may well have been one of her motives in agreeing to the York meeting. But events moved too fast for her and the Guises were in no mood to listen to peace. They had the support of their old rival Montmorency and of many other moderate Catholics who were becoming alarmed by the growth and pretensions of the Prince of Condé's Huguenot faction during the tolerant regency of Catherine de Medici. The head of the house of Bourbon, Anthony of Navarre, was also on their side for more selfish reasons. Thus reinforced, they brushed Catherine aside, seized control of King and government, and soon began to overmatch the Huguenots in the field. Before long they might be full masters of France and free to resume the British ambitions which the Tumult of Amboise and the death of Francis II had interrupted. Moreover, Philip II of Spain, anxious to check the contagion of heresy spreading from France into his own Netherlands, seemed inclined to support them. Unless something was done speedily to uphold Condé, it looked as if Mary might soon have the whole power of France to back her, while Spain looked on in benevolent neutrality. If, however, Elizabeth was going to intervene against the Guises in France, she could not well at the same time hobnob with their niece at York. So in July 1562 she told Mary that the meeting could not take place that year.

Two months after this envoys arrived from Condé to beg urgently for help in men and money. In their need, they were apparently persuaded to go beyond their instructions and to offer, in return for help, possession of Dieppe and Le Havre as pledges for the eventual cession of Calais. This was not an altogether novel proposal. Two years earlier, after the failure of the Conspiracy of Amboise, some of the Huguenots had made a similar suggestion. At that time Cecil had advised strongly against entering 'into that bottomless pit' of expense of force and treasure within the King of France's own mainland and with no support there 'but a devotion popular upon opinions in religion'.[13] Especially, remembering Boulogne, he had advised against seeking to seize and hold any place in France. As the treaty of Edinburgh had just been signed then, the matter had been dropped. But now the circumstances were different and the temptation too strong. Even Cecil felt that Condé was fighting England's battle as much as the Lords of the Congregation had been in 1560, while Dudley and Throckmorton were strenuously urging war. Might not the Huguenots be built up into an effective counterpoise to the Guises in France just as the Scots Protestants had been built up in Scotland? And might not Calais be recovered into the bargain?

There, however, lay the fatal difference. In 1560 Elizabeth had sought nothing from the Scots. Now, in occupying Le Havre and demanding Calais, she outraged French national feeling. Many of the Huguenots could not stomach it, while Guise in September offered them a large toleration if they would deny entry to the

English. In December Catherine de Medici made a similar offer to Condé if he would help to drive the English out. Condé was not yet prepared to trust Guise or the Queen Mother, but he showed how troubled his conscience was by urging Elizabeth to abandon her claims. This was ominous, but worse was to come. The King of Spain warned Elizabeth sternly not to support heresy in France. She, to appease him, refused to let her troops at Le Havre join Condé in the field and protested to de Quadra that she was intervening not for religion but for Calais. Then, on December 19th, the Huguenot field army, unaided by its English allies, was destroyed at Dreux. Condé himself was taken prisoner by the Catholics and Montmorency by the Huguenots. As Anthony of Navarre had been mortally wounded a month earlier and his son Henry was a mere boy, Guise was left almost without a rival and it looked only a matter of time before he turned his forces against the English in Le Havre.

Mary's hopes of a friendly meeting with Elizabeth were plainly not encouraged by these developments. There were, too, other things to try her patience that winter. In October 1562 Elizabeth had lain for two days at death's door with smallpox and Mary knew that, in the fevered debates among Privy Councillors about the succession, barely a voice had been raised in her favour. Then in January 1563 Parliament met and there was a real danger that, in the anxiety caused by Elizabeth's illness, it would drive the English Queen to some decision fatal to Mary's claims. Mary therefore dispatched her Secretary, Maitland, to London to press again for her recognition as heir presumptive and for leave to plead her cause before Parliament. That would indeed be to force Elizabeth's hand. Mary did offer in return her mediation to secure peace with France and the restitution of Calais. But the fact that Guise was making similar overtures to the new English ambassador, Sir Thomas Smith, made this offer somewhat suspect. Maitland, moreover, had talks with the Spanish ambassador in London before he went on to the French court. It was suspected that his secret purpose in these visits was to sound de Quadra about the possibility of Mary marrying Philip II's eldest son Don Carlos and Catherine de Medici and the Guises about a match with Charles IX of France.[14]

For these intrigues could not be kept entirely secret. Possibly, too, hints of them were deliberately allowed to leak out in the hope that the threat of such marriages would move Elizabeth to concede Mary's demands. If so, they failed of their purpose, for again the fates were against the Queen of Scots. In February 1563 Guise was assassinated. His eldest son was also a mere boy. Two of his brothers, Aumale and the Grand Prior, died a few days later; a third, Elbœuf, was besieged in Rouen; and the fourth, the Cardinal of Lorraine, was away at the Council of Trent. The Guises suddenly had become as leaderless as the Bourbons and the Montmorencies. The way was clear for Catherine de Medici to take control again, clear too for Condé to join her in expelling the English in return for the granting of toleration to the Huguenots. With Catholics and Huguenots united against them, the English in Le Havre were doomed. An outbreak of plague hastened their doom and at the last moment south-westerly gales held up the supplies and reinforcements which might have prolonged resistance for a few more weeks. On July 29th, 1563 Le Havre surrendered. Eight months later Elizabeth at length abandoned her dreams of regaining Calais and by the treaty of Troyes (April 1564) brought this unhappy adventure to a close.

It had not been entirely profitless. It had reminded governments that were willing to wound, how dangerous it was to strike. It had taught the English a salutary lesson in the realities of power and the dangers of relying too much upon 'a devotion popular upon opinions in religion'. Henceforward Elizabeth, though always ready to encourage French, Scottish, and Netherlands Protestants as useful pressure groups, would openly support them in rebellion only as a last desperate remedy when she could come to terms with their lawful rulers in no other way. The affair had also taught Catherine de Medici and moderate men in France how dangerously their religious quarrels could tempt English intervention on the Huguenot side and Spanish on the Catholic. Catherine was therefore prepared not only to grant toleration to keep the peace at home but also to seek an understanding with Elizabeth, even if that meant doing little for Mary Stuart and denying her Charles IX as a husband. Catherine's attempts to arrive at a similar good relationship with Spain were to prove less successful, for despite the Protestant alarm over her meeting with the Duke of Alba at Bayonne in 1565, her return to power revived all Philip II's old suspicions of France. That, of course, drove her the more towards friendship with Elizabeth. And while Mary Stuart was thus losing her French support, her hopes of a Spanish marriage were dashed by the growing madness of Don Carlos. She could no longer hope for the King of France or the Prince of Spain and there was no other continental suitor of sufficient greatness to frighten Elizabeth into recognizing her claims.[15] Anglo-Scottish relations were becoming still more a purely British matter, further disentangled from continental complications.

All this brought Mary very little nearer to her goal. For, while the foreign dangers that might accompany her recognition diminished, the domestic difficulties grew more apparent. Her formal recognition would mean setting aside Henry VIII's will. That would require the consent of Parliament, for the will owed its validity to an Act of Parliament and could hardly be set aside without parliamentary sanction. How very difficult this would be to obtain, had been shown by the 1563 Parliament, which had been no more favourable to Mary's claims than the Privy Council had been in October 1562. Elizabeth had given a non-committal answer to its petition for her own marriage and had also managed to steer it off any legislative enactment about the succession. But as feeling against Mary was strongest in the more Puritan south and south-east where parliamentary seats lay thickest, this was clearly no temporary obstacle. So, in the autumn of 1563 Elizabeth instructed Randolph to explain the position to Mary. She hinted that, privately, she thought Mary's claim the strongest. She had stopped Parliament from doing anything to bar it and she desired to further the union of the two realms. But she hinted also that, if Mary wanted to be Queen of England, she must be ready to accept Protestantism at least as the established religion of the country. Moreover, any suggestion of Mary marrying one of 'the children of France, Spain, or Austria' would make recognition impossible, though a suitable match abroad or with an English nobleman might make it possible to have her claim examined and, if found good, furthered by such means as Lords and Commons would be content with.[16]

In March 1564 Elizabeth went a step further and named the suitable English nobleman – Lord Robert Dudley, soon to be made a little more eligible by elevation to the Earldom of Leicester. She had been dropping very broad hints of this for a year past and her offer was probably well intentioned. Yet it was hardly likely that Mary would bring herself to marry Elizabeth's 'horsekeeper', especially as even now Elizabeth would not promise full and formal recognition as the reward. She must, Cecil reiterated in December 1564,[17] be ruled by her country's laws and by the consent of Parliament. That, indeed, was the crux of the matter. To promise more would be to promise more than she could perform and probably what she was really aiming at was a tacit understanding with Mary that would not involve formal recognition or public declaration. Apart from Elizabeth's own lifelong reluctance to name her successor, it might well be in Mary's best interest to avoid clear-cut decisions, to keep the issue blurred. Let her rely upon Elizabeth's goodwill (as James VI was to do later) to prevent any rival claimant stealing a march on her and let her hope that in time her own moderate courses in Scotland would lull the fears, perhaps even win the confidence, of the English people. She was, after all, a Queen and the next heir by blood.

It was hardly to be expected that the impatient Mary and the logical Scots would be content to trust to time and to blur the issue in this way. And, indeed although Mary's behaviour at this time 'suggests not politics but a biological urge that would not be denied',[18] her next move – her marriage to Lord Darnley (July 1565) – could be interpreted as designed to build up support in a quicker, if more risky, manner. Darnley's father, the Earl of Lennox, had been during her infancy the Hamiltons' rival for the Scottish succession if she should die childless. Lennox had sought Henry VIII's aid, had been attainted as a traitor, and since 1544 had lived in exile in England. There he had married Lady Margaret Douglas, daughter of Henry's elder sister Margaret (Mary's grandmother) by her second husband the Earl of Angus. Darnley could therefore claim, through both his parents, a place after Mary in the Scottish succession and, through his mother, in the English too. Moreover, the strong inclination of the Lennoxes to the old religion made him a figure around whom English conservative opinion might be mobilized in support of Mary's recognition as Elizabeth's heir presumptive. Indeed, when the marriage took place, some of Elizabeth's Councillors were much alarmed lest it should encourage the supporters of the old religion, 'upon which only string the Queen of Scots' title doth hang'. They thought 'that the peril was greater by this marriage with Lord Darnley ... than with the mightiest prince abroad', since he had 'for the cause of religion and other respects made a party here' so great, as he boasted, that Elizabeth 'dare not attempt to contrary this marriage'.[19]

Nevertheless, it would be rash to equate Elizabeth's intentions with the opinions of her more Protestant Councillors and she never quite shared their doubts about the loyalty of her Catholic subjects. Besides, there is a hint in Throckmorton's letters that the Darnley match was not so ill taken there by Her Majesty and her Council as they pretended. The French ambassador, too, suspected that Elizabeth 'disguised the pleasure which she really had at heart to see it go on'.[20] Certainly Mary was not unjustified in expressing surprise at the angry reaction that her marriage aroused. It is true that Elizabeth had sent Lennox to the Tower for practising it in 1562. Yet he was back again at court in good favour next year. In 1564, too, Elizabeth was well aware that the practice was on foot again, as her hint to Melville about the Scots preferring 'yonder long lad' (Darnley) showed.[21] Yet in September 1564 she had helped Lennox to return to Scotland and recover his estates there. Then in February 1565 she gave Darnley leave to join his father. A month later she informed Mary that not even marriage to Leicester would bring a declaration of her title as heir to England until Elizabeth had either herself married or announced her determination never to marry.[22] She could hardly have done more to ease the way to the Darnley marriage, short of openly pressing for it.

Elizabeth's purposes, however, are here more than usually unfathomable and the influences working upon her more than usually confused. She cannot have foreseen the tragedies that were to ensue upon this marriage. But perhaps she did regard it as further insulating Scottish affairs from continental politics. Mary's cause would certainly look less attractive to foreign princes when she could no longer offer herself as a bride with a kingdom as her dowry. Elizabeth may even have felt that, in so far as the Darnley marriage would rally English support for Mary's recognition as her successor, this, too, was a step in the right direction. And, of course, by making Mary out to have married in defiance of her wishes, she gave herself an excuse for refusing to listen any longer to the Scottish Queen's nagging requests for a recognition that it was not yet practicable to promise.

Whatever Elizabeth's motives, it looked awhile as if she had misjudged the situation. Even before the Darnley marriage, Mary had broken with her Protestant advisers and by August 1565 Moray, Châtelherault, and Argyle, fearing as they said for their lives, were in open rebellion. But most of the other Protestant lords stood aside and the Protestant congregations would not take arms for the men who had brought back their Catholic Queen and her Mass. Besides, Mary had again publicly promised not to alter the 1560 religious settlement without Parliament's assent; while Darnley, though he had married her by Catholic rites, had withdrawn before Mass was celebrated and had since been seen several times at Protestant preachings. Nor was Mary relying merely upon Catholic support. She had restored to Gordon the Earldom of Huntly, but Gordon now professed himself a Protestant, as did Bothwell, who was also rising to influence at court. So, few were yet prepared to rise against her and, although Elizabeth secretly sent the rebel lords £3,000, by October 1565 the 'Chase About Raid' was over and they were exiles in England.

Mary's intentions at this point are almost as unclear – were so perhaps even to herself – as Elizabeth's over the Darnley marriage. In August and September 1565 she did secretly appeal to France and Spain for help. So it is possible that, as the Protestants suspected, she was encouraged by news of Catherine de Medici's meeting with Alba at Bayonne (June 1565) and the rumours of a Catholic league which grew out of it. Possibly she did look upon her victory over Moray as a first step towards the re-establishment of Catholicism in Scotland and upon her marriage to Darnley as a first step towards a Catholic reaction against Elizabeth in England. But if so, she also had misjudged the situation both abroad and at home. For the two great Catholic powers were still too suspicious of each other to act together and too afraid of each other to act separately. Philip II, with his Netherlands on the verge of open rebellion, would only promise a little money secretly through the Pope and that only if Mary did not claim Elizabeth's throne during the English Queen's lifetime. In addition, he warned her sternly not to let French forces into Scotland. The French, though they warned Elizabeth not to attack Mary, devoted their diplomacy towards reconciling the two Queens. Thus it became tolerably clear that neither of the great Catholic powers would intervene unless Elizabeth made open war upon Mary – and Elizabeth had no intention of letting Moray involve her as Condé had done.

Mary therefore was left to do the best she could with such support as she could rally inside her own realm. On those terms she could hardly hope to carry through a revolution. The Protestants, although for the most part they had refused to rise with Moray, were watching her with alert suspicion, ready to take alarm at the first whiff of a Popish plot. Without their support and loyalty, the ill assorted coalition of northern Gordons, Lennox Stewarts, and Bothwell's borderers was not likely to make the royal power very effective. Indeed, the tone of Mary's appeal to the Pope in January 1566[23] suggests that she herself despaired of mastering her realm without prompt and substantial foreign assistance. By then, too, she knew that her marriage was a grievous mistake. Darnley, who combined an excess of aristocratic arrogance with complete political ineptitude, had already made himself intolerable even to his wife.

Over the next twelve months their estrangement deepened into disaster. First, Darnley, denied the kingly power which he thought his due, conspired with a group of Protestants, allied to the Lennoxes by blood or marriage and headed by Morton and Ruthven. Together they carried out the murder of Mary's latest confidant, her Italian secretary Rizzio, and brought back Moray and the Chase About Raid exiles (March 1566). That done, Darnley promptly deserted his fellow-assassins and was outwardly reconciled to Mary. Until the birth of their son, the future James VI, on June 19th, 1566, the pretence of reconciliation was more or less preserved. Meanwhile, however, Mary had rallied around her all the leading nobles, united in common hatred of Darnley, and once she was safely out of childbed her estrangement from her husband became more bitter and more obvious than ever. By October Maitland (now again her Secretary) was writing to her ambassador in Paris that it was 'a heartbreak to her to think that he should be her husband and how to be free of him she sees no outgate'.[24] The words had a sinister ring, all the more as Mary was showing greater and greater favour to Bothwell, a fierce Border Earl only too inclined to use the sword or dagger on Gordian knots. Bothwell was also among the group of nobles who in November 1566 at Craigmillar agreed to 'free' their Queen from her husband. Thus, when on February 9th, 1567, Darnley was mysteriously murdered at Kirk o' Field, just outside Edinburgh, few people had much doubt who was his murderer. Mary, however continued to favour Bothwell, allowed him to attend the Privy Council meeting at which his own trial was arranged, allowed him to pack Edinburgh with his henchmen and make that trial a farce. Then, after his collusive divorce of his wife, she let him kidnap and marry her (May 1567). All this seemed to prove that, if Bothwell was the murderer of Darnley, Mary must have been his accomplice. The populace and the greater part of the nobility were outraged and when the Protestant Morton and the Catholic Atholl took up arms, they soon attracted a following that Mary and Bothwell's dispirited adherents were unable to withstand. At Carberry Hill on June 15th, 1567, the Queen was taken prisoner, while Bothwell escaped into exile. Refusing to renounce her marriage, Mary was compelled by the confederate lords to abdicate in favour of her year-old son James VI. Moray, who with a suspiciously well timed discretion had started off abroad on the eve of Darnley's murder, was recalled to take over the government as Regent.

It looked as if the Scottish crisis had worked itself out in the manner most advantageous to England. Mary Stuart, the Catholic rival for Elizabeth's crown, was discredited as well as dethroned. Scotland's government was in the hands of the faction which, because of its Protestantism, must almost of necessity seek a close alliance with England. Moreover, in the infant James VI, who would now be brought up in the Protestant faith, that faction had a candidate for the English succession far more acceptable than the Catholic and half-French Mary. He was also a candidate who for many years to come would be too young to tempt his supporters into hastening his succession by shortening Elizabeth's days. Another long step had been taken towards making Great Britain politically as well as geographically an island.

All this had happened without any overt interference by Elizabeth. She had kept in fairly continuous touch with Mary before Carberry Hill, urging her repeatedly to clear her honour by vigorous measures to discover and punish her husband's murderers. She had been kept pretty well informed of all that was going on. For example, Bedford and Randolph sent advance information from Berwick of the plot against Rizzio (Moray and his fellow-exiles were then at Newcastle) and later there was a steady flow of news about Mary's relations with Darnley, Bothwell, and the Protestant lords. But while the English government watched events closely and anxiously, there is little evidence that it did much to shape them. Events, indeed, moved too fast and too confusedly to be matched by any coherent policy. 'Scotland,' Cecil once complained, 'is a quagmire: nobody seems to stand still.'[25] Now, however, after Carberry Hill it seemed that all Elizabeth needed to do was to stand still herself and accept what had happened, so much to her advantage, in Scotland. That was what all her Councillors advised, what every reason of state and common sense urged upon her. It was what foreign ambassadors expected of her and what other foreign princes themselves were doing. Catherine de Medici made no bones about trying to preserve French influence in Scotland by offering to support Moray and by suggesting that Mary might be shut up in a French convent. Philip of Spain wrote off the Scottish Queen as too defamed and too irresponsible to be worth countenancing. Even the Pope decided to deal with her no more 'unless indeed in times to come she gives some proof of better life and religion'.[26]

Elizabeth was deaf to all such arguments. Remembering perhaps the accusations hurled against herself when she had wanted to marry one of her nobles who was widely suspected of wife-murder, she was less willing than most people to assume Mary guilty of her husband's death. True, she was deeply grieved that Mary should commit such disastrous follies in Scotland just when in England signs of support for her recognition as heir presumptive were beginning to appear, at least among the nobility. She believed also that in these Scottish tragedies 'some power existed in herself and that for the punishment of horrible and abominable facts one prince and neighbour might use compulsion with another'.[27] Hence her pressure on Mary to divorce Bothwell, to punish Darnley's murderers, and to accept conditions that would firmly and finally establish the Protestant settlement and the English alliance. But she would not allow that the Scots might imprison, let alone depose, their lawful Queen. Subjects must 'touch not the Lord's anointed'. So, after Carberry Hill, while the Edinburgh populace were mobbing Mary with shouts of 'burn the whore', Elizabeth sent Throckmorton to threaten Moray with her direst displeasure unless he released the Queen and restored her to a nominal sovereignty. She even instructed the reluctant Throckmorton to get in touch with the Hamiltons and other possible Marian supporters and it seemed that she was only deterred from armed intervention by Cecil and Throckmorton's warnings that such action would be instantly answered by Mary's execution. In the end she had to admit that there was little she could do, but she steadily refused to recognize James VI as King or Moray as Regent.

Elizabeth's behaviour in all this certainly was 'more creditable to her heart than to her understanding'.[28] In trying to shield the honour and dignity of a foolish, and probably guilty, Queen she jeopardized the peace of two nations. She also prepared for herself a dilemma from which she was not to escape with her own reputation untarnished. On May 2nd, 1568, Mary escaped from imprisonment and made a bid to regain her throne. She rallied some support, but not enough to match the Regent Moray's power. So, eleven days later, she was again defeated in battle at Langside and, no longer trusting her life in Scottish hands, she fled over the Border into England. Elizabeth's first impulse was to receive her at court as the lawful sovereign of Scotland. But Mary had arrived just when, as we shall see later, England's relations with Spain were beginning to deteriorate seriously and when France was sliding towards a new war of religion which might well put the Catholic Guise faction again into control there. Elizabeth was intelligent enough to realize that at such a time it would be folly to involve herself in a needless quarrel with the *de facto* government of Scotland. She must stop talking nonsense about restoring Mary by force. She could not even allow this Catholic pretender to her own throne to take refuge with Catholic powers abroad or to remain in full freedom among the largely Catholic population of northern England.

That left only two courses open to her. One was to accept Mary's guilt in the murder of Darnley and to proclaim it as justification for keeping her under restraint in England, while recognizing James VI as lawful King of Scotland. The other was to try, as in 1567, to negotiate with Moray and the Scots some compromise that would leave the government in their hands but restore Mary to nominal sovereignty. It was this second course that Elizabeth set out upon. She proposed that the two parties should send envoys to meet her own commissioners at York. There the Scots would justify their rebellion; Mary's envoys would answer them; and Elizabeth would then decide upon her own action, which (deliberately or otherwise) she led Mary to believe could only take the form of her restoration to the Scottish throne. The

Scots, however, were as determined as in 1567 not to have Mary back. They would not come to such a conference unless they were sure that the verdict would at least not go against them. And to show how strong their case was, they sent copies of their bill of charges against Mary and of the 'Casket Letters' written, so they alleged, by Mary to Bothwell at the time of Darnley's murder. This evidence, if genuine, was damning and it seems clear that Cecil now gave Moray the assurances required. He would hardly have dared to go so far without Elizabeth's knowledge.

When, therefore, at York in October 1568 Moray and the Scots produced their charges and the original Casket Letters, Mary's envoys found that it was their mistress who was being arraigned for murder rather than her subjects for rebellion. No wonder that she regarded herself as tricked or that her envoys refused to answer. Yet Moray and the Scots were not to be satisfied either. Their charges were heard at York and at a further conference at Westminster (November) which a number of English peers also attended on its final day. The Casket Letters were examined at considerable length, compared with letters of undoubted authenticity from Mary to Elizabeth, and apparently accepted as genuine by all who saw them – by Norfolk, Sussex, Arundel, and Northumberland as well as such Protestants as Cecil and Bacon. Nevertheless, the conferences ended without a verdict. In the evidence which the English Councillors and peers had seen and accepted, Elizabeth had her excuse for not restoring Mary, for keeping her more or less a prisoner in England, and for not taking any action against Moray and the new regime in Scotland. But that evidence was not published. Not until 1571 was it to be printed and then only semi-officially in Buchanan's *Detection*. So, except for those peers and Councillors who had been invited to the Westminster conference, Elizabeth's refusal to pronounce openly for either side cast over Mary's apparent guilt a veil of doubt. It was just enough to keep the Marian faction alive in Scotland, as a magnet for all the discontents that seethed in that quagmire of family feuds and religious rivalries. It was just enough to make Mary herself a magnet for all the inly-working discontents of the English north country.

Since the summer of 1567 Elizabeth, in Scottish affairs, had allowed sense to be overruled by sentiment, plain national and dynastic interest to be outweighed by high-faluting notions of the divinity that should hedge a Queen. As a result, the Scottish

problem, which seemed to have solved itself at Carberry Hill, was
to require yet another armed English intervention and, before that,
the conservatism of northern England was to flare out in open
rebellion.

Chapter 21

Defence and Trade, 1558-68

THE first ten years of Elizabeth's reign, despite a number of mistakes in policy, had brought a very substantial improvement in England's position in the world. At the same time this had been underpinned by appreciable progress towards settling the nation's religion, strengthening its defences, and stabilizing its economy, the foundations upon which its independence ultimately rested.

Despite the vocal discontent of the Puritans, something had been done to steer the nation's religious life into the middle way, where the new national Church could satisfy its inner need for a life of its own, without outraging the conservatism of a large part, perhaps still the larger part, of the population. The chief danger here was of stirring Catholic resentment, since the Catholics might then be goaded into active disloyalty and to looking abroad for help, whereas the Puritans, however dissatisfied, could look only to Elizabeth. So the Queen and her reluctant Archbishop Parker had frustrated or damped down Puritan efforts to dispense with clerical vestments and other outward symbols of continuity with the old ways and had taken no drastic measures to enforce Catholic conformity to the new order. The religious temperature had been deliberately kept low and this, though it had a debilitating effect upon the Church, at least quietened dissension in the state, allowed secular unity to grow and religious passions to die down.

In matters of defence, only limited progress had been made by 1568 in reorganizing the land forces.[1] Two Privy Council committees had looked into the northward and southward defences in 1558–9 and some strengthening of the fortifications of Berwick, Portsmouth, and the Isle of Wight had resulted. General musters of the county forces had been held on at least four occasions between 1559 and 1565 in an effort to enforce the obligations to make everyone show the arms and equipment required of them under Mary Tudor's 1558 statutes. Thanks mainly to Gresham's purchases in the Netherlands, there was also a considerably larger, though still inadequate, stock of firearms, armour, and

278

munitions. But little, if anything, had yet been done, it seems, towards training the men in their use or indeed towards training the men at all. This was due perhaps more to the reluctance of the counties to add to their burdens than to any apathy or fear of arming the people on the part of the central government. In 1560 Gresham had complained that 'we have men enough if they were armed and trained to the wars that now be raised.'[2] In 1568 there were still very few of them so trained and armed.

However, the land forces were only the second line of defence. The first line, now more than ever, was the navy. 'It is the flower of England's garland,' Throckmorton told Cecil, ' ... it is your best and best cheap defence and most redoubted of your enemies and doubtful friends.'[3] Well aware of this, Elizabeth's government had already done a good deal to make the navy once more an efficient force. They had not increased the number of the Queen's ships, which remained around two score as against the fifty-three left by Henry VIII in 1547. But five old and rotting vessels had been replaced and the rest made sound and seaworthy, as Winter had proved in January 1560. Despite Puritan qualms, an Act had also been passed through the 1563 Parliament to encourage the fisheries, that great nursery of seamen, by making Wednesday an additional fish day. All told, England's power at sea was again redoubtable enough to remind her enemies of the lessons of 1545.

That more had not been done to rearm and train the county levies or to increase the navy, was largely due to the government's lack of money. Economy was the order of the day. Expenditure was cut from the £267,000 of Mary's last half year to £109,000 in Elizabeth's first six months,[4] thanks largely to the ending of the war. But Mary had left debts of nearly £200,000, a third of them to the Antwerp bankers at fourteen per cent interest. Then Elizabeth's intervention in Scotland in 1560 cost her well over £178,000, her intervention in France in 1562–3 well over £170,000. Another £106,000 was paid out for the navy in the two years 1559–60 alone and £50,000 for the fortification of Berwick in the three years 1558–60. The large forces that still had to be kept on the Scottish Border after the treaty of Edinburgh cost £256,000 in the seven years from Michaelmas 1560 to Michaelmas 1567, and during those years Ireland was costing the English Exchequer from £20,000 to £26,000 a year.[5] Altogether, Elizabeth's inherited debts and extraordinary expenditures in the first ten years of her reign must have amounted to well over £1,000,000.

Now, Mary's improvements in financial administration had raised the crown's land revenues to nearly £70,000 in Elizabeth's first year. Her revised book of rates (May 1558) increased the yield of the customs to nearly £83,000 in that year,[6] though it was to fall sharply as a result of the 1563-4 quarrel with the Netherlands. Yet even when feudal dues, profits of justice, and clerical first fruits and tenths (now restored to the crown) were added, these 'ordinary' revenues left little margin over the ordinary costs of government. They could contribute little to such extraordinary expenditures as those of these first ten years. Parliament did add to them the grant of a subsidy and two fifteenths and tenths, say £195,000, in 1559; a slightly larger sum in 1563; and a smaller one in 1566. But grants of this sort, on the customary scale and assessment, could not entirely close the gap. It was closed partly by borrowing, partly by the sale of £260,000 worth of crown lands.[7] Such living on capital was not a happy solution, but these were no years in which to test the loyalty of the Queen's subjects by new and more stringent forms of taxation. To ask for the accustomed grants three times in eight years was quite as far as government dared to go, at least until the national economy was stabilized and trade moving forward again.

A first step in that direction was the recoinage of 1560, which gave the country once more a stable and honest currency – and the crown a useful profit of perhaps £45,000.[8] Measures were also taken to stimulate industrial development, by patents of monopoly and other means. These, like the measures designed to stabilize labour conditions and deal with vagrancy and unemployment (such as the statute of apprentices and the poor law of 1563) were matters of domestic policy. Some of them, nevertheless, could have an important bearing upon foreign policy by lessening England's dependence upon foreign countries for the means to defend herself and to maintain her economy. Thus an organized search for native supplies of saltpetre, and the encouragement of the home manufacture of gunpowder, might lessen dependence upon Antwerp for munitions.[9] The development, with the help of German capital and skill, of copper and calamine mining and the beginnings of a brass and copper industry meant the beginning of home manufacture not only of brass cannon but also of copper wire for wool cards for the cloth industry.[10] Patents for the home manufacture of salt might reduce dependence upon French supplies and those for the production of alum might, it was hoped, free Protestant English clothmakers from having to rely upon supplies from the Papal States. By 1568 even the more successful of these enterprises were only just taking root. For example, it was only in that year that the brass and copper syndicates, which included a number of Privy Councillors, showed their first returns upon an outlay of over £25,000. None the less, by encouraging capital into such undertakings, the government was helping the country to stand on its own feet militarily and industrially.

All these things contributed to foreign policy without being part of it. In the fostering of overseas trade, however, foreign policy had a direct concern. One of its objects was still the traditional one of seeking to confirm and strengthen the position of English merchants at Antwerp and in the Netherlands market. In the 1560s this became a matter of considerable importance.[11] Two circumstances were aggravating then the perennial jealousy of the Netherlands clothmakers against the English Merchant Adventurers. One was the sharp increase in English export dues upon unfinished cloth resulting from the 1558 revised book of rates, an increase that was naturally passed on to the Netherlands cloth-finishing industry. The other was that several thousands of Netherlands textile workers had already fled to England to escape the religious persecution in their own country. The Privy Council had settled them in Norwich, Colchester, Canterbury, and elsewhere on condition that they employed and taught their skills to English workmen. As a result, England was now manufacturing and exporting increasing quantities of those finer cloths of which the industry of Flanders, Artois, and Brabant had possessed a monopoly. The English 'new draperies' were beginning to compete for the Netherlands market with the native product. Then in 1562–3 a third grievance was added. On the outbreak of the first French War of Religion many English privateers had taken up the commissions to prey upon French Catholic trade which the Prince of Condé issued. In 1563 they were reinforced by more privateers operating under the general letters of marque which Elizabeth also issued during her quarrel with France. To the privateers, however, all foreigners were French, particularly if they were Catholic. So, as in fact the richest and most numerous foreigners in the Channel were Spaniards or Netherlanders, it was they who suffered most. Their losses eventually mounted, so they were to claim, to two million ducats. The privateers' methods, too, were rough and brutal and at least one Spanish crew was tied up in its ship's sails and thrown overboard to drown.[12] In Spanish ports there was fierce retaliation against visiting English sailors, although, as these were usually (at least for the time being) innocent traders, this only exacerbated Anglo-Spanish relations.

In the Netherlands the merchants' and cloth-finishers' complaints to the Governess, Margaret of Parma, received a ready hearing from her chief minister, Cardinal Granvelle. Granvelle did not share the timid anxiety of Philip II, and of the Duke of Alba's faction in Philip's Council, to avoid at almost any cost an open quarrel with England. An imperial statesman, son of Charles V's great minister and schooled in those more confident days, he would have curbed Elizabeth's growing independence and brought her realm back to the Roman faith by forcible means. The support given by English merchants to the opposition at Bruges and elsewhere against his scheme for reorganizing the Netherlands bishoprics and enforcing the placarts against heresy, convinced him that those merchants were among the principal spreaders of Protestant ideas in the Netherlands. Elizabeth's intervention in 1562 on behalf of the French Huguenots, the other great source of the contagion, convinced him that the English government was behind the nefarious activities of its traders, perhaps even organizing a Protestant league. He believed, too, that the English were so dependent upon their Netherlands trade that they could hardly survive without it and that by stopping that trade he might bring Elizabeth to her knees and her realm back to Catholicism. So in the autumn of 1563 he used an outbreak of plague in England as an excuse for temporarily banning the import of English cloth. Elizabeth at once retaliated by forbidding all imports from the Netherlands and forbidding exports except in English ships. Thereupon in December the Netherlands government answered by closing its ports not only to English cloth but also to English ships and by forbidding a wide range of exports to England.

In 1564 the growing opposition of the Netherlanders to

Granvelle's rule forced Philip to recall him and in November trade with England was reopened. Yet negotiations, which dragged on into 1567, produced no real settlement of the questions in dispute. For in fact the days of England's trade to Antwerp, indeed the days of Antwerp's greatness, were already numbered. As long ago as 1550, as we saw, the economic dangers of relying too exclusively upon Antwerp had become apparent. The 1563–4 dispute and embargoes had re-emphasized the political dangers. And now the mounting hostility of the Netherlands to Spanish rule began to plunge the country into an anarchy by no means encouraging to trade. By forcing the dismissal of Granvelle the Netherlands opposition had won a dramatic initial victory, but it had still failed to extort from Philip II any real change in the system of government or any moderation of the laws against heresy. The greater nobles, led by William of Orange and the Counts of Egmont and Horn, answered Philip's obstinacy by, in effect, going on strike. But this was an abdication of leadership. It brought a virtual breakdown of government and it allowed less moderate elements to come to the fore, among them the militant Calvinist minority. The resulting disorder reached its peak in the summer of 1566 with the wild image-breaking and desecration of Catholic churches that culminated in the sack of Antwerp cathedral. With the Netherlands, from Artois to Utrecht, in this condition, it was clearly time for England's merchants to seek less turbulent 'vents' for their traffic.

The government had already begun to encourage that movement, along the paths explored long ago by Henry VII and followed more recently by Northumberland. The first step was taken by the Merchant Adventurers. In 1564, while still excluded from the Netherlands, they made an agreement with Emden, just across the frontier in Germany. Emden, seeing itself as a future Antwerp, welcomed with open arms their summer fleet of some fifty ships. But the town had few natural advantages as a distributing centre; the government of the Netherlands put it out of bounds to their merchants; the Hansards, whom Elizabeth in 1563 had forbidden to carry English cloth to the Netherlands, boycotted it in retaliation; and the Italians also stayed away. So the venture was not a success. Individual Adventurers went as far afield as Cologne and Frankfort to find a sale and even then the Company was left with, it was said, 24,000 cloths on its hands until the reopening of Antwerp allowed them to be disposed of there. For the moment it looked as if Granvelle was right in thinking that England could not do without Antwerp.

One immediate result of this abortive attempt to break away was the granting of a new charter to the Merchant Adventurers in July 1564. This extended their field of trade to include Germany as well as the Netherlands. It gave them an improved organization, with fuller control over the admission of members, and it tightened their monopoly of trade within their widened field. Combined with the restrictions on the Hansards, it went some way towards implementing the proposals that Gresham had put forward in Northumberland's time. Thus reorganized and strengthened, the Adventurers were better equipped to try another move when the 1566 disturbances again made Antwerp unattractive. This time they were more successful. Despite the opposition of the other Hanse Towns, Hamburg in July 1567 granted them a charter with wide privileges to settle and to trade there for ten years. Only four ships of that summer's fleet went to Hamburg, but the trade was established. The agreement was a major breakthrough for the Merchant Adventurers, who handled by far the greatest part of what was by far England's greatest export trade. As a distributing centre, Hamburg was not equal to Antwerp at its zenith, but it was probably the best alternative in north-western Europe, a principal gateway for German and Baltic trade. There the Adventurers would find foreign buyers in satisfactory numbers and for the next ten years at least they could feel that their traffic was assured. English trade had broken out of its dependence upon Antwerp and English foreign policy was to feel the benefit in a greater freedom of manoeuvre.

Besides effecting a decisive breakaway from the Netherlands, the 1567 Hamburg agreement also established that break into the Hanseatic monopoly in Germany which the English had been seeking for a century. And not only north-western Germany, but also the Baltic,[13] where the growing power of the Danish and Swedish monarchies and the seizure of Narva (1558) by the Russians had shattered Hanse supremacy and let in rival German and Dutch shipping. Elizabeth had not accepted her persistent suitor Eric of Sweden's offers to make Viborg and Reval centres for English trade to the Eastlands and Russia. But even before the Hamburg agreement English ships had begun to join the other invading foreign traders and from 1560 England's trade with the Baltic lands was carried for the most part in English vessels. Some of these belonged to London Merchant Adventurers, but many were owned by merchants of East Anglian and north-eastern ports trading individually. This unregulated traffic fluctuated considerably during these early years and never approached in volume the Merchant Adventurers' main trade. Yet at least here were useful additional 'vents' for England's cloth, while the vital timber and naval stores, for which the Baltic area was the traditional source of supply, were now being brought back in English ships. At the same time that England was breaking loose from its economic dependence upon the Netherlands, it was also shaking off its dependence upon the Hanse.

Dependence upon the Hanse, and upon the Baltic area, was further lessened by the good progress of the Muscovy Company's trade, for timber and naval stores, besides furs and, if needful, corn, could now be imported from Russia in exchange for English cloth and other manufactures. Indeed, far greater things than these seemed to be within the Company's grasp when in 1562 Anthony Jenkinson successfully made his way down the Volga and across the Caspian Sea into Persia. Here might be something even better than the North-East Passage to Cathay, which had been the Company's original objective in 1553. The voyage around the North Cape to Archangel and the journey through Russia and across the Caspian to Persia, India, and the Middle East were admittedly long, arduous, and risky. Yet it seemed possible for this route to become a serious rival to the long Portuguese sea route around the Cape of Good Hope. If it did, the gains could be enormous. With hopes running so high, in 1566 the Muscovy Company's monopoly was confirmed and strengthened by Act of Parliament and in the following year the Tsar conferred upon it the exclusive right of trading into the northern parts of his dominions. Thus by 1568 this company, too, was well established and flourishing. The volume of its trade, some dozen or fifteen ships a year, was again small as compared with the main trade of the Merchant Adventurers. But it also provided a useful additional 'vent' for English exports, assured an alternative supply of timber and naval stores to that offered by the Baltic.[14]

These developments in Germany, the Baltic, and Russia, did not, of course, fully make up for the loss of the great Antwerp market. They obviously resulted in a great expansion of the field of trade, but certainly not in these years in any expansion of its total volume. The important thing, however, was that they did provide sufficient alternatives to render the closure of the Netherlands trade bearable. England's overseas commerce, in fact, had been successfully re-deployed within a very few years and in a manner that freed the country from its excessive economic dependence upon the Spanish Netherlands and the north German Hanse. It was, in the commercial sphere, an achievement comparable with the virtual solution of the Scottish question in the political field. For it, most of the credit no doubt must go to England's, and especially London's, merchants. Nevertheless, those merchants owed much to the help and encouragement of their government, and the government reaped its reward in a considerably greater freedom of action for its foreign policy.

It was just in time, for only a month after the Merchant Adventurers' agreement with Hamburg, the Duke of Alba's arrival in the Netherlands opened a new era in Tudor foreign policy. But before we turn to that, there is one other side of England's maritime development in these years that we must notice. This is the southward and westward enterprises which, because of the results they were to produce in the next centuries, have bulked larger in the history books than in themselves they deserve. For they involved as yet only a tiny fraction of England's shipping and capital and contributed only a very small amount to the volume of England's trade, though they did a little contribute to the worsening of relations with Spain. We have already seen how the establishment of trade to Morocco and the voyages to Guinea, begun under Northumberland, had evoked strong protests from Portugal which Philip of Spain had supported. Under Elizabeth those West African voyages continued, with government support. When the Portuguese again protested, Elizabeth answered that the mere fact of being the first discoverers of those lands gave them no right to exclude others from trading or settling there. Only where the Portuguese were in effective occupation would she recognize their sovereignty.[15]

Long ago Henry VII had enunciated the same doctrine, but now there were Englishmen ready to act upon it and to carry it across the Atlantic to the West Indies and Spanish America, in many parts of which the Spaniards were no more thick on the ground than the Portuguese in West Africa. Not only Englishmen but Frenchmen too, and Huguenots at that, were of this mind. Already the Huguenots were planting a colony in Florida, dangerously adjacent to the homeward route of the silver fleet, while others were privateering in the Caribbean. Philip II, lacking a war navy of ocean-going sailing ships – his strong Mediterranean naval forces were composed of oared galleys useless for ocean work – found these intruders very difficult to deal with and it was here that an Englishman, John Hawkins,[16] saw his opportunity. He came of a Plymouth family long engaged in the Spanish and southwards trades. He now proposed to develop a triangular traffic, to West Africa to buy or capture Negro slaves; on to the West Indies and America to sell them to the Spanish colonists who were suffering from an acute labour shortage; and back to England with American goods bought out of the proceeds. In this he had the full support of Elizabeth, who invested one of her ships in the undertaking and sent Hawkins out with her commission. There was, of course, one obstacle. Spain claimed a monopoly of all American trade, as Portugal did of all West African. The Spanish government was indeed engaged in tightening this monopoly. Hawkins, however, seems to have thought that he could get round this difficulty. First he would demonstrate his ability to supply the Negro slaves the Spanish colonies needed. Then, he apparently hoped, the Spanish government might grant him an *asiento* or contract to supply the slaves in return for his help with his ships both against the Turks in the Mediterranean and against the French and other intruders in the Caribbean. After all, Portuguese syndicates had been granted such *asientos*, so why not Spain's old allies, the English?

Between 1562 and 1568 Hawkins put these ideas into practice by making three voyages himself and sending out a fourth. As he expected, the Spanish colonists welcomed his slave cargoes and readily traded with him. The local officials were also at first ready enough to forget their duty if he would land a few men and a gun or two, to give them the excuse of bowing to irresistible force. But the Spanish government showed no signs of welcoming his intrusion, without a by your leave, into this forbidden field and each successive voyage provoked more peremptory orders to the local officials against trading with him. His shows of force had gradually to come nearer to real compulsion and Philip II was clearly indisposed to engage this new poacher as his gamekeeper. On the contrary, in 1565 he scraped together a few ships and wiped out the Huguenot settlement in Florida. Two years later he began to arm twelve galleons, the Indian Guard, to protect the silver fleets.

In spite of all this, Hawkins, with the continued support of the Queen, persisted. In 1568 he was again in the Caribbean with two of the Queen's more elderly warships, the *Jesus* and the *Minion*, and four other vessels. There were the usual difficulties, usually overcome by the usual brief display of force, and on the whole business was still good. But before facing the homeward journey across the Atlantic, the ships, especially the old and leaky *Jesus*, needed attention and on September 16th, 1568, he put into San Juan de Ullua, on the coast of Mexico, to refit. Two days later, when most of his ships were in no condition to fight or flee, a Spanish squadron of thirteen vessels, carrying the new Viceroy of Mexico, appeared. Hawkins could have closed the port against them but, holding the Queen's commission, was not prepared to risk so open an act of war against the King of Spain's representative. So an agreement was made and the Spanish ships admitted. Soon afterwards the Spaniards broke faith, fell upon the English, and opened fire upon their helpless ships. Hawkins himself got away in the *Minion* and one of his young lieutenants, Francis Drake, in the little *Judith*. But the *Jesus*, three other vessels, a good part of the proceeds of the voyage, and a large number of men were lost.

These voyages of Hawkins and the treacherous attack that ended them, coming on top of English privateering and piracy in home waters and Spanish reprisals against English sailors in Spanish ports, certainly did nothing to sweeten Anglo-Spanish relations. Also, as it happened, the San Juan de Ullua incident coincided in time with the outbreak of a sharp quarrel between the English and Spanish governments at the close of 1568. Many have therefore regarded that incident as a major cause of this quarrel and so have seen the Elizabethan conflict with Spain as in origin largely oceanic and colonial. It is doubtful, however, whether much was known in England by the close of 1568 about what had happened at San Juan de Ullua. Drake in the *Judith* only reached Plymouth on January 20th, 1569, Hawkins in the *Minion* on January 25th, though uncertain rumours from Spain had preceded them. Certainly neither government was in fact greatly influenced in its attitude by what Hawkins had done or by what had been done to him. Both Elizabeth and Philip were more or less resigned to the doctrine of 'no peace beyond the line' and, wherever that line might be, the Caribbean was generally accepted as being beyond it.[17] Nor were either country's vital interests as yet involved in this rather small scale Caribbean clash.

The real reason for the Anglo-Spanish quarrel was in fact European and continental, not oceanic and colonial. It arose over the Netherlands, not over the West Indies. It had its origins, not in Hawkins's disaster in Mexico in September 1568, but in the Duke of Alba's arrival, with the main army of Spain, at Brussels in August 1567.

Chapter 22

The First Quarrel with Spain

THE Duke of Alba's arrival in Brussels in August 1567 was one of the turning points of western European history. For a century to come, the anxiety of Spain to secure the communications with its army in the Netherlands, and the anxiety of Spain's enemies to cut those communications, were to be constant and dominant features in international relations. The immediate effects upon English foreign policy were no less marked. Hitherto, for centuries, France had been the national enemy. It is true that English relations with the French government of Catherine de Medici had somewhat improved since 1564. It is also true that since Elizabeth's accession Anglo-Spanish relations had been ruffled by her independent policies, by growing religious differences, by difficulties over Netherlands trade, and by bickerings at sea. Yet before August 1567 in the minds of English statesmen the greatest potential danger still threatened from France. What they most feared was still the suspected designs of the Guise faction to use Mary Stuart and Scotland as stepping-stones to the conquest of Elizabeth's throne. These fears, and England's commercial dependence upon Antwerp, had made them careful, if not to secure Spain's alliance, at least to avoid her hostility.

Alba's arrival in the Low Countries changed all that. Within five years it brought about a diplomatic revolution that allied England with France against Spain and made Spain rather than France appear to most Englishmen as the prime national enemy. This was not due to any aggressive intentions towards England on Philip II's part: indeed, rather the contrary. There was, admittedly, among his Councillors an aggressive group, headed by Ruy Gomez, Prince of Eboli, and by Cardinal Espinosa.[1] This group would have appeased the Netherlands by yielding a large measure of the home rule that those provinces desired. They would then have concentrated more actively upon bringing England back into the Roman and Habsburg fold. All the Spanish

290

ambassadors to Elizabeth, with the doubtful exception of de Silva, either shared these views or came to share them as they watched the Elizabethan settlement take root and as they listened to the growing despair of the English Catholics. In England, they also believed, lay the roots of the Netherlands' heresy and discontent, which would wither away if hope of English support were cut off. 'England once disposed of,' de Quadra had written to Granvelle in 1561, 'His Majesty can restore order elsewhere at his leisure.'[2] Granvelle, as we have seen, needed no telling.

However, there was also among Philip's Councillors another group, headed by Spain's foremost soldier, the Duke of Alba himself. These men held that the most urgent task of the monarchy was to establish its own authority and the Catholic faith effectively in all the King's dominions. In the Netherlands, as elsewhere, local liberties must be curbed or destroyed, heresy stamped out, and the provinces subordinated, by force if necessary, to direction from Madrid. Philip perhaps inclined to these views anyway. But it was probably his pious horror at the excesses of the Netherlands Calvinists in 1566 – and unusually good returns from the American silver mines – that decided him in 1567 to adopt Alba's policy so wholeheartedly and to send Alba himself to execute it. The decision was thus one of domestic policy, not of foreign policy, and it was far from being designed as an immediate threat to Elizabeth. Philip was in fact as mindful as ever of Charles V's warnings about the vital importance of not losing English friendship. His jealousy of France, his fear that Mary Stuart's claims might be used to make Great Britain French, still reinforced his father's counsels. Now, with this great effort in the Netherlands on his hands and a major conflict with the Turks impending in the Mediterranean, he could less than ever afford to add a quarrel with England to his burdens. Alba, too, became more than ever convinced by experience in the Netherlands that Spain must at all costs avoid an open conflict with England.

Yet to Elizabeth and her Councillors Spanish policy could hardly appear quite so innocuous. At a time when the new link with Hamburg had been forged but not yet tested, the Netherlands were still the main market for England's trade and Alba's military rule could well prove disastrous to their economy. Even more disturbing was the strategic menace. Alba brought with him some 10,000 Spanish infantry. These were speedily reinforced by German, Italian, and Walloon levies to 25,000 men and eventually to over 50,000. With such forces he might soon turn the hitherto harmless Netherlands into the garrison area of the main army of Spain. For it was the main field army of Spain that Alba brought with him and its arrival meant a significant shift in the centre of gravity of Spanish military power. Elsewhere, in Italy, North Africa, Spain itself, there were bodies of garrison troops. Here in the Netherlands was now the real striking force of Spain by land. It was lodged 'in the very counterscarp of England' – the words are Cecil's[3] – just across the Narrow Seas from Dover and little more than a hundred sea miles from London. If Alba were allowed to master the Low Countries, with all their wealth and shipping, he would be in a position to accomplish what Granvelle had lacked power to attempt. A great Catholic Spanish army in full control of the Netherlands was at least as alarming to England as a great Catholic French army in full control of Scotland.

Nor could it be safely assumed that Alba's ultimate purpose was less hostile than Granvelle's had been. After all, before Alba left Italy he and Philip knew that law and order had already been restored in the Netherlands. The image-breaking and social disorders had provoked such a reaction that by the spring of 1567 great nobles, lesser nobles, and burghers had rallied to the government and crushed the last armed Calvinist resistance.[4] Shocked by the religious and social anarchy of 1566, they were in no mood to argue longer with their Spanish overlord. In 1559–61 Egmont and Horn had been in the forefront of the fuss over a few thousand Spanish troops left in the Low Countries after the peace of Câteau-Cambrésis. Now they were utterly deaf to William of Orange's warnings against the danger of letting Alba's great army come in unopposed. All this made it hard for nervous neighbours to believe that Philip was really sending Alba with so large a whip merely to flog so dead a horse.

Nevertheless, although Alba arrived in Brussels in August 1567, it was not until December 1568 that Elizabeth took any action. This does not necessarily mean that she was not at all alarmed.[5] But she, and Cecil, had learned caution in helping Protestant rebels in foreign lands, even when those rebels had considerable backing from the native nobility and populace. When it came to a clash of arms, the Scots had shown in 1559–60 how feeble such movements could be, the French Huguenots in 1563 how un-trustworthy. And what little was left of the Netherlands opposition by August 1567 had the backing of neither the Netherlands nobility – apart from the exiled William of Orange and his family – nor of the great mass of the Netherlands people. What open resistance there was, was mostly Calvinist, and Elizabeth at this moment felt more than usually ill disposed towards Calvinists. She was angry with the Scottish Protestant lords who had played so leading a part in forcing their lawful Queen to abdicate. She was no less angry with her own Puritan subjects. They had been in the vanguard of the parliamentary agitation in 1566 for her marriage and the settlement of the succession. They had carried that agitation to the point of holding up the grant of badly needed taxes for eleven weeks, until they had extracted from her a promise that 'I will marry as soon as I can conveniently, if God take not him away with whom I mind to marry.'[6] No doubt largely in anticipation of such pressure, and to lend verisimilitude to such an answer, she had already reopened negotiations with the Arch-duke Charles.[7] And while the Puritans were so prominent in badgering her to marry and settle the succession, they were also stubbornly resisting Archbishop Parker's injunctions (1566) about the wearing of surplices and matters of that sort. These things did not dispose her to sympathy with the defeated Calvinist minority in the Netherlands and she spoke repeatedly to de Silva in praising terms of Alba's mission.

Yet what Elizabeth said to Spanish ambassadors was not always evidence of her real views and here it does look as if the lady did protest too much. For there was another consideration that she must have taken into account. The arrival in the Netherlands of Alba and the army of Spain was at least as disturbing to the French government as it was to the English. If the Netherlands coast was little more than a score of miles from Kent or a hundred from London, the Netherlands frontier was little more than eighty miles from Paris and in those eighty miles there were few serious natural obstacles to hold up an invading army once it was across the Somme. Alba's arrival with his army in Brussels, therefore, was likely so to heighten French jealousy of Spain that, combined with the efforts of William of Orange to arouse the Netherlands, it would make English intervention superfluous. England's security and independence during the sixteenth century always benefited when rivalry between Habsburg and Valois sharpened, and now that rivalry looked likely to sharpen markedly.

Here, however, religion once again came in to play its baleful part. While Alba was marching from Genoa to Brussels, all along France's eastern frontier, the French government in alarm raised a force of Swiss and other troops to shadow him. The Huguenots thereupon took fright, seeing in these levies the first fruits of the great Catholic conspiracy hatched, as they persuaded themselves, by Alba and the Queen Mother at Bayonne in 1565. They rushed to arms in September 1567, plunging France into a second War of Religion and, after a brief armed truce between March and September 1568, into a third which was to go on until August 1570. So from September 1567 it was doubtful whether France could do much to hinder Alba; by September 1568 it was certain that she could do nothing.

This collapse of France nullified William of Orange's hopes of relighting the Netherlands revolt in 1568. The Netherlanders themselves, held down by Alba's army, could do little without outside help, but William did manage to hire a considerable army in Germany, increased a little by Protestant adventurers from England, Scotland, and France. It was as a volunteer with this army that Black John Norris, one of the warrior sons of Elizabeth's old friend Lady Norris, began the career that was to make him outstanding among Elizabethan soldiers. Nevertheless, William of Orange's hope of breaking Alba's grip depended largely upon the appearance of a threat from France that would seriously distract the Spanish forces. The uneasy armed truce in France, and the mounting power of Catholic influence there, ruled this out. The Huguenots could spare only a few volunteers under de Cocqueville to threaten Alba's rear, and the French government, not daring to add a quarrel with Spain to its troubles, had de Cocqueville rounded up before he even reached the frontier. All therefore depended upon the ability of William's levies to defeat Alba's veterans. His younger brother, Louis of Nassau, in a diversionary attack into Groningen, did begin by defeating a Spanish force at Heiligerlee in May 1568, only to be routed in turn by Alba at Jemmigen in July. So, when William with the main army invaded eastern Brabant, he was soon faced by Alba's concentrated strength. Alba, avoiding a needless battle, shepherded him up and down the Maas until his money ran out and his unpaid troops deserted. Inside the Netherlands hardly a man had dared or cared to lift a finger to help such unpromising liberators and by November William was back in Germany discredited and with his army gone.

In all this Elizabeth, busied with Scottish problems, had taken little or no part. Remembering 1562-3 she had not allowed Condé to draw her again into French religious quarrels, though Leicester and with him some of her more old-fashioned Councillors had again found the bait of Calais alluring. Also, although William of Orange had sent messengers to her, he had not asked for her help nor had she made any motion towards offering it. Yet there were signs that she was not wholly uninterested. Perhaps the first came as early as October 1567 when, after protesting for a year to the Spanish ambassador that she would allow no more expeditions to Spanish-held America, she allowed Hawkins to sail with her commission and two of her ships on his third, ill fated, voyage to Africa and the West Indies. It could have been intended as a veiled warning to Philip, though it could easily be disavowed if need be. In November 1567 there was another hint, when the marriage negotiations with the Archduke Charles petered out over his very moderate demand for the right to hear Mass secretly if he became Elizabeth's husband.

Then, in the summer of 1568 there was a sharp quarrel over Philip's curt expulsion of the English ambassador-resident in Spain, Dr John Man. Man, who had been appointed to Madrid in January 1566, was a rather odd choice anyway. In 1540 he had lost his fellowship at New College, Oxford, on suspicion of heresy, in 1562 he had become Warden of Merton College, and in 1566 Dean of Gloucester. Diplomacy was hardly his *métier*. It was not tactful at a Madrid dinner party to call the Pope 'a canting little monk'[8] and the theological fury and virulent personal abuse acceptable in academic controversy came ill from an ambassador. In the spring of 1568 Philip retaliated by forbidding him to use the Anglican service privately in his house. Then, after protesting to Elizabeth at Man's recalcitrance, he expelled him from his court without waiting for her reply. What gave this brusque action a sinister look was that at almost the same time Philip replaced de Silva by a new resident ambassador to England, Guerau de Spes. De Silva was the one Spanish ambassador whom Elizabeth ever came to regard as a true friend of Anglo-Spanish amity. De Spes, so she heard from several sources, had been much in company of late with the arrogant Count of Feria and the English Catholic exiles who gathered round him and his English wife. It certainly looked a change for the worse.

In fact, English suspicion of Philip was not entirely fair. Man's own tactlessness was an adequate explanation of his expulsion. De Silva had long been begging for his own recall – four years was about as long a residence as most sixteenth-century ambassadors' purses would bear. There was nothing in de Spes's instructions, so far as we know them,[9] to suggest that he was meant to be the agent of a new and more hostile policy towards Elizabeth. But, unfortunately, when de Spes arrived in September 1568, he soon began to show marked signs of wishing to act in a manner quite different from that of de Silva. So he strengthened English suspicions just at the moment when the new civil war in France and the collapse of William of Orange's campaign seemed to remove the last obstacles to Alba's rapid and total success in the Netherlands. And even if Spanish intentions towards England were inoffensive now, would they remain inoffensive once Alba was complete master of the Low Countries?

Just when that question was becoming urgent, Elizabeth was presented with an unexpected opportunity for action. In mid-November the Channel weather and the Channel privateers scared four small Spanish ships into taking shelter in Plymouth and a fifth in Southampton. Aboard them was £85,000 lent by the bankers of Genoa to Philip II and on its way to Antwerp to pay Alba's army.[10] Once in those English ports with such a cargo, the Spaniards dared not sail again, for the privateers gathered round them like wasps round a honey pot. Yet Alba badly needed the money. He had expected to get all he needed from the Netherlands and to send a 'river of silver' back to Spain into the bargain. Instead, the cost of his army, now getting on towards 50,000 men, and the expenses of the campaign against William of Orange had far outrun the income that he had managed to wring from the provinces. His troops' pay was many months in arrears and without money the great military force upon which his power depended might soon and suddenly break in his hand. De Spes therefore begged Elizabeth to provide an armed escort for the loan. At first she agreed, but then it was most conveniently discovered that legally the money remained the property of the

Genoese bankers until it was delivered in Antwerp. Now Elizabeth, too, was short of money. The difficulties of trade with the Netherlands had sharply reduced her customs revenue.[11] She had waived a third of the grant proposed in 1566 in a vain effort to divert the Commons from the subject of her marriage. Also, Alba's rule had so dislocated the Antwerp money market that no loan could be raised there. The Genoese, however, were willing to transfer their loan to her and on December 28th, 1568, she told de Spes (as he had begun to suspect a week or more earlier) that she had decided to borrow the money herself.[12]

Whatever legal excuses Elizabeth could put forward, she could hardly have expected Alba to regard this as a friendly action. Indeed, one of her unavowed motives in it was almost certainly to make his position more difficult. Yet neither the Queen nor Cecil, who was probably its real initiator, seem to have expected quite so violent a Spanish reaction. For that de Spes was in part responsible. He had already on December 21st written to Alba[13] urging the seizure of all English ships and goods in the Netherlands and Spain, as well as more direct measures to support Mary Stuart and the English Catholics and to overthrow Cecil and the 1559 religious settlement. Alba, in the first flush of anger, adopted the first part of this advice. On December 29th he seized all English ships and goods in his ports and embargoed all trade with England. Elizabeth promptly retaliated with similar measures against Netherlands shipping and property. The seizures and counter-seizures soon spread to Spain itself and Anglo-Spanish, as well as Anglo-Netherlands, trade came to a sudden standstill.

This sharp Anglo-Spanish quarrel quickly provoked no less sharp a clash within the English Council, a clash whose outcome was to be decisive for the future of English foreign policy. For some time dissatisfaction with Elizabeth's government had been mounting on many sides in spite of, and in part because of, the overall success of these first ten years. What was especially resented and criticized was the Queen's repeated failure to honour her promises to marry and settle the succession. Over this Council and Parliament, peers and Commons, Puritans and Catholics, were united in feeling that she was neglecting her plain duty. She was, they felt, selfishly and wantonly letting the morrow take care of itself because she would not, as would they and their children, be there to see and suffer what it might bring forth.

Elizabeth was now thirty-five. If she was to marry and have children, the time was growing short. Yet the revived negotiations with the Archduke Charles, on almost all counts her most eligible suitor, had dragged along since 1564 with little appearance of urgency. Late in 1567 they came to a halt over obstacles that few of her Councillors regarded as insuperable.[14]

To increase her subjects' anxiety and exasperation, the choice of her successor then became more obscure than ever. In January 1568 Lady Catherine Grey died and, although she left two small sons, those two bastardized infants could hardly be even the figureheads of a faction. Meanwhile the disasters that befell Mary Stuart, and the crimes charged against her, made her less than ever acceptable to one large section of Englishmen and clouded her attraction for the rest. Yet Elizabeth, by listening to those charges and then refusing to pronounce a verdict, had cloaked Mary's ill fame in just that haze of doubt which was needed to keep her cause from foundering utterly. She had also deprived herself of a valid excuse for keeping Mary prisoner. So she now faced the problem of either getting her back to Scotland with security for her life but with no power, or else finding some means other than close imprisonment of rendering her harmless in England. As Moray, despite continual pressure, would not hear of having her back in Scotland, only the second alternative was really open and already at the York conference some English and Scots had toyed with Maitland's idea of marrying her to the Duke of Norfolk. Unable to champion Mary and unwilling to condemn her, Elizabeth by her shifts and subterfuges had already exasperated her loyal Puritan Councillor Sir Francis Knollys into exclaiming that it was time to end this feeble female government and for the Queen to let the men of her Council take over the management of affairs.[15] Now she was driving England's only Duke, and others besides him, to dabble in conspiracy to ward off the perils that they saw impending.

The seizure of the Genoese loan and the resulting quarrel with Spain brought these discontents to a head. Everyone, it seems, felt that the day of reckoning between Elizabethan England and the great Catholic powers was at hand. Cecil, in a memorial written early in 1569,[16] anticipated the early triumph of Alba in the Netherlands and of the Catholics in France. Then there would follow that French or Spanish or joint Franco-Spanish action to restore Papal authority in England which only the repeated domestic misfortunes of the Catholic monarchies had delayed so long. Like most of those who had served their apprenticeship in the dark days of Edward VI and Mary Tudor, Cecil had as yet little faith in England's ability to withstand this onslaught. 'The realm', he believed, 'is become so feeble by long peace as it were a fearful thing to imagine, if the enemies were at hand, of what force the resistance would be.' The only remedy, as he saw it, was to keep those enemies at arm's length by every means short of actual war. Therefore he wanted a defensive alliance with the Protestant rulers of Denmark, Sweden, Germany, and Scotland. He wanted also to do everything possible, short of openly dispatching English troops, to aid and encourage the French and Netherlands rebels who still stood in arms between England and her Catholic foes.

Almost all his colleagues agreed with Cecil's diagnosis, but only a few were prepared to swallow his remedy. They justly doubted whether the sluggish mass of German and Scandinavian Lutheranism could be sufficiently moved. The French and Netherlands Calvinists were rebels of no great strength. No, it was not that way that safety lay, but in the prompt reversal of Cecil's policy. Let good relations be restored promptly with England's old and natural ally, Spain. Let Mary Stuart be married to the Duke of Norfolk or some other loyal Englishman so as to render her harmless during Elizabeth's lifetime yet keep her available as successor if Elizabeth should die childless. So thought Norfolk and Arundel, Pembroke and Sussex, and many others, even Leicester whose favour with Elizabeth they hoped to exploit. For the most part their meaning was loyal enough. They wanted, not to overthrow Elizabeth, but to save her from Cecil and from herself.

But to reverse Cecil's policy meant first overthrowing Cecil and Elizabeth was not likely to part easily with her most trusted minister. No one could doubt that, especially after the way she rounded upon Leicester when on February 22nd, 1569, as spokesman for the opposition, he urged her to call Cecil to account for the general discontent and for endangering the realm.[17] She would be even less easily persuaded to agree to Norfolk marrying Mary Stuart, her leading nobleman marrying the claimant to her throne. Cecil's opponents thus knew that their views would be unpalatable to Elizabeth. They could hardly hope to impose them unless Cecil's policy turned out badly enough to compel her to discard both it and him. It was only a short step from hoping for such an outcome to helping it to come about. But that short step would take them across the narrow line dividing opposition from treason and not all of them were able to walk so daintily. Norfolk in particular, related to Catholics though not one himself, was susceptible to the pressure of those who, like Arundel, Lord Montague, and the northern Earls of Northumberland and Westmorland, hoped to use the agitation to restore the old religion and put Mary Stuart at once upon Elizabeth's throne. It was these men who, through an Italian banker Ridolfi, got in touch with the half-imprisoned de Spes and begged him for Spanish support.[18] If Alba could not spare troops, at least let him seize the English cloth fleet that would sail in the spring for Hamburg. That, de Spes believed, would of itself cause a revolution and if the French would also close their ports to English trade the revolution would be swift and easy.[19]

Matters did not in fact turn out as badly as either Cecil or his opponents feared. They all paid too little heed to something that Henry VIII had never quite forgotten even in the perilous days of 1538–40 and that Elizabeth, too, never quite forgot – the persisting secular jealousy between the two great Catholic powers. In April the French government did send the Cardinal of Guise to discuss joint economic action with the King of Spain. Philip, knowing that the English Catholics looked only to him and wanted no truck with France, rebuffed the French attempt to nose into his preserves. They should, he coldly told the Cardinal, settle their own domestic troubles before meddling in other people's. At that very moment Fénélon was urging Catherine de Medici to warn Alba that, while she was willing for him to do his utmost to recover his losses, she could not allow him to make any invasion or enterprise within the English realm.[20]

Moreover, while joint Franco-Spanish action was very much more remote than Cecil and his colleagues feared, so too was separate action by Spain. Besides his jealousy of France, Philip was distracted by the great Morisco revolt in Granada, which broke out in December 1568 and was not to be finally crushed until the autumn of 1570. With the Turkish fleets and the Barbary corsairs gathering again to threaten Spain's hold on the western Mediterranean, the revolt could not be regarded lightly and it made Philip the less inclined to get involved against Elizabeth. In February 1569 he did tell de Spes that he might consent to her deposition if a real opportunity offered. But he left it to Alba to decide whether there was an opportunity and what, if anything, could be done about it.[21] Alba himself was growing daily more certain that nothing could be done. For Elizabeth's seizure of the Genoese loan was having its effect. In March 1569 the Duke, to find pay for his army, resolved to impose on the Netherlands a one per cent capital levy and also a five per cent tax on land sales and a ten per cent tax on all other sales, the 'twentieth penny' and the 'tenth penny'. These taxes would be oppressive enough in themselves to the provinces' commercial life. But the tenth penny and twentieth penny were especially resented because, unlike the usual single sum grants of the estates, they were to be perpetual taxes which would provide the government with a revenue independent of the estates' control. So great, indeed, was the outcry, even among Alba's own Councillors, that the Duke agreed to postpone the new taxes in return for substantial grants of the traditional type. All this made him less than ever disposed to add a conflict with England to his problems and on May 15th Philip, after consulting his Council, endorsed Alba's view. 'It was undesirable to embark upon a war with the Queen, as however great the damage we may do her, she will not by this means restore what she has taken.' She must therefore be treated gently, though her fear of a declaration of war should not be entirely removed.[22]

Most of these jealousies and doubts were, of course, hidden from English eyes. Nevertheless, as 1569 wore on, the course of events did much to strengthen Elizabeth's confidence. The closing of the French ports in January, and the defeat and death of Condé at Jarnac in March, did cause her to disavow the very substantial aid that her subjects were unofficially giving to the Huguenots.[23] It also caused her to revoke the subsidies which she had sent Henry Killigrew to promise to the Calvinist Elector Palatine if he would organize a German Protestant army to help the Huguenots. But the Huguenots, under their new leader Admiral Coligny, soon recovered from Jarnac and Elizabeth's alarm passed. Meanwhile towards Spain she was unflinching. When Alba sent d'Assonleville in February to negotiate about the seizures, she and Cecil took this as a sign of weakening and refused to discuss the matter with anyone except a fully accredited envoy from Philip himself. That would show the English Catholics how little they could hope for from the King of Spain! Also, to increase Alba's nervous concern for his communications with Spain, she spoke of her determination to enforce her claim to dominion over the Narrow Seas. Moreover, in the matter of seizures, Elizabeth was very clearly having the best of the business. The Spanish and Netherlands ships and goods seized by the English were worth far more than the English ships and goods seized in Spain and the Netherlands. At the same time, English privateers, co-operating with Huguenots and Netherlanders under Condé's and Orange's commissions, practically closed the Channel and Narrow Seas to Spanish shipping. Then in May the Merchant Adventurers' half-yearly cloth fleet, under escort of the Queen's navy, reached Hamburg unmolested and Hamburg, unlike Emden in 1564, proved able to take all they could sell and at good prices. England's commerce could at last manage without Spanish Antwerp.[24]

The course of events, far from forcing Elizabeth to discard Cecil, was thus confirming her confidence in his judgment. The hope of reversing his policy towards Spain was dwindling daily. Yet something might still be done for the project of marrying Mary to Norfolk and settling the succession. This design had taken hold of Norfolk's imagination, much as the witches' pro-phecies take hold of Shakespeare's Macbeth.[25] England's first peer now, he saw himself as destined to be King-consort of Scotland soon and King of Great Britain hereafter. Leicester still urged him on, hoping as his own reward to win at last the consent of his peers to his own marriage with Elizabeth. Pembroke and Arundel and Sussex were still his allies and Moray in Scotland had agreed to the match in the belief that it chimed with Eliza-beth's purposes. Then in May 1569 Elizabeth's anxiety to rid her-self of her embarrassing guest took shape in a demand to Moray that he would take Mary back as Queen of Scotland upon con-ditions that would render her harmless for the future.[26] Here perhaps was an opportunity for Norfolk to realize his ambition without overleaping the line that divided intrigue from treason. For how better render Mary's restoration harmless than by marry-ing her off to a loyal English nobleman? Had not Elizabeth herself suggested it in 1565 and even once named Norfolk, along with Leicester, as a suitable husband for Mary?

The opportunity was the more welcome because at this moment Norfolk's relations with the leaders of the more treasonable wing of the opposition were far from good. In May 1569 his six-year-old stepson and ward Lord Dacre was accidentally killed when vaulting over a rickety wooden horse. Norfolk at once claimed the extensive Dacre lands in Cumberland, Westmorland, and York-shire for the boy's three sisters, who were also his wards and whom he planned to marry to his own sons. His claim was contested by the girls' uncle Leonard Dacre, one of the leading northern Catho-lics. In the impending lawsuit between them, Cecil as Master of the Court of Wards must play a considerable part. It is hard to believe that either Cecil or Norfolk was blind to this considera-tion.[27] Norfolk needed at least to disarm the hostility of the Master of the Court of Wards. Cecil could not fail to see in this a chance to win the Duke back to loyal courses or to discredit him and his faction in Elizabeth's eyes – and in any event a chance to worm out his secrets. So at the end of May the two patched up their quarrel. Cecil made some vague promises about listening to Norfolk's views on Anglo-Spanish relations and judgment on the Dacre inheritance went in Norfolk's favour (though upon the evidence before the commissioners the verdict seems to have been a fair one). The Duke let Cecil into the secret of his proposed marriage to Mary and Cecil, who knew a good deal of that secret already, urged him to inform Elizabeth as early as possible and to act only with her consent.

Leicester, however, whose real purposes now became increas-ingly ambiguous, persuaded Norfolk to wait for Moray to open the subject when he answered Elizabeth's demand for Mary's return to Scotland. Meanwhile, to prepare the ground, a number of peers and Councillors, perhaps including Cecil,* at the begin-ning of June sent to ask Mary whether she would refer her cause wholly to Elizabeth; satisfy her in all points about her title to the English throne; establish by Act of Parliament in Scotland the religion established in England; dissolve the Scottish alliance with France in favour of a perpetual league with England; and wholly follow Elizabeth's will in the matter of the Norfolk marriage.[28] Mary, sincerely or not, answered all the questions satisfactorily. Then on July 27th,[29] in Cecil's absence, Norfolk secured a vote of the Council in favour of Mary's release and

* He endorsed the paper recording their questions.

marriage to an English nobleman. All was ready for Moray's envoy to come and open the question with Elizabeth herself.

But Moray had changed his mind. Late in July he held a convention at Perth which voted against Mary's restoration on any terms and declared it treason in any Scotsman to uphold her authority. If Elizabeth's consent to the Norfolk match was to be obtained, the Duke and his friends must now broach the matter to her themselves. The moment was not inopportune. It was just possible that her anger at Moray's refusal might tempt her to listen. Norfolk however, held back by Leicester, could never quite screw his courage to the speaking point and Mary was too far off to play Lady Macbeth to her ineffectual suitor. Elizabeth, who had a shrewd idea of what was afoot, gave him several openings during August 1569, but each time some small distraction was enough to tie his tongue. After one attempt he fell into an ague and 'was fain to go without tarrying dinner and get me to bed.'[30] All that he managed to do was to deepen Elizabeth's suspicions of his loyalty. In the end it was Leicester who, perhaps unable to bear it longer, confessed the story to the Queen on September 6th. She at once sent for Norfolk and absolutely forbad the match. She would, she remarked, herself be in the Tower within four months if it were allowed. Ten days later Norfolk left court without leave, first for London, then on to Kenninghall, his house in Norfolk. Elizabeth, fearing he was about to rebel, commanded him on his allegiance to return at once. Some weeks earlier he had indeed approved a plan for Northumberland and Dacre to seize Mary and raise the north in his support. But now again his courage failed him. After another bout of ague and another spell in bed, he bade his friends not rise and himself rode meekly off to London where he was promptly sent to the Tower.

The conservative opposition was now in rout all along the line and it is just possible that this might have been the end of it if Elizabeth had not in November 1569 summoned Dacre and the northern Earls to court, after learning from Norfolk's confession of their correspondence with de Spes. Dacre obeyed but Northumberland and Westmorland, goaded on by their wives and followers, rebelled. For two or three weeks, until the southern levies came up, the Earl of Sussex, President of the Council in the North, and his few loyal northerners were in some jeopardy at York. But the north was almost as reluctant to fight against Elizabeth as to fight for her. Those northern counties had shown 60,000 men at the summer musters. Not more than 7,000 turned out in November to fight for the rebel Earls and the old faith.[31] By December those 7,000 were dispersing to their homes and before Christmas the Earls themselves fled over the Border. Two months later Elizabeth sent Hunsdon with a small force from Berwick to arrest Dacre, now back in Cumberland. In a brilliant little action near Naworth on February 20th, 1570, Hunsdon, though he failed to capture Dacre, dispersed his supporters and forced him, too, to flee across the Border. Five days later, and five months too late, Pope Pius V in Rome sealed a bull excommunicating Elizabeth and absolving her subjects from their allegiance.

So the revolt ended in feeble and depressing failure. It could have been more dangerous if it had been better led, in particular if Norfolk had shown boldness and resolution. More northern Catholics might have given it active support if the Pope had excommunicated the Queen before it began instead of after it ended. Yet the leadership only reflected the debility of the Catholic cause, and the dependence upon Norfolk – not yet, if ever, a Catholic – was a consequence of that debility. The delay in the Papal excommunication was only one more consequence of the jealousy between the Catholic powers which was always one of Protestant England's chief safeguards. Indeed, the more deeply we consider the significance of the revolt and of its feeble failure, the more easily we shall understand the new feeling of strength and confidence that gradually developed in Englishmen during the ensuing years.

Chapter 23

The Ridolfi Plot and
St Bartholomew's Day

FOR two or three years after the revolt of the north, as during
the two or three years before it, English foreign policy remained
chiefly concerned with the Netherlands and Scotland. We have
seen how important it was for England's security to get the
Spanish army out of the Netherlands and to keep the French out
of Scotland. The revolt gave those needs a new urgency. For it
brought home sharply to Elizabeth, and still more sharply to her
ministers, the dangers that could result if the Spaniards fomented
English Catholic discontent in retaliation for English pressure
upon Alba, or if the French fomented it to restore Mary Stuart
and French influence in Scotland. The rebellion had uncovered
the dealings of some of the English Catholics with the Spanish
ambassador de Spes and had revealed how much they looked to
Spain for support. At almost the same time the assassination of the
Regent Moray by one of the Hamiltons (January 1570) had thrown
Scotland back into confusion, revived the Marian faction's hopes
there, and produced disturbing signs of fresh French intervention.
Nor, after the Pope's bull of excommunication, could Elizabeth,
and still less her ministers, entirely rid their minds of the fear that
Mary's Catholicism might some day bring together Spain and
France, English Catholics and Scottish Marians, in a crusade
against Protestant England. On the other hand, it was also clear
that, if Elizabeth could attain her purposes in the Netherlands and
Scotland, nothing would do more to take the heart out of the
domestic opposition, which already was fast losing hope of ever
achieving anything without substantial foreign aid. And with the
domestic opposition crushed, foreign threats too would lose most
of their menace. Accordingly, the year 1570 witnessed the beginning of new and more determined efforts to settle the
Netherlands and Scottish questions.

Over the Netherlands, Elizabeth continued and increased the

pressure upon Spain which had begun with the seizure of the Genoese loan. She could not contemplate attempting by force of arms to expel Alba's army and restore the provinces to their ancient liberties and former harmlessness. But by diverting trade from Antwerp and by encouraging the privateers to sever the Netherlands' sea communications with Spain, she could hope to make Alba's position so difficult that Philip might have to modify his policy. For as the 1569 grants from estates ran out, Alba's financial difficulties again grew serious. To impose his new taxes must provoke great discontent, perhaps worse, and William of Orange was already preparing a new expedition from Germany, partly financed by the sale of the privateers' prizes at Dover, Plymouth, and La Rochelle. Yet Alba could look for very little help from Spain, where the Morisco revolt continued until the autumn of 1570 and was followed by costly preparations for the Lepanto campaign against the Turks in the Mediterranean. Moreover, in the seizures and counter-seizures that followed the diversion of the Genoese loan into Elizabeth's coffers, the balance of gain was increasingly on England's side. Spanish traders were suffering far more than their English counterparts who were now able to re-route much of their traffic safely to Hamburg.

So the pressure upon Spain was maintained and it seemed to be having its effect. For now that the northern revolt had failed, Philip appeared more than ever anxious not to offend Elizabeth further. He refused to let the Papal bull of excommunication be published in his dominions. In May 1570 he even sent an assurance through his ambassador in France, Alava – de Spes was no man for such messages – that the traditional Anglo-Spanish amity would never be broken through any fault of his.[1] It was a little unfortunate that this assurance reached the English government just when a bold English Catholic gave them their first news of the bull by nailing a copy of it (supplied through Ridolfi by de Spes's chaplain)[2] to the Bishop of London's door. Nevertheless, Spanish actions in general chimed with Spanish words. Alba quietly accepted the dismissal empty handed (December 1569) of a second envoy, the soldier Ciapino Vitelli, whom he had sent over in the autumn of 1569 about the seizures – and perhaps to make contact with the northern rebels. Then in the summer of 1570 he had to assemble a large quantity of shipping to escort Philip's new bride, Anne of Austria, from Antwerp to Spain. With the privateers swarming in the Channel, this was necessarily a major operation and de Spes took advantage of it to spread rumours that Anne's escort would carry ten or fifteen thousand troops for a descent upon England. Alba, however, sent assurances – again through Alava – that nothing of the sort was intended, adding gratuitously that his master was much annoyed at the Pope's ill considered bull.[3] The ending of the third French War of Religion (August 1570) caused him to coo more gently still towards England, despite the failure of further, semi-official, negotiations about the seizures. Thus, when Anne of Austria did sail for Spain in October, the ninety ships of her escort exchanged only courtesies with the Queen of England's ships and in the New Year Alba sent yet a third official envoy, Sweveghem, to seek a settlement about the seizures.

Sweveghem, though allowed to remain in England, got no further than his predecessors, for Elizabeth still refused to negotiate with Alba. Indeed at that moment she mistrusted Philip too, since rumours had just reached her that he was encouraging a renegade English pirate, Thomas Stukeley, to organize an invasion of Ireland. This gave her the excuse to put off Sweveghem and to send Sir Henry Cobham to Madrid to require that the King of Spain send her an envoy specially accredited from himself to deal about the seizures. And besides having hard things to say about Alba and de Spes, Cobham was to demand the expulsion of English rebels and refugees from the King's dominions. If Philip yielded to such demands from the Queen who had seized his loan and was still harbouring his rebel Sea Beggars, then the English Catholics would indeed be shown how little they had to hope from Spain.

While she was thus maintaining a firm, even arrogant, attitude towards Spain over the Netherlands, Elizabeth began again to take a conciliatory line towards France over Scotland. Under pressure from her Council,[4] she did recognize that she could not let the Protestant party there perish. So, in April 1570, she sent Sussex to harry the Marian Borderers for sheltering her northern rebels and in May Sir William Drury to chastise the Hamiltons on the same pretext. Yet she knew that armed English intervention in Scotland, however she excused it, would be resented by France and she could not afford to offend France when she was being so very rude to Spain. She also doubted the Scottish Protestants' strength and she still hoped to get Mary Stuart off her hands on some safe but honourable terms. Accordingly, to the despair of Cecil and Sussex, late in May she recalled Drury and opened a new round of negotiations for Mary's release and restoration. News of the Pope's bull of excommunication, and then the peace impending in France, only strengthened her determination. In July she did agree to, indeed urge, the appointment of Lennox as Regent in Scotland. She also assured him that she would make no settlement with Mary without the Scots' assent. But she insisted upon the negotiations and even when, in February 1571, they reached deadlock, she still refused to give formal recognition to the little James VI as King of Scotland. As she had bluntly told Cecil back in May 1570, she meant no longer to team up with his 'brothers in Christ' but to come to some good arrangement about the matter with the King of France.[5]

After the ending of the third French War of Religion (August 1570), she found those who now shaped Charles IX's policies ready to welcome her advances. In the minds of Catherine de Medici and the *politiques* the events of 1562-4 had already conjured up the spectre of French domestic broils inciting English intervention on the side of the Huguenots and Spanish intervention on the side of the Catholic Guises. Alba's arrival in the Netherlands and Elizabeth's support of Protestant privateering in the Channel sharpened their alarm, while the inconclusive civil wars of 1567-70 discredited the extreme Catholic remedy of removing the danger by exterminating the Huguenots. So the French government was now reverting to its earlier policy of seeking a modus vivendi between Catholic and Huguenot. This was bound to affect France's foreign relations. For just as the Guises stood for support of Mary Stuart and of the Catholic cause in Great Britain, so did the Huguenots stand for support of William of Orange and of the rebel, and now largely Protestant, cause in the Netherlands. Doubtless Catherine hoped to steer a middle course in these foreign matters no less than in home affairs. Nevertheless, her new policy must worsen relations with Spain and that made it desirable to improve relations with England.

To make the most of this favourable atmosphere, Elizabeth began towards the end of 1570 to take up the idea, put forward earlier by some Huguenot leaders, of a marriage between herself and Charles IX's younger brother Henry, Duke of Anjou. Late in December, better dressed than usual, she broached the subject to the French ambassador, la Mothe Fénélon.[6] The French responded cautiously, for Elizabeth's past record in such affairs was not encouraging. Nevertheless, the bait was irresistible. Such a match would mean a crown for the restless Anjou. It would bind England and France in an alliance so close that neither need fear anything from Spain. It would more than offset the decline of French influence in Scotland and might even justify a break with Rome if the Pope proved too Spanish. So in March 1571 Catherine made a formal proposal for Anjou.

In England the match had the warm support of Cecil, who in February 1571 was elevated to the peerage as Baron of Burghley. He always believed that the best and simplest answer to the English succession problem was for Elizabeth to marry and have children of her own. She was now thirty-seven, but in Burghley hope on this subject sprang eternal. 'There would', he argued, 'long be possibility of children' and the English people would hope for them even longer. So the succession debate would be buried for many years to come, 'a happy funeral for all England'. Of course Anjou, the victor of Jarnac, had hitherto shown himself a strong Catholic. Yet Burghley, along with many Huguenots and the new strongly Protestant English ambassador to France, Francis Walsingham, believed that he would soon succumb to Anglicanism once he was in England. Even if he did not, his marriage to Elizabeth so soon after her excommunication would be a stinging blow to the Papacy from one of the two great Catholic powers. And while the Pope's malice would 'vanish in smoke', Spain's hostility would be checkmated. The match would also go far to ruin Mary Stuart and the Catholic cause in England, while assuring toleration for the Huguenots in France. For all this, Burghley was prepared to take the risk of the young Anjou outliving Elizabeth to become King of England, and perhaps of France as well. Walsingham was no less enthusiastic and even Leicester, ever unwilling to see Elizabeth married to anyone but himself, professed to support the match.[7]

It is hard to believe that Elizabeth was much moved by any of these reasons that so excited Burghley and Walsingham. It is indeed hard to believe that she was serious about the matter at all, that she was not laughing up her sleeve at all the fuss they were making about it. No doubt she was conscious of the possibilities that they saw in it and she would certainly appreciate the usefulness of having active negotiations for her marriage in progress when Parliament met, as it had to meet in April 1571 to make a grant towards her recent expenses. Yet she also knew – and if she did not, Norfolk, Arundel, and plenty of others would soon tell her – what a blow to ancient and deep-seated English prejudices such a French marriage would be. Many Protestants too, perhaps with underhand encouragement from Leicester, were alarmed at Anjou's Catholicism. A French husband therefore might be even more unpopular than a Spanish and Elizabeth did not mean to repeat Mary Tudor's error.

What, then, was Elizabeth's game? Perhaps the best clue to her meaning is provided by a remark she made to Fénélon in July 1570 when she heard that peace was about to be made in France. She then foretold that within two years the French Catholics might again drive their King into war to root out the Huguenots.[8] It was an astonishingly accurate prediction, as St Bartholomew's Day (August 24th) 1572, was to prove so bloodily. But it also showed an instinctive lack of faith in the constancy of French policy, however benevolent its present intentions. This mistrust would reinforce her inveterate dislike of committing herself irrevocably, especially to matrimony, and it would explain much in her conduct which baffled and exasperated her ministers during the next two years. It looks, in fact, as if she meant to exploit French goodwill to the utmost as long as it lasted, to extract from it the greatest possible advantage both over Mary Stuart and Scotland and in her dispute with Spain where Cobham's mission was one of its first fruits. But she could not feel sure enough of French stability to enter into an alliance so close that it would rule out a reconciliation with Spain. This looked a dangerous game to play and Burghley was terrified lest his Queen by blowing hot and cold towards Anjou might so offend French pride as to make France an even more bitter enemy than Spain. In fact, it was safe enough. For as Elizabeth clearly saw, 'the knotty point of religion'[9] could always be relied upon to provide a way of retreat with honour for either party. Hence from an early stage she firmly insisted that Anjou must conform to the English Church and could not be allowed even a private and secret Mass. Over this the negotiations reached deadlock in July 1571. But probably in Elizabeth's eyes they had by then achieved their purpose, for the French were beginning to hint at the possibility of an alliance without marriage.

In political affairs, however, it is seldom possible to solve old problems without creating new ones and the Anjou marriage negotiations created several. In the first place, it drove the already dispirited English Catholic leaders to desperation. Norfolk, too, released from the Tower but more or less confined to Howard House in London, saw in it the final blow to his hopes. Yet few of these despairing souls could quite believe that the King of Spain would stand meekly by in face of the threat which so close an Anglo-French alliance implied to his Low Countries and to Habsburg and Catholic interests generally. Surely now the Spaniards must at last come over to help them? So they listened readily to a plan concocted by Ridolfi, the Florentine banker, for a new Catholic rising in the coming summer to put Mary upon Elizabeth's throne. To touch it off and assure its success, Ridolfi looked to Alba to land six thousand men, with arms, munitions, and money at Harwich (which he thought was in Norfolk) or maybe at Portsmouth (which he placed in Sussex).[10] Mary had approved these plans in January 1571 and communicated them to the ever-willing de Spes. In March Ridolfi induced Norfolk to agree to them and, although the Duke would sign nothing, he did authorize Ridolfi and de Spes to write credentials and instructions in his name.[11] With these and Mary's letters, and a highly optimistic list of probable supporters among the nobility, Ridolfi left London on March 25th to persuade Alba, the Pope, and the King of Spain to play their allotted parts.

The Pope proved enthusiastic and neither Philip nor Alba could altogether ignore proposals that purported to be backed by most of the English peers and whose success would be so much to Spain's advantage. Besides, Philip and his Councillors at this moment were much nettled by the message Cobham had delivered. Kings and grandees of Spain were not used to being addressed in so high a tone and Cobham had been haughtily dismissed.[12] But they had also just recently received a very different English visitor, an agent from no less a person than John Hawkins. He brought an offer that Hawkins would desert to the Spaniards with a considerable squadron of ships in return for a substantial payment and the release of his shipmates who had been captured at San Juan de Ullua.[13] Hawkins was in fact acting with Burghley's knowledge and approval. But he managed to get testimonials from Mary Stuart as well as the gullible de Spes and he seems to have deceived Philip completely. This, of course, gave Ridolfi's plans a much more attractive look. With Hawkins's ships to escort Alba's expeditionary force, an invasion of England came nearer to practical politics. But it would still be necessary to assure the invaders an unopposed landing and a safe base. That was a job for Norfolk and his friends and it meant that their rising must be well on the way to success before the Spaniards struck their blow, all the more so because a premature invasion would merely drive England and France closer together and so precipitate the very dangers Spain was most anxious to avert. Philip and Alba were therefore agreed that 'the first steps must not be taken by us' and when Ridolfi reached Madrid late in June 1571 he was promised Spanish aid, but only after Elizabeth had been assassinated or made prisoner and Norfolk and his friends were in control of the government.[14]

By now reports of some great conspiracy to dethrone Elizabeth by Spanish aid were flowing in to Burghley from the Netherlands, where Ridolfi had babbled to others besides Alba and his Councillors; from France, where the Huguenots rifled a Spanish courier's baggage; from Italy, where Ridolfi had boasted of his plans to the Grand Duke of Tuscany who passed the information back to Elizabeth. Moreover, the self-important Ridolfi had an itching pen as well as a babbling tongue. From Brussels late in April he wrote, quite unnecessarily, to report progress to the Bishop of Ross (Mary's ambassador to Elizabeth) and to Norfolk and the Catholic Lord Lumley. The messenger, Ross's servant Charles Bailly, was stopped and searched at Dover and, though the letters were spirited away, he confessed under torture that he had brought them – one to Ross, two others to English noblemen whose identities were concealed under the cipher symbols 40 and 30 and whose names he did not know. He confessed also that they concerned a plot for a rebellion supported by a Spanish invasion.[15]

Burghley could feel reasonably sure that any invasion must involve Hawkins's co-operation and that Hawkins could be trusted to deal ruthlessly with Alba's defenceless transports. The real danger lay at home and until he could discover who 40 and 30 were, there was little he could do to meet it. Ross, when examined, pretended the figures stood for Mary and de Spes, which was clearly false.[16] But late in August 1571 some of Norfolk's servants were caught forwarding money from Mary's friends in France to her supporters in Scotland. Their examinations led to the discovery of the key to Norfolk's cipher, hidden under the roof tiles of Howard House, and also, hidden under a doormat, a ciphered letter from Mary about Ridolfi's plans. Norfolk was at once sent back to the Tower and Ross and many others rigorously interrogated. This time the Bishop confessed all he knew, adding that he believed Mary had poisoned her first husband, Francis II, had been an accomplice in Darnley's murder, and was no fit wife for any man. Well might his examiner, Dr Thomas Wilson, exclaim 'Lord! what a people. What a Queen! What an ambassador!'[17] And, we may add, what conspirators and what an opposition! Elizabeth Tudor was indeed fortunate in her enemies.

The evidence against Norfolk was damning and on January 16th, 1572 his peers convicted him of treason. Elizabeth's reluctance, and perhaps the hope of further confessions, delayed his execution for another five months, but with the reassembly of Parliament the clamour for his head rose so high that the Queen had at last to send him to the block (June 1572). The evidence against Mary was also damning and, if Parliament and Council had had their way, she too would have been executed. But to execute the Queen of Scots, the sometime Queen of France, must intolerably strain Anglo-French friendship, whatever Charles IX's private views. So there Elizabeth drew the line. She would not even assent to a bill that would have barred Mary from the English succession. Nevertheless, with Norfolk's arrest and conviction, 'the last combined effort of the English aristocracy to undo the Reformation and strangle the new order of things'[18] was nipped in the bud. Philip II's lack of interest in Hawkins's renewed overtures indicated pretty clearly that the Spanish invasion plan was off as well.

Clearly, too, now was the time to step up the pressure on Spain. So in December 1571 the turbulent de Spes was ignominiously expelled. In a sense this made little difference, for the ambassador had not had audience with the Queen for almost two years and his relations with her Council had long been acrimonious and intermittent. Also, Sweveghem and a Spanish merchant, Antonio de Guaras, were allowed to stay in London,

doing what they could semi-officially about the seizures. Nevertheless, de Spes's expulsion amounted to a formal severance of
diplomatic relations. It was another turn of the screw.

To point it more sharply, Elizabeth now sent Sir Thomas
Smith to France to follow up French hints of an alliance without
marriage. Burghley was not altogether happy about this. He saw
his hopes of solving the succession problem and 'avoiding the
inevitable ruin of this monarchy' slipping away. He feared, too,
that without the marriage 'the French amity shall serve to small
purpose but to make us ministers of their appetites and, those
fulfilled, to cast us off'.[19] What particularly alarmed him was that
the hints of a league without a marriage coincided with Charles
IX inviting the Huguenot leader Coligny to court and listening
to his advocacy of schemes for intervention in the Netherlands.
These schemes were the work of William of Orange's brother,
Louis of Nassau, who since 1568 had been organizing the Netherlands privateers at La Rochelle. What he proposed was an alliance
of France, England, and the German Protestants to assist the new
enterprise that William was preparing for the summer of 1572.
Together the allies should expel the Spaniards from the Netherlands and then partition those provinces, Flanders and Artois
going to France, Holland and Zeeland to England, and the rest
under William to the Empire. Charles IX's Council had approved
the project in July 1571 on condition that England and the
Germans would play their parts and accordingly in August Louis
had broached the matter to Walsingham. Walsingham, and
Leicester when he heard of it, recommended the project strongly
'in respect of the spiritual fruit that may thereby ensue'.[20]

But it was the political fruit that worried Burghley. Like the
Queen, he was anxious to get the Spanish army out of the Netherlands, but not at the price of installing the French in its place.
For, as Sussex succinctly put it, 'the case will be hard with
the Queen and with England if ever the French possess or the
Spaniards tyrannize in the Low Countries.'[21] Controlling the
Netherlands, the French might dominate western Europe and
be intolerably dangerous neighbours. For in those provinces they,
unlike the Spaniards, would have no long lines of communication
back to their home base to make them vulnerable. Instead, even
if they only possessed Flanders, they would have uninterrupted
control of the coastline east as well as west of the Straits of Dover.

This must seriously weaken England's hold upon the Narrow Seas and make a French invasion, or French aid to Scotland, much easier. England's vital eastward trade would also lie open to attack. Nor could English occupation of Holland and Zeeland do much to offset these dangers and anyway those two provinces, even if they could be occupied, would be as burdensome to hold as ever Calais or Boulogne had been. It was all very well for Walsingham and Leicester to prate about 'the advancement of the gospel' and casting the proud Spaniard into the fire 'that he may know what it is to serve against God'.[22] But the plain fact was that French Huguenot interest in William of Orange and the Netherlands could easily prove no less dangerous to England's security than French Catholic interest in Mary Stuart and Scotland.

Elizabeth must have shared Burghley's fears about Count Louis's schemes, for no direct answer was made to his overtures. Moreover, although Sir Thomas Smith's instructions have not survived, it is clear that he and Walsingham were told to seek only a defensive league with France. They were also instructed to attempt to resuscitate the Anjou match, but this was probably mere artistic embellishment, Elizabeth acting out her part to the end. For when Anjou proved uncooperative and Catherine put forward his younger brother Francis, Duke of Alençon, as a more amenable suitor, Elizabeth showed a marked lack of interest in that undersized and pock-marked youth twenty years her junior. With these preliminaries out of the way, agreement on the defensive character of the alliance was easy enough, for neither side felt sufficient confidence in the other to make it offensive and so risk a breach with Spain. Also French enthusiasm for an offensive against the Habsburgs was cooling somewhat. The defeat of the Turks at Lepanto (October 1571) had impressively demonstrated Spanish power and the Ridolfi plot had reminded Catherine that the Guises could play in France the role for which the ineffective Norfolk had been cast in England.

All this, however, strengthened the arguments for a defensive alliance with Elizabeth and two points alone seriously delayed the final treaty. The English wanted to insert, in the clause promising mutual aid against attack by any third party, the words *etiamsi religionis causa*. Charles IX felt that this would be unduly provocative to his Catholic subjects and in the end

Elizabeth accepted instead his offer of an assurance in a private letter. The second point concerned Scotland, which could hardly be ignored in an Anglo-French treaty of alliance. There the Marians had seized Edinburgh in May 1571 and in September had done to death a second Regent, Lennox. By then, too, the unravelling of the Ridolfi plot had revealed how much Mary and her friends there were looking for aid to Alba rather than to France. This compelled Elizabeth to abandon her attempts to mediate between the warring factions and come down on the side of the new Regent, the Earl of Mar.[23] She tried therefore to get the French to recognize the Regency as at least the *de facto* government of Scotland. The French were reluctant to throw over Mary so positively and here, too, a compromise had to be accepted whereby 'the realm and state of Scotland' was included in the treaty without naming either Mary or the Regency. This was, nevertheless, a substantial success for Elizabeth, since the omission of any reference to Mary amounted to the abandonment of her cause by the French government. On these terms the treaty was finally concluded at Blois on April 19th, 1572.[24] Elizabeth had got what she wanted. She had insulated the Scottish question and she had gained a French shield without committing herself to draw her own sword against Spain. Or, as Smith put it, 'if Spain will now threaten ... , it will be afraid hereafter, seeing such a wall adjoined; ... if the House of Burgundy will be friend ... , yet nothing is done on your Majesty's part to break the amity.'[25] Elizabeth was in a position to play her game both ways.

She was indeed already beginning to do just that. In January 1572 some person unnamed hinted to Antonio de Guaras that the time was ripe for fresh talks about the seizures of goods and shipping. Then, late in March, Burghley himself asked de Guaras to inform Alba that the English government was ready for a settlement.[26] Alba jumped at the chance and invited Burghley to suggest the heads of an agreement. Nothing came of this immediately, for by now a new development had occurred. On March 1st Elizabeth had ordered out of her ports the Netherlands privateers under the Count de la Marck who were operating in the Narrow Seas. Followed as it was by Burghley's overture to de Guaras, this could be, and was meant to be, interpreted as another friendly gesture towards Alba and Spain. Its sequel, however, casts a shadow of doubt over such an interpretation.

For, after cruising round for some weeks, la Marck on April 1st suddenly pounced upon the town of Brielle in south Holland. Brielle's inhabitants fled almost to a man, the town had no regular garrison, and the Sea Beggars thus became masters of an easily defensible base in their own Low Countries.

Was this an accidental and unforeseen consequence of la Marck's expulsion from English ports? Or was it an enterprise concerted by him with the English government under cover of that expulsion? These are questions on which different historians have come to completely opposite conclusions and on which, in truth, the evidence hardly suffices for a conclusive answer.[27] The privateers were undoubtedly becoming a serious nuisance to ordinary traffic, English as well as foreign. Yet merely to move them elsewhere was no solution. Besides, they and the western and La Rochelle privateers were effectively cutting Alba's communications with Spain. It does not seem very likely that Elizabeth would choose just this moment to relax that pressure, whatever ostensible gestures of friendship she might otherwise be making. Also, landswoman though she was, she could not expect the Beggars, like some fleet of Flying Dutchmen, to remain for ever at sea. She may have thought that they would go off to join their comrades at La Rochelle. Yet, again, it looks odd that she should thus ease the pressure in the Narrow Seas, the straitest bottleneck in the Netherlands' communications with Spain. It looks even odder that the man sent to Dover to order the Beggars off was John Hawkins. It is perhaps oddest of all that they went when ordered, so quietly and with so little protest.

At all events, once in Brielle, la Marck begged the English government to allow arms and munitions to be sent to him and to let volunteers from the Netherlands refugees in England come over to join him. His requests were readily granted and not only refugees, but also a growing number of English volunteers, led by a young Welsh captain, Thomas Morgan, began to stream across the North Sea. Thus reinforced, the Beggars were able to seize Flushing, which gave them a tight hold upon the waterways to Antwerp, and to fan out over a considerable part of the two coastal provinces of Holland and Zeeland. Their task was made easier by the universal hatred of the tenth and twentieth pennies, the new perpetual taxes which Alba had proposed three years ago and which in February 1572 his financial straits had at last compelled him to impose upon the Netherlands. This had not turned the mass of Netherlanders into active rebels, but it did make most of them adopt the attitude of the Gouda militia, who when the Beggars appeared before their town threw down their arms, shouting that they would not fight for the Duke of Alba and the tenth penny. Defence against the Beggars therefore depended almost entirely upon Alba's regular troops. But the Duke knew that across his eastern frontier William of Orange was mustering 20,000 or more German mercenaries and that across his southern frontier Louis of Nassau was gathering another force of refugees and Huguenots. He could therefore afford only small and scattered garrisons for the northern provinces. He had to leave most of their seaboard towns defenceless against the Beggars.

So the Revolt of the Netherlands began – not in the way that Louis of Nassau was planning and the French government had envisaged, but as a movement coming in from the sea and owing its initial impulse to Elizabeth of England. Whether Elizabeth had provided that impulse deliberately or accidentally, its immediate results were very much to her liking. 'Here is all covert means to let them of the Low Countries pass home to the help of the liberty of the country; and I wish it were done rather by themselves than by others that percase would not suffer them long to enjoy their liberty when it should be recovered.' Thus did Burghley write to Walsingham on April 23rd and he cherished the hope that, if William of Orange could seize the opportunity created by the Beggars, the Netherlands by their own exertions might force out Alba's army and regain their ancient liberties.[28]

But what pleased England, must also tempt France. Late in May, Louis of Nassau with a few thousand men, mostly French Huguenots, crossed the Netherlands frontier and seized Mons and Valenciennes. Alba could not feel sure that the whole power of France would not soon follow Louis and to meet this, by far his worst, danger he had little choice but to concentrate still more of his troops in the south. He was then able to win back Valenciennes and lay siege to Mons, but he had perforce to leave the road open for William to march in from Germany and to leave the provinces north of the Maas to the mercy of the Beggars. And in those northern provinces, too, French volunteers were pouring in to reinforce the Beggar bands.

With these footholds secured and with Alba battling for his life, would the French King succumb after all to Coligny's arguments for open intervention? This was the question now uppermost in the minds of both Alba and the English government. The time looked near when Elizabeth must decide whether to draw the sword alongside France or to proffer the olive branch to Spain. The decision she adopted may be seen in a paper of advice drawn up by Burghley early in June. If, he advised, the Duke of Alba seemed able to hold his own against France, England should 'let both sides alone for a time'. If not, and if 'the French proceed to seek to possess the maritime coasts and frontiers', then Alba should be

> informed secretly of the Queen's Majesty's disposition to assist the King his master by all honourable means she might in the defence of his inheritance, so as it may appear to her that he will discharge his subjects of their intolerable oppression, restore them to their ancient liberties, reconcile his nobility to him, deliver them from the fear of the Inquisition, and continue with Her Majesty the ancient league for amity and traffic in as ample sort as any others, Dukes of Burgundy, heretofore have done.[29]

In this document we have the first and clearest official outline of the policy towards the Netherlands which Elizabeth was to follow with remarkable consistency for the remainder of her reign.[30] It was a policy not at all to the taste of Protestant zealots like Walsingham, who wanted England and France to lead a crusade to establish an independent Netherlands, cast the Spaniards into the fire, and bring the triumph of the Huguenot cause in France and of the Protestant cause in Europe. Elizabeth cared little for those things. She wanted to retain Spain as a counterpoise to France. She wanted the Netherlands, though restored to their ancient liberties, to remain Spanish so that they would not become French. She had no great faith in the Huguenots' ability to impose their will upon France. She had too much humanity and common sense to wish for a Protestant crusade that must unleash a general religious war over the whole continent, a war, too, in which the Protestants would be by no means predestined victors. Her concern was England and, whatever the religious zealots, the pious men of blood, might say, she would not gamble England's future on so barbarous and unpredictable a holocaust. Above all, she mistrusted the constancy of French policy, the hinge upon which the whole gamble would turn. Events were soon to justify her mistrust.

For the occasion to carry out the policy of Burghley's memorandum quickly came and the justification of its wisdom speedily followed. At the end of June 1572 Alba forwarded through Antonio de Guaras a letter from Philip to Elizabeth, thanking her for expelling his rebel Sea Beggars. With it the Duke sent a letter of his own, suggesting yet once more negotiations to settle Anglo-Spanish differences. Elizabeth welcomed the overture and, also through de Guaras, suggested that she might seize Flushing and hold it for the King until Alba could take it over. She did not mention the conditions listed in Burghley's memorandum.[31] But these could come later: the main thing now was to reopen a line to Alba and prevent a breach with him over the dispatch of another thousand or more 'volunteers' early in July to counter French influence in Zeeland. With these volunteers went Sir Humphrey Gilbert, with secret instructions to bring all the English there under stricter discipline, to hold them near the coast, and in particular to use them to keep the French out of Flushing.[32]

The enmity and suspicion which resulted between Gilbert's men and their French allies did little to encourage Charles IX to expect Elizabeth's help if he drew the sword openly. Nor did her ambiguous and sometimes contradictory answers to Catherine's renewed proposals for her marriage to Alençon. Along with this came two setbacks in the Netherlands. Through most of July William of Orange was held up between the Rhine and the Maas for lack of pay to get his army marching and on July 25th a French force under the Huguenot Genlis, on its way to succour Mons, was cut to pieces by the Spaniards. Meanwhile storm clouds were gathering in France. A considerable majority of the French nobility and an overwhelming majority of the French people, especially in Paris and the great cities, were Catholics. They were growing more and more outraged by Coligny's dominance at court and by the prospect of the King adopting a militant Huguenot foreign policy. The gathering in Paris of many leading nobles, Catholic and Huguenot, with their retinues for the wedding of the King's sister Margaret to the young Henry of Bourbon, the Huguenot King of Navarre, made a violent explosion all too likely by crowding together all the different pressure groups in the hot and restless capital.

Anjou shared the Catholics' disgust and Catherine, the Queen Mother, feared that, unless Charles could be saved from Coligny's influence, a new Catholic outburst must sweep away the Valois dynasty, tear France asunder, and invite a more dangerous Spanish and English intervention than in 1562–4. To persuade Charles quickly enough looked impossible. So Catherine instigated the Guises to remove Coligny. The Guisard assassin, however, on August 22nd botched his job and only wounded the Huguenot leader. To complete his work, and prevent the investigation which the Huguenots clamoured for and which must reveal her own complicity, Catherine with Anjou's aid persuaded the feeble and impressionable Charles that the Huguenots were plotting to kidnap him and destroy her and the Catholic leaders. Reluctantly the King consented to the immediate execution of the chief Huguenots. At dawn on August 24th, St Bartholomew's Day, the slaughter began. The Parisian populace joined in with a will, to be emulated in the following days by the people of other Catholic cities. What had started as an attempt to assassinate one man, swelled to a horrifying and nation-wide massacre. Yet the Huguenots were not exterminated and during the next five years France plunged into a fourth, a fifth, and a sixth War of Religion, marked off from each other only by brief intervals of fevered and uneasy truce.

To suggest, as Froude does, that these terrible events might have been averted if Elizabeth had married Anjou or Alençon and had joined Charles IX in attacking Spain openly in the Netherlands, is surely as far-fetched as his guess that she might thereby have averted the Thirty Years War and the French Revolution.[33] Nothing she could have done would have stayed the build-up of explosive forces inside France which really caused the tragedy and which had made it increasingly improbable that Charles IX ever would attack Spain, whatever England did. Indeed, it was largely because Elizabeth anticipated some such debacle, had predicted it to within a month two years beforehand, that she was so careful not to commit herself. It was William of Orange and Louis of Nassau who had gambled on the constancy of French policy and it was they, not Elizabeth, who now paid the price. Without substantial French aid their prospects were little better than in 1568 and during the autumn of 1572 their second enterprise went the way of their first. Mons surrendered in September and William's army, too, disintegrated. This time, however, he and the remnant of his forces were able to continue the fight on Netherlands soil. The revolt which he and Louis had planned had collapsed. But that which Elizabeth, wittingly or unwittingly, had touched off in Holland and Zeeland was still alive. There William was able to continue the struggle to recover the 'liberty of the country'. In so doing he also played a part in making the next five or six years for England the least troubled of Elizabeth's reign.

Chapter 24

High Water Mark

FOR the better part of twelve years after the St Bartholomew Massacre, from 1573 until 1585, England was able to go her way in peace. Plots there were and rumours of wars, especially after 1580; but not since the later days of Henry VII had the country enjoyed so long a freedom from domestic rebellion and foreign conflict. The first five of those years in particular, from 1573 to 1578, were the calmest and most secure of all Elizabeth's reign. During them, Froude says with pardonable exaggeration, 'the annals of England are almost a blank.'[1]

Nevertheless, even during these first five peaceful years the debate on foreign policy was as lively as ever and English diplomacy had seldom been more active. The reasons for the debate and activity are clear enough. As Walsingham once said, the cause of England's quietness 'proceeded of her neighbours' unquietness'.[2] Now, to Elizabeth, her neighbours' unquietness and their mutual jealousies appeared as more or less permanent facts of international life. At least for the foreseeable future they could be relied upon still to preserve her in comparative quietness. Her instinct therefore was to play upon them by diplomacy in order to shape the patterns of power in Europe more to her liking, yet to involve herself as little as possible in overt action or substantial expense. To the more zealous, and nervous, Protestants among her Councillors, however – men convinced of the undying malice of Spain and Rome and the Guises and lacking faith in the strength of Dutch and Huguenot resistance – the internal problems and mutual jealousies of England's foreign foes seemed no more than transient distractions. Sooner or later they would disappear and 'the two great monarchies of Europe' would turn 'not only to disquiet but also to displace Her Majesty'.[3]

So Walsingham, who became joint Principal Secretary with Sir Thomas Smith in December 1573 (Burghley had been promoted to Lord Treasurer in July 1572), was continually agitating, generally with Leicester's support, for more active intervention in

France, the Netherlands, and Scotland. Not infrequently events for a moment played into his hands and alarmed the Queen into toying with his ideas, all the more because past years had taught her to trust none of her neighbours too far. The alarms soon passed, but their effect was to give her policy a superficial appearance of feverishness. Its movements looked as erratic as those of a sailing boat in light and variable airs, constantly trimming its sails to catch each puff of shifting breeze even while aiming always at the same mark. Happily we need not follow in detail these gyrations and hesitations, which were so exasperating and often unintelligible to men of Walsingham's forthright temper. For us what matters is the course Elizabeth set herself rather than the track she followed.

Her aim remained remarkably constant – to restore the Netherlands to the semi-independent status they had enjoyed under Charles V; to keep the French out of those provinces and Scotland; and to do these things without involving England in war or burdensome expenditure. On the first news of the Massacre she did put her navy to sea; begin to put ready another 8,000 men to reinforce Gilbert in Zeeland; think of sending £20,000 to Orange; and actually send Killigrew to invite the Regent Mar, very secretly, to take back Mary Stuart for trial and execution in Scotland.[4] But the extreme alarm soon passed and even while it lasted she was careful, having a Spanish quarrel already on her hands, not to break with the French King. It soon appeared that Charles IX and his mother were equally anxious to avoid a breach with her. After all, Catherine's purpose in touching off the Massacre had not been to launch a Catholic crusade against England, but to prevent a Huguenot crusade against the Netherlands which by splitting France in two would have invited Spanish and English intervention there. Moreover, the Huguenots, despite the loss of so many of their leaders and thanks in part to the help which Elizabeth allowed her subjects to send them unofficially, soon showed such resilience that in June 1573 Charles again patched up a peace with them. From that time forward it became increasingly clear, as France slipped nearer and nearer to anarchy, that the King had not the power nor the Catholics as yet the organization to beat them down, however shrilly and often Walsingham might cry out that their case was desperate.

The death of Charles IX (May 1574) and the accession of the

strongly Catholic Anjou as Henry III did cause some new doubts. These led to negotiations with the Calvinist Elector Frederick of the Palatinate for a German army to aid the Huguenots and eventually to a secret loan of £15,000 for that purpose. They led also to vague and unkept promises to Henry of Navarre and young Condé, the new Huguenot leaders, and to fresh talk of marrying Alençon, now temporarily their ally. But Henry III's realm was too far out of hand for him to quarrel with England and in March 1575 he gladly renewed the treaty of Blois. In 1576 there was again suspicion that he might encourage Alençon to be troublesome abroad rather than at home by taking advantage of the sudden breakdown of Spanish power in the Netherlands. Elizabeth was quick to warn them both that if they moved in on the side of the Netherlanders, she would have to move in on the side of Spain.[5] Again, however, France collapsed into a civil war that ruled out foreign adventures. The war did not end until September 1577, just when Elizabeth was considering another loan to the Huguenots to help to prolong it and keep the French still occupied at home. It was not until July 1578, when Alençon did at last begin to meddle in the Netherlands, that French policy began to give Elizabeth any serious cause for anxiety.

In the meantime she had taken advantage of French impotence to bring about the destruction of Mary Stuart's cause in Scotland. Killigrew could not persuade the Scots to take back their Queen for trial and execution except on terms which would have manifested all too publicly Elizabeth's complicity. But he did induce Huntly and the Hamiltons to submit to Morton, who had become Regent on Mar's death (October 1572). Then in May 1573 Sir William Drury led another English force, with a siege train, to help Morton batter Edinburgh castle into surrender. Elizabeth had hesitated long over this step. The expense irked her (the balls fired by her cannon were carefully collected up when the siege was over). Fénélon, too, had been quick to remind her that to dispatch troops into Scotland unilaterally would be a breach of the treaty of Blois.[6] When it came to the point, however, France acquiesced. So the last Marian garrison surrendered, and never again were Scotsmen to draw their swords for Mary Stuart. At least until Morton's fall (1578) and the arrival of Esmé Stuart (1579) to seduce the boy James VI for a time into wayward courses, England's postern gate was firmly closed and surely guarded.

Thus, while the Anglo-French alliance survived, the possibility of French interference in Scotland or the Netherlands lingered during these five years only as a shadow that occasionally clouded Elizabeth's imagination. In that time she had also set about re-establishing normal relations with Spain on terms which would restore the Netherlands to their ancient liberties. Here, too, she met with a marked readiness to agree. For the Spaniards had learned from the long siege of Haarlem (December 1572 to July 1573), which cost them 12,000 men, how tough a job lay before them in Holland and Zeeland. It was the tougher because Philip, with the Channel closed, had not yet found a way to send money, let alone reinforcements, regularly and safely from Spain.[7] Alba felt that, with the resources at his disposal thus limited, he would never suppress the revolt if England came in openly. He was therefore in favour of peace with Elizabeth at almost any price. Even, he wrote to Philip in March 1573, even if she broke her promises and continued 'to favour the rebels and pirates ... there is a great difference between open action and underhand'.[8] Hence as early as October 1572 the Spaniards renewed their overtures for a settlement. Through de Guaras Burghley made England's terms quite plain once more. Elizabeth would settle accounts about the seizures, take measures to reduce privateering and piracy, no longer shelter Philip's rebels. In return Spain must expel English rebels and refugees and assure English traders freedom from the Inquisition. At the same time the Queen's interest in the Netherlands' liberties was made plain again by her repeated offers to mediate between the Spaniards and Orange.

These terms were too stiff for Spain to accept at once, but in the spring of 1573 a limited agreement for two years was concluded. Trade was reopened and negotiations begun which eventually produced the convention of Bristol (August 1574), settling the claims and counter-claims arising out of the seizures. On the political side, too, Spanish policy was gradually modified. In November 1573 Alba was replaced by Don Luis de Requesens who abolished the Council of Blood, offered to abolish the tenth penny, and opened negotiations with Orange on the basis of a return to the traditional liberties and forms of government. Then in the spring of 1575 he banished the English rebels and refugees from the Netherlands and agreed that English traders should not be molested for their religion. Spain had thus, it seemed, acceded to almost all Elizabeth's demands and for the time Anglo-Spanish relations regained much of their former friendliness. In the summer of 1574, by the Queen's command and to Walsingham's consternation, a Spanish fleet was even welcomed in English ports on its way up Channel with supplies and reinforcements for Requesens.

Indeed the difficulty now was rather with William of Orange than with Spain. He stood out for liberty of worship for the Netherlands Protestants, the one thing above all others that Requesens had no power to grant. So the peace negotiations, and Elizabeth's hopes of a good settlement, broke down. In addition, William's attempts to blockade the Scheldte brought a good deal of interference with England's reopened trade to Antwerp and sharpened Elizabeth's animosity into almost open hostility. Worst of all he was appealing to France for aid. Yet Elizabeth dared not cast him off entirely before a lasting settlement was achieved. And he now needed help more than ever. Holland and Zeeland's resistance was heroic but desperate. They had saved Alkmaar in 1573. In 1574 they had destroyed off Bergen such naval forces as Requesens possessed; had cleared the last Spanish garrison out of Walcheren; and by cutting the dykes had raised the siege of Leiden. But they were slowly losing ground and by the end of 1575 were getting very near the end of their resources. It seemed only a matter of time before Requesens's weary soldiery trampled out their resistance. Could the King of Spain then be trusted to keep his promises, withdraw his army, and respect Netherlands liberties?

Perhaps he could: but certainly he would be more likely to do so if Elizabeth could mediate a settlement along those lines while Holland and Zeeland were still in arms. And for that the time seemed to be running out. It might be running out in another sense too. For there were signs that a pause was coming in France's long series of civil wars and that, if it came, Henry III would not be sorry to see his turbulent brother Alençon seek adventure abroad. William of Orange (not, perhaps, without Walsingham's secret encouragement)[9] was already trying to tempt him to seek it in the Netherlands, while the exhaustion of Requesens's troops and of Philip's finances – in 1575 he had to suspend payments to his creditors – made the moment opportune. We have seen how Elizabeth tried underhand to prolong France's 'unquietness', but this made her all the more anxious to achieve a settlement in the

Netherlands as quickly as possible. So the end of 1575 and beginning of 1576 brought renewed and more widespread efforts at mediation, backed by resounding threats to either party that, if they would not listen, England would go openly to their rival's support.

Before these efforts bore fruit, events overtook them. In March 1576 Requesens died suddenly. In April Philip named as his successor no less a person than Don John of Austria, illegitimate son of Charles V and victor of Lepanto. But it was late November before Don John reached Luxembourg and by then the whole scene had changed. In July the Spanish army, left without a master and without pay, mutinied and began to hold the country to ransom. Threatened by military anarchy, the whole Netherlands rose in self-defence. In October representatives of most of the provinces came together in a States General at Ghent. The Spanish soldiery were now running wild and on November 4th and 5th, in the 'Spanish Fury', they sacked Antwerp. At once, on November 8th, the States General concluded with Holland and Zeeland the Pacification of Ghent. This recognized William of Orange as Stadholder of those two provinces and called in his forces to help the rest expel the Spanish troops and restore their own ancient liberties as in the time of Charles V. The laws against heresy were suspended and religious differences were left to be settled by the States General in quieter times, which meant that Calvinist ascendancy in Holland and Zeeland was tacitly accepted. All the provinces acknowledged the King of Spain as their sovereign, but they refused to admit his new governor-general, Don John, until he accepted and confirmed the Pacification.

To strengthen their position they also asked Elizabeth to intercede with Spain to get the Pacification accepted. In addition they asked her to grant them a loan of £100,000 if Don John should refuse. Her response was prompt and clear, in marked contrast to her previous shifts and hesitations. She rushed Sir John Smith off to urge Philip, and Edward Horsey to urge Don John, to confirm the Pacification, threatening to support the States General by force if they refused. Even more convincingly, she sent the States £20,000 and promised the other £80,000 if Don John did refuse. In fact the situation left him little option except to agree and in February 1577, by his ill named Perpetual Edict, he accepted the States General's terms.

This was the high water mark of Elizabeth's Netherlands policy, perhaps indeed of her policy as a whole. In outward appearance at least, the Pacification and the Edict gave almost all she had striven for – a united Netherlands governing themselves, enjoying their ancient liberties as in the days of Charles V, and free from Spanish troops, yet still acknowledging the sovereignty of Spain. At the same time France, plunged into yet another civil war, was a danger to no one but herself, and Scotland was ruled by the firm hand of the Anglophil Regent Morton. Moreover, England still had her defensive alliance with France and she had regained something of the old amity with Spain.

It was, of course, too good to last, and even now there were two disturbing flaws in the Netherlands situation. One was that the Perpetual Edict contained nothing to satisfy Holland and Zeeland in the matter of religion. William and those two provinces therefore stood aloof from the general welcome to Don John, just as they had stood aloof from the overtures of Requesens earlier. The second flaw was due to Don John's own ambitions. There were well founded rumours that his secret purpose was to pacify the Netherlands so that he could use the Spanish forces there to conquer England, marry Mary Stuart, and put her and himself upon Elizabeth's throne. His close contacts with exiled English Catholics, and his attempt to persuade the States to send the Spanish troops home by sea, lent weight to these rumours. Elizabeth therefore remained watchful and her warnings helped the States to insist upon the troops leaving by land for Italy instead of by sea for Spain – or England. Left without forces, baulked in his great design (which Philip had never heartily approved), and unable to win over Orange, Don John soon grew weary of being a mere figurehead and began also to fear for his personal safety. At last he could bear it no longer. He slipped away from Brussels, rallied a few Walloon troops, and on July 24th, 1577, seized Namur citadel. Then he sent to recall the Spanish army. Rumour also had it that the Duke of Guise was raising forces for him in France.

Elizabeth immediately sent over William Davison, a man made in the Walsingham mould, to urge the States General to place Orange in command and to offer them forces and money if Don John repudiated his Perpetual Edict. They thereupon sent the Marquis of Havré in September to ask again for the loan of

£100,000 and for 5,000 foot and 1,000 horse under the Earl of Leicester. With unusual alacrity the Queen promised, within four days, £80,000 on top of the £20,000 sent earlier. She also agreed to send the required forces if Guise moved to Don John's support. Now, however, the States General hung back. Catholics for the most part, they were reluctant to put themselves under the Calvinist William of Orange or to strengthen his party with Protestant English troops. Instead, though they invited William to Brussels, in October they called in the Austrian Archduke Matthias, the Emperor's younger brother, to take Don John's place as their Governor. Their coolness and tardiness naturally chilled Elizabeth's enthusiasm.

For, clearly, in the Netherlands religion was again beginning to cut across politics. To Walsingham and men of his opinions (it is remarkable how often he used in his letters some such phrase as 'God's glory and next the Queen's safety'[10] – always in that order) this was a reason for joining in at once, while the Protestant forces were still in arms and before the Catholic forces were fully mobilized. The last thing, however, that Elizabeth wanted was to precipitate a general religious conflict, and she feared that to send over English troops might do just that. Besides being virtually a declaration of war against Spain, it would sharpen the divisions among the Netherlanders and perhaps drive many Catholics to join Don John or, worse, to call in the French. For in September 1577 the latest civil war in France had ended and the French king's brother, Francis of Alençon – or of Anjou, as we must now call him – was already putting out feelers to the States General. To risk a war with Spain in order to maintain a United Netherlands was one thing; to plunge into a Netherlands faction fight which might invite French intervention, was quite another. So Elizabeth withdrew her offers to Havré and turned again to mediation. In December 1577 she sent Thomas Wilkes to Spain to demand the recall of Don John and the maintenance of the Pacification. Then she sent Sir Thomas Leighton to the Netherlands to persuade both the States and Don John to an armistice until she received Philip's answer.

Philip's decision was made clear long before his answer arrived. Not unnaturally, he regarded the appointment of Matthias as an act of open rebellion and his reply to it was to send back the Spanish army from Italy to the Netherlands under the conduct of

Alexander Farnese, Prince of Parma, son of Margaret of Parma, the former Governess of those provinces. Thus reinforced, Don John on January 31st, 1578, routed the States General's ill disciplined and ill led levies at Gembloux and set once again about the task of reducing the Netherlands to obedience.

This renewal of the war was a sharp setback to Elizabeth's hopes. It must make mediation more difficult. Also Gembloux threw the States General into such disarray that, if nothing were done to help them, it seemed likely they would either succumb to Don John or call in Anjou. Elizabeth could hardly send English troops till she got Philip's answer, but in March she did offer either to stand surety for a loan of £100,000 or to lend £40,000 herself to bring in John Casimir of the Palatinate with 11,000 German and Swiss troops, provided that her name was not allowed to appear. The States accepted her second offer with reluctance. Casimir would not be ready for a couple of months or more and they wanted men now, even Englishmen. Nor would the Calvinist John Casimir and his 11,000 Protestant troops be very welcome to the Catholic majority when they did come. For the Gembloux disaster had dangerously inflamed the religious division among the Netherlanders. In the great cities of Flanders and Brabant, in Ghent especially, the Protestant Orangist minority began to seize control by insurrectionary movements, sometimes supported by the armed forces of Holland and Zeeland. In Utrecht and Gelderland the same thing was happening and Catholics everywhere feared that their town and provincial governments might soon be taken over by the Calvinists as those of Holland and Zeeland had been taken over in 1572. This fear was already driving a few to reconcile themselves to Don John; it was driving many more, especially in the Walloon, French-speaking provinces, towards Anjou.

At this point Elizabeth received Philip's answer to her demands sent in December by Wilkes. It was brought by Bernardino de Mendoza, who had been one of Alba's captains and had come over on a mission from Requesens in 1574. He was now to stay as Spain's resident ambassador, the first since de Spes's expulsion in 1571. He was to explain that Philip, much against his will, was forced to take up arms again to pacify his Netherlands and to 'maintain therein the Roman Catholic religion and my authority'. He was, however, to assure the Queen that 'we never desired to gain any advantage or fresh power there, other than what was enjoyed by my father, the Emperor.' He was therefore to beg her, as a good ally and neighbour, to prohibit 'any sort of help or countenance, direct or indirect, being sent from her country to the States'. He was to 'endeavour to keep her in a good humour and convinced of our friendship'. And, as a final proof of that friendship, Philip instructed Mendoza that 'if any English Catholics approach you, you will receive them kindly, consoling and encouraging them in general terms to persevere, but you will not enter into any negotiation or plans with them against the Queen.'[11]

There is no real reason to doubt that these confidential instructions expressed Philip's true meaning towards England. Elizabeth, of course, could not feel so sure what his meaning was. Nevertheless, Mendoza's arrival did give her renewed hope that, at least on the side of Spain, there was still some room for mediation. For, if Mendoza spoke truth, Philip was ready to accept almost all the conditions which she regarded as essential to England's security. The danger now seemed to be that the States General, under growing Protestant pressure, and Don John, with the Spanish army back again, might prove less amenable than Philip. If so, had the States the strength and unity to defend themselves without foreign aid? What was happening at Ghent and elsewhere after Gembloux was already driving many Netherlands Catholics to look around for defenders against both Don John's Spanish soldiery and William of Orange's Calvinist followers. The Archduke Matthias had failed them. Lacking personality as well as means, he was even falling himself under William's spell. This was why many Catholics, particularly the French-speaking nobles of Artois and Hainaut, were turning to the Duke of Anjou and France. So many, indeed, that the States General, too, were driven to negotiate with him for fear that, if they did not, he might detach the Walloon provinces from the union, perhaps even (as Walsingham feared) take them over to Don John.

As always, fear of France gaining possession of the Low Countries spurred Elizabeth to action even more than fear of Spain tyrannizing there. Yet how was she to stop Anjou? Undoubtedly the best way would be to bring the States to agreement with Don John before their necessities drove them to call in the French. So in April 1578 she sent Wilkes to attempt mediation once again. Once again it failed and most of her Councillors then agreed that the only course was to outbid Anjou by offering more substantial aid.

She did lend another £5,000 in April and allow the purchase of a large quantity of munitions in England. But that was as far as she would go. To give aid enough to outbid Anjou must wreck her good relations with Philip, even if it did not provoke open war with Spain. Besides, she had already lent the States £25,000, and another £40,000 to hire John Casimir, with little or nothing to show for it. Why risk wrecking her own finances by lending still larger sums to those whose credit was so low that they could hardly borrow £20,000 at Antwerp even at twenty-five per cent interest? Why pour good money after bad into this seemingly bottomless abyss?

Moreover, was Anjou really so dangerous? He had sent a secret envoy, back in March, to soothe her fears and protest his devotion. In May Sir Edward Stafford, on a special mission to Paris, found Henry III anxious enough to see his turbulent brother occupied outside the realm but too conscious of the precarious situation in France to challenge Spain by giving him open support in the Netherlands. Anjou's Netherlands scheme was pretty clearly a private venture, not an enterprise of the French crown. If, therefore, Elizabeth could find some way to control the Duke, might she not use him safely to fight her battles in the Low Countries at his own expense and without burning her fingers? And what better way than reviving the old project for her own marriage to him? Despite her past record she was still, as Walsingham said, 'the best marriage in her parish'[12] and Anjou's secret envoy had given her cause to hope that the Duke might swallow the bait.

Still, she was not quite sure and there could be no doubt that a peace between Don John and the States would be a better solution. So in June 1578 she sent Walsingham and Lord Cobham to make a final attempt at mediation. They were not, however, to oppose an agreement between the States and Anjou, only to advise the States to see that he did not come in with power enough to overrule them. They were also to assess the States' power and, if they found it inadequate even with the aid of Anjou and Casimir, they might promise that Elizabeth would send an English army if she were given Sluys and Flushing as security. Here, then, were the three strings to Elizabeth's bow – peace between the States and Don John for preference; failing that, Anjou; in the last resort, if even Anjou's aid were inadequate, open English assistance.

The two ambassadors' reports in July 1578 made the first course look hopeless and the third unnecessary. The States demanded not only their ancient liberties and the withdrawal of all Don John's troops, but also the recognition of Matthias as their Governor and the reference of religious matters to themselves for settlement. Even Walsingham felt that Don John could not with honour concede such terms[13] and Elizabeth, when she heard them, raged furiously against the States. At the same time Walsingham wrote that 'the more I consider the state of this country, the harder I find it for the King of Spain ever to recover the full possession thereof unless God should take away the Prince [of Orange].'[14] He meant to encourage the Queen to action. Instead he seems to have encouraged her to remember that the two provinces of Holland and Zeeland had held off Alba and Requesens for four years. Surely the entire Netherlands could do at least as well against Don John?

Moreover, at this moment two more envoys from Anjou brought her a formal proposal of marriage and an assurance that he would undertake nothing without her liking. Angry with the States and feeling fairly sure of Anjou, she now refused to send any forces to the Netherlands or even to honour her earlier pledge to stand security for loans up to £100,000, unless they delivered Sluys and Flushing as security. Her Councillors were aghast and ten days later their clamour did induce her to offer 10,000 or 12,000 troops or the rest of the £100,000 loan if Walsingham and Cobham felt that there was real danger of Anjou becoming master of the Low Countries or going over to Spain. It was too late, for on August 13th, 1578, the States General came to terms with Anjou. The terms, however, were reassuring. The States accepted him only as an ally, as 'defender of Belgic liberties'. He was to have no share in their general government nor any right to treat with any province separately, though he might conquer for himself any lands east of the Meuse (i.e. Luxembourg, Limburg, and southern Liège), and would be preferred before all others as sovereign if the States should cast off their allegiance to Spain. In return he was to provide 10,000 foot and 2,000 horse for three months and thereafter 3,000 foot and 500 horse until the war ended. If he could be held to these terms, he would be no great danger to England and Elizabeth, as soon as she heard them, again withdrew her offer of troops and would stand bond only for the £28,000 the States had already borrowed in Antwerp. Even for that she required jewels and plate of equivalent value as security.

335

That this was the outcome of Elizabeth's personal policy there can be no doubt. All through the summer of 1578 she had gone her own devious way, generally in defiance of the advice of almost all her Councillors. She had, so far as possible, kept them in the dark about her dealings with Anjou and even Burghley was not immediately let into her secret. 'Our conference with Her Majesty about affairs is both seldom and slender,' Leicester wrote on August 1st[15]. Sussex and Sir Nicholas Bacon seem to have been on her side and Burghley's attitude, torn between his traditional suspicion of France and his perennial desire to see the Queen married, is not always clear. But the majority were certainly in favour of giving prompt and substantial aid to save the States from both Don John and Anjou.

Yet it is hard to deny that in judging the situation and its possibilities Elizabeth, for all her maddening hesitations and gyrations, was right and her Councillors wrong. She could not persuade the States and Don John to peace and, as Sussex put it, 'for the Queen to be the head of the war is more, I fear, than she can go through withal or the realm will maintain.'[16] To go openly to the States' defence would be to challenge Spain openly to war and for that England was as yet hardly prepared. Almost any other course that would prolong the Netherlands resistance to Spain without enabling the French to impatronize themselves of those countries, was preferable at this stage. And in the Anjou courtship Elizabeth had found such a course. It was to give her another seven years to make her realm more ready for war. It might well have given her longer still but for a series of historical accidents that destroyed for a time the premises upon which her policy, indeed most of Tudor policy, was based.

Chapter 25

The Years of Peace

THE years of peace between 1573 and 1585 were also decisive years in the work, begun in the fifteen sixties, of settling the nation's religion, strengthening its defences, and stabilizing its economy.

In religion it was now that the great mass of Englishmen, even if they did not all become active Protestants, turned their backs finally and conclusively upon Rome. Most people find a winning cause attractive and the new generation now coming to manhood could barely, if at all, remember any church service other than that according to the 1559 Prayer Book. They could perhaps remember little about the fires of Smithfield either. But what many of them had read in Foxe's 'Book of Martyrs' must have seemed amply confirmed by what they heard of Alba's rule in the Netherlands and of the Massacre of St Bartholomew's Day in France. Young Philip Sidney, for example, soon to become the paragon of Protestant chivalry, was born in the year of Mary Tudor's Spanish marriage and named after his godfather Philip of Spain. The Mass was officially banned in England when he was four and his first visit abroad landed him in Paris in August 1572.

Even in Catholic families the Mass had been known for a generation only as a forbidden and more or less furtive ceremony. It was a ceremony, too, that seemed doomed soon to lapse for want of celebrants. For as the old priests died off, there were none to replace them. There was nowhere in England where successors to them could be trained. In fact, in the fifteen seventies Catholicism in England bore all the marks of a dying cause. It was also a cause depressed by a sense of its own impotence after the successive failures of the conspiracy against Cecil, of the northern rebellion, and of the Ridolfi plot. Only, it seemed, by a successful foreign invasion could England ever be won back to the old faith. And that was a solution that most English Catholics were too conscious of their Englishness, or too lukewarm in their Catholicism, to contemplate. All therefore, that most of them asked was to be left to vegetate in peace, without being compelled to choose between their temporal and their spiritual allegiances.

Pope Pius V's 'roaring bull' of excommunication and the answering legislation of the English Parliament made even that difficult. Many did struggle to avoid the unwelcome choice between creed and country, but more and more compromised with conscience and conformed at least outwardly, as the state required. As the Puritans, even those who now desired to replace episcopacy by presbyterianism, were still working for further reform from within, the Queen's Church was gradually becoming in fact as well as in law the Church of all Englishmen.

This was, of course, too good to last and towards 1580, in religious matters as in foreign affairs, the tide began to run less strongly Elizabeth's way. We need do no more than mention the growing assertiveness of the Puritans, for although that troubled the Queen increasingly, it rather strengthened than weakened England's unity in face of the Catholic powers. The beginning of a Catholic revival was a different matter, for that could re-create a treasonous faction inside the country and open a gate for a foreign invader. That, it seems clear, was not the original purpose of the exiled William Allen, a former principal of St Mary's Hall, Oxford, when in 1568 he founded a seminary at Douai in the Spanish Netherlands for the mission of reconverting England. It was certainly not the purpose of most of the dedicated young priests who from 1574 slipped across the Channel from Douai, and later from Reims, in growing numbers and varying disguises. The first Jesuits who came to reinforce them in 1580, led by two more exiles from Oxford, Edmund Campion and Robert Parsons, did have permission to discuss political matters with 'those whose fidelity has been long and steadfast'.[1] But even this licence was withdrawn from the Jesuits who followed them. Few underground resistance workers, indeed, have had purer motives or a more heroic history and, of the two hundred and fifty who between 1577 and 1603 were executed for treason or died in prison, almost every one honestly believed that he was dying for the faith.

Yet this was a tribute to their own unworldliness and to the thoroughness of their indoctrination rather than a just judgment upon what they were doing. For their tragedy was that the actions of their Church's leaders and the reactions of the English government made it impossible to keep religion and politics apart. Pope

Pius V's bull had excommunicated not only Elizabeth but also all
who continued to obey her and recognize her as their sovereign. It
thus commanded resistance and legalized rebellion. The Explanation, which Pope Gregory XIII (1572–85) authorized Campion
and Parsons to publish in 1580, did release the English Catholics
from this anathema and these obligations, but only until the
'Enterprise of England' could be launched and the invader was
ready to hurl Elizabeth from her throne. Then they would still be
expected to play their parts.

Nor was it Pope Gregory's fault that they had to wait until
1588 for this. Within a few months of the Explanation his trusted
Secretary of State, the Cardinal of Como, gave written approval to
a project for Elizabeth's assassination.[2] Before that, the Pope had
encouraged Don John of Austria's invasion plans in 1577 and in
1578 he fitted out a ship and troops for the renegade Stukeley to
raise a rebellion in Ireland. The ship, like many of these Catholic
projects, was so ill found that it almost sank halfway, and at Lisbon
Stukeley and his men went off to find their deaths alongside King
Sebastian of Portugal in Morocco. However, the Irish rebel James
Fitzmaurice Fitzgerald and the Pope's nuncio, the Jesuit Dr
Nicholas Sander, with Portuguese and Spanish connivance,
scraped together another motley force at Lisbon and Ferrol. With
this they reached Ireland in July 1579. The Earl of Desmond and
some Irish rallied to them and for a year or more part of Munster
was in their hands. Not till November 1580 did Lord Grey capture
Smerwick, their last stronghold, and execute its defenders as
pirates. It was never, perhaps, a very dangerous affair, but it cost
Elizabeth over £250,000[3] and it was a clear act of war by the Pope.
Coinciding as it did with Campion's and Parsons's mission, it made
nonsense of the pretence that the missionaries were only winning
religious converts and not making potential traitors as well.

That, at any rate, was how most Englishmen saw it and the
plots of the next few years strengthened their conviction. There was
the project which Allen and the Jesuits Parsons, Holt, and Crichton
discussed with Guise and Mendoza in 1582–3 for the Catholic
powers to invade England through Scotland, whither Holt and
Crichton were dispatched to prepare the way. It was for complicity
in this project and for designing the Queen's death that Francis
Throckmorton was arrested in 1583 and executed early next year.
In 1583, too, there was the wild plot of Somerville, a mentally

unstable Warwickshire gentleman, who announced to all and sundry that he was on his way to London to assassinate the Queen. In 1585 there was William Parry, another would-be assassin, who had a letter of approval from the Pope's Secretary. He had failed to take his chance because, he said, the Queen looked so like Henry VIII that he could not do the deed – though just possibly he was trying to fool both sides, for he had certainly been working for both sides. Besides the plots there was a growing stream of printed propaganda, much of it under Parsons's direction, much of it merely devotional, but much of it political as, for example, the scurrilous *Leicester's Commonwealth* (1584). All this plotting and propaganda was happening at the same time as the missions of the seminarists and Jesuits and under the same patronage and direction. It is hardly surprising, therefore, that the government and most Englishmen regarded them as all tarred with the same brush.

The outcome was that the Catholic cause in England was at once saved and ruined. The missionaries converted some back to the old faith and strengthened the hard core of true believers. They thus made sure that English Catholicism would not die out as it had seemed doomed to die out in the fifteen seventies. But the increasing severity of the penal laws, which the plots and missions provoked in the fifteen eighties, trimmed off the large fringe of timid or conventional old Catholics and left Catholicism as the creed of a devoted minority, a backwater more and more cut off from the main streams of national life. More fatal still, because the Pope had chosen to attack Elizabeth with the arm of the flesh as well as with spiritual weapons, the missionaries were bound to appear to most Englishmen as recruiting sergeants for his secular arm. Or, as Burghley put it in his *Execution of Justice in England* (1583), if they pretended 'that none are traitors that are not armed, they will make Judas no traitor, that came to Christ without armour, colouring his treason with a kiss'.[4] So patriotism became more and more identified with Protestantism in English minds and, however sharp the differences between Anglicans and Puritans, they stood shoulder to shoulder in unity when the King of Spain began to prepare his Armada to execute the bulls of Rome.

With this growth in unity went a marked growth in strength. In matters of national defence the fifteen seventies witnessed the beginning of a modernization of the land and sea forces that was to increase their efficiency considerably by the time war came in

1585. Alba's arrival in the Netherlands in 1567 and the serious deficiencies revealed by the mobilization against the northern rebels in 1569 at last aroused serious alarm about the county levies upon which defence by land depended.[5] As early as 1567 there were suggestions for forming a corps of harquebusiers. Then in 1569 the government proposed to enlist four or five thousand men, equip them with modern firearms, and give them three or four weeks' training a year, the cost being borne by a special levy upon the clergy, local and central officials, and other well-to-do people. This, however, was too alien to English tradition, and smacked perhaps too much of a standing army, to get anything but a cold reception from the county gentry, who as local commissioners of musters were the men in charge of local military administration. They objected to the 'importunate charges' of such a scheme and no less to its principle of selective taxation. So it had to be dropped.

The government then turned to refurbishing the traditional county forces. It was, of course, neither possible nor necessary to equip and train all the 'able men' in the counties with modern weapons, with firearms and pikes. The most that could be done, or needed to be done, was to equip and train a selected number, the 'trained bands', in each county. Accordingly, in 1573 the Privy Council ordered 'a convenient and sufficient number of the most able to be chosen and collected' at the musters in each county and then to be 'tried, armed, and weaponed, and so consequently taught and trained'. At the same time it insisted upon the obligation of everyone to provide or help to provide, according to his ability, weapons and armour as the 1558 statutes required. More than that, it steadily increased the quotas for all classes until they were well above the statutory levels.

All this, however, cost money and the cost fell upon the counties and towns rather than upon the central government. It meant not only making steadily rising assessments of the quantities of weapons and armour individuals had to provide, but also levying steadily rising local rates for training, powder, and so forth. It therefore produced much grumbling and passive resistance. Dorset, for example, at first agreed to train five hundred men once a quarter, but soon cut the number to one hundred. Indeed, it looks as if, after the first impulse in 1573, training to a great extent lapsed until alarms about Don John's invasion schemes brought fresh government pressure in 1577. Thereafter, particularly as the skies darkened in the fifteen eighties, the Privy Council succeeded in insisting upon regular training for eight or ten days a year, though it had to consent to many counties reducing their numbers of men to be trained in order to make sure that at least some men really were trained. Along with this went some improvement in organization and command. In December 1583 the 'maritime' counties of the south and south-east were ordered to levy rates to put their trained bands on an active footing. In April 1584 the men were organized into companies, at first coinciding with divisions and later with hundreds in each county. The companies were put under captains who were responsible for their mustering and training. In the summer of 1585 Lords Lieutenant, with deputy lieutenants in place of the old commissioners of musters, were put over them. With the coming of war, this organization was gradually extended until it covered the entire country.

It was, however, upon the navy that the first responsibility for national defence rested. And during these years the navy underwent something like a revolution. Much of the driving force behind this revolution came from John Hawkins, backed by the steady and understanding support of Burghley.[6] It was not until January 1st, 1578, that Hawkins became Treasurer of the Navy, the principal official of the Navy Board. But his influence was at work some time before that for, apart from his contacts with Burghley, he had married the daughter of old Benjamin Gonson, his predecessor as Treasurer of the Navy, while the Surveyor, Sir William Winter, had been his business associate in the West Indian ventures.

The first change was in the design of the new ships built from 1570 onwards. They became longer and leaner, narrower in proportion to their length, and without the towering forecastles that made the older ships so unhandy in a strong breeze and so liable to strain and leak in rough seas. The new vessels were usually of rather smaller tonnage, but faster, handier, and more seaworthy, able to sail a little nearer the wind and able to keep the sea for longer periods. They were also more heavily gunned with guns of longer range, ship-sinkers rather than ship-boarders. The outstanding example was the *Revenge*, of four hundred and fifty tons, completed in 1577. Drake regarded her as the finest warship of her day and under Grenville's command in 1591 she was to justify that claim in her final blaze of glory off the Azores. Nor was it only the new ships that embodied these new principles. For, particularly after Hawkins became Treasurer, many of the older ships were modified, in many cases virtually rebuilt, on the new lines. Thus although the number of the Queen's ships was not much increased – there were twenty-two in 1578 and twenty-five by 1587 – their quality and fighting power were greatly improved. What is more, the greater part of the Queen's navy was transformed from a short-range, Narrow Seas, almost a coast-defence, force into a high-seas fleet capable of operating at long range as an ocean-going fighting navy.

Moreover, during Hawkins's Treasurership all the ships were brought to the highest pitch of soundness and efficiency, as the Armada campaign was to prove. Besides the fighting ships, eighteen ocean-going pinnaces were built by 1587. These were capable of acting as a scouting screen between England and the Spanish coast to give advance warning of a hostile fleet's approach. On land, too, the ancient network of beacons was reconstituted and elaborated to flash the warning on from Land's End or the Lizard to the burghers of Carlisle. Nor were the seamen forgotten. In 1585 their wages, when the Queen's ships were in commission, were raised from 6s. 8d. to 10s. a month. The extra charge was partly offset by the reduction in the crews from one man for every ton and a half of ship to one man for every two tons, a reduction which improved design made possible. All this was done without any increase, in fact with a decrease, in the Queen's expenses. For by cutting out the waste and graft that had grown up in the naval administration since Henry VIII's day, Hawkins reduced the over-all expenditure on the upkeep of the fleet from around £10,000 a year to barely £6,000. This was far from popular with his colleagues and subordinates, including Winter and his brother, the Clerk of the Ships, who had found the maintenance of the Queen's navy a very profitable family business. Nor were the new ships popular with the Narrow Seas officers like William Borough. But the results spoke for themselves.

Hawkins had given the Queen an instrument of war which was not only capable of defending England against invasion and of cutting Spain's communications through the Channel to its army in the Netherlands. He had provided one which might also reach out to harry Spain's communications across the Atlantic to the silver mines of America. That this was indeed in his mind is clear from his offer in 1570 to go with ten ships of his own and two of the

Queen's to lay for the homeward-bound silver fleet with (as he reckoned) its cargo of £6,000,000 of bullion. His offer was not taken up at that time, but the idea lived on and had much to do with the re-shaping of the Queen's navy in the following years into a weapon for bringing Spain to its knees as well as for just repulsing its assaults. By sea, even more than by land, the years of peace had brought a very considerable increase in England's strength for war.

It has sometimes been argued that more should have been done, that Elizabeth should have had a navy as large as her father's instead of half as large; that she should have formed at least the nucleus of a standing army. But she had no monastic lands to sell, no profits from debasing the coinage, to swell her severely limited income. The 1569 rebellion cost her over £93,000; two Irish rebellions in the fifteen seventies not far short of £500,000. By 1575 she had repaid all her own and her sister's loans and could borrow, if she needed to, at 8 or 9 per cent when Philip of Spain had to pay 12 or 18 per cent. By 1584 she had put by a reserve of close on £300,000 of 'chested treasure'.[7] But in the event of war that would not go far, for as Burghley had noted some years back, it took three times as much to put an army in the field as it had done in Henry VIII's time.[8] In fact by 1589, after four years of war, the £300,000 had shrunk to £29,000 and by 1590 it was gone.[9]

Of course, judged by later standards, taxation was not heavy during these years of peace. The Parliaments of 1572, 1576, and 1581 each made grants that brought in something over £170,000 apiece, collected over three years. The total amount so collected in the ten years 1575–84 was £348,000. This was less than a third of the £1,092,000 that was to be collected in the ten years 1593–1602.[10] But those were years of war. In peacetime the taxpayer still believed that the crown should and largely could 'live of its own'. When we remember this, and the resistance of the counties to the rates for the trained bands, it is indeed mildly surprising that the government got as much as it did from Parliament with so little serious trouble.

No doubt the country could have paid more. In 1584 John Hawkins firmly believed that 'the substance of this realm is trebled in value' since Elizabeth's accession.[11] Yet even if his guess was right, what is statistically possible is not always politically wise. The experience of 1566 did not make Elizabeth any the more

344

anxious to come cap in hand to Parliaments which were all too ready to meddle in such delicate matters as religion, the succession, and her own marriage. Nor does the outcry over monopolies in the last years of her reign, or that over impositions under James I, or the fiscal policies of Charles I's 'personal government', suggest that she would have been wise to seek greatly to augment her 'ordinary' revenues. It may well be that England, through Elizabeth's parsimony in these years of peace, gained more in political unity than it lost in military and naval preparedness.

It may be, too, that it gained more in economic strength. For comparatively light taxation played its part in fostering the developments which had started in the fifteen sixties. The progress of home manufactures continued to lessen England's dependence upon imports from abroad and to increase the variety of her exports. The rapid decrease in the Staplers' exports of wool, from about 3,000 sacks a year before 1565 to under 200 a year in the fifteen eighties,[12] reflected in part the renewed growth of the woollen cloth manufacture, especially in the 'new draperies' which could find wider markets abroad than the older cloths. Other manufactures were also going ahead, many of them of vital importance to national defence. Firearms, pikes, and corslets for the trained bands no longer need be bought at Antwerp. Iron and brass artillery was even being exported, not always legally. Gunpowder, too, could sometimes be spared for export, though much of the saltpetre needed for its manufacture still had to be imported. England's economic independence was also increased when home-manufactured copper wire began to be available for wool-carding and cloth-finishing, when English-made glass became obtainable for glazing windows, and when home-manufactured salt began to take the place of imports from the disturbed areas of western France. Coal, too, was beginning to provide an alternative fuel to the diminishing wood supplies for domestic use and some industrial uses.[13]

Nevertheless, whether or not all this merits description as the beginning of 'an early industrial revolution', Elizabethan England was far from being an industrial society. Its well-being still depended principally upon its agriculture, its wealth upon its commerce. The dying down of the mid-century agrarian agitation suggests that agriculture was now recovering its balance, an important element in national stability. Meanwhile the redeployment of overseas trade continued along the lines sketched out earlier.

By far the most important part of this trade was, of course, the woollen cloth export handled by the Merchant Adventurers. For, even twenty years later, a parliamentary report of 1604 described them as having 'the managing of the two-thirds part of the clothing of this realm'[14] and cloth in the fifteen sixties made up four-fifths of all English exports.[15] As we have seen, the Adventurers in 1567 had found in Hamburg a fairly adequate substitute for Antwerp and until 1577 it was thither that they sent their main fleets. With Antwerp also reopened to them in 1573, despite interference from Holland and Zeeland cruisers, and with Emden still being visited by some north-country Adventurers, the middle fifteen seventies were on the whole fairly satisfactory years for England's principal exporters. Things grew less easy when in 1577 the jealousy of the other Hanse Towns prevented Hamburg from renewing its ten years' agreement. The Adventurers then had to move back again to Emden until in 1587 they found a new base on the Elbe, just below Hamburg, at Stade. The Spanish Fury at Antwerp in 1576 and the desertion of that city by many Italian, Spanish, and Portuguese merchants during the ensuing troubles, also added to their difficulties. The opening of a new 'vent' at Middelburg in Zeeland in 1582 was some slight compensation. Also the ten years at Hamburg had allowed them to knit their own connections with other German centres inland and the changes of their headquarters had encouraged their members to forage for themselves. Nevertheless, all this had loosened the Fellowship's control, and their trade, though still substantial, was no longer up to the levels of the great days at Antwerp.

However, while the Adventurers were running into difficulties, other 'vents' were being opened or widened. The Baltic and Eastland trade prospered, despite the opposition of Danzig. In 1579 the merchants engaged in it were incorporated as the Eastland Company, which strengthened their organization and bargaining power. At the same time they moved their headquarters from Danzig to Elbing, a Polish town which, like Emden, did not belong to the Hanseatic League. The King of Poland, on bad terms with Danzig himself, welcomed them, although for years to come English and Hanseatic agents waged a running diplomatic battle at his court. Meanwhile during most of the fifteen eighties the Eastland

Company flourished. Its trade was worth perhaps no more than an eighth of the Merchant Adventurers', but it provided a useful outlet for English finished cloth (the Adventurers exported most of their cloths 'white', or unfinished) and a no less valuable source of supply for timber and naval stores. We have seen how the Muscovy Company had already firmly established another useful trade with Russia in those same commodities. That, too, still prospered, although from 1583 the Dutch also began to creep into it and from 1580 the outbreak of war between Persia and Turkey frustrated the hopes of pushing trade overland to the middle East.

Moreover, the penetration of English trade into the Baltic and Russia, which had begun in the fifteen fifties and fifteen sixties, was paralleled in the fifteen seventies and fifteen eighties by a similar penetration into the Mediterranean and Levant. Direct trade with Spain was, of course, reopened in 1573 and a Spanish Company got its charter in 1577. But English ships now pushed beyond the northern and western ports of Spain into the Mediterranean, where very few had been seen for twenty years. The growing demands of the populations of southern Europe for north European corn, fish, and cloth could no longer be met through Antwerp. Venetian shipping resources had been too strained by the war of Cyprus (1570-71) and the Lepanto campaign, and Spain's communications through the Channel were too precarious, for them to fetch these commodities for themselves. So from 1573 English ships again appeared in growing numbers in the western Mediterranean, particularly at the new port of Leghorn where the Grand Duke of Tuscany made all merchants welcome. They soon found, too, that there was a ready demand, not only for English cloth of the better sorts, but also for English lead and tin – tin was needed to make bronze, from which the best cannon were manufactured.

It was this that induced the Sultan of Turkey to listen to the proposals of a group of London merchants in 1578 and in 1580 to grant 'capitulations' permitting them to trade to his dominions. In 1581 Elizabeth incorporated them as the Turkey Company and gave them a monopoly of this trade for seven years, besides herself investing in their venture. Two years later the Venice Company was incorporated for trade to the Venetian dominions. The two were amalgamated in 1592 as the Levant Company. Meanwhile the older established trade to Morocco continued to provide

347

valuable supplies of sugar and, more important, saltpetre in return for cloth, iron, timber, and shipbuilding materials. Here, too, the leading merchants were in 1585 formed into the Barbary Company, though like all the other monopolistic companies they met with considerable competition from interlopers who were unable or unwilling to join their chartered circle.

This spreading of English trade in English ships to the Baltic and Russia, to the Mediterranean, Levant, and North Africa, did something to compensate for the Merchant Adventurers' difficulties. Added to their German and Netherlands trade, it helped to falsify the belief of Granvelle and others that English commerce could not do without Antwerp. It meant that England no longer had nearly all her commercial eggs in one basket and a Spanish basket at that. Besides the gain in economic independence, there were incidental political advantages too. The Adventurers' ten years' residence at Hamburg, which so aroused the jealousy of Danzig and Lübeck, further undermined the cohesion of the already declining Hanseatic League. The Eastland Company's trade brought closer and on the whole friendly relations with Protestant Denmark and Sweden, despite occasional disputes about Danish tolls on ships passing through the Sound. It also forged new links with Poland and East Prussia. All of this was to be of some value later when, during the war, Spanish diplomacy tried to get north Germany and the Baltic closed to English and Dutch trade. Southwards, too, by 1585 the English had made their services too valuable for the Spanish war to close the Mediterranean to their shipping, while the trade to Turkey and north Africa provided links with possible, if in Christian eyes disreputable, allies against Spanish power. The presence of an English resident ambassador at Constantinople, paid by the Turkey Company, and of English agents in Morocco, was never in fact to bring active help from the Muslim states in the war against Spain, but it was to be a continual source of anxiety and expense to the Spanish government.

What was to be more directly helpful, when war eventually came, was the reinforcement of English sea power that resulted from this wider spreading of overseas commerce. The ships that carried the Merchant Adventurers' cloth exports on the comparatively short runs to Antwerp, Middelburg, or even Hamburg, were usually fairly small vessels of fifty to one hundred tons. Their crews gained no great sea experience and the ships themselves were for the most part too small to be any real reinforcement to the Queen's navy.[16] On the other hand, those employed in the Levant trade were often quite large and well armed, for they had to make longer voyages through more dangerous waters where they might at any time have to defend themselves against Muslim corsairs. The largest of them, the *Merchant Royal* (400 tons), was not so very greatly inferior to the Queen's *Revenge* (450 tons). There were others of two hundred tons or more among the fourteen ships of all sizes that the Turkey Company had in regular trade in 1585 and the nineteen of the Venice Company. To these larger Levanters could be added a number of privately owned ships of similar size, designed primarily for trade but with an eye on their possible use as privateers too. Some, like the London *Hercules* (300 tons), belonged to merchants; others to noblemen or gentry who in these days found shipping a good investment – such were the *Galleon Leicester* (400 tons), Sir Walter Raleigh's *Roebuck* (300 tons), and the perhaps smaller *Castle of Comfort* whose successive owners included Sir Henry Compton, John Hawkins, and Sir Richard Grenville. Together such ships as these formed, like their predecessors in Henry VIII's day, a real 'royal naval reserve', an R.N.R. whose best units could take their place alongside the Queen's warships in a fleet action, were indeed in 1588 to share with them the main burden of the fighting against the Armada. The spreading out of England's commerce thus helped to restore England's strength at sea, her first line of defence against invasion.

Meanwhile westward enterprises across the Atlantic continued to build up a body of seamen with the oceanic experience to use that strength offensively in the way that Hawkins thought it might be used if war with Spain should come. But after 1568 raiding here took the place of trading and between 1569 and 1572 a number of Englishmen, as well as a still larger number of French Huguenots, were marauding in the Caribbean. In part this was simply the Channel privateers going farther afield as Spanish trade in home waters dried up. But a good deal of it seems to have been organized by Hawkins, the Winters, and others holding official positions.[17] Drake's 1571 and 1572–3 voyages were probably part of this unofficial campaign by officials, an oceanic counterpart to Gilbert's 'volunteers' in Zeeland.

Certainly the 1572–3 voyage looks more than a private marauding venture. Drake's force was tiny, two small ships and seventy-
three men. But his objective was the year's shipment of gold and
silver from the mines of Peru. This was sent up the Pacific coast by
sea as far as Panama and then transported by mule trains across
the isthmus to Nombre de Dios on the Caribbean side. There a
convoy of large ships, the *galeones*, came each summer to carry it to
Havana, where they joined the other annual convoy, the *flota*,
from Vera Cruz with the bullion of Mexico. The combined
convoys were then escorted by the ten or twelve warships of the
recently formed Indian Guard across the Atlantic to Cadiz. It
was this combined convoy that Hawkins had offered to attack in
1570.

Drake, of course, could not attempt that. His eye was on the
weak land link across the isthmus of Panama, where a small and
less official-looking force might still hope for a rich haul. For the
only Spanish settlements there were Panama, Nombre de Dios, and
a small halfway post at Venta Cruces. After providing garrisons for
these and escorts for the mule trains, the Spaniards could barely
muster two or three hundred men and the nearest help was far
away. Also there were on the isthmus hostile tribes of Cimaroons,
runaway Negro slaves who had intermarried with the Indians.
With help from these and from another English privateer, James
Ranse, Drake surprised Nombre de Dios but failed to carry off – or
perhaps to find – much booty. Then, with the help of a Huguenot,
le Testu, early in 1573 he captured one of the mule trains. He
lacked men to carry away all the bullion but the share he brought
home in August 1573 was worth £20,000.

By then Elizabeth had patched up her quarrel with Spain and
for the next few years she made some effort to divert her sailors away
from Spanish America. The raids did not cease, but those we hear
of were small-scale private ventures, mostly concerned with plundering coastwise shipping. John Oxenham, who had been with
Drake in 1572–3, did in 1576–7 cross the isthmus of Panama, build
a pinnace on the Pacific side, and intercept one or two ships
coming up from Peru. But he, too, had only a small force, two
ships and fifty-three men, which in August 1577 was overwhelmed
by the Spaniards. The more serious and official enterprises were
diverted to projects less offensive to Spain. Projects there were
galore. The Muscovy Company's hopes of finding a North-East

Passage to Cathay did not die until the attempt of Pett and Jackman in 1580 finally proved it impracticable. The idea of finding a North-West Passage around the north of America also came to life again with Martin Frobisher's three voyages of 1576–8 and was to inspire three more notable attempts by John Davis in 1585–7. There were schemes for planting colonies in Newfoundland and on the American coast northward of the Spanish settlements, schemes which cost Sir Humphrey Gilbert his life in 1583 and which Raleigh and Grenville were to bring briefly to realization in Virginia in 1585 and 1587. Grenville and William Hawkins also proposed in 1573–4 to sail through the Straits of Magellan to discover and settle Terra Australis Incognita, the great southern continent that was supposed to stretch north-westwards across the Pacific from the Straits to New Guinea. Their proposal was rejected. To let loose in the Pacific a man of Grenville's nature and privateering record was probably regarded as too great a risk when Anglo-Spanish relations were steadily improving.

By the end of 1577, however, the European situation had changed again. Peace had just been made in France and war had broken out between Don John and the States General in the Netherlands. If that war was to be ended in a manner satisfactory to England and before the French could intervene, pressure had to be put upon Philip of Spain. So, in December 1577 Elizabeth sent Wilkes to Madrid to press her demands more urgently. In the same month she allowed Drake, an even more dangerous man than Grenville, to sail for the Pacific with three fighting ships and one hundred and sixty men. This was no unauthorized private venture. Drake sailed with the Queen's commission and instructions and with the financial backing of Leicester, Walsingham, Hatton, Lord Admiral Clinton, John Hawkins, and the Winters. In so far as his expedition included none of the Queen's ships, it was less obviously an act of state than Hawkins's West Indian voyages, more easy to disavow than Winter in 1560. Yet there can be no doubt that it was a deliberate act of royal policy. Moreover, although ostensibly Drake went to carry out the Terra Australis project, before he sailed he obtained (or so he later said) the Queen's approval to other plans which she bade him keep secret, especially from Burghley.

Just what those plans were, we can only guess, though they clearly involved acts hostile to Spain and perhaps to Portugal. One important object may have been to explore, and if possible to open, a route through the Magellan Straits to the Spice Islands of Indonesia. This would have annoyed the Portuguese, but it is hard to see why it should have been kept secret from Burghley. On the other hand, Drake certainly knew of Oxenham's intentions, though not yet of his failure, and Oxenham's men boasted to the Spaniards that they themselves were 'nothing compared to what is coming'.[18] Possibly, therefore, Drake hoped to join Oxenham and establish a Pacific base from which his ships could blockade the silver route from Peru to Panama, even perhaps to hold the isthmus itself, as a Spanish officer reckoned three hundred Englishmen could well do indefinitely. A blockade of the Peruvian silver would have handicapped Don John in the Netherlands even more than the seizure of the Genoese loan had handicapped Alba and it is tempting to guess that this is what Elizabeth had in mind when she approved Drake's secret plans.

If that guess is right, then this voyage must be added to the considerable number of Drake's enterprises that produced brilliant results but fell short of achieving decisive strategic success. For after passing safely through the Straits of Magellan in September 1578, two of his three ships were forced back by fierce north-westerly gales. One of them disappeared for ever; the other's crew forced their commander to return to England. So Drake was left alone in the Pacific with only the ship he stood up in, his flagship, the 120-ton *Pelican*, now renamed the *Golden Hind*. He himself had been driven so far south and east that he knew there could be no continent south of the Straits, but only open sea joining the Pacific to the Atlantic. This and the north-westerly gales discouraged any further thoughts of Terra Australis and he cruised on up the west coast, plundering shipping, surprising coastal towns, and capturing one of the rich but almost unarmed treasure ships from Peru to Panama. Aboard this ship, the *Cacafuego*, was silver enough to ballast the *Golden Hind* on her journey home.

In one sense it was all so easy and simple, for the Spanish settlements on the Pacific coast were quite unprepared and almost defenceless, while even the ships sent to pursue him were often totally unarmed. The Spaniards, indeed, were taken completely by surprise. On one beach a landing party found a man quietly sleeping beside thirteen bars of silver and 'we took the silver and left the man'[19] – apparently still fast asleep. But with only one ship and, as he now learned, Oxenham already captured, Drake could not attack Panama or the isthmus. He did in April and May 1579 sail north far enough to satisfy himself that the western entrance to the North-West Passage was not so far south as the geographers supposed. Then he spent some weeks refitting the *Golden Hind* on the Californian coast, making friends with the local Indians, and putting up a brass plate to proclaim that this New Albion now belonged to the Queen of England. (A crudely inscribed brass plate was appropriately picked up near San Francisco in 1937.) That done, in July 1579 he sailed off across the Pacific and Indian Oceans, round the Cape of Good Hope, and home to Plymouth on September 26th, 1580, the first Englishman to circumnavigate the globe.

As a feat of navigation and daring this voyage outtopped all the other achievements of the Elizabethan seamen. Few investors, too, have ever done better than the Privy Councillors and others to whom Drake brought back a return of perhaps 4,700 per cent. The Queen's share alone was not less than £160,000, as much as nine months' ordinary crown revenue or the proceeds of a normal parliamentary grant. The voyage had also revealed the riches and defencelessness of the Spanish Pacific settlements and the practicability of breaking into the Portuguese monopoly in the Spice Islands, though it had damped hopes of an easy westward passage to those Islands. And all this had been achieved with a single 120-ton ship, whose 63-foot keel would fit easily on to a modern cricket pitch.

Soon, too, it became apparent that Drake would not lack imitators. In 1581 a group of investors, including Burghley, Leicester, Drake, and the Muscovy Company, began to prepare an expedition to sail by way of the Cape of Good Hope and India to the Moluccas to exploit Drake's trade treaty with the Sultan of Ternate. It sailed under Edward Fenton in May 1582, four ships, including the powerful 400-ton *Galleon Leicester*. But as soon as Fenton reached the south Atlantic, many of his crews clamoured to follow the *Golden Hind*'s route through the Straits of Magellan and up the Peruvian coast. Fenton, who had express orders not to go that way, vacillated. One of his captains, John Drake, who had been round the world in the *Golden Hind*, made off for the Straits, only to be captured by the Spaniards in the River Plate. With the rest Fenton turned back to England.[20] The ruin of his expedition showed how strong was now the lure of

Spanish silver. It was becoming increasingly difficult to divert adventurous Englishmen away from the plunder of Spanish America to the cold search for a North-West Passage or the hard colonizing labour of Virginia or even to the sober and solid cargo-carrying of European trade.

For Spain, with the Netherlands now a wasting liability instead of a rich asset, the prospect of heavier and more frequent English attacks upon her American colonies and her American silver supplies was certainly a growing irritation. Yet we must not make too much of this. As a modern historian of Spain remarks: 'Drake's operations ... annoyed Philip II but they did not deprive him of a single colony or enable England to gain any. Even the prizes taken were minute compared with the treasure which continued to reach Spain and the trade which she still controlled.'[21] And Philip's immediate reactions were still defensive. Just as he had answered Hawkins's voyages in the fifteen sixties by forming the Indian Guard to escort his silver convoys across the Atlantic, so now his answer to Drake was to plant colonists in a fortified post to guard the Straits of Magellan, to establish standing patrols of armed ships along the Caribbean coasts, and to improve his advance warning system of small, fast dispatch boats, or *avisos*. It was not what happened in the Caribbean or the Pacific that brought England and Spain to war in 1585, but what was happening in the Netherlands and France. To that side of the story we must now turn back again.

Chapter 26

The Road to War

By the fifteen eighties England had worked out answers to most of the problems created by the loss of her possessions across the Channel and by the growth there of the two great Habsburg and Valois monarchies. Her government and people had abandoned their ancestors' dreams of continental empire and had felt their way to a more modern and insular policy relying largely upon sea power. They had also established the conditions to make that change practicable. They had developed a power at sea that could dominate their home waters and they had begun to envisage how it might be used offensively at long range on and across the oceans. They had begun to develop in the trained bands a fairly adequate second line of defence on land that was within the capacity of the government's limited finance and the country's limited manpower. Behind these improved defences the nation had regained the unity and sense of common purpose which had been lost or impaired during the religious changes and economic difficulties of the mid-century. The widening spread of its overseas commerce had ended its excessive dependence upon the Netherlands market and upon the Hanseatic and Venetian carriers. The Reformation in Scotland and the new relationship resulting from it had closed England's postern gate and thereby rounded off her strategic insularity. The rise of the French Huguenots and the Dutch Calvinists, while it had not after all made the Catholic governments of France and Spain forget their mutual secular jealousy, had offered to Elizabeth useful levers to press upon their kings. Despite considerable provocation therefore, both France and Spain had shown during the fifteen seventies anxiety only to avoid an open quarrel with England. Thus far the new approach to foreign policy had proved its validity.

There were, of course, darker shadows in this happy picture. Scottish politics were never entirely stable and they grew less stable for a time as the young James VI grew towards manhood. The anarchic condition of Ireland was a standing temptation to foreign powers, slow though they were to yield to it. The Catholic minority in England, revitalized by the missionary priests and encouraged as potential traitors by the Pope, could still hope for Mary Stuart's accession to revive their cause. Elizabeth's continued refusal to settle the succession tempted a few of them to listen to plans for hastening their liberation by calling in the armies of the Catholic powers. And if neither France nor Spain seemed eager to answer their calls, that only increased the attraction of plots for Elizabeth's assassination.

These, however, were but small shadows on a bright prospect. It needed a series of catastrophic changes, touched off (as at the end of Henry VII's reign) by a series of princely deaths, to blot out the generally promising picture under the clouds of war. But for these unhappy accidents, Elizabethan England might have gone on gathering strength through yet more years of peace.

The first of these accidents was the death of young King Sebastian of Portugal in battle against the Moors at Alcazar in August 1578. His successor, the only remaining representative of the royal house in the male line, was his great-uncle Cardinal Henry, an elderly epileptic who himself died on January 31st, 1580. An illegitimate son, Don Antonio, of Henry's elder brother Luiz, then claimed the throne. He had the support of a nationalist faction among the nobles and perhaps of the mass of the people. But the man with the strongest hereditary claim and the best means to enforce it was Philip II of Spain, the son of Henry's eldest sister. Philip had prepared carefully and now acted promptly. By September 1580 Spanish troops under the Duke of Alba had overrun Portugal; in April 1581 the Portuguese Cortes recognized Philip as their King; and Don Antonio had to seek refuge first in France and then in England.

The acquisition of Portugal brought Spain an alarming accession of strength. It gave her control of the entire Iberian peninsula. It added to her own great colonial empire in the west the rich Portuguese colonial possessions in the east and along the African coast. It added Portuguese control of the spice trade to her own control of the American silver mines. All this, too, coincided in the earlier fifteen eighties with an unprecedentedly large output from those American mines,[1] which gave Philip an unwonted amount of financial elbow room. His total revenues probably now exceeded those of all the other European states put

together. Of no less strategic significance was his acquisition of
the Portuguese royal navy, with its dockyards and its reserves of
skilled mariners. Two of the twelve Portuguese fighting galleons
were barely fit for service. But the other ten, added to those of
the Spanish Indian Guard, could give Philip an ocean-going war
fleet almost equal in numbers to the royal navy of England. At
last he was on his way to possessing the means to challenge
Elizabeth on the high seas, to justify him in considering the
possibility of a sea-borne invasion of her realm. It is small wonder
that Alba's conquest of Portugal in 1580 caused something of
the same alarm in England, and indeed in France, as his arrival
in the Netherlands in 1567.

Philip, of course, still had those rebellious Netherlands on his
hands. In Portugal itself there was popular discontent and, though
most of the Portuguese overseas possessions quietly submitted, the
Azores – one of the vital links in the transatlantic sailing routes –
had declared for Don Antonio. Philip was not yet therefore in a
position, or a mood, to challenge England. Above all, he still
feared what France might do if he committed himself to a struggle
with Elizabeth.

Nevertheless there were disturbing signs in 1580 that he might
be on his way to committing himself and that, if he did, he might
hope to rally Catholic Europe to his side for the 'Enterprise of
England'. In September another eight hundred Papal troops,
mostly Italians but with some Spaniards among them, arrived
from Coruña to reinforce the Irish rebels in Munster. By then,
too, in Scotland Darnley's cousin Esmé Stuart, who had come
over from France in the previous autumn, had won the young
James VI's favour and gained for himself the Earldom of Lennox.
He had drawn together those – and they were many – opposed
to the strong-handed Protestant leader, Morton, whom they
arrested in December 1580. Lennox now professed himself a Calvinist, but he had been a pupil of the Jesuits and was vehemently
suspected of being the agent of the Duke of Guise and the Pope.
In England itself the Jesuits Campion and Parsons, as well as a
hundred or more seminary priests, were busily at work. And, as
if to provide Philip with a pretext for joining in, on September
26th Drake sailed into Plymouth with his shipload of stolen
Spanish silver. Worst of all, through most of the year it seemed
possible that if Spain were to attack England, she would not

have to worry overmuch about the reactions of the French government. For in February 1580 a seventh War of Religion had broken out in France. It was, it is true, a less serious affair than its six predecessors. It was more in the nature of an aristocratic revolt by Henry of Navarre and Condé and it found little support among the Huguenot towns and churches. Yet it could easily swell into another serious religious conflict. If it did, it might well force the French King into the arms of the Guises and of the Catholic League which since 1576 had been steadily gaining support in the cities and provinces of northern and eastern France.

In France, indeed, lay the crux of the matter. If the now over-mighty Philip of Spain was still to be discouraged from attacking England, the first thing necessary was to end the new civil war in France and keep Henry III out of the power of the Guises. To this end Elizabeth did her best to restrain Navarre and in June 1580 she refused Condé any help towards raising troops in Germany. But there was another card, too, that she could play – the Anjou courtship. The course of that courtship, since its revival in the summer of 1578, had not run altogether smooth. At the close of that year Anjou, together with the Archduke Matthias and John Casimir, had withdrawn from the Netherlands. The summer's adventure had run down his resources and, like an unsuccessful gambler pursuing a rich heiress, he now pressed his suit all the more ardently. His agent Simier during the winter and spring of 1579 made great progress in wooing Elizabeth by proxy. He was less successful in persuading her and her Council to agree to the Duke's terms for the marriage settlement, which included being crowned as king and given an income of £60,000 a year.[2] But in August 1579 Anjou himself had come over for twelve days and the affair seemed then to take on a new serious-ness. Unprepossessing though the Duke was – his nickname of her Frog was not the most flattering that Elizabeth could have chosen for him – he appeared to make even better progress in person than Simier (Elizabeth's Monkey) had as proxy.

With Elizabeth, of course, we can never feel quite sure. 'For her own mind, what that really was,' a seventeenth-century writer confessed, 'I must leave as a thing doubly inscrutable, both as she was a queen and a woman.'[3] And if her mind was inscrutable to the next century, modern historians may be pardoned for failing to fathom her heart. Nevertheless there was an emotional element about this phase of the Anjou courtship that suggests more than mere diplomatic manoeuvring. Elizabeth, as she herself had said, was human and she was now in her forty-sixth year. In the spring of 1579 Burghley was still arguing for her marriage on the ground that, by the evidence of her physicians and her women, she might yet for some years hope for children. He was still hopeful in a memorandum that he wrote in October, perhaps still hopeful in January 1580. But that seems to be the last time that he was to use such an argument.[4] It may be that here we have the explanation of Elizabeth's outbursts of tears and repeated shifts from 'yes' to 'no', sometimes within the space of a few hours. It may explain the rapid and unpredictable changes of mood and purpose which baffled her exasperated Councillors and often bore no very obvious relation to the diplomatic circumstances. Again and again she gives the impression of a woman under unusual emotional stress, reluctant to make up her mind yet clutching at straws to avoid finally casting away her last opportunity. All this, nevertheless, bedevilled the course of her policy and we must try to follow its main drift without getting too much caught up in these emotional side eddies.

One of Elizabeth's main difficulties – or excuses? – was that the prospect of her marrying the Catholic heir presumptive of France aroused vociferous and widespread opposition in England. Admonitions, letters, pamphlets, poured in against it. The best known was the Puritan John Stubbe's *Discovery of a Gaping Gulf whereunto England is like to be swallowed by another French Marriage if the Lord forbid not the banns*. When he was punished by having his right hand chopped off, he loyally waved his hat with his left and shouted 'God save the Queen.' But there was no echoing shout from the silent crowd around the scaffold. In the Privy Council, too, only Burghley, Sussex, and perhaps a couple more favoured the match, though when berated by their furious and tear-shedding mistress they all professed to be ready to help arrange it if she insisted.[5] Formal articles were, in fact, agreed on in November 1579. By then, however, Elizabeth too seemed to be losing interest, whether impressed by the outcry or making it an excuse for her reluctance to commit herself finally. So for some months the matter had died down.

Possibly it would have died away altogether but for the Spanish conquest of Portugual, the outbreak of the seventh French War of Religion, and the attendant alarms of 1580. Those events gave it a new usefulness. Anjou still hoped, if not for Elizabeth's hand, at least for her subsidies, while Henry III's alarm at the growing power of Spain made him more eager than before to commit the English Queen to a French marriage. Playing on these hopes and fears, Elizabeth in the summer of 1580 gave Anjou to understand that she could only contemplate an alliance with him if his brother, the French King, granted good terms to the Huguenots. This perhaps played some small part in bringing the war in France to a speedy end in November 1580. Henry III, who anyway had no love for the Guises, was thus enabled for a little while longer to keep his head above the waters of French religious faction.

But it was also very desirable that Henry III should be clearly committed to stand alongside England in face of the growing power of Spain, committed, if possible, to do something to check that growing power. 'We think it good', Elizabeth wrote a little later, 'for the King of Spain to be impeached both in Portugal and his Islands and also in the Low Countries, whereto we shall be ready to give such indirect assistance as shall not at once be a cause of war.'[6] She gave the French an earnest of her good intentions, so far as Portugal and the Islands were concerned, by allowing Drake in the summer of 1581 to prepare an expedition in Don Antonio's name to secure the Azores as a base for operations against the Spanish silver fleets and the Portuguese East Indiamen. Before she would let Drake sail, however, she insisted that she must have assurances of French support if Spain reacted violently. Philip had rejected Mendoza's advice to take reprisals when she had refused to restore Drake's plunder and had knighted him aboard the *Golden Hind* (April 1581). But an expedition to so strategically tender a spot as the Azores would be less likely to pass unnoticed.

Besides, it was not enough to 'impeach' the King of Spain at sea, in his Islands. He should also be impeached by land, in his Netherlands. Here Anjou could again be useful. For in September 1580 the rebel provinces, after much negotiation, had invited him to become their sovereign instead of Philip of Spain. Elizabeth's reaction to the news of this offer was significant. She wrote to Anjou urging him to accept it only if he was assured that the French King would provide him with the means for effective action and would 'abandon the friendship of the King of Spain'. When in January 1581 he ratified his agreement with the States, again her only complaint was that he had broken his promise not to do so until he was assured of his brother's help and of 'forces equal to so great an enterprise'.[7] Clearly she was now more alarmed by the growing overmightiness of Spain, and by the French King's sluggishness in opposing it, than by her normal fear of the French possessing the Netherlands. She was prepared to acquiesce in Anjou's intervention there, provided that Henry III would finance him and support him in a manner that would involve France in a clear and unmistakable commitment to the anti-Spanish side. But as in 1570 she had no faith in the permanence or stability of French policy. She was not prepared therefore to tie herself irrevocably to such a weathercock of an ally, least of all when it was likely to involve her herself in a war with Spain.

The French answer to her promptings was to profess complete readiness to join heartily with England, even to the point of open war with Spain, as soon as Elizabeth actually married Anjou. This frank offer has been contrasted with Elizabeth's shifty dealings, but probably it was less honest than it seemed. Henry III knew too well the disordered state of his own realm and finances to contemplate seriously making war on Spain. He knew Elizabeth well enough to guess that she might mean marriage as little as he meant war. So why not play her at her own game? If he could not induce her to marry Anjou, he might still drive her to finance the Duke's Netherlands enterprise as a form of damages for breach of promise. If he succeeded, Anjou would cease to be a nuisance in France; Elizabeth rather than Henry would be responsible for what he did against Spain; and Henry would have peace at home and abroad.

That this was the French line began to appear even more clearly when in July 1581 Elizabeth sent Walsingham over with ambiguous instructions which he interpreted, probably correctly, as directing him to save her from both war and marriage yet to procure French co-operation in underhand opposition to Spain.[8] Walsingham made little headway, but at least his mission made clear how reluctant Henry was to risk an open breach with Spain. Elizabeth therefore refused to risk a breach herself by attacking the Azores and in August she countermanded Drake's proposed expedition when Philip warned her that support of Don Antonio would be treated as a *casus belli*.[9] But she became correspondingly more anxious to involve Anjou in the Netherlands. Without Henry's full and open support he could hardly impatronize himself there, yet his intervention must still suggest to Philip II a considerable degree of Anglo-French solidarity. So in August 1581 Elizabeth even sent Anjou £30,000 herself.[10] Thus enabled to pay the troops he had levied, he crossed the Netherlands frontier and seized Cambrai, which the Spaniards had besieged but from which they withdrew to avoid a direct clash with the French. After that small success Anjou's money ran short and, putting his troops into winter quarters, he came again to England in October 1581 to see what more he could collect there.

He stayed for more than three months, drawing from Elizabeth ever more fervid demonstrations of affection. Once, in front of the whole court, she kissed him, gave him a ring, and swore he should be her husband.[11] By then, however, the indications are that she was acting, or over-acting, a part and that her true purpose was to get Anjou off to the Netherlands still unmarried, and Henry III committed at least indirectly to the anti-Spanish side, at the lowest possible price to herself. At last, in February 1582 she succeeded in packing off Anjou after a suitably tearful parting at Canterbury followed, if we may believe Mendoza, by a little dance of joy in the privacy of her chamber.[12] It cost her £10,000 in cash and a bond for £50,000 to follow (of which £30,000 was in fact to be paid).[13] But Anjou's arrival in Antwerp, escorted across by Leicester and a distinguished troop of English nobles, was a demonstration of Anglo-French solidarity impressive enough to reinforce Philip of Spain's doubts about the wisdom of quarrelling with England. At the same time, too, Henry III allowed Catherine de Medici, who had a remote claim of her own to the Portuguese crown, to dispatch an expedition under Filippo Strozzi to take Don Antonio to the Azores. The French alliance and the Anjou courtship were still serving their purpose and postponing a little longer the day when Philip of Spain would at last resolve to settle his long account with Elizabeth of England.

Nevertheless they were not without their side-effects. One of these was the temporary eclipse of the English party in Scotland. Throughout 1580 Elizabeth had tried to prod Morton and the

Protestants into getting rid of Lennox. She sent repeated half-promises of help, which she neither kept nor meant to keep, for with Spain conquering Portugal she could not risk offending the French King by unilateral action in breach of the 1572 treaty. After Morton's arrest (December 1580) she did, in the spring of 1581, prepare forces at Berwick. But Henry III pressed her not to intervene, while Morton had alienated and Lennox charmed so many Scots that an English invasion might well unite nearly all against the old enemy. Besides, Lennox's public profession of Calvinism and private assurance of goodwill to England half-convinced the English ambassador, Thomas Randolph, of his harmlessness.[14]

So Lennox was left unmolested and around him conspiracy was soon woven. Back in February 1580 Mary Stuart's ambassador in France had approached Vargas, the Spanish ambassador there, about sending Spanish troops to support Lennox. Philip, busy with Portugal, had refused. The execution of Morton in June 1581, for complicity in Darnley's murder – a conviction that implied Mary's innocence of that crime – revived her friends' hopes and those of the more militant English Catholics. Mendoza, unable to promise direct Spanish aid against Elizabeth lest it rouse Henry III as well, advised them to concentrate upon converting James VI and Scotland to Catholicism in the hope that he would then take the lead in liberating his mother and converting England. Mary agreed and sought to smooth the way by suggesting that she and James should share sovereign power during her lifetime – a project which she also discussed with Elizabeth. During the winter of 1581–2 two Jesuits, Crichton and Holt, who had come to England with Campion and Parsons, went to Scotland to see how the land lay.

They found Lennox co-operative but not hopeful of James's conversion. So, on their report in May 1582, Guise, Parsons, Allen, and Vargas's successor Tassis, framed a scheme to send 8,000 Spanish and Papal troops to help Lennox to restore Catholic supremacy in Scotland as a preliminary to an invasion of England on Mary's behalf. The scheme fell through, for Philip II would have nothing to do with so airy a project. By then, too, Elizabeth's suspicions were aroused and Lennox had involved himself in a quarrel with the Kirk that quickly revived the Protestant party in Scotland. In August 1582 the Protestant leaders kidnapped

James in the Raid of Ruthven and arrested Lennox's chief hench-man James Stuart, lately created Earl of Arran. Lennox, in terror for his life, fled back to France to die there next year, and for the moment the danger in Scotland was averted.

Guise and the Jesuits, in consultation with Mary, Mendoza, and Tassis, then changed their plan. Besides sending a force to Scotland, Guise himself would lead a direct surprise invasion of southern England, combining it with attempts to assassinate Elizabeth. The invasion, however, still depended on Spain for four or five thousand troops from the Netherlands, for transports, and for money. Once again Philip, in September 1583, refused to countenance a Frenchman invading England and this plot also fell through. In November, however, one of the plotters, Francis Throckmorton, was apprehended and the Tower rack drew from him all he knew. He knew a great deal and his con-fessions implicated not only Mary Stuart, Guise, and the Earls of Arundel and Northumberland, but Mendoza as well. The ambassador tried to brazen out the charges. 'Don Bernardino de Mendoza', he blustered, 'was not born to disturb kingdoms but to conquer them.'[15] But the evidence was strong against him and in January 1584 Elizabeth ordered him to leave her realm within fifteen days. She did send William Waad, a clerk of the Council, to Madrid to explain her reasons, but Philip refused to see him or hear his message and sent him packing even more abruptly than Elizabeth had dismissed Mendoza.

Philip's patience, however, was not yet quite exhausted. Irritat-ing as the indirect opposition of England and France might be, it did not immediately threaten any mortal danger. Anjou in the Netherlands had been more a nuisance than a menace. The Azores were safe, for in July 1582 the combined Spanish and Portuguese fleet under Spain's greatest sailor, the Marquis of Santa Cruz, had destroyed Strozzi's expedition in an old-fashioned boarding action. The Spanish occupation of the Islands was then completed in July 1583.

Nevertheless, this victory excited Santa Cruz into suggesting in August 1583 that next year he should lead an armada from Spain to destroy 'the heretic woman' of England and put Philip II on her throne. Philip listened so far as to order the laying down of new galleons, the hiring of some large Biscayan and Italian ships, and the preparation of biscuit.[16] He also consulted the Prince of Parma, who had become Governor-General of the Netherlands on the death of Don John of Austria in October 1578. Parma, too, thought an invasion of England not impracticable, although he considered that it would be better to complete the conquest of the Netherlands first and that anyway a surprise attack by 34,000 men from Flanders would be more likely to succeed than a direct invasion from Spain.[17] So by now Philip had two plans to ponder over. Both his best admiral and his best general regarded the 'Enterprise of England' as feasible, the one enthusiastically, the other more cautiously. Granvelle, too, who had been recalled to Philip's Council in 1579, favoured it, for he still believed now as in the fifteen sixties that in England lay the root of all the evils in the Netherlands. Philip himself was not yet quite sure that it was either safe or necessary to lay the axe to the root of those evils. He still feared that, if he attacked England, he might bring France upon his back and he was again beginning to hope that Parma might soon trample down the Netherlands rebellion.

For the second great change which came over the continental situation during the years following Spain's conquest of Portugal was the collapse of that United Netherlands which had come into existence with the Pacification of Ghent in 1576. This had been from the start a union of incompatibles, brought together by an overriding common fear of the mutinous Spanish soldiery. There was little else in common between the revolutionary and Calvinistic burgher oligarchies of Holland and Zeeland and the conservative and Catholic nobles and magistrates of the other provinces. Moreover, each side could look for substantial support in the other's territory. As late as 1587 Thomas Wilkes regretted that nine-tenths of the population even of Holland were Catholics. In the other, Catholic, provinces, particularly in the great cities of Brabant and Flanders, there were, on the other hand, considerable and very active Calvinist minorities that looked to Holland and Zeeland for support. William of Orange had tried to smooth over these differences, but under the pressure of Don John's successes in 1578 the cleavage had widened until in January 1579 the United Netherlands split into the rival Unions of Arras and Utrecht. In May 1579 the Catholic Union of Arras, comprising the two Walloon provinces of Artois and Hainaut, made their peace with Don John's successor, Alexander Farnese, Prince of Parma. They were to permit only the Catholic religion, but their ancient liberties were guaranteed, no foreigners were to be appointed to offices there, and no foreign troops to be garrisoned there. These terms were all that most Catholic Netherlanders wished for and they accordingly exerted a powerful attraction in the other provinces too.

The political conditions for Spanish military success were thereby much improved and Parma, a young commander as remarkable for his statesmanship as for his generalship, was just the man to make the most of them. For a time he remained hampered by having still to base his army in remote Luxembourg and Liège. But in 1581, under the threat of Anjou's intervention, the Arras Union asked him to bring his troops to their defence. As we have seen, he judged it wiser to lose Cambrai than to meet the heir presumptive of France head-on. But he had acquired a base from which he could advance down the Lys and Scheldte into the heart of Flanders and Brabant. That same summer the Catholic Stadholder of the north-eastern provinces, Rennenberg, also made his peace with Parma, bringing over Groningen and a large part of Overijsel and Gelderland. Here was another valuable base, one from which the Union of Utrecht's eastern flank might be turned.

But first Flanders and Brabant had to be subdued and in 1582 Parma began their conquest. The States General of the Utrecht Union could do little to stop him. Their finances were in chaos and most of their troops were used up in garrisoning their towns, partly because the largely Catholic inhabitants were not to be trusted, partly because the town authorities were their best pay-masters and would seldom pay much except for services locally rendered. Anjou's arrival in February brought much rejoicing but no great relief. He would have been no match for Parma any-way and he had not even the means to try. Elizabeth gave him only enough money to be a nuisance to Spain and had no intention of giving him enough to make him effective master of the pro-vinces. Henry III was equally unhelpful, though he did allow his favourite Biron to take in a few more troops in November. Holland and Zeeland, the chief paymasters of the Union, could find too little money for their own troops to spare much for his and, jealous of their independence, denied him all real authority, despite Elizabeth's misguided efforts to coerce them by demanding that they repay her earlier loans. Driven to impotent desperation,

Anjou in January 1583 attempted to seize power by a military coup. But in this 'French Fury' he failed to kidnap Orange or to capture Antwerp and the great cities of Flanders. In June he crept back to France and the States were again left to their own resources.

Meanwhile Parma had overrun that part of Flanders that lies south of the Lys. Then, after a pause for preparation in 1583, in 1584 he overran the rest and most of Brabant as well. By the end of the year Antwerp, Ostend, Sluys, and Brussels were the only places left in the States' hands south of the Maas and Waal. Antwerp and Ostend were already beleaguered and Brussels was to capitulate in February 1585. With so much of the country east of the Ijsel already in Spanish hands thanks to Rennenberg's 1581 'treason', the situation was growing very like that of 1572–6 when Holland and Zeeland stood alone against Alba and Requesens.

This military collapse of the Utrecht Union was serious enough. What made it truly alarming was the additional prospect of political collapse that resulted from the assassination of William of Orange in July 1584. It was he who had held the Union together and very few, even in Holland and Zeeland, believed that the now 'headless commonwealth' could long survive unless it could find some princely leader to fill his place. There was no one within the Union who could fill it, for William's son Maurice was still a schoolboy and no other native nobleman stood head and shoulders above the rest as William had done. The princely head, it seemed, must be a foreigner, a foreigner too who could bring substantial military and financial help. Only the Queen of England and the King of France fulfilled those requirements. Yet if either accepted the part, it was hard to see how Philip could regard it as anything but a declaration of war. On the other hand, if neither of them accepted it, the final reduction of the whole Netherlands under Spanish rule looked to be only a matter of time.

At this juncture, with the issues still poised between peace and war, a third great change in the continental situation relieved Philip of the fear of France that had for so long restrained him from breaking with England. On May 31st, 1584, Anjou died. In himself he was hardly worth the tears that Elizabeth decorously shed for him each day for three weeks on end.[18] But he was heir presumptive to his brother Henry III of France who was, and was almost certain to remain, childless. The two brothers were the last of the Valois line and the next heir by blood and law was Henry of Bourbon, King of Navarre, the Huguenot leader. The prospect of having a Huguenot for their king was more than most French Catholics could stomach. To the Catholic League and the Guise family it was intolerable. Accordingly they prepared to take up arms to prevent it. They meant to force Henry III to disinherit Navarre, crush the Huguenots, and recognize as his heir Navarre's uncle the Cardinal of Bourbon, an elderly 'wineskin of a man' but a Catholic. Lacking confidence in their own unaided strength, on December 21st, 1584, they concluded the secret treaty of Joinville with the King of Spain. By this treaty they accepted Philip as their protector and he promised them 50,000 crowns a month to help them achieve their purposes. So was removed the last restraint holding Spain back from action against England. Philip knew that for some time to come he had nothing to fear from France.

Yet even now immediate war between England and Spain was not inevitable. Philip still had two courses open to him. He might take advantage of French impotence either by completing the reduction of the Netherlands or by attacking England. Of the two, the reduction of the Netherlands looked the easier and more promising, provided that the rebels there did not obtain substantial assistance from Elizabeth. On that proviso, though, the issue between peace and war now hinged. For Philip's decision about the Enterprise of England now depended chiefly upon Elizabeth's attitude to the Dutch revolt.

In England, of course, the intentions of the League and the treaty of Joinville were not yet known and until the spring of 1585 there still seemed a possibility that Henry III might help the Dutch either openly or underhand. Nevertheless, his refusal of their first offers in July 1584, just when William of Orange was assassinated, compelled Elizabeth to consider seriously the possibility that Henry would in the end do nothing. Should she then go alone to their rescue? Could she afford to let them fall to Spain if France would not help to save them? The answer depended partly upon what the constitution of the Netherlands would be, but more upon how Philip was likely to behave, if once the revolt were crushed. The terms that Parma granted to the reconciled provinces, and to the towns he was taking, did suggest that Philip still meant what he had said in his instructions to Mendoza about seeking no more power there than Charles V had possessed. Yet with the revolt suppressed, Parma's army would be free for other enterprises and would have the resources, ports, and shipping of the Low Countries at its command. Would Philip then use them for the Enterprise of England? That was the crucial question.

Some of Elizabeth's Councillors, perhaps a majority of them, headed by Walsingham and Leicester, were sure that this was just what Philip would do.[19] They saw in his persecution of Netherlands Calvinists, in the intrigues of his ambassadors, in his connivance at Papal attempts in Ireland, clear proof of his 'insatiable malice' against all things Protestant. Therefore he must not be allowed 'to grow to the height of his design and conquests'. Whether France would help or not, England should step in at once to maintain those who were fighting what was no less England's battle than their own.

Other Councillors, headed by Burghley, were not so sure. The Dutch, they pointed out, were rebels and in seeking to suppress them Philip was only doing 'a thing that any prince would do'. If his ambassadors plotted with English traitors and he connived at Papal enterprises, had not Elizabeth given underhand help to the Dutch and Anjou and refused to give back Drake's spoils? True, Philip persecuted Protestants savagely in his own dominions, but had he ever shown great enthusiasm about crusading for his faith in other princes' realms? Why not therefore give him the benefit of the doubt and thereby avoid precipitating a war which would be enormously expensive, which might be disastrous to trade, and which was perhaps not yet inevitable?[20] After all, 'if the Queen would meddle no more in matters of the Netherlands, but most strongly fortify her kingdom ... gather money, furnish her navy with all provisions, strengthen the Borders towards Scotland with garrisons, and maintain the ancient military discipline of England'[21] – if she did these things and assured herself of Scotland, England would be impregnable, come what might. And if what came was war, she might well be better off without having the United Provinces to drain away her limited resources, like an infinitely more costly Boulogne. For that loose and headless confederation of 'popular' states, with few nobles to lead them, reluctant to open their own purses, and all too ready (as Anjou had found) to quarrel with their foreign helpers, could easily prove more a liability than an asset.[22]

Until the early summer of 1585 Elizabeth's policy reflected the doubts of Burghley more than the convictions of Walsingham. She was still worried about the danger of France acquiring the Netherlands. So, while repeatedly urging Henry III to help them himself or to join her in helping them, she secretly encouraged the Dutch not to make their offers to him too generous, to seek his support as another defender of their liberties rather than as their absolute sovereign.

The spring and early summer, however, brought a radical change in the outlook. On February 27th Henry III finally refused the Dutch offers and declared his inability to help them because his own estate was 'so tickle and so unsound within itself that he was to fear lest in going about to get upon others he should put in a venture to "leese" himself.'[23] On March 20th the Catholic League rose in arms and issued their declaration of Peronne, calling upon Henry III to reform his government and extirpate heresy. On that same day Walsingham first got wind of the treaty of Joinville.[24] Then at the end of May Philip suddenly seized all English ships in Spanish ports, though many of them had come under his safe conduct with corn to relieve a shortage caused by a crop failure in Spain. This news was brought early in June by the *Primrose* of London, which escaped by capturing her would-be captors. Late in June Henry III submitted to the League by the treaty of Nemours. By then, in the Netherlands, Malines had yielded to Parma and besieged Antwerp was parleying with him.

These events, particularly Henry III's capitulation to Guise and the League, revolutionized the situation. Now that the King of France had apparently become the puppet of the King of Spain's hired man, it was no longer just the Netherlands but also France, indeed Europe, that was in danger of subjugation. The elderly Cardinal Charles of Bourbon could prove a stalking horse for Spanish hegemony of the continent, just as the old Cardinal Henry of Portugal had been for Spanish hegemony of the Peninsula. And if Spain should control all western Europe from the Ems or the Elbe to Gibraltar, it was less easy to feel confident in England's impregnability. It looks as if the revelation of these new dangers now converted Burghley to a policy of action: certainly during this summer of 1585 he protested very vigorously

against insinuations that he was opposed to aiding the Dutch.[25]
The Queen, too, reluctantly concluded that she could no longer
stand as a spectator on the side-lines.

It remained for her to decide in what ways she should intervene.
In June 1585 a Dutch embassy arrived to offer her their sovereignty; Ségur was begging her for 200,000 crowns (about £63,000,)
to help Navarre hire a German army; and Edward Wotton was
in Scotland bargaining with James VI and Arran (now back in
favour) about a league and a pension. Elizabeth could not, however, play fairy godmother to the entire continent. So, on the
arrival of the Dutch envoys and the disturbing news of Antwerp's
parley, she reduced her original offer to Ségur of 100,000 crowns
to 50,000 and made that conditional upon the King of Denmark
and the German Protestants contributing their shares as her
envoys were already urging them to do.

She also refused the Dutch offer of their sovereignty, which
would have meant an unlimited liability for their defence as well
as being a more flagrant offence to Philip. But on August 10th,
1585, by the treaty of Nonsuch[26] she did take them into her
protection. She agreed to send and pay, so long as the war lasted,
an auxiliary force of 5,000 foot and 1,000 horse. Its commander
was to be an Englishman of quality and rank who, with two other
Englishmen, should sit with the Council of State as the Provinces'
executive government. As security for the eventual repayment of
her expenses, she was to garrison at her own cost the port towns
of Flushing and Brielle; and if an enemy fleet entered the Narrow
Seas, the States were to assist her with as many ships of war as
she herself put forth.

Finally, Elizabeth also took action by sea. For this, Philip's
seizure of the corn ships provided a legitimate excuse, besides
turning the English traders to Spain from petitioners for peace
into advocates of war. So Drake was unleashed, with a strong
squadron including two of the Queen's ships, to visit the ports of
Spain and release the seized ships and their crews. It was tacitly
understood that then he might go on to execute a plan, such as
Hawkins had several times suggested, to raid the ports and shipping of the Caribbean and to make a cast for the silver fleet.

The vanguard of the English auxiliary forces, under Sir John
Norris, reached the Netherlands by mid-August and the rest soon
followed, though too late to save Antwerp. In September no less

a person than the Earl of Leicester was named as their General, though he did not actually go over until December. In September, too, Drake spent twelve days plundering Vigo and Bayona in north-west Spain, before sailing off to sack more towns in the Cape Verde Islands on his way to the Caribbean. About the same time a small squadron under Sir Walter Raleigh's brother raided the Spanish and Portuguese fishing fleets on the Newfoundland banks, capturing many boats and six hundred mariners. These warlike acts made it clear that, if Spain meant to complete the reduction of the Netherlands, she would have to fight the English both there and at sea. Philip, therefore, with France no longer to be feared, began to think more favourably of Granvelle's advice, of going to the root of the trouble by dealing with England first. It was, after all, very tempting to see there the solution to all his problems. For the conquest of Portugal, the collapse of the United Netherlands, and the collapse of the French monarchy had left England as the one obstacle to Spanish hegemony of western Europe. So during the autumn of 1585 Philip II began to think seriously of the Enterprise of England and in January 1586 he instructed Santa Cruz to begin detailed planning and preparation for an Armada to execute it.

The new ideas of basing England's policy and defence primarily upon insularity reinforced by sea power had proved adequate to uphold her interests and independence so long as the accustomed jealous equilibrium persisted between the great powers of the continent. Those ideas were now to be tested by war when the continental balance was overturned and only the French Huguenots and the Dutch rebels stood in arms between England and the overmightiness of Spain.

Chapter 27

The Beginning of the War
with Spain

FROM the beginning of open, if undeclared, war between England and Spain in the summer of 1585 until the defeat of the Spanish Armada in the summer of 1588, English policy and strategy conformed broadly to the pattern set by the decisions that we have just been discussing. This is not to say that Elizabeth now, any more than in earlier years, followed a clear and undeviating course. In war as in peace she was ultimately guided by deep-seated and fairly consistent instincts more than by reason. Yet her vigorous and highly educated intellect prevented her from ever trusting unhesitatingly to her intuition. The pale cast of thought sicklied o'er many a resolution and she was always liable to be half-convinced by reasonings which, on a particular issue at a particular time, conflicted with her instincts. War only made this conflict within herself more acute. So, while the overall pattern of her policy remained remarkably consistent, the twists and turns of its detail became even more elaborate and involved and at times self-contradictory.

She appreciated clearly that the overriding consideration was now the danger of invasion from Spain or the Netherlands or from both at once. Walsingham might assure her gaily, as he did in March 1586, that Spain's naval preparations 'will prove nothing this year and I hope less the next'.[1] Nevertheless, her strongest instinct was always to husband England's limited naval, military, and financial resources and to keep them to the utmost possible extent in hand to meet this greatest of all dangers.

This did not mean that she waited altogether passively for the blow to fall. It did not, for example, rule out the use of a few of her own ships and a larger number of privately owned vessels for counter-blows to disrupt Spanish naval preparations or to lay for the silver fleets, although as the invasion danger came nearer she became more reluctant to let her sea forces go far from home waters. Nor did it blind her to the importance of denying the Armada advanced bases or harbours of refuge along the coasts opposite to her own. It was the Netherlands ports that concerned her most, for it was there that the Armada and the main field army of Spain might most dangerously join forces for an invasion of England. She was concerned also about the French Channel ports, but these were less likely to be used as Spanish invasion bases. Besides, whereas the Dutch held still the most vital of the Netherlands ports, the Huguenots, Spain's chief enemies in France, held none of the Channel ports and lacked the strength in those regions to seize them.

Accordingly Elizabeth relied mainly upon diplomacy in France and concentrated her military assistance upon the Dutch. Even there she was insistent that her help should be strictly limited to what she had promised in the treaty of Nonsuch and that her forces be employed primarily to preserve the maritime parts of the United Provinces from Spanish conquest. For she was determined not to let her defensive concern with the continental ports draw her into large-scale continental offensive commitments. As things were in France and the Netherlands, English intervention there was more likely to goad Philip II into hastening the Armada than to deter him from dispatching it. England therefore could not now afford to exhaust her resources in fighting French and Dutch battles before her own supreme test came, any more than before the Battle of Britain in 1940 she could commit her air forces unreservedly to the Battle of France. So Elizabeth's strongest instinct was to husband her strength to the uttermost until – or in case – the great test came. That instinct underlay and explains most of her parsimony and hesitations during these years.

No doubt, too, her reluctance to waste her strength was encouraged by lingering hopes that the present quarrel, like that of 1568–72, might after all be ended by peaceful negotiation. For, even before Leicester reached Holland, peace feelers were being put out from both sides.[2] In November 1585 Walsingham got Dr Hector Nuñez, a Portuguese physician in London, to write to the former Portuguese ambassador Castilio. In December the Spanish governor of captured Antwerp, Champagny, Cardinal Granvelle's brother, moved from the other side. He encouraged an Italian merchant there, Carlo Lanfranchi, to get Andrea de Loo, a Flemish merchant in London, to make overtures to Burghley.

About the same time Sir James Croft got a kinsman of his in the Netherlands, William Boddenham, to approach Parma, though his overture was soon linked to that of de Loo and also brought under Burghley's control. Burghley also encouraged the exiled Genoese financier, Horatio Palavicino, to open a correspondence through his brother-in-law, Lazaro Grimaldi, with Prince Andrea Doria of Genoa.

All this was done with a great parade of secrecy, for neither side wished to appear as suing for peace. Besides, the English had to be careful not to alarm their Dutch allies. This was the more necessary because Burghley and Croft, with the Queen's warm approval and to get the de Loo and Boddenham negotiations moving, emphasized the matters on which agreement was easiest. They gave, for example, vague and perhaps deliberately misleading assurances on the more difficult questions, such as toleration for the Dutch Protestants. We need not necessarily assume from this that the Queen or her Councillors were ready to yield easily on the crucial point of religion, any more than Philip II was when after the Armada he allowed similarly misleading approaches to be made to the States themselves.[3] But clearly such tactics would arouse Dutch suspicions and for that reason some attempt seems to have been made to keep Leicester, and perhaps Walsingham as well, in the dark. Nevertheless, before he left England Leicester perceived 'that your peace with Spain will go fast on' and at the end of March 1586 Burghley gave him a rough outline of what was afoot.[4]

By then half a dozen or more Councillors had been let into the secret of the de Loo and Boddenham negotiations. One of them, Lord Cobham, had just been approached by yet another Italian merchant, Agostino Grafigna, sent over by La Motte, the governor of Gravelines. Like the other go-betweens, Grafigna apparently embroidered upon the answer that he carried back to Flanders. At all events, Parma himself now joined in the game and sent back Grafigna and Boddenham with letters expressing his willingness to listen to the Queen's pleas for peace. To be put in the position of suing for peace was not, however, at all what Elizabeth meant and her answer (July 8th) sharply disabused Parma of any such notions. With this, the de Loo-Boddenham-Grafigna negotiations came for a time to an abrupt halt. The correspondence of Walsingham with Castilio and Palavicino with Doria also led to nothing very promising.

Meanwhile things had gone sadly wrong in the Netherlands. For this, Leicester was chiefly to blame. From the first he had wanted the Queen to accept the sovereignty over the Provinces and back in April 1585 she had upbraided him for encouraging the States to offer it to her. Before he left England on December 3rd, 1585, he was grumbling at the limited authority allowed him by her instructions.[5] Six weeks later, without consulting her, he accepted from the States General the office of Governor-General. He thus assumed the title and authority which the King of Spain's representative had formerly held. This plainly implied that the Provinces acknowledged Elizabeth as their sovereign and Leicester as her viceroy. It was an attempt, almost certainly deliberate, to thrust upon her by the back door the sovereignty that she had categorically refused when the States' envoys had publicly offered it at the front. It was therefore not only a flagrant defiance of her instructions but also a complete contradiction of her declared policy. For in her speeches to the States' envoys, in her published *Declaration* of her reasons for aiding them, and in her explanation to Parma, she had vigorously affirmed that she was intervening only to uphold the Provinces' ancient liberties and that she had no intention of usurping the sovereignty over them.

The whole history of her policy is proof that in this she meant what she said. The Netherlands that she always wanted to see established were the Netherlands of the Pacification of Ghent, a self-governing dominion under the King of Spain's nominal sovereignty. She had no wish at all to take over from him the burden of defending them against France. For that reason she wanted neither to make them English nor to make them independent. And, as she said, 'none knew her determination therein better than' Leicester.[6]

It is then hardly surprising that his action provoked from her an explosion of wrath that Henry VIII might have envied. Her immediate reaction was to insist that Leicester must at once resign his new title as publicly and formally as he had received it. Burghley, Walsingham, Hatton, and other Councillors delayed the dispatch of these orders and managed gradually to persuade her that so drastic a measure might altogether break up the States' disordered government. But it was not until June that she finally let the matter drop and left Leicester to make what he could of his rashly assumed authority.

What he made of it was little enough. This again was largely because he would not be content to cut his coat according to the Queen's cloth. Before, as well as after, he went over, both he and the States were abundantly warned – even by Walsingham – 'not to attend any greater support from hence' than the payment of the forces promised by the 1585 treaty,[7] a sum which he well knew was reckoned at £126,000 a year. This sum was about equal to half Elizabeth's ordinary annual income, or to three-quarters of the grant that Parliament had been making roughly once every four years. It was therefore quite as much as she could possibly reckon to spare on this one sector of the war.

Leicester, however, showed no sign of understanding this.[8] One of his first acts was to raise his own pay from £6 to £10 3s. 4d. a day, with corresponding increases for all the other officers and captains. This added at a stroke £8,000 to the Queen's estimated yearly charge of £126,000. Then, too, he advanced to some 8,000 English volunteers in the States' pay money intended for the Queen's troops. For, though many Dutch burghers were prospering, the States' public finances were in such chaos that they thought they were doing well if they paid their troops six months out of twelve. The Queen's treasurer at war, too, found it a slow business getting back from them for the pay of her troops the £25,740 that she had spent on levying their volunteers in England. In these and other ways Leicester and the States between them bedevilled the Queen's army finances within a very few months.

The levy, transport, and pay of her troops to October 11th, 1585, had cost £32,060. A further £20,000 was issued in November and again £24,000 in March 1586. This £44,000, with the £25,740 due from the States, ought to have paid the troops in full for the six months to April 11th, 1586, and left £6,740 over. Instead they were paid in full only to December 11th and at least one-third of their pay for the other four months, some £9,000, was still owing to them. After six months the army finances were thus already almost £16,000, or 25 per cent, above estimate. Elizabeth's answer to this was to tighten her purse strings. After paying out another £45,000 in July, she refused to send any more until late October. Nevertheless it was to take the £30,000 she then sent, and £15,609 from the next issue in February 1587, to make a full pay to October 11th, 1586. The total bill charged up against her during the year from October 12th, 1585, to October 11th,

1586, was thus over £160,000 instead of the £126,000 which she had reckoned was the most she could afford.

Elizabeth had, it is true, managed to keep the actual payments out of her Exchequer down to £115,000 during that year. But she did this by leaving her troops to live after December 11th, 1585, on imprests, or 'lendings', advanced against their pay at irregular intervals. There was some effort to pay these lendings every week. But 'bare weekly lendings', even if they sufficed to provide victuals for the soldiers, still left the captains little or nothing to spare for keeping their companies up to strength in men, weapons, and equipment. Thus, despite the eagerness of the English in the States' pay to transfer to the Queen's pay roll, the effective strength of her forces soon dwindled. This ought to have lessened her charge, for deductions (or 'checks') were supposed to be made from a company's pay for any defect in numbers or equipment. But apart from frauds by the captains and corruption among the officers of musters, Leicester 'forgave' all checks up to December 11th, 1585,[9] and those for the next ten months were returned at only £2,642. Five or six times that sum might have been a truer figure, for even in June 1587 – after the States had discharged all but 1,800 of the English volunteers – the 5,000 foot were admitted to be 1,000 short and the 1,000 horse numbered little more than 500. Small wonder if the Queen tightened her purse strings.

Meanwhile Leicester landed himself in other difficulties in the Netherlands. Never very good at personal relations – except with Elizabeth – he fell out with all his ablest officers and advisers. His relations with the States' leaders were even worse. The row over the Governor-Generalship, the growing weakness of the auxiliary forces, the rumours of peace talks, had disillusioned them about their English allies. Leicester's attempt to control their finances through a finance chamber of his own creatures and his efforts to stop their lucrative trade with the enemy turned disillusion into hatred. The States hampered him, opposed him, cut back his authority all they could. He retaliated by building an opposition faction out of exiles from the southern provinces to whom the States and cities of the north denied office and influence; out of the more extreme Calvinists who disliked the States' tolerant religious attitude; out of the 'popular' elements excluded from the urban and provincial oligarchies; out of soldiers who hoped to get more regular pay from the Queen than from the States. Men of this faction, led by Gerard de Prounincq, had seized control of the city of Utrecht, and Leicester was thinking of using Colonel Sonoy and others of the party to seize four or five towns in north Holland.[10]

It is surprising that, in the midst of these quarrels, Leicester made any showing at all against Parma. Yet he did achieve something. In April Sir John Norris and Count Hohenlohe relieved Grave on the Maas. Parma, however, took that town in May and Venlo in June. Having thus secured the Maas crossings into Cleves, he pushed on to secure those over the Rhine east of Nijmegen. These would enable him to link up with Colonel Verdugo, Count Rennenberg's successor, in Overijsel and Groningen and to establish his hold upon the crossings over the Ijsel, where he already held Doesburg and Zutphen. Once over the Ijsel, he could turn the States' left flank and roll up their main line of defence along the great rivers Maas and Waal. The danger momentarily stilled the quarrels between Leicester and the States. The Queen also sent Thomas Wilkes over to appease matters and the States now promised Leicester £20,000 a month for four months to take the field. By the end of August he had scraped together 7,000 men, English and Dutch, and moved into Gelderland. He was too weak to challenge Parma to battle, but he did take Doesburg and a fort dominating Zutphen. Parma saved Zutphen itself, after a wild cavalry skirmish in which Sir Philip Sidney was mortally wounded. But Leicester had secured the Ijsel line more firmly and had prevented the laying open of the States' eastern flank.

Even so, this was not a great deal to show for a year's war effort that had cost the States and the Queen between them £400,000.[11] Leicester perhaps still believed that if only Elizabeth would substantially increase her forces and wage vigorous offensive war against Parma, peace through victory was just around the corner.[12] Few, however, shared his illusion. Dr Bartholomew Clark, one of the two English members of the Dutch Council of State, doubted if even two or three years of 'sharp war' would drive the Spaniards to seek peace and he pointed out that 'these hundred years and more never any King [of England] was able to continue wars beyond sea above one year.' He therefore thought it best 'to enter no further ... than to defend that which already standeth with us'.[13] Leicester's recall in November 1586 showed that this was also Elizabeth's opinion.

The general situation outside the Netherlands gave additional justification for caution. Elizabeth had perhaps hoped, as Walsingham certainly had,[14] that Drake would bring back from the West Indies profits on the scale of 1577–80. But, 'the reason best known to God', Drake missed the 1585 silver fleets, whose last ships sailed into Cadiz as he left Vigo. Worse still, a pointless digression to the Cape Verde Islands infected his men with a virulent fever. This so reduced his forces that, after sacking Santo Domingo and Cartagena, he had to abandon hope of taking Panama and Havana and of catching the 1586 consignments of silver in the Caribbean. By July he was home with nothing decisive accomplished and the loss to the Queen of £5,000 on her investment.

By then, moreover, other demands upon her purse were growing more clamant. In Scotland after the fall of Arran (October 1585) the growing personal authority of the young King James VI at last began to provide a stable element in the quagmire where for so long, as Burghley had once complained, 'nobody stands still.' Elizabeth had steadily refused to waste her money on the shifting factions among the Scottish nobility, but she was a little readier to spend something to bind to her a king who seemed to be master in his own house. She would not give a lot, for she considered James's hope of the English succession her best hold over him. Nevertheless, in July 1586 she concluded an alliance with him and confirmed the pension of £4,000 a year that she had offered him in the previous summer.

At the same time Henry of Navarre also induced her to loosen her purse strings. It will be remembered that in July 1585 she had offered him 50,000 crowns to help raise an army in Germany. She had, however, made her offer conditional upon the Danes and the German Protestants paying their share of the £100,000 which John Casimir reckoned would be needed. Also, although in February 1586 she did send Palavicino to Germany with the 50,000 crowns,[15] her main effort in French affairs had been directed towards persuading Henry III to break with the League and turn to Navarre. Unfortunately Henry III, little as he loved the Guises, dared not ally himself with the Huguenots. So when the campaigning season opened, Elizabeth had to reconsider her policy, all the more as the German negotiations were hanging fire and there were persistent hints that Navarre might turn Catholic.[16] In June she authorized Palavicino to raise her contribution to

100,000 crowns (about £31,000) if it were absolutely necessary. It was necessary, for the Danes refused to contribute at all, the few German princes who promised anything were very slow to pay, and Navarre himself could provide only a fraction of what he had promised. All this so delayed matters that it was not until January 1587 that the levy of men began and within another month Navarre's agents were pestering Elizabeth for yet another 100,000 crowns. Without it, they said, the army could not march.

They could hardly have asked at a worse moment, for during the past few months crises had blown up on all sides. To see why, we must return briefly, and for the last time, to Mary Stuart. After the Parry plot Mary's secret correspondence with her friends had been completely cut off. Early in 1586, however, she found that letters could be smuggled in and out in the barrels of beer supplied weekly to her household. In June she received in this way a letter from a young English Catholic, Anthony Babington.[17] He asked her approval for a plot for a rebellion, supported by a Spanish or French invasion and accompanied by the assassination of Elizabeth. Mary replied early in July. Her letter has disappeared, probably burnt by Babington as she directed. But before it reached him, a copy had been made for Walsingham. For it was in fact Walsingham who had organized the beer-barrel post and everything that went in and out by it passed through his hands. Mary had fallen into his trap even more completely than he could have hoped. As she herself admitted, she had approved of the invasion and rebellion plans; according to Walsingham's copy of her letter, she had approved of the assassination too. If she had, she was liable to the death penalty prescribed by the 1585 Act against any claimant to the succession found guilty to being privy to an attempt upon Elizabeth's life.

Of course Mary denied it, but the weight of the evidence is against her. Even Elizabeth was convinced enough to bring her to trial in mid-October before a special commission of peers, judges, and Councillors. They pronounced her guilty and Council, Parliament, and nation clamoured for her head even more stridently than in 1572. While Elizabeth hesitated, another plot was discovered – or invented – involving the French ambassador. This so far decided her that on February 1st, 1587, she signed Mary's death warrant. Yet even then, she tried to get old Sir Amias Paulet, Mary's keeper, to do away with his prisoner unofficially. Paulet, a 'precise fellow'[18] and no Bothwell, refused. So Burghley and his fellow Councillors, without consulting Elizabeth further, took it upon themselves to see the warrant duly executed. On February 8th, 1587, twenty years all but a day after Darnley's murder, Mary Stuart was beheaded.

There is no denying that in thus destroying the 'bosom serpent' Burghley and his colleagues had served Elizabeth and England well. The four years before Mary's death had brought four serious plots; the sixteen years that followed saw only the dubious affair of Doctor Lopez in 1593. Abroad, among the exiles, desperate talk still continued, but without support from the Catholics at home there was no great danger in that. And the Catholics at home had no desire to kill Elizabeth in order to make the Calvinist James VI or the Spanish Philip King.

When the news reached Elizabeth, however, it produced a veritable tornado of anger. The chief sufferer was Davison, who had been appointed a second Principal Secretary in September and who, in Walsingham's absence through a timely illness, had carried the warrant to the Queen for signature and then to the Council for execution. He was sent to the Tower and sentenced to an enormous fine. Next to him, Burghley bore the brunt of the storm. It was four weeks before Elizabeth again received him at court, four months before she ceased to rail at him. In all this royal anger there was probably an element of genuine grief and indignation over a distasteful, if necessary, action. But much of it was a show put on for the benefit of the neighbours. For Mary Stuart was not only a Catholic who had been slain by Protestants; she was also a sometime Queen of France and Scotland who had been executed by Englishmen. Her death therefore roused ancient national, as well as more recent religious, passions in those countries. James VI and Henry III might well have no wish to break with Elizabeth, but they must find it hard to resist their subjects' clamour if they were not given some explanation that they could at least pretend excused them from openly hostile action.

By protesting so violently that the Council had acted without consulting her; by imprisoning, fining, and even threatening to hang one of her Secretaries (even if the more expendable one); and by disgracing for weeks her most trusted minister, Elizabeth did her best to provide that excuse. It was hard on Burghley. It was harder still on Davison whose career was blasted, though he was released after eighteen months, never made to pay his fine, and allowed to go on drawing a Secretary's stipend and even until 1590 a Secretary's share of the Signet Office fees. Nor was it more convincing than Charles IX's excuses for the St Bartholomew Massacre. But like those, it served its turn. After a flurry of protests James VI, with his eye on the English succession and with the English £4,000 a year in his pocket, remained true in his fashion to the English alliance. Henry III also after similar protests and the seizure of English ships at Rouen, evaded the League's pressure to denounce his treaties with England.

Nevertheless it was some months before Elizabeth could feel reasonably sure of James, while the uproar in France ruled out any hope of inducing Henry to break with the League and made it dangerous to irritate French national sentiment further by assisting a German invasion on behalf of the Huguenots. Moreover, while these storms with Scotland and France were blowing themselves out, others were gathering elsewhere. In that critical February, when Navarre's agents were demanding another 100,000 crowns and James VI was pressing for another £1,000 a year and recognition as Elizabeth's heir, a Dutch embassy arrived to ask for the doubling of the English auxiliary forces and a loan of £60,000. Hard on their heels came news of the betrayal of Deventer by Sir William Stanley and the Zutphen fort by Rowland Yorke, which put the Ijsel crossings in Parma's hands and uncovered the flank of the main Dutch defence line. By now, too, even Walsingham could no longer doubt that the reports of great preparations in Spanish ports and the growing concentration of Parma's army in Flanders presaged an early attempt to invade England.

Once again therefore, as in 1585, Elizabeth had to review her whole policy and carefully balance one demand against another. The pattern that emerged was much the same as before. Her first reaction was to avoid all new continental commitments and to husband her resources for home defence. In spite of the advice of Walsingham, Leicester, and even Burghley, she refused to give a penny more to James, to the Huguenots, or to the Dutch. She did, however, make some offensive use of her sea power. Already, in the previous autumn, Hawkins had been out with five of her ships and thirteen others, probably in the hope of catching between the Azores and Spain the silver fleet that Drake had been unable to wait for in the Caribbean. He put to sea in August 1586, soon after

Drake's return, but the discovery of Babington's plot caused alarm about French intentions and led the Council to keep him patrolling in the Channel for two or three weeks. Either this or a storm which later beat him back from the Azores – unfortunately we know very little about this voyage[19] – caused him to miss both the returning Portuguese East Indiamen and the 1586 American silver convoys. When he returned in October he had achieved very little.

Next spring Drake was more successful. He set out in April with four of the Queen's galleons, another galleon, four of the Turkey Company's ships, and a dozen others. At that moment the Armada was neither concentrated nor ready to put to sea. Santa Cruz, with the main body of galleons, was in Lisbon; there were more ships including the Mexican *flota*, at Cadiz; and other ships and stores were coming round from the Mediterranean. Drake's main task was to disrupt these preparations and delay the concentration. He went first to Cadiz. Ignoring the shore batteries and brushing aside twelve galleys that tried to bar his entry, he swept into the harbour and destroyed between two and three dozen of the larger ships, including most of the *flota*. He then moved north to Cape St Vincent, where by storming Sagres castle he secured himself a good anchorage. He did not dare to enter the Tagus to flush the ill prepared Santa Cruz out of Lisbon, but off Cape St Vincent he could catch everything passing northwards, including the barrel staves for the Armada's water casks. After two months at sea, however, his supplies ran low and his men fell sick, all too frequent occurrences on his expeditions. He could not stay out very much longer, but he did manage to run to the Azores and capture a rich Portuguese East Indiaman, the *San Felipe*. So he was able to bring back to his shareholders on June 26th a booty of £140,000 of which £40,000 went to the Queen. What was more his Azores raid drew Santa Cruz out to convoy the returning East Indiamen and American *galeones*. Santa Cruz took with him all the ships he could get to sea, about forty in all, and he did not get back to Lisbon until October. By then it was too late, especially after the dislocation Drake had caused, to refit and re-store for an invasion of England that year.

Sir Francis Drake had certainly 'singed the King of Spain's beard' and it has been argued that, if Elizabeth had listened to her sailors, she might soon have made Philip as harmless as the shorn Samson. All she had to do, Drake and Hawkins assured her, was to keep up this pressure at sea. The silver fleets would pay for it and it would make a Spanish invasion of England impossible. This strategy, however, of using sea power at long range across the oceans and as an independent arm, was both novel and revolutionary. By now it was not quite untried, but it was still quite unproven. For its achievements so far had been spectacular rather than decisive. Neither Drake in 1585–6 nor Hawkins in 1586 had actually caught the silver convoys. In 1586 and 1587 neither had managed to keep their comparatively small squadrons at sea off the Spanish coast as long as three months. They had not therefore maintained an effective blockade of the Spanish ports and not even Drake dared (either in 1587 or later in 1589) to break into Lisbon as he had broken into Cadiz.

Yet Lisbon, as Drake was beginning to appreciate, was the key to the situation. There lay the main fighting ships of Spain. The English sailors could not smoke them out, and to bottle them up would require squadrons relieving one another in relays every two or three months and each at least as strong as those of Hawkins in 1586 or Drake in 1587. That could well use up two-thirds of the Queen's navy and twice as many armed merchantmen. Moreover, it is very doubtful whether Elizabethan ships had the sailing qualities and signals equipment for such work, or Elizabethan seamen the discipline and the health. Santa Cruz would certainly have found it no harder to elude Drake and Hawkins than, two centuries later, Villeneuve found it to elude Nelson. And from Lisbon he could sail westwards in full force to the Azores to reinforce the Indian Guard and bring in the silver ships, as he had just done; or he could go north against England while one-third of the Queen's ships were refitting and another third away between Spain and the Azores.

This would have mattered less if Elizabeth had had the money to copy her father and to double or treble the size of her navy royal. But with the small margin of superiority that she in fact possessed, she could not gamble her own and her realm's security upon Drake's and Hawkins's theories. Far-sighted men are often blind to the obstacles at their feet and, just as the 1914–18 War produced ideas about the use of air power that could only be realized with the aircraft and technical equipment of 1944–5, so the Elizabethan war produced ideas about the use of sea power that needed the fleets of Nelson's day for their effective execution. Elizabeth was perhaps too conscious of the obstacles at her feet.

But, like Burghley, she knew that her fighting ships were 'the wall of England'[20] and that if this wall were overthrown England would lie naked to her enemies. There was therefore much to be said for keeping those ships under hand in home waters. Even at care and maintenance in the Medway they were more available than when cruising to the Azores or refitting in dry dock. On so vital a matter Elizabeth had to play safe.

Moreover, early in June 1587, just before Drake got back from Cadiz, a new danger appeared closer home: Parma laid siege to Sluys. His choice of objective was significant. He might have exploited Stanley's and Yorke's treasons by thrusting westwards across the Ijsel through Gelderland and Utrecht towards the heart of Holland. With the growing forces at his disposal, amounting by September to 30,000 men available for service in the field, he might thus have put the United Provinces in desperate jeopardy. That he massed his troops in Flanders and attacked Sluys instead, indicated that the Spaniards meant to attempt the Enterprise of England before they settled with the Dutch. It indicated too that the Enterprise was likely to take the form not – or not only – of a direct invasion from Spain but of a combined operation in which Santa Cruz's navy from Spain would cover or co-operate with an invasion by Parma's army from Flanders. It suggested that Parma was hoping to secure the Armada a base in the Netherlands. Sluys could not provide that. It was no more a deep-water port, capable of harbouring great ships in large numbers, than Dunkirk or Nieuport which he already possessed. But Sluys, on the southern shore of the Scheldte estuary, was an obvious stepping-stone to Flushing, and Flushing could well serve as an Armada base besides opening the Scheldte right up to Antwerp.

Here, then, was a threat that Elizabeth could not ignore. Drake might have delayed the Armada, but he had not destroyed it. Indeed, by delaying it, he had given Parma the time to secure it a base in the Low Countries. This had to be prevented and Elizabeth tried to prevent it in two ways. She sent Leicester back with reinforcements to save Sluys and hold Flushing and the northern shores of the Scheldte estuary. She also reinvigorated the peace talks and tried to persuade Parma to an armistice during the negotiations and before he had time to take Sluys or Flushing.

Hitherto, since Leicester's return to England, Elizabeth had been most unwilling to increase her aid to the Dutch. She had

rejected their envoys' requests in February. In March she did send
one of her Privy Councillors, Buckhurst, to report on the situation
and to try to heal the Provinces' dissensions. His reports urged her
to send Leicester back to provide a head and authority in government, and to send money to pay her troops. Wilkes on the Council
of State, and other English leaders in the Netherlands, agreed. Yet
even in May Elizabeth would offer no more than to lend the States
£15,000 and to send Leicester back if they would put £100,000 in
his hands for the summer's campaigning. It was the siege of Sluys
that decided her to act. Thereupon she made Leicester a personal
loan of £6,000, gave him £30,000 to pay her troops, and sent him
back with 5,000 more men to reinforce her now sadly depleted
auxiliary companies. More than this, she authorized him to
demand from the States full authority to administer their war
funds, to command their forces, and to issue ordinances with the
Council of State's advice. If they refused, he might appeal over
their heads – or behind their backs – to the individual provinces
and towns. He was also to induce them to join in the peace negotiations that she was attempting again to set on foot.[21]

For Elizabeth was now trying hard to revive the peace negotiations that she had brought to an abrupt halt in the previous
summer. She had tried to revive them earlier in 1587 in the hope,
it would seem, of frightening Henry III of France with the spectre
of an Anglo-Spanish reconciliation and so scaring him off taking
too strong a line over Mary Stuart. Some highly optimistic report-
ing by de Loo and by Croft's servant Morris then suggested to her
that Parma might agree to an armistice and that he had full powers
from his master to conclude a peace. It had also led Parma to
believe that she would not press the point of religious toleration for
the Dutch. Burghley's firm denial of any such intention might have
halted the talks again. But, just as Parma attacked Sluys, letters
came from the King of Denmark offering his mediation and
inviting both sides to send commissioners to a peace conference at
Emden. Elizabeth jumped at the chance and offered to send her
commissioners at once provided Parma would agree to an immediate armistice.[22] The proviso and its timing show clearly that this
new warming-up of the peace talks was largely a tactical device for
saving Sluys. It was the diplomatic counterpart of Leicester's
military effort.

This is not to say that there were not other good reasons for seeking peace if it could be had. One was the effect of the war on trade. The Spanish and Portuguese markets were closed to English merchants. The Straits of Gibraltar and the western Mediterranean were now hostile waters. Much of northern France was also hostile and all France was in chaos. Parma's conquest of Belgium and control of the Rhine above Nijmegen cut off access to Germany through the Netherlands. Hansard hostility closed Hamburg, restricted access up the Elbe, and made difficulties in the Baltic. Also for reasons only remotely (if at all) connected with the war, the Muscovy Company's trade to and through Russia was contracting; the North-East Passage had proved impracticable; and Davis's brilliant explorations (1585–7) had failed to open a North-West Passage. So English merchants found it increasingly difficult to sell their cloth and other goods abroad. With their stocks piling up unsold, they stopped buying from the clothiers. The clothiers could offer less and less work to the weavers and spinners. The sheep-owners found dwindling sales for their wool. The war, in short, was reproducing the economic effects of the fifteen fifties depression. Might it not also produce the same social fruits of popular discontent and rebellion? Desperately the Privy Council in December 1586 had tried to compel the Merchant Adventurers to go on buying cloth even if they could not sell it – though the Queen would not hear of subsidizing them to do that. Now in May 1587 the cloth export trade, except to Emden and the Baltic, was thrown open to all English merchants and at reduced customs rates to foreign merchants as well. Yet it was clearly recognized that these were at best only palliatives. The stagnation of trade was the result of foreign war, not of domestic monopolies, and the only 'sovereign remedy' was peace.[23] Not, however, peace at any price. For while Elizabeth pressed for an armistice as the condition of dispatching her peace commissioners, she also made it clear both to the Danish King and to Parma that the Dutch must be consulted and, if possible, represented, and that a continued Spanish refusal to grant them liberty of worship would prove an insuperable stumbling block to agreement.

In the event, neither Leicester nor the peace negotiations achieved anything. Leicester had queered his own pitch before he left England. He had written urging his partisans to make ready to support his demands for authority from the States and unfortunately the States obtained copies of these letters and of his instructions as well. From these they drew the natural, if unjust, conclusion that Elizabeth had sent him less to save Sluys than to seize control of their country, so that by betraying them to Spain she might the more easily buy her own peace. This suspicion sealed the fate of Sluys. Leicester was hamstrung by the reluctance of the States to co-operate, especially by their reluctance to supply the shallow-draught boats needed for the relief operations. Parma, evading the Queen's demands for an armistice, was thus able to take the town on July 26th.

After that, the situation in the United Provinces went from bad to worse. Leicester, more than ever exasperated at the States, made a half-hearted attempt to snatch power from them. At Amsterdam, Leiden, Naarden, Enkhuisen, and elsewhere in Holland and Zeeland his partisans tried to seize control as Prounincq had done earlier at Utrecht. These attempts failed, but they brought the Provinces to the brink of civil war and over the brink of anarchy. The eastward provinces – Utrecht, Gelderland, Overijsel – were jealous of a States' government dominated by the far richer province of Holland and were beginning to drift away from the union. The States' ill paid garrisons at Medemblik, Arnemuiden, Veere, Geertruidenberg, Heusden, and Workum were on the verge of mutiny. If Leicester could have taken them into the Queen's pay, as many of them desired; if he could have used the Queen's troops boldly to back his partisans and assure the defence of the eastward provinces, he might have fused all the discontents into the instrument of his own supremacy. But all this would have cost money, much money, and while Elizabeth was ready to let Leicester see what his Dutch partisans could do for him, she was determined not to pay them a penny for doing it. All, therefore, that Leicester and his faction did was to make any effective government impossible. Once this became clear, he was recalled. By December 1587 he was back in England and his Dutch partisans were left to make their peace as best they could with the States.

Chapter 28

The Coming of the Armada

By the autumn of 1587 few could doubt that the Armada preparing in Spain was intended for the invasion of England. Nor,
despite Drake's raid, could they now doubt that it would come in
1588. Even Leicester recognized that it was time for Elizabeth to
'look to her own case and specially to strengthen herself at home
by all the means and ways she can and that forthwith, chiefly by
her navy'.[1] Home defence, however, would also be a costly business. Burghley reckoned that to mobilize for only three months
thirty-six of the Queen's ships and pinnaces, with fifty others,
would cost £66,000. To mobilize for two months one army of
10,000 men to guard the coasts and another of 20,000 to defend the
Queen would cost the Exchequer £52,000, besides the charge on
the counties for their levy, equipment, and bringing together. This
took no account of the need to strengthen the forces in Ireland, on
the Scottish Border, and in the south-coast garrisons, which might
come to another £24,000.[2] And, of course, in the event double
these numbers of sea and land forces were to be mobilized, even if
some for shorter periods.

Clearly, therefore, the Queen had now to watch more carefully
than ever her continental commitments. The heaviest by far were
those in the Netherlands. In her alarm at Parma's attack on Sluys,
she had given Leicester a second chance to end the United
Provinces' disarray by asserting his authority as their Governor-
General. As a result, the second year's aid to the Dutch had been
no less expensive than the first. Between October 12th, 1586 and
October 11th, 1587 the amount actually paid over had risen to
close on £164,000. Some of this went on settling the first year's
debts. Nevertheless, in November 1587 the Privy Council estimated – and almost certainly underestimated – the total bill for the
two years at £313,000 instead of the £252,000 (£126,000 a year)
which they had anticipated when the 1585 treaty was signed.[3] On
top of this there was £47,695 spent in the fifteen months from September 1586 upon ships to keep the Narrow Seas towards Flanders.[4]

Yet what had all this achieved? Leicester had quite failed either to assert his own authority or to heal Dutch dissensions. His partisans had proved too weak to wrest control of Holland and Zeeland from the States party without much more active and expensive support from the English than Leicester could afford to give. Their attempts had only distracted the States from the war against the Spaniards, while stirring many garrisons to mutiny and widening the division between the Hollanders and the eastward provinces. Possibly the extra 5,000 English troops that Leicester had brought over, though they failed to save Sluys, had helped a little to deter Parma from attacking Flushing and Bergen-op-Zoom. Yet the real deterrent to Spanish attacks upon the vital Zeeland islands was not the English land forces but the States' naval forces. Indeed, any deterrent effect that the extra 5,000 English had, was more than offset by the hopes given to Parma by the mounting suspicion and hostility which their presence inspired in the States, by the persistent rumours of Dutch plots to expel the English garrison from Flushing. Neither Leicester nor the extra troops were likely to accomplish anything that could not equally well be achieved by the ordinary auxiliary forces and a good understanding with the States.

Accordingly, the extra 5,000 troops were discharged from October 11th, 1587, and in November Leicester was recalled. He returned to England early in December, almost his last act being to remit 'checks' amounting – so the muster-master later alleged – to nearly £24,000.[5] On December 17th he resigned all his authority in the Netherlands. His successor, Lord Willoughby, although he continued to sit along with another English councillor in the Dutch Council of State, was instructed 'only to deal in those things that concerneth the regiment and government of Her Majesty's forces, without intermeddling in anything that concerneth the government of the said countries'.[6] In March 1588 a new establishment fixed the total charge of the Queen's forces in the Netherlands at £125,389 a year.[7] This was the original 1585 figure, but at the same time Willoughby was told that the Queen was not disposed to make a full pay to her army for the year ended October 11th, 1587, which would have required nearly £44,000. Instead, apart from a small imprest to the captains and a supply of clothing for the men, the companies were to continue to make do on bare weekly lendings. This did nothing to remedy their wants and weakness. It meant, too, that by October 11th, 1588, the sum required to settle their accounts and make them a full pay to that date rose to over £70,000. But in the meanwhile the financial relief to the Queen's Exchequer was considerable and immediate. The new policy – or, rather, reversion to the original 1585 policy – almost halved the Queen's expenditure in the Netherlands during the crucial and costly Armada year. From October 12th, 1587 to October 11th, 1588, the actual payments made for the army there were barely £88,000.[8]

The political effects emerged more slowly. In part this was due to the delay in publishing Leicester's resignation. No one seems to have felt that there was any urgency about this and through a series of accidents the States were not informed until March 1588.[9] In the meantime the Queen's scolding remonstrances to them about their ill-treatment of Colonel Sonoy and others helped to obscure the fact that she no longer had any intention of encouraging the designs of Leicester's partisans. It was not therefore until the spring that relations between the States and the English began to improve or the States made much headway in reasserting their authority. Once Leicester's resignation was known, however, progress was fairly rapid. The suspicion that the States were planning attacks on the cautionary towns died down. Elsewhere Willoughby, on the Queen's orders, helped to conclude an agreement with Colonel Sonoy and to end the mutinies in the other garrisons. Even so, it was not until mid-June that the turbulent Germans in Geertruidenberg were appeased and the danger of military anarchy was over.

Political unity was of even slower growth. By the late spring opposition to the States in Holland and Zeeland was broken and routed, but the eastward provinces still remained distracted and aloof. They were slow to send their deputies to the States General, even slower to vote their small contributions, and not until late August were Utrecht, Overijsel, and Friesland to name their representatives on the Council of State. The chief reason for this, and for the slow growth of the States' confidence in their English allies, was the continued peace negotiations between the Queen and Parma. Those negotiations had failed to save Sluys by securing an armistice in June–July 1587. Yet after taking Sluys Parma attempted nothing else for almost fifteen months and during that time there was in the Netherlands something very like an uncovenanted cessation of arms. We, who can read Parma's correspondence with the King of Spain,[10] know the real reason for that. Until almost the end of 1587 Philip, despite the dislocation that Drake had caused, was still urging his Armada to sea and its eventual postponement in 1587 only strengthened his determination that it must sail in 1588. Parma therefore had to hold his army ready all that time to join in the invasion of England. He could not risk committing it, even for a few weeks, to any serious operations in the Netherlands.

This was, however, less obvious to the Queen and her advisers in 1587-8. Parma's preparations and the massing of his troops in Flanders were patent enough. But back in April 1587 Walsingham had heard that he 'could not make any great attempt this year for want of victuals'.[11] His inactivity after taking Sluys could be taken as confirming that information and as betokening his enforced sincerity in the quest for peace. Moreover, there were clear signs that the 'great disette of grains' in the Spanish Netherlands, and the fear that Leicester's troops might spoil the promising 1587 harvest, were making the commons there long ardently for peace.[12] There was some hope, too, that the native nobility might press Parma to it, even perhaps that he might be induced to throw in his lot with them and set himself up as their sovereign independent of Spain.[13] His own assertions that he was only suspending his operations because of Elizabeth's promise to send over her peace commissioners, and his protests that her delay was losing him the campaigning season, lent some slight encouragement to such hopes, without unduly encouraging the Queen to any greater haste.

Elizabeth had in fact named her commissioners as early as July 1587, but she was reluctant to send them over before she had persuaded the States to join in the negotiations. After all, though her ultimate object was no doubt a general peace, her immediate tactical purpose was still to postpone Spanish attacks on Flushing and the Zeeland islands by securing a formal cessation of arms in the Netherlands. Her repeated emphasis on an immediate armistice, as a necessary preliminary to a peace conference, clearly shows that. Yet she could hardly expect Parma to agree to an armistice if the States were not a party to it. Their obstinate reluctance to join in or even countenance the negotiations therefore held up matters for months. Eventually in February 1588 the Queen lost patience and sent her commissioners to Ostend without waiting longer for the States' concurrence. By then even she could

hardly expect a peaceful outcome and in the event the envoys'
negotiations, which dragged on until the Armada was actually in
the Channel, proved a farce from the start. Twelve weeks passed
before the two sides could even agree upon their meeting place.
When, late in May, their conferences began at Bourbourg, just
outside Ostend, they were still unable to agree upon a cessation of
arms and it soon became obvious that the Spaniards would not so
much as consider the Queen's conditions for a peace.

Yet, although the envoys' negotiations proved a farce, they were
not necessarily a mistake. They caused no slackening in England's
defence preparations. They brought exact and up-to-date information about Parma's preparations. The Earl of Derby's shipmaster
had a good close look at the shipping in Dunkirk when he brought
over beer for the Earl, who conveniently found the local brew
unpalatable. Dr Dale sent home, only ten days before the Armada
arrived, a detailed account of Parma's land and sea forces.[14] More
important, if Parma wished, as he clearly appeared to wish, to keep
negotiations going until the Armada came, then he could not use
the time to seize a base for the Armada in the Netherlands by
attacking Flushing as last year he had attacked Sluys. Also the
negotiations 'served to expose the duplicity of the Spaniards and
might almost have been devised with that intent'.[15] Parma had to
send hastily to Spain for the powers to treat which he had pretended to possess. The minimum terms upon which the English
envoys insisted – even the over-pacific Sir James Croft of the 'long
grey beard with a white head witless'[16] – were familiar enough.
They were in essence the terms of the 1576 Pacification of Ghent –
withdrawal of foreign troops from the Netherlands and settlement
of the religious question by a Netherlands States General. They
were the terms which Elizabeth had been pressing Philip II to
accept ever since 1568. For the Spaniards to refuse them out of
hand was a confession of their insincerity in the peace negotiations.
Monarchs and statesmen of the later sixteenth century had a
curious anxiety to stand well in the world's opinion and the farce at
Bourbourg at least provided some useful grist to the English
propaganda mill.

It did, however, have unfortunate effects upon the Dutch. The
hope of an early peace made the largely Catholic populations of
the weak and poverty-stricken eastward provinces more than ever
reluctant to submit to the domination of the wealthier and more

powerful Hollanders. At the same time the States of Holland and Zeeland feared that Elizabeth was about to leave them in the lurch, if not actually to betray them to Parma and buy her own peace by delivering Flushing, Brielle, and Bergen to the Spaniards. This caused them to concentrate more exclusively upon their own defence, which only added to the grievances of the exposed and thinly garrisoned eastward provinces. It also caused Holland and Zeeland to concentrate their naval forces in their own home waters for fear of a sudden onslaught by the Spaniards or a sudden betrayal by the English. As a result, the Dutch warships promised by the 1585 treaty never joined the English fleet in the main Armada actions. Worse still, the English did not feel that they could trust their allies even to maintain the blockade of Parma's few poor ships and many invasion barges at Dunkirk. So when the Armada came, a powerful squadron, containing eight of the Queen's ships under Sir Henry Seymour, was to be kept chafing in the Straits of Dover, unable to play its part alongside Howard and Drake until the very last days of the great sea battle.

That was the price England paid for Leicester's bungling and Elizabeth's peace negotiations. Yet at least the Armada was to find no friendly harbour in the Netherlands waiting to shelter it. Once it was through the Straits of Dover, there was nowhere for it to go but homewards by the long and perilous route around the north of Scotland and the west of Ireland. For that, perhaps, the £400,000 and more which Elizabeth had spent in the three years' help to the Dutch was not too great a price to pay.

Westwards of the Straits of Dover, in France, Elizabeth's commitment had been much smaller and the situation was much more precarious. Henry of Navarre and the Huguenots were still in arms and had won a notable victory at Coutras in October 1587. The German levy, however, towards which the Queen had contributed £31,000, had in November come to an ignominious end after a most inglorious campaign. In part this was Navarre's fault. He had refused to join forces with them and tried to use them instead to create a diversion in Lorraine and eastern France. Their presence there had indeed distracted the Duke of Guise and a sizable part of his forces. But their disintegration meant that in 1588 Navarre and the Huguenots would stand alone against the undivided power of the Catholic League. This outcome, and the reasons for it, did nothing to enamour Elizabeth either of German levies or of

Huguenot allies and she accordingly maintained her firm refusal to contribute anything more to their cause. An ambassador from Navarre, who came in March 1588 to beg for another 100,000 crowns for another German levy, was sent off with a very cold answer.

Instead, the Queen, through her ambassador in France, Sir Edward Stafford, increased her efforts to persuade Henry III to break openly with the League and join forces with Navarre and the Huguenots. During 1587 such persuasions had evoked little response, possibly because Henry, as he secretly told Stafford later, hoped that Navarre's German levy would force the Guises to a settlement on his own terms. That hope was now dashed. Also the Guises were beginning to demand his more whole-hearted co-operation and he knew that the Parisian Leaguers were organizing in their support. Accordingly he at last turned to Elizabeth for help, the more earnestly because her peace negotiations with Spain made him fear lest she, too, might soon fail him. Owing to the large gaps that exist, on both the English and the French sides, in the diplomatic correspondence for these months, we have to piece together the story from none too adequate evidence. However, it was apparently upon a hint from the French ambassador that in January 1588 Elizabeth instructed Stafford to approach the King again. He had audience on February 10th and five days later received the King's answer, begging the Queen to persuade Navarre to submit to him and become a Catholic. This, he said, would deprive the League of its chief pretext and enable him to help England against the Spaniards. Henry amplified his request at a very secret nocturnal meeting with Stafford on February 24th.[17] Now, Elizabeth obviously could not urge Navarre to turn Catholic, but she did respond by offering Henry III her help, and her credit to raise forces in Germany, if he would arrest the Guises as traitors and break openly with the League. Stafford communicated these offers on March 28th, but found Henry III as nervous as a kitten at the thought of such drastic action.[18]

It seems fairly certain that Stafford also communicated information about these moves, though not always very accurately or very promptly, to the Spanish ambassador in France. This was none other than Bernardino de Mendoza, a man dedicated to revenge upon England for his ignominious expulsion in 1584. Some historians have seen in this clinching proof of Stafford's alleged 'treason'.[19] And, indeed, it is by no means impossible that Stafford may have been a traitor. Yet it is difficult to repress a doubt concerning his guilt on this occasion. For in this matter he and Mendoza had a common purpose – to provoke an early showdown between Henry III and the League. Mendoza was working for it with the Guises and the Paris Leaguers. He wanted thereby to put the League in full control of at least northern France, so that when the Armada came the Channel ports would be in friendly hands and Parma would be relieved of his anxiety about the French troops on his flank in the royalist Duke of Épernon's governments of Picardy and Normandy.[20] Stafford wanted it – assuming he was a loyal Englishman – for precisely opposite reasons and was working for it through Henry III. Yet he clearly felt that Henry quite lacked the boldness to break with the Guises of his own accord. He equally doubted whether Navarre was likely to do much to screw the King's weak courage to the sticking point. It was suspicious that he and Henry III had both wanted the Germans in 1587 to come no further west than Lorraine. Also, the furtive comings and goings of secret agents between the two made Stafford suspect the more that Navarre was only held back from making his peace with the Guises as well as the King by fear of Condé stepping into his place as Huguenot leader if he apostasized – and at the end of February Condé died, it was suspected by poison.

Yet if Henry III would not break with the League of his own accord and Navarre, converted or unconverted, was unlikely to persuade him to a breach, there was another way. The League might be encouraged to break with Henry III. And how better than by judiciously disclosing to their mentor Mendoza Henry's dealings with the English Jezebel? That this was Stafford's design, is no more than an hypothesis. Yet it does fit the facts, and it is just about as much in character with what we know of him, as the hypothesis that he was selling his country's secrets to pay his gambling debts.

The upshot was perhaps not quite what either ambassador hoped. At the end of April Guise entered Paris and on May 2nd the city rose for him in the Day of Barricades. But next day the King slipped away. Guise had not quite managed the swift seizure of the king's person and the King's government which Mendoza had wanted. Moreover, Henry had fled south-westwards to Chartres, a step towards Navarre and the Huguenots. Elizabeth promptly

did her best to move him the rest of the way. Mendoza heard –
presumably from Stafford – that on the first news of the Barricades
she assured the French ambassador that, if Henry would join her
and Navarre against Spain and the League, she would throw all
her forces by sea and land into the struggle. Possibly her offers were
not quite so lavish, but she did at once send Thomas Bodley to offer
her help. Henry, however, in reply professed to have no doubt of
his ability to chastise his enemies with his own forces. In fact, his
nerve was failing again. His Declaration of May 19th manifested
that he dared not join forces with the Huguenots and was prepared
to treat with the League. Elizabeth tried once more, sending Sir
Thomas Leighton to urge him to denounce the Guises as traitors
and to ally with Navarre. According to Mendoza, Leighton was
also to offer the aid prescribed by the 1572 treaty, or indeed all the
Queen's forces, to maintain the French crown; or to pay Swiss and
German troops for six months if on religious grounds Englishmen
would be unwelcome. There is nothing of this in the draft of
Leighton's instructions and it is suspiciously like the advice given
at this time to Stafford by one of the King's intimate advisers.[21]
Incidentally, again according to Mendoza, Stafford now secretly
offered Guise English subsidies against the King in the hope that
the Duke might be tempted to listen and might then be discredited
in Catholic eyes.[22] Guise did not listen. But if Stafford could try
that sort of trick on him, perhaps we need not suspect quite so
deeply his dealings with Mendoza.

None of these English efforts succeeded. Late in May Henry III
moved, northwards, first to Mantes and then to Rouen. There his
negotiations with the League ended in his almost total capitulation
on July 5th. He signed a new Edict of Union, swearing to exterminate the Huguenots, to acknowledge no heretic as his successor, and
to renounce his English alliance. This capitulation was a victory
for Mendoza: but its timing was not. The Armada had sailed from
Lisbon on May 18th. But for the contrary winds and gales that
first delayed its progress and then drove it into Coruña until July
12th, it would have arrived in the Channel while Henry III was
still at large at Chartres. As it was, when the Armada at last
sighted the Lizard on July 19th, Spain's Leaguer allies had still
not had time to make themselves complete masters even of
northern France. Le Havre had declared for them in June, but the
governors of Dieppe and Calais were hostile to them, while they

had failed to seize Boulogne, thanks in part to support given by the English fleet to that town's governor Bernet, a creature of Épernon's. From the point of view of England's defence, the barriers here along the northern coast of France were certainly even more fragile and precarious than those in the Netherlands. Here Elizabeth had cut things very fine indeed. Yet at least, westwards of the Straits of Dover as well as eastwards, the crucial Channel ports, those nearest to Parma's army, were neither freely at the Armada's disposal nor organized for its relief and supply. And with the Huguenot party, thanks to these upheavals, still intact, the power of France, if not enlisted on the English side, was not available to the Spaniards either.

In England's rear, Scotland, too, was reasonably assured. Elizabeth would not listen to the pleas of Leicester, Walsingham, even Burghley, that she should increase James VI's pension. In July she did send an ambassador to him and early in August this ambassador, William Ashly, made unauthorized promises which in the end it cost her £3,000 to repudiate. Yet in fact she was right to trust to James's interest in the English succession to keep him on her side. He had no desire to see his inheritance conquered by the Spaniards, less desire to help them to its conquest. He was strong enough to control his own realm and only the Armada's victory could have turned him unwillingly Spanish.

Indeed, upon the success or failure of England's defence against the Armada all things now depended. And despite the peace negotiations, despite the heavy expenses in the Netherlands, England's defences were ready for the test. We have already seen what had been done on land, through the Lords Lieutenants and their Deputy Lieutenants within the various counties, to rearm, organize, and train the trained bands and to perfect the beacon warning system. From 1585 arrangements were also pressed forward for the mobilization and deployment of those county forces on a national scale.[23] A detailed survey of possible enemy landing places, made in 1585, had led to the throwing up of earthworks and staking of some beaches to supplement the string of coastal castles developed from Henry VIII's time. At first it was intended that the levies of the coastal counties, supported by these fixed defences, should meet the enemy as he landed and slow down his advance as much as possible, so as to give the inland levies time to concentrate towards the point of danger. Only the trained bands, it was further decided in 1587, would be used for this, the untrained men being mobilized for police duties in the rear. In the spring of 1588, however, the influence of veteran officers from the Low Country wars – and realization of the sheer number of possible landing places – led to the adoption of different tactics. The counties of various regions were grouped together and their mobilization focused upon certain important ports. In this way, although the enemy's first landing would not be heavily opposed, large defending forces would rapidly gather not far from the point of danger – 19,200 men around Plymouth, 14,000 around Poole, 16,000 around Portsmouth, and so forth – to crush him before he could establish a secure bridgehead. Behind these there was to be, besides a substantial force guarding the Queen, another large army concentrating inland, ready to reinforce them and bring the enemy to battle before he could reach London.

Happily, perhaps, for England, the enemy was not to land in 1588 and no such battle was to occur. For all these forces were what in later days would have been called 'territorials', part-time soldiers, not full-time professionals comparable with the famous Spanish *tercios* in the Netherlands. Yet we should not allow Shakespeare's comic description of Falstaff's levies to make us too scornful of the Elizabethan trained bands. Falstaff was levying men for foreign service and, except for a time in the fifteen nineties, Elizabethan foreign levies were not usually taken from the trained bands. They mostly came from 'the outcasts of the city and the suburbs'[24] and from the untrained men of the counties. Even so, when those raw levies, after a few weeks' service, faced the Spanish infantry in the Netherlands, or the mercenaries of the Catholic League in France, their prowess was not far below that of 'the scum of the earth' who served under Wellington in the Peninsula two centuries later. The trained bands, a citizen force chosen from men of some substance and trained to handle their weapons, would perhaps have given no worse an account of themselves if the sailors had let the 1588 Armada shepherd Parma's army across the Narrow Seas. Parma himself, who had tested the mettle of English soldiers in the Netherlands and was wont to make a special note when a town had Englishmen in its garrison, at least anticipated no walk-over. 'If I set foot on shore,' he wrote to Philip II in March, 'it will be necessary for us to fight battle after battle ... and in a very short time my force will thus be so much reduced as to be quite inadequate to cope with the great multitude of enemies.'[25]

The trained bands, however, were only England's second line of defence. The first line was her naval forces, above all the Queen's twenty-five fighting galleons, or battleships as they would later have been called. We have seen how Hawkins and his colleagues had already reshaped and rearmed these, with their scouting pinnaces, into much the most up-to-date and formidable fighting fleet then in existence. We have seen, too, how the reaching out of trade to distant markets, and the attractions of plundering the Spaniard, had built up a substantial reserve of large merchantmen and privateers capable of fighting alongside the Queen's ships. There was nothing comic about Elizabethan England's sea power, whatever might be thought of her military power on land. In fact, by the close of 1587 there were only two question marks against it. When should it be mobilized? How should it be used?

To mobilize too soon could be as dangerous as to mobilize too late. At sea wooden hulls soon became encrusted with barnacles and weed. Gales might strain timbers and start leaks as well as damage rigging and spars. Disease spread rapidly in the unhygienic and overcrowded shipboard conditions and England could not afford to lose too many of her sailors when the mobilization was on such a scale as this. Mobilization on this scale also created enormous supply and victualling problems. It was not entirely the government's fault, nor was it entirely due to financial stringency, that the fleet could only be victualled for a month or so at a time. There is no evidence that this was a deliberate device to keep men like Drake in leading strings. To collect and transport the quantities needed was no small task, particularly when the fleet was based in the remote west at Plymouth. Given the pace of cart horses on sixteenth-century roads, especially in wet seasons, the best means of transport was by sea. But in the stormy summer of 1588 even sea transport from the Thames westwards to Plymouth was made slow and uncertain by the prevailing Channel winds. Nor was it possible to solve the problem by accumulating stores ahead of time. The sixteenth century had few means of preserving victuals, even grain.[26] Thus, although a large amount of beer was gathered at Plymouth, it all became undrinkable. Here Spanish experience is also illuminating. They victualled their ships for six months, only to find that 'meat and fish and biscuits, packed into casks when the sailing had been set for October, turned out by May to be inedible by even the most tolerant standards.'[27]

The shorter the time, therefore, between mobilization and action, the better. Many English Councillors had urged the Queen to put her ships to sea as early as October 1587. In December, upon a new alarm, she did order their mobilization and within a fortnight her fleet was fully manned and ready for battle. It was a remarkable feat, one that no other nation could then have emulated, one that fully justified the Queen in cutting her corners rather close. So, when the alarm died down in January, the crews on the royal ships were reduced to half-strength. This left enough men to handle them and, while saving on wages, lessened the dangers from overcrowding and reduced the strain on the supply organization. It was not until news came in March that the Armada was to sail next month, that full mobilization was again ordered and an embargo laid on all shipping. If the Armada had arrived late in April as Philip intended, this would have been excellently timed. As it turned out, owing to delays by weather and its own deficiencies, the Armada did not reach the Channel until July 19th. By then the English fleet had been mobilized not for one month, but for four, and some at least of its problems sprang directly from this Spanish tardiness.

One problem, of course, was what the fleet should do while waiting for the Armada to sail. Here, as with the deployment of the trained bands, new ideas triumphed. Back in 1584 Burghley had sketched out purely defensive dispositions, with part of the fleet covering the west country, a second part the Isle of Wight, and a third in the Downs.[28] The mobilization of December 1587 envisaged instead concentrating the main fleet in the Narrow Seas, close to its Medway bases, while Drake with thirty ships (including seven of the Queen's) made a reconnaissance in force to the Spanish coast from Plymouth. The partial demobilization of January held up this project. In April, however, Lord Admiral Howard with the main fleet was ordered first to Portsmouth, then to Plymouth. When he arrived at Plymouth on May 23rd and added Drake's squadron to his force, he had under him, there at the western end of the Channel, practically the whole strength of England by sea, except for Seymour's squadron keeping watch on Parma.

Nor was this all. Drake in a letter of March 30th had urged that the Queen had no reason 'to fear any invasion in her own country' and that what they should do was 'to seek God's enemies and Her Majesty's wherever they may be found ... for that with fifty sail of shipping we shall do more good upon their own coast than a great many more will do here at home'. This was 'the first recorded exposition of the policy which has been Britain's ever since',[29] of what was to become classic naval doctrine. Yet, despite its novelty and its boldness, the Queen and her Councillors so far yielded that early in May they left the decision to Lord Admiral Howard and his council of war. And after some debate Howard and his council agreed with Drake. By the end of May the whole fleet at Plymouth was under orders to sail for the Spanish coast as soon as the ships were victualled and the winds served. Howard's ships, however, carried less than three weeks' victuals until their store ships could get round from the Thames. Nor did the winds serve. On May 30th the fleet did put to sea, but a week later all were back in Plymouth after beating vainly against strong westerlies at the mouth of the Channel. At this point Elizabeth was smitten by doubts and sent fresh orders restraining Howard from venturing too far to the southward. But these orders were soon rescinded and it was not the Queen but the winds that in the event restrained the English fleet. Late on June 23rd, it put to sea and took station in the Western Approaches. But not until July 7th did the wind allow it to set course for Coruña, where the June gales had driven the Armada to take shelter to repair damage and replace its rotting victuals. A mere two days later the wind backed and began to blow hard from the south-west. So, by July 12th, the English fleet was back in Plymouth, its victuals shorter than ever. On that very day the Armada came out of Coruña on what was to prove for fully half its 130 ships their last voyage. By the afternoon of July 19th they were off the Lizard. The supreme test had come, but England stood ready by sea, and even by land, to face it.

The news, indeed, must have drawn a long sigh of relief from Lord Treasurer Burghley. At home as abroad, expenses had been kept to a minimum. In April most of the cost of preparing the shipping requisitioned to reinforce the Queen's ships had been shifted from the Exchequer to the coastal towns in the form of ship money. In the same way the cost of the land armies was so far as possible thrown upon the counties, which were responsible for keeping their troops so long as they remained within the county

boundaries. Thus the 20,000 men from the trained bands that were
to form Leicester's army at Tilbury were not called up until July
23rd, when the Armada was already off Portland. Those from the
more distant counties were still on the road when they were halted
on August 3rd and by August 10th all but 6,000 were sent home.
For the army to guard the Queen, the government relied mainly
upon the retinues of the nobility, officials, and courtiers, drawing
no more than 5,000 men for a brief period from the counties.

The relief to the Exchequer was considerable. But ship money
was very far from popular in the coastal towns and the burden on
the counties was great. Burghley on July 18th wrote that for many
places these 'unsupportable charges towards musters' totalled as
much as four parliamentary subsidies and such local evidence as
survives bears out his estimate. Already, he added, 'I see a general
murmur of people and discontented people will increase to the
comfort of the enemy.' This 'murmur' which he 'saw' would make
it 'very unreasonable to demand new subsidies' from Parliament,
especially as the second instalment of the last grant was just about
to be collected.[30] Anyway, there was no time to call a Parliament
and get in its grants before the enemy arrived. Yet the Exchequer
was well-nigh empty. Its issues, which had been under £150,000 in
the financial year 1582-3, had risen to over £367,000 in 1586-7
and in this critical year 1587-8 rose still higher to £420,000. The
reserve of 'chested treasure', £299,000 at Michaelmas 1584,
dwindled to £55,000 by Michaelmas 1588.[31] Already in January
1588 letters under the privy seal had gone out demanding from the
better-to-do taxpayers a loan of £75,000, while another £30,000
had been borrowed from the City in March.

Burghley, badgered by Howard and Hawkins for money to keep
the fleet together, by Marmaduke Darrell for money to victual it,
by Seymour for pay to keep his crews from mutiny, by Leicester
for the army's needs at Tilbury, saw no hope of borrowing more at
home or of getting money in time from abroad. Yet he urgently
needed £40,000 or £50,000 to maintain the Queen's fleet and
armies. 'A man could wish', he wrote to Walsingham, 'if peace
cannot be had, that the enemy would not longer delay but prove
(as I trust) his evil fortune. For as these expectations do consume us,
so I would hope ... upon their defeat we might have one half year's
time to provide for money.'[32] He wrote this letter on July 19th
– the very day that the Armada appeared off the Lizard. So narrow

in the end was the financial margin, despite all Elizabeth's parsimony over the past three years. The £70,000 that she owed to her troops in the Netherlands, the £31,000 that she had refused to grant to Henry of Navarre's ambassador, take on a different significance when they are viewed against this background. They were not the products of miserly cheeseparing. They were the narrowly calculated price of victory and survival.

Conclusion

THE story of the defeat of the Invincible Armada has been told too often and too well[1] to need retelling here. That eleven-day sea fight up the Channel and through the Narrow Seas was very far from ending the war. Indeed, the war was to drag on for another sixteen years, years that brought for England a slow disillusionment, straining both the fabric of government and the patience of the people. It proved easier to avoid defeat than to achieve victory. That, however, is another story, though one that does need retelling. For us, the Armada battle in 1588 is the climax to the much longer story whose course since 1485 we have been following. For those hundred years and more England's rulers – and her sailors, soldiers, and merchants – had been gradually working out the answers to the problems posed by the loss of their continental dominions and by the growth of the mighty monarchies of France and Spain. The Armada campaign was the conclusive testing and proof of the soundness of those answers. An invasion attempt, made in unprecedented strength, was beaten off, beaten off by sea power alone. No English soldier fired a shot on land against the enemy and not one Spaniard set foot on English soil except as a prisoner. Barely half the Spanish ships were able to struggle home and in all their long voyage they did not sink a single English boat.

For the English it was indeed a famous victory. It proved that an insular policy based upon sea power was practicable even in these desperate circumstances. It showed that England could successfully, and almost singlehanded, maintain her independence against the mightiest of continental Leviathans. The moral effect, the boost to national confidence, was great. Even the older generation, conditioned to a cautious timidity by the perils of the fifteen fifties and fifteen sixties, no longer half expected to lose the war. For the younger generation the only question now was how to win it.

Those, however, who knew most about the course and nature of the Armada battle were the least inclined to immoderate exultation. This was to be expected. For the Armada battle was the first great fleet action ever fought between sailing warships. Naturally, therefore, it was a confused and muddled affair, with both sides fumbling to improvise effective fleet tactics and organization in the heat of the conflict. Yet there was something else, more disturbing to the English sailors. They had out-sailed, out-manoeuvred, and out-fought the Spaniards as they had always expected to do. But they had neither broken the Armada's formation nor destroyed its ships by their gunfire as they had believed with equal confidence that they would. Knowing that the Spaniards carried heavier guns, but of shorter range, than their own, they had stood off and fought the Channel actions at a range beyond the reach of the Spanish broadsides. At that distance, however, their own shot proved too light to do more than superficial damage.

The result was 'so much powder and shot spent, and so long time in fight, and in comparison thereof so little harm'.[2] By the time they reached Calais roads on July 27th not a single Spanish ship had been sunk by gunfire. One had limped off to Le Havre before the fleets even made contact; a second had been blown up by accident, or by a disgruntled member of her crew; and a third surrendered to Drake after being disabled in a collision. When the English fireships went in at Calais, a fourth Spaniard was wrecked and in the ensuing panic the Armada lost all formation. As it had also almost run out of cannon-balls, the English were now able to close the range and do more effective execution. Off Gravelines on July 29th at least three galleons were sunk and others severely damaged by English gunfire. After that, however, the English, too, were almost out of ammunition. The whole battle, in short, was yet another warning of the risks of trusting too completely to the bold strategic theories of revolutionary thinkers before those theories had been tested and proved in actual operations. It was, perhaps, after all fortunate for England that the wind had backed southwesterly on July 9th and that the first great fleet action between sailing warships was therefore fought off the English rather than off the Spanish coast.

For what turned defeat into disaster for the Spaniards was that, after their battering off Gravelines, they were so very far from home. It was on the long haul back to Spain, often in rough weather, around the north of Scotland and the west of Ireland, that most of their ship losses occurred. English gunnery had no doubt made the task of the winds and waves easier. But had the Armada after Gravelines been able to find shelter and supplies in Flushing or Antwerp, or even refuge in the Firth of Forth, it might have remained a formidable threat and Burghley might have gone on sighing for his 'one half-year's time to provide for money'. The whole campaign, indeed the whole war, emphasized how little, even now, England could afford for strategic reasons to turn her back completely upon the continent or to ignore Scotland. It thus reinforced the lesson taught by the trade depression which the war produced: the lesson that, although England was an island, it was still none the less part of the European community.

In short, by 1588 it was already clear that in normal times, when the balance between the two great continental powers stood even, England was safe enough provided she kept up her navy, made sure of Scotland, and kept control over Ireland. She could then generally rely upon Spain to stand by her against France or France against Spain. The events of 1588 made it no less clear that England could not afford to dissociate herself entirely from the continent. In particular she could not afford to stand by indifferently if the continental balance broke down and allowed one of the two great monarchies to rise to a position of dominance. Certainly the defeat of the Armada demonstrated that even in those abnormal conditions her sea power was now a reasonably sure shield for her independence. Nevertheless, the strain and burden of standing alone, or almost alone, against such an enemy were heavy to bear and not lightly to be incurred. The surest way to avoid the burden and strain was to keep an ever-watchful eye upon the continental Powers, to see that the balance never swung too sharply towards either the one or the other, above all to keep the coast between Brest and Emden from falling under a single master.

These were the answers to the problems posed by the fifteenth-century changes in England's strategic circumstances. By 1588 those answers were clear and tried. The pattern was set that English foreign policy was to follow for the next three and a half centuries, until new revolutions in the art of war made sea power no longer an adequate defence and insularity no longer a practicable policy.

Notes

Chapter 1

1 G. Mattingly, *Renaissance Diplomacy*, p. 77.

2 A. Ruddock, 'Trinity House at Deptford in the 16th century', in *Eng. Hist. Rev.*, XLV (1950). 458–76.

3 e.g. *Letters and Papers of Henry VIII* (hereafter *L. and P.*), I. ii. nos. 1858, 1870, 1875, 1894.

4 Sir J. Dalrymple, *Memoirs of Great Britain* (ed. 1790), III. iii. 59, quoted in Sir Winston Churchill, *Marlborough*, I. 420.

5 *Cal. S. P. Venetian*, VIII. 345.

6 G. Mattingly, *Renaissance Diplomacy*, chapter 21.

7 *Bacon's Works* (ed. Spedding), VIII. 198.

8 W. Camden, *Annales* (Leyden, 1625), p. 780.

Chapter 2

1 *Bacon's Works*, VI. 238.

2 J. S. C. Bridge, *Hist. of France*, I. 66.

3 For a discussion of this apathy, see J. D. Mackie, *The Earlier Tudors*, pp. 9–12.

4 A. Conway, *Henry VII's Relations with Scotland and Ireland, 1485–1498*, chapter 1.

5 Bridge, *Hist. of France*, I. 165.

6 Quoted ibid., p. 167, from *Lettres inédites de Maximilien*, pp. 146–7.

7 *Bacon's Works*, VI. 68. It seems more probable that it was England's interest that chiefly moved Henry to uphold the Breton cause, rather than (as W. Busch, *England under the Tudors*, I. 47–54, suggests) the dynastic desire to secure thereby a Spanish match for his eldest son. Henry's remarks to the Papal collector Gigli in January 1489 show that at least he was fully alive to the importance to England of keeping Brittany out of French hands (*Cal. S. P. Venetian*, I. 177–8). It is perhaps also relevant that he did not ratify the treaty of Medina del Campo until October 1490 and then only with amendments which the Spaniards would not accept (Mackie, *Earlier Tudors*, pp. 94–7).

8 *Cal. S. P. Spanish*, I. 21–4.

9 T. Rymer, *Foedera, etc.*, XII. 362–72.

10 F. C. Dietz, *English Government Finance, 1485–1558*, p. 55.

Chapter 3

1 Grey of Fallodon, *Twenty-Five Years*, I. 51.

2 A. F. Pollard, *Reign of Henry VII from Contemporary Sources*, I. 82–3.

[3] A. Conway, pp. 48–52.

[4] Kildare was virtually superseded by James Ormond and Thomas Garth in December 1491. Archbishop Fitzsimmons formally took his place as Lord Deputy in June 1492, to be himself succeeded by Lord Gormanston in September 1493. For these years and for Poynings's administration, see especially A. Conway, chapters 3 to 7 and appendices.

[5] See also chapter 5 below.

[6] H. A. L. Fisher, *Political Hist. of England*, V. 69.

[7] Hall, *Union of Two Noble Families*, p. 477.

[8] *Rotuli Parliamentorum*, VI. 545.

[9] *Cal. Carew MSS.*, V. 180–81.

Chapter 4

[1] J. Leland, *Collectanea*, V. 373–4.

[2] *Cal. S. P. Spanish*, I. 306.

[3] Ibid., p. 309.

[4] Ibid., p. 328; A. F. Pollard, *Reign of Henry VII*, III. 78 note; A. F. Pollard, *Henry VIII*, p. 174.

[5] Dietz, *English Government Finance*, p. 85.

[6] *Cal. S. P. Spanish*, I. 358–9; also *Letters and Papers of Henry VII* (ed. J. Gairdner), II. 147.

[7] Rymer, *Foedera*, XIII. 123–32.

[8] G. Mattingly, *Catherine of Aragon*, pp. 76–7, 82.

[9] *Cal. S. P. Spanish*, I. 409.

[10] *Letters and Papers of Henry VII* (ed. Gairdner), II. 323.

Chapter 5

[1] *Bacon's Works*, VI. 172; Mackie, *Earlier Tudors*, p. 218.

[2] At the beginning of the reign the proportion was much larger – Dietz, *English Government Finance*, pp. 25, 86.

[3] *Bacon's Works*, VI. 95.

[4] W. Money, *Hist. of Newbury*, p. 184.

[5] *Statutes of the Realm*, II. 502.

[6] Ibid., pp. 534–5.

[7] G. Connell-Smith, *Forerunners of Drake*, pp. 40–55.

[8] The latest account is H. van der Wee, *Growth of the Antwerp Market and the European Economy* (3 vols., 1964). For briefer accounts, S. T. Bindoff, 'The Greatness of Antwerp' in *New Cambridge Modern History*, II. 50–69; G. D. Ramsay, *English Overseas Trade*, chapter 1.

[9] Pollard, *Reign of Henry VII*, II. 285–309.

[10] Rymer, *Foedera*, XII. 713–20.

11 *Cal. S. P. Spanish*, I. 21.

12 Connell-Smith, *Forerunners of Drake*, pp. 53–5.

13 Sir J. Clapham, *Concise Econ. Hist. of England*, p. 166.

14 M. E. Mallett, 'Anglo-Florentine Commercial Relations 1465–91' in *Econ. Hist. Rev.*, XV. 250–65.

15 J. A. Williamson, *Cabot Voyages and Bristol Discovery under Henry VII* (Hakluyt Soc., 1962).

16 Dietz, *English Government Finance*, p. 25; G. Schanz, *Englische Handelspolitik*, II. 37 ff.

Chapter 6

1 The story comes from P. Sarpi, *Hist. of the Council of Trent*, published in Italian in 1619 and first translated into English in 1629; Mackie, *Earlier Tudors*, p. 234.

2 *Utopia* (ed. Everyman), p. 13; *Erasmi Epistolae*, II. 69.

3 Fisher, *Political Hist. of England*, V. 160.

4 Garrett Mattingly's view of the young Henry VIII (*Catherine of Aragon*, pp. 106 ff) seems to me altogether more convincing than that of Pollard (*Henry VIII*, pp. 67–9).

5 *Cal. S. P. Spanish*, II, 50; cp. *L. and P.*, I. no. 674.

6 For Bainbridge's diplomatic activities at Rome, see D. Chambers, *Cardinal Bainbridge*, especially pp. 22–71.

7 *L. and P.*, I, no. 162 (p. 84).

8 Ibid., no. 127.

9 *Cal. S. P. Spanish*, II. 50; also *L. and P.*, I. no. 793.

10 *Cal. S. P. Venetian*, II. 63; also *L. and P.*, I. no. 430.

11 *L. and P.*, I. no. 129.

12 Ibid., no. 725; see also ibid., nos. 734, 793, 880.

13 Mattingly, *Catherine of Aragon*, pp. 96–128, for her part in the diplomacy of 1509–14.

14 A. Ferrajoli, 'Un breve inedito', in *Archivio della Reale Società Romana di Storia Patria*, XIX (1896). 425–31.

15 But see note 17 below.

16 Quoted in D. Chambers, *Bainbridge*, p. 45, from Brit. Mus., Cotton MSS., Vitellius B. II. fo. 45.

17 Dietz, *English Government Finance*, pp. 90–93, 225–7. Dr B. P. Wolffe ('Henry VII's Land Revenues and Chamber Finance', in *Eng. Hist. Rev.*, LXXIX (1964). 225–54) estimates from the Chamber accounts that Henry VII spent on jewels and plate between £200,000 and £300,000, 1491–1509. He adds, too, that 'there is no means of knowing how much of this expenditure on jewels and plate was for the normal use and display of monarchy, how much was intended for the King's gifts, and how much went towards a royal hoard. But one may reasonably suppose that within it was contained the full value of that legendary "golden fleece" which Henry is reputed to have left to his son.' If so, and if the estimate of over £900,000 as the cost of Henry VIII's first French war in the years 1511–14 is correct, there is a considerable problem about where the money for that war came from. Parliamentary and clerical taxation apparently provided only some £217,000 towards it and there cannot have been any great surplus out of the ordinary revenues of perhaps

£150,000 a year. The 'legend' of Henry VII's savings was not current merely among foreigners. On Sept. 1st, 1516 Tunstal and Sir Richard Wingfield wrote to Wolsey that 'if the King our master had in ready money much more than ever hath been left him by his father of good memory, this were a way, as we think, to void his coffers' (C. Sturge, *Tunstal*, p. 39).

[18] See Mattingly, *Catherine of Aragon*, pp. 127, 320–21, and references there, as against Pollard, *Henry VIII*, p. 76 and *Wolsey*, p. 19.

Chapter 7

[1] *L. and P.*, II. i. no. 227.

[2] Ibid., no. 411.

[3] *Lords Journals*, I. 57.

[4] *L. and P.*, II. ii. appendix, no. 38.

[5] Dietz, *English Government Finance*, pp. 92, 225; J. Wegg, *Richard Pace*, chapters 4 and 5.

[6] *L. and P.*, II. i. nos. 1814, 2270, 2487, 2500.

[7] G. Mattingly in *Journal of Modern Hist.*, X (1938). 1–30; also his *Catherine of Aragon*, pp. 146–9, and *Renaissance Diplomacy*, pp. 167–71.

[8] *L. and P.*, II. ii. no. 4453.

[9] Ibid., no. 4540.

[10] Ibid., no. 4438; *Cal. S. P. Venetian*, II. 560.

[11] *Mémoires de Florange* (ed. 1913), I. 272.

[12] *L. and P.*, III. i. nos. 1149, 1150.

[13] Ibid., III. ii. nos. 1508, 1509; *Cal. S. P. Spanish, Further Supplement to vols. I and II*, pp. xvii–xviii.

Chapter 8

[1] Pollard, *Wolsey*, pp. 124 ff., 161–4.

[2] W. Bradford, *Correspondence of Charles V*, p. 22.

[3] *L. and P.*, III. i. no. 728 (p. 256).

[4] Ibid., no. 432.

[5] *Cal. S. P. Venetian*, II. 470.

[6] *L. and P.*, III. i. no. 1150 (p. 425).

[7] Ibid., no. 1370.

[8] See, in particular, ibid., no. 1150.

[9] A. Ruddock, 'Trinity House at Deptford in the 16th century', in *Eng. Hist. Rev.*, XLV (1950). 458–76.

[10] See Mattingly, *Catherine of Aragon*, pp. 152–63.

[11] *L. and P.*, III. ii. no. 3346.

[12] *Cal. S. P. Spanish*, II. 597; also Pollard, *Wolsey*, p. 127.

[13] Dietz, *English Government Finance*, p. 94.

[14] R. B. Merriman, *Life and Letters of Thomas Cromwell*, I. 30–44.

[15] Roper, *Life of More*, p. 34.

[16] Ibid., pp. 12–14.

[17] Hall, *Henry VIII* (ed. Whibley), I. 317.

[18] Dietz, *English Government Finance*, p. 225.

[19] Their instructions, *L. and P.*, IV. no. 1212; extracts in M. St Clare Byrne, *Letters of Henry VIII*, pp. 31–8.

[20] Hall, *Henry VIII*, II. 40.

[21] Ellis, *Original Letters* (3rd series), I. 369–75.

[22] *L. and P.*, IV. i. no. 1319.

[23] Hall, *Henry VIII*, II. 44.

[24] As quoted in C. Sturge, *Tunstal*, p. 94, note 2.

Chapter 9

[1] Mattingly (*Catherine of Aragon*, pp. 180–82) suggests that if Henry's real concern had been about the succession and a male heir, his obvious course would have been to try to marry Mary to James V. This would not have called for his own divorce from Catherine and therefore, Mattingly suggests, what decided Henry to seek the divorce was probably his determination to marry Anne Boleyn. We do not know just when Henry fell in love with Anne, but June 1525 would be a very early date for his determination to *marry* her. Yet in June 1525 his preferment of Richmond and his lack of interest in a Scottish match for Mary seem already to point towards solutions in which Catherine and Mary would have little part. There was also the objection of James's young years. Altogether it does seem more likely that Henry fell in love with Anne when he was already looking around for a new wife, than that he only realized his need for a new wife when he fell in love with Anne.

[2] Ibid., p. 132.

[3] *Cal. S. P. Venetian*, III. 662.

[4] Above, p. 52.

[5] G. Constant, *Reformation in England*, I. 53, note 63.

[6] *L. and P.*, IV. ii. no. 2482.

[7] Ibid., no. 2558; *State Papers of Henry VIII*, I. 181.

[8] Pollard, *Henry VIII*, p. 170.

[9] *Cal. S. P. Venetian*, IV. 365.

[10] *L. and P.*, IV. ii. no. 3326.

[11] Ibid., no. 3400.

[12] Ibid., no. 3682.

[13] Ibid., no. 4310.

[14] Ibid., no. 3930.

[15] Dietz, *English Government Finance*, p. 102.

Chapter 10

[1] *L. and P.*, IV. iii. no. 6290.

[2] Rymer, *Foedera*, XIV. 435–8.

[3] *L. and P.*, V. no. 1187.

[4] Ibid., VI. no. 230.

[5] Ibid., no. 230 (2).

[6] Ibid., no. 1427.

[7] Ibid., nos. 568, 570.

[8] Ibid., no. 1426.

[9] J. A. Froude, *Hist. of England* (Silver Library ed.), I. 394.

[10] *L. and P.*, VII. nos. 217, 286, appendix no. 8.

[11] Ibid., VI. nos. 1079, 1150.

[12] Instructions for Mundt and Heath, ibid., VII. no. 21; for Paget, ibid., no. 148.

[13] Summary in Fisher, *Political Hist. of England*, V. 358–61; Merriman, *Life and Letters of Thomas Cromwell*, I. 220–22.

[14] *L. and P.*, VII. nos. 784, 785.

[15] Ibid., no. 1060; *Papiers d'état de Granvelle*, II. 136.

[16] *L. and P.*, VII. no. 1483.

[17] Ibid., IX. nos. 213, 1016.

[18] Merriman, *Life and Letters of Thomas Cromwell*, I. 214.

[19] Dietz, *English Government Finance*, pp. 103–43, 221.

[20] *L. and P.*, X. no. 141 (p. 51).

Chapter 11

[1] *State Papers of Henry VIII*, I. 571.

[2] *L. and P.*, XI. no. 780.

[3] R. Reid, *King's Council in the North*, p. 126.

[4] G. Elton, *England under the Tudors*, p. 155.

[5] *L. and P.*, XIII. ii. no. 1134.

[6] As quoted in Froude, *Hist. of England*, III. 149.

[7] *L. and P.*, XIV. i. no. 670.

[8] B. H. St J. O'Neil, *Castles and Cannon*, pp. 41–64, with photographs of several of these works.

[9] *L. and P.*, XIV. i. no. 373. It is significant that next year, when the foreign danger was passing, an Act of Parliament limited this concession to goods loaded in English ships.

[10] Ibid., no. 103.

[11] G. Elton, 'Thomas Cromwell's Decline and Fall', in *Cambridge Hist. Journal*, X (1951). 150–85.

[12] *L. and P.*, XV. no. 976.

Chapter 12

1 *Sadler State Papers* (ed. Clifford), I. 3–13.
2 *L. and P.*, XVII. no. 1204.
3 Ibid., XVIII. i. no. 106 (p. 72).
4 Ibid., no. 144.
5 Ibid., no. 217.
6 *Declaration* printed at London, 1542; also in Hall, *Henry VIII*, II. 320–38.
7 *Sadler S. P.*, II. 560.
8 *L. and P.*, XVIII. i. nos. 102, 104, 305.
9 Ibid., no. 804; Rymer, *Foedera*, XIV. 786–96.
10 *L. and P.*, XIX. i. no. 314.
11 Ibid., nos. 319, 327.
12 Ibid., no. 136.
13 Ibid., nos. 619, 714.
14 *Tudor Royal Proclamations* (ed. P. L. Hughes and J. F. Larkin, 1964), I. 345–6.
15 Connell-Smith, *Forerunners of Drake*, pp. 127–96.
16 Sir J. Corbett, *Drake and the Tudor Navy*, I. 31–8.
17 *L. and P.*, XX. ii. no. 88.
18 Ibid., XXI. i. 1014.
19 Dietz, *English Government Finance*, chapters 12 and 13.
20 Pollard, *Political Hist. of England*, VI. 10.

Chapter 13

1 Pollard, *England under Protector Somerset*, pp. 132–4.
2 Quoted ibid., p. 232 from S. P. Domestic, Edward VI, 4/33.
3 J. Foxe, *Acts and Monuments* (ed. Pratt, 1870), VI. 25.
4 C. S. L. Davies, 'Provisions for Armies, 1509–50', in *Econ. Hist. Rev.* (2nd series), XVII. 234–48.
5 *Tudor Tracts* (ed. Pollard), p. 77.
6 *An Epistle to the Nobility (etc.) of Scotland* (ed. J. A. H. Murray, 1872).
7 P. Hume Brown, *Hist. of Scotland*, II. 32–3.
8 Ibid., p. 33.
9 Ellis, *Original Letters* (3rd series), III. 292.
10 J. Strype, *Ecclesiastical Memorials*, II. ii. 435.
11 Ibid., p. 429.
12 Home castle held out until Dec. 1549 and Broughty until Feb. 6th., 1550 (Pollard, *Somerset*, p. 265; *Diurnal of Occurrents*, pp. 49–50; *Acts of the Privy Council* [ed. J. R. Dasent], *1547–50*, p. 407).
13 Strype, *Ecclesiastical Memorials*, II. ii. 416–18.
14 Ibid., pp. 294–5.
15 Pollard, in *Cambridge Modern History*, II. 499.

Chapter 14

[1] Strype, *Ecclesiastical Memorials*, II. ii. 482.

[2] e.g. Pollard, 'The Reformation Parliament as a Matrimonial Agency', in *History*, XXI (1936). 219–29.

[3] *Troubles connected with the Prayer Book of 1549* (Camden Soc., new series, XXXVII), pp. 148–88.

[4] Hall, *Henry VIII*, II. 357.

[5] P. Janelle, *L'Angleterre catholique à la veille du Schisme*, pp. 14–15.

[6] See, e.g., J. R. Hale's introduction to Sir John Smythe's *Certain Discourses Military* (Ithaca, N.Y.; 1964), especially pp. xli–lvi.

[7] Dietz, *English Government Finance*, pp. 167–74, 178, 186–7, 191.

[8] F. J. Fisher, 'Commercial Trends and Policy in 16th century England', in *Econ. Hist. Rev.*, X (1940). 95–117.

[9] F. Edler, 'Winchcombe Kerseys in Antwerp, 1538–44', ibid., VII (1936). 57–62.

Chapter 15

[1] Strype, *Ecclesiastical Memorials*, II. ii. 297.

[2] *Literary Remains of Edward VI* (ed. Nicholls), II. 284–5, 291.

[3] Quoted in Conyers Read, *Mr Secretary Cecil*, p. 68.

[4] Strype, *Ecclesiastical Memorials*, II. ii. 382–3.

[5] *Literary Remains of Edward VI*, II. 308–9.

[6] *Cal. S. P. Foreign, Edward VI*, pp. 65, 72, 75—6.

[7] Strype, *Ecclesiastical Memorials*, II. ii. 384.

[8] *Cal. S. P. Foreign, Edward VI*, p. 137.

[9] As quoted in Froude, *Hist. of England*, IV. 544.

[10] See Pollard, *Political Hist. of England*, VI. 56.

[11] Dietz, *English Government Finance*, pp. 140, 190–91, 206.

[12] Ibid., pp. 183, note 17, 188–201.

[13] Ibid., p. 179; Froude, *Hist. of England*, V. 128.

[14] See his letter to Northumberland, quoted in Froude, *Hist. of England*, V. 131–4.

[15] *Acts of the Privy Council*, III. 487.

[16] Connell-Smith, *Forerunners of Drake*, chapters 7 and 8.

[17] T. S. Willan, *The Muscovy Merchants of 1555*.

[18] *Literary Remains of Edward VI*, II. 432–3.

Chapter 16

[1] S. T. Bindoff, *Tudor England*, p. 166.

[2] *Machyn's Diary* (Camden Soc., XLII), p. 178.

[3] *Wriothesley's Chronicle* (Camden Soc., new series, XI), II. 101–2.

[4] As quoted in Froude, *Hist. of England*, V. 263, from *Poli Epistolae*, IV.

[5] *Cal. S. P. Spanish*, XI. 230.

[6] Ibid., pp. 244–5.

[7] Ibid., p. 328.

[8] E. H. Harbison, *Rival Ambassadors at the Court of Queen Mary*, p. 105.

[9] Strype, *Ecclesiastical Memorials*, III. ii. 339.

[10] *Cal. S. P. Spanish*, XI. 363.

[11] Rymer, *Foedera*, XV. 377–81, 393–403.

[12] Quoted in Harbison, *Rival Ambassadors*, p. 106.

[13] Ibid., pp. 111–13 and references there.

[14] *Cal. S. P. Spanish*, XII.85.

[15] Harbison, *Rival Ambassadors*, p. 129; Froude, *Hist. of England*, V. 333 note.

[16] *Chronicle of Queen Jane and Queen Mary* (Camden Soc., XLVIII), pp. 38–9.

[17] Harbison, *Rival Ambassadors*, pp. 132–3.

[18] It may be that 'Pembroke had allowed [Wyatt] to advance until retreat had been cut off' (Pollard, *Political Hist. of England*, VI. 110). Yet even if the Queen's troops had orders to avoid action and to let Wyatt through, they none the less showed a suspicious alacrity in obeying such orders and were remarkably ready to make way for the rebels.

[19] *Cal. S. P. Spanish*, XI. 334–5.

Chapter 17

[1] *Papiers d'état de Granvelle*, IV. 359–67.

[2] *Cal. S. P. Venetian*, V. 581–2.

[3] Foxe, *Acts and Monuments*, VI. 704.

[4] For details see Harbison, *Rival Ambassadors*, appendix II.

[5] *Acts of the Privy Council*, V. 56.

[6] *Cal. S. P. Spanish*, XIII. 105.

[7] For these debates see Harbison, *Rival Ambassadors*, pp. 216–22.

[8] *Cal. S. P. Spanish*, XIII. 93–4.

[9] *Cal. S. P. Venetian*, VI. i. 212.

[10] R. Hakluyt, *Principal Navigations* (Dent ed.), VI. 246–63.

[11] Brit. Mus., Lansdowne MSS., II. no. 33; Strype, *Ecclesiastical Memorials*, II. ii. 437.

[12] Examination of William Crowe, quoted in Harbison, *Rival Ambassadors*, p. 290.

[13] Ibid., p. 274.

[14] Pollard, *Political Hist. of England*, VI. 146.

[15] S. P. Domestic, 8/52.

[16] H. Clifford, *Life of Jane Dormer*, p. 70.

Chapter 18

1 *Hist. MSS. Comm., Salisbury MSS.*, II. 462.

2 Sir J. Harington, *Nugae Antiquae* (ed. 1804), I. 362.

3 *Cal. S. P. Spanish, Elizabeth*, I. 3–4.

4 P. Forbes, *Full View of the Public Transactions*, I. 34.

5 *Cal. S. P. Spanish*, I. 7.

6 A. L. Rowse, 'Alltyrynys and the Cecils', in *Eng. Hist. Rev.*, LXXV (1960). 54–76.

7 *Cal. S. P. Foreign, Elizabeth*, XXII. 327.

8 Peacham, *The Compleat Gentleman* (ed. 1634), p. 45.

9 Naunton, *Fragmenta Regalia* (ed. 1641), p. 12.

10 Quoted from S. P. Domestic, Elizabeth, 1/7, in Conyers Read, *Mr Secretary Cecil and Queen Elizabeth*, p. 119.

11 *Hardwicke State Papers*, I. 167.

12 Wright, *Queen Elizabeth and her Times*, II. 457.

13 Quoted in *Dict. National Biog.*, s.v. Mason, Sir John.

14 *Cal. S. P. Foreign*, II. 3; for Paget, *Hist. MSS. Comm., Salisbury MSS.*, I. 151.

15 S. P. Domestic, 1/77.

16 *Cal. S. P. Venetian*, VI. 1049.

Chapter 19

1 *Cal. S. P. Foreign*, I. no. 1008.

2 *Tudor Tracts* (ed. Pollard), p. 332.

3 Forbes, *Full View*, I. 28.

4 *Cal. S. P. Spanish*, I. 21–3.

5 Rymer, *Foedera*, XV. 505 ff.; Forbes, *Full View*, I. 68–81.

6 See in particular Sir J. Neale, *Elizabeth I and her Parliaments*, I. 51–84.

7 J. R. Tanner, *Tudor Constitutional Documents*, p. 141; J. B. Black, *Reign of Elizabeth I* (2nd ed., 1959), p. 16.

8 See Conyers Read, *Cecil*, pp. 139–41.

9 *Sadler S. P.*, I. 681.

10 *Cal. S. P. Foreign*, I. no. 1028.

11 *Cal. S. P. Spanish*, I. 81.

12 cp. Dr Wootton's letters of Nov. 18th, 1558 and Jan. 9th, 1559 in *Cal. S. P. Foreign*, I. no. 7, and Forbes, *Full View*, I. 18–19; also Feria in *Cal. S. P. Spanish*, I. 51.

13 *Sadler S. P.*, I. 568.

14 Ibid., pp. 634–6.

15 S. P. Domestic, 7/65.

16 N. Williams, *Thomas Howard, 4th Duke of Norfolk*, p. 265, note 2.

17 *Cal. S. P. Foreign*, II. pp. 197–8.

18 Ibid., no. 483; *Sadler S. P.*, I. 654–5.

19 *Cal. S. P. Foreign*, II. no. 497.

20 S. Haynes, *Burghley Papers*, pp. 217, 220.

21 Wright, *Queen Elizabeth and her Times*, I. 24.

22 *Parker Correspondence*, p. 105.

23 Neale, *Elizabeth*, p. 71.

24 Forbes, *Full View*, I. 313.

25 Ibid., p. 295.

26 Haynes, p. 231; for Elizabeth's hopes, ibid., pp. 229, 230, 235.

27 Rymer, *Foedera*, XV. 569–71; the draft in Haynes, pp. 253–5.

28 Neale, *Elizabeth*, p. 102.

29 Forbes, *Full View*, I. 455–6.

30 Rymer, *Foedera*, XV. 593–7.

31 J. Mariejol in E. Lavisse, *Hist. de France*, VI. i. 207.

Chapter 20

1 Quoted in Froude, *Hist. of England*, VI. 435 from S. P. Ireland, 2/39 (*Cal. S. P. Irish*, I. 162).

2 Pollard (*Political Hist. of England*, VI. 181) believed it; but see Conyers Read, *Lord Burghley and Queen Elizabeth*, pp. 210–11; Neale, *Elizabeth*, pp. 220, 239–40, 244–5.

3 Neale, *Elizabeth*, p. 81.

4 I. Aird, 'The Death of Amy Robsart', in *Eng. Hist. Rev.*, LXXI (1956). 69–79.

5 *Hardwicke S. P.*, I. 164.

6 See C. G. Bayne, *Anglo-Roman Relations 1558–65*, pp. 73–116.

7 *Hardwicke S. P.*, II. 185–6.

8 Sir James Melville's *Memoirs*, p. 122.

9 *Cal. S. P. Spanish*, I. 70.

10 *Hardwicke S. P.*, I, 174; *Cal. S. P. Scottish*, I. 595.

11 *Letter from Mary to Guise* (ed. J. H. Pollen), p. 38.

12 Read, *Cecil*, p. 237; D. Hay Fleming, *Mary Queen of Scots*, p. 292, note 35.

13 *Cal. S. P. Scottish*, I. 445.

14 *Cal. S. P. Spanish*, I. 305–12.

15 Ibid., pp. 308, 312, 340–41; Labnoff, *Lettres ... de Marie Stuart*, I. 296–7.

16 *Cal. S. P. Scottish*, II. 19–20, 27.

17 Ibid., p. 104.

18 Read, *Cecil*, p. 316.

19 Brit. Mus., Cotton MSS., Caligula B X. no. 108; *Cal. S. P. Foreign*, VII. 384–7.

20 Ibid., p. 371; Fleming, *Mary Queen of Scots*, p. 338; see also *Cal. S. P. Spanish*, I. 424.

21 Melville's *Memoirs*, p. 120.

22 Murdin, *Burghley Papers*, p. 758.

23 Fleming, *Mary Queen of Scots*, pp. 378–9.

24 Ibid., pp. 139–40.

25 Quoted in Read, *Cecil*, p. 378 from S. P. Ireland, 20/67.

26 J. H. Pollen, *Papal Negotiations with Mary*, p. 397.
27 R. Keith, *Hist. of Scotland* (ed. 1844), II. 667.
28 Froude, *Hist. of England*, VIII. 216-17.

Chapter 21

1 L. O. J. Boynton, *English Military Organization 1558-1638* (unpub. Oxford D.Phil. thesis, 1962), pp. 55-65.
2 *Cal. S. P. Foreign*, II. 310.
3 Forbes, *Full View*, I. 416.
4 Pollard, *Political Hist. of England*, VI. 186-7.
5 These are the figures given in F. C. Dietz, *English Public Finance 1558-1641*, pp. 7, 10-12, 426 (the figure for the navy is given as £105,025, ibid., p. 437). Other estimates, made soon after Elizabeth's death, agree on £178,000 for Scotland 1560, but give £245,000 or £246,000 for France 1562-3 – S. P. Domestic, 287/59; *Hist. MSS. Comm., Salisbury MSS.*, XV. 2.
6 Dietz, *English Government Finance 1485-1558*, pp. 206, 208.
7 Dietz, *English Public Finance 1558-1641*, pp. 19, 382, 392.
8 Read, 'Profits in the Recoinage', in *Econ. Hist. Rev.*, VI (1936). 186-93.
9 E. W. Bovill, 'Queen Elizabeth's Gunpowder', in *Mariners Mirror*, XXXIII (1947). 179-86.
10 H. Hamilton, *Brass and Copper Industries to 1800*.
11 There is a good short account in chapter 4 of E. E. Rich's introduction to *The Ordinance Book of the Merchants of the Staple*. See also Ehrenberg, *Hamburg und England im Zeitalter der Königin Elisabeth*, pp. 64 ff., and B. Hagedorn, *Ostfrieslands Handel*, I. 162 ff.
12 Froude, *Hist. of England*, VIII. 30.
13 G. D. Ramsay, *English Overseas Trade*, chapter 4.
14 The latest account is T. S. Willan, *Early Hist. of the Russia Company*.
15 *Cal. S. P. Foreign*, VIII. 466-7, 589-90.
16 The best account of him is J. A. Williamson, *Sir John Hawkins* (the 1st ed., 1927, is in some respects more complete than the 1949 revised ed.).
17 G. Mattingly, 'No Peace beyond what Line?', in *Trans. R. Hist. Soc.* (5th series), XIII. 145-62.

Chapter 22

1 J. H. Elliott, *Imperial Spain*, pp. 225-6, 253-7; J. Lynch, *Spain under the Habsburgs*, I. 190-92.
2 As quoted in Froude, *Hist. of England*, VI. 539.
3 *Somers Tracts* (ed. W. Scott, 1809), I. 169.
4 P. Geyl, *Revolt of the Netherlands*, pp. 95-9.
5 *Cal. S. P. Spanish*, I. 659, 661.
6 Neale, *Elizabeth and her Parliaments*, I. 147.

[7] For these final negotiations with the Archduke, see *Queen Elizabeth and some Foreigners* (ed. V. von Klarwill), pp. 176–299; also N. N. Williams, *Norfolk*, pp. 88, 92–5, 100–3, 129–32, and Read, *Cecil*, pp. 326–37.

[8] *Cal. S. P. Spanish*, II. 29.

[9] Ibid., pp. 66–8.

[10] Read, 'Queen Elizabeth's Seizure of Alba's Pay Ships', in *Journal Mod. Hist.*, V. 443–64.

[11] Dietz, *English Public Finance*, p. 308.

[12] *Cal. S. P. Spanish*, II. 91–3.

[13] Ibid., pp. 90–91, 95–8.

[14] Williams, *Norfolk*, pp. 130–32, quoting S. P. Domestic, 44/42, 46, for Norfolk's views.

[15] *Cal. S. P. Scottish*, II. 602–3.

[16] Haynes, pp. 579–86.

[17] Fénélon, *Correspondance*, I. 233–7.

[18] *Cal. S. P. Spanish*, II. 111.

[19] Ibid., pp. 136–7.

[20] Fénélon, I. 333–6.

[21] *Cal. S. P. Spanish*, II, 108–9, 109–10.

[22] Ibid., p. 150.

[23] *Cal. S. P. Foreign*, VIII. 573.

[24] Ehrenberg, *Hamburg und England*, p. 110.

[25] The parallel is drawn by Williams, *Norfolk*, p. 145.

[26] *Cal. S. P. Scottish*, II. 647.

[27] Williams, *Norfolk*, pp. 117–19.

[28] *Cal. S. P. Scottish*, II. 651.

[29] For this dating and that of the ensuing events, see Williams, *Norfolk*, pp. 155–9 and notes.

[30] Norfolk's confession, *Cal. S. P. Scottish*, IV. 35.

[31] Read, *Cecil*, p. 467.

Chapter 23

[1] A. Teulet, *Relations politiques de la France et de l'Espagne avec l'Écosse* (ed. 1862), V. 176; *Cal. S. P. Spanish*, II. 254.

[2] *Hist. MSS. Comm., Salisbury MSS.*, I. 555; K. de Lettenhove, *Relations politiques des Pays Bas*, V. 652.

[3] *Cal. S. P. Foreign*, IX. 291.

[4] *Cal. S. P. Scottish*, III. 95, 136–7.

[5] Fénélon, III. 188.

[6] Ibid., p. 418.

[7] *Cal. S. P. Foreign*, IX. 383, and Read, *Burghley*, p. 32; for Walsingham, Digges, *Compleat Ambassador*, p. 83; for Leicester, Fénélon, IV. 22–3.

[8] Fénélon, III. 239; Cecil thought much the same, *Cabala* (ed. 1691), p. 166.

[9] Digges, p. 88.

[10] *Cal. S. P. Rome*, I. 393–405; Murdin, pp. 32–51.

[11] Murdin, pp. 32–51, 117–23.

[12] *Cal. S. P. Spanish*, II. 307–12, 313–17.

[13] Williamson, *Hawkins*, pp. 243–53.

[14] *Correspondance de Philippe II sur les affaires des Pays Bas* (ed. Gachard), II. 185–8.

[15] Murdin, pp. 9–12.

[16] Ibid., pp. 14–15.

[17] Ibid., pp. 20–54, 57; Digges, p. 137.

[18] Froude, *Hist. of England*, IX. 521–2.

[19] Digges, pp. 129, 133.

[20] Ibid., pp. 121, 123–8.

[21] *Cal. S. P. Foreign*, XIII. 120; Burghley wrote: 'necessary for England that the state of the Low Countries should continue in their ancient government, without either subduing it to the Spanish nation or joining it to the crown of France' (Read, *Burghley*, p. 188).

[22] Digges, p. 128.

[23] *Cal. S. P. Scottish*, IV. 1.

[24] Leonard, *Recueil de traités de paix*, II. 584–92.

[25] Digges, p. 180.

[26] K. de Lettenhove, VI. 352–4.

[27] J. B. Black, 'Elizabeth, the Sea Beggars, and the Capture of Brielle', in *Eng. Hist. Rev.*, XLVI (1931). 30–47; Williamson, *Hawkins*, pp. 261–7 and *The Tudor Age*, p. 315; Pollard, *Political Hist. of England*, VI. 331–2. Louis of Nassau had sought Elizabeth's aid for a rather similar project in the spring of 1571 – Read, *Mr Secretary Walsingham and the Policy of Queen Elizabeth*, I. 148–50.

[28] Digges, pp. 189, 203.

[29] K. de Lettenhove, VI. 421.

[30] Wernham, 'English Policy and the Revolt of the Netherlands', in *Britain and the Netherlands* (ed. J. S. Bromley and H. Kossmann), pp. 29–40.

[31] K. de Lettenhove, VI. 434.

[32] Ibid., pp. 483–6; *Cal. S. P. Foreign*, XVII. 497–8.

[33] Froude, *Hist. of England*, X. 22.

Chapter 24

[1] Froude, *Hist. of England*, X. 328.

[2] Digges, p. 268.

[3] Ibid.; Read, *Walsingham*, I. 238, 239.

[4] Murdin, pp. 224–5.

[5] *Cal. S. P. Foreign*, XI. 303.

[6] Fénélon, V, 308–10.

[7] He did send 500,000 ducats overland through France at the end of 1572 – Lynch, *Spain under the Habsburgs*, I. 132.

8 *Correspondance de Philippe II sur les affaires des Pays Bas* (ed. Gachard), II. 320.

9 Read, *Walsingham*, I. 324–5, 334.

10 Ibid., p. 133.

11 *Cal. S. P. Spanish*, II. 553–7.

12 Read, *Walsingham*, I. 402–3.

13 K. de Lettenhove, X. 588.

14 Ibid., p. 589.

15 Ibid., p. 678.

16 Ibid., p. 775.

Chapter 25

1 A. O. Meyer, *England and the Catholic Church under Elizabeth*, p. 142.

2 Ibid., p. 271.

3 £254,960 according to a 1603 estimate – *Hist. MSS. Comm., Salisbury MSS.*, XV. 2. Between March 30th, 1579 and Michaelmas 1586, £350,000 was paid out of the English Exchequer for military expenses in Ireland; between 1558 and 1588, £940,933, according to Dietz, *English Public Finance*, p. 37.

4 Quoted in Read, *Burghley*, p. 254.

5 For this and the following paragraphs, L. O. J. Boynton, *English Military Organisation 1558–1638* (unpublished thesis, 1962) is the only satisfactorily comprehensive study.

6 See, in particular, Williamson, *Hawkins*, pp. 305–82.

7 Dietz, *English Public Finance*, pp. 16, 27–8, 37, 47–8; *Hist. MSS. Comm., Salisbury MSS.*, XV. 2; D'Ewes, *Journals of all the Parliaments of Elizabeth*, p. 245.

8 Brit. Mus., Cotton MSS., Caligula B X. no. 127.

9 Dietz, *English Public Finance*, p. 55.

10 Dietz, *Exchequer in Elizabeth's Reign*, pp. 83–5, 87–9.

11 Wright, *Queen Elizabeth and her Times*, II. 232.

12 E. E. Rich's introduction to *The Ordinance Book of the Merchants of the Staple*, pp. 67–8.

13 J. U. Nef, *Rise of the British Coal Industry*, I. 165–89.

14 *Commons Journals*, I. 219.

15 Ehrenberg, *Hamburg und England*, p. 8.

16 'These two-day voyages twice a year, where every pedlar may practise, whereby there is scant either a good mariner or a good ship maintained' – *Hist. MSS. Comm., Pepys MSS.*, p. 39.

17 Williamson, *Hawkins*, pp. 266, 271.

18 *Documents concerning English Voyages* (Hakluyt Soc., 1932).

19 Hakluyt, VIII. 59.

20 *The Troublesome Voyage of E. Fenton* (Hakluyt Soc., 2nd series, CXIII).

21 Lynch, *Spain under the Habsburgs*, I. 302.

Chapter 26

[1] See the table in Elliott, *Imperial Spain*, p. 175.

[2] Murdin, pp. 319-21.

[3] Introduction by A. H. to Digges, *Compleat Ambassador* (1658).

[4] Read, *Burghley*, pp. 208-11, 221, 256; Murdin, pp. 322-31, 336.

[5] Murdin, pp. 336-7.

[6] *Cal. S. P. Foreign*, XV. 279.

[7] *Hist. MSS. Comm., Salisbury MSS.*, II. 358-9, 481.

[8] Digges, p. 391.

[9] *Cal. S. P. Spanish*, III. 159-61.

[10] Read, *Walsingham*, II. 78.

[11] *Cal. S. P. Spanish*, III. 226.

[12] Ibid., p. 243.

[13] Read, *Walsingham*, II. 99.

[14] Ibid., pp. 165-6.

[15] *Cal. S. P. Spanish*, III. 516.

[16] F. Duro, *La Armada Invencible*, I. 241-3.

[17] *Correspondance de Philippe II sur les affaires des Pays Bas* (ed. J. Lefèvre), II. 405-6, 428-9.

[18] *Cal. S. P. Foreign*, XVIII. 579.

[19] See the various memoranda relating to the Privy Council discussions in October 1584, ibid., XIX. 95-9; *Hist. MSS. Comm., Salisbury MSS.*, III. 67-70.

[20] Burghley, March 18th, 1585, in Brit. Mus., Harleian MSS. 168 fo. 102.

[21] Camden, *Annales*, p. 410.

[22] Brit. Mus., Harleian MSS., 168 fo. 102.

[23] *Cal. S. P. Foreign*, XIX. 315.

[24] Ibid., pp. 371-2.

[25] Read, *Burghley*, pp. 318-22.

[26] Dumont, *Corps universel diplomatique*, V. 454-5.

Chapter 27

[1] *Leicester Correspondence* (ed. Bruce; Camden Soc., XXVII), p. 187.

[2] The best account of the earlier (1585-6) negotiations is that by Mrs S. C. Lomas in her preface to *Cal. S. P. Foreign*, XX. See also Read, *Burghley*, chapters 17 and 20, and *Walsingham*, III, chapters 13 and 15.

[3] Instructions to San Clemente, May 6th-16th, 1590 – *List and Analysis of S. P. Foreign*, I. para. 740.

[4] Read, *Walsingham*, III. 125; *Leicester Corresp.*, p. 200.

[5] Read, *Walsingham*, III. 96, 125.

[6] *Cal. S. P. Foreign*, XX. 323.

[7] Ibid., p. 172.

[8] See, in particular, Neale, 'Elizabeth and the Netherlands 1586-7', reprinted in his *Elizabethan Essays*, pp. 170-201. Some of my figures differ slightly from his. For methods of payment, musters, etc., see C. G. Cruickshank, *Elizabeth's Army*.

[9] *Cal. S. P. Foreign*, XX. 394.

[10] Ibid., XXI. ii. 63.

[11] Ibid., p. 248.

[12] Ibid., pp. 62-4, 182-3, 195.

[13] Ibid., pp. 247-9.

[14] *Leicester Corresp.*, pp. 191, 341.

[15] L. Stone, *An Elizabethan; Sir Horatio Palavicino*, chapter 4 for his negotiations.

[16] e.g. *Cal. S. P. Foreign*, XXI. i. 47-8.

[17] The best account is Read, *Walsingham*, III. 1-70.

[18] Nicholas, *Davison*, p. 278.

[19] Williamson, *Hawkins*, pp. 414-16.

[20] *Cal. S. P. Foreign*, IX. 513-14.

[21] Ibid., XXI. iii. 120-3.

[22] Ibid., XXI. i. 323; XXI. iii. 111, 161-2, 185.

[23] Nicholas, *Hatton*, pp. 470-72; more accurately in Read, *Burghley*, pp. 379-80. See also J. D. Gould, 'The Crisis in the Export Trade 1586-7', in *Eng. Hist. Rev.*, LXXI (1956). 212-22.

Chapter 28

[1] *Cal. S. P. Foreign*, XXI. iii. 424.

[2] Read, *Burghley*, p. 420.

[3] *Cal. S. P. Foreign*, XXI. ii. 199; XXI. iii. 57, 425; S. P. Holland, 19 fo. 211; *Acts of the Privy Council*, XV. 176.

[4] *Cal. S. P. Foreign*, XXI. iii. 465.

[5] S. P. Holland, 34 fo. 117.

[6] *Cal. S. P. Foreign*, XXI. iii. 452.

[7] Ibid., XXI. iv. 156.

[8] Ibid. XXI. iv. 168-9; XXII. 275-7.

[9] Ibid., XXI. iv. p. xiii.

[10] *Correspondance de Philippe II sur les affaires des Pays Bas* (ed. Lefèvre), III. 230 ff.

[11] *Cal. S. P. Foreign*. XXI. iii. 18

[12] Ibid., pp. 52, 76.

[13] See Read, *Walsingham*, III. 265-6 for these intrigues.

[14] *Cal. S. P. Foreign*, XXII. 3, 34-7.

[15] Ibid., XXI. iv. p. xxxvii.

[16] *Armada Papers* (Navy Records Soc.), I. 49.

[17] *Cal. S. P. Foreign*, XXI. i. 510, 519-28; *Cal. S. P. Spanish*, IV. 222.

[18] *Hist. MSS. Comm., Salisbury MSS.*, III. 315-17.

[19] On the general question of Stafford's 'treason', see Read in *American Hist. Rev.*,

XX (1915). 292–313 and XXXV (1930). 560–66; Pollard in *Eng. Hist. Rev.*, XVI (1901). 572–7; and Neale in *Eng. Hist. Rev.*, XLIV (1929). 202–20, reprinted in *Elizabethan Essays*, pp. 146–69.

[20] L. Jensen, *Diplomacy and Dogmatism: Mendoza and the French Catholic League*, pp. 133–40.

[21] *Cal. S. P. Spanish*, IV. 319; *Cal. S. P. Foreign*, XXI. i. 629–30, 633–6.

[22] *Cal. S. P. Spanish*, IV. 319–20.

[23] Again, the best account is Boynton, chapters 3 and 4.

[24] *Cal. S. P. Foreign*, XXIII. 381.

[25] *Cal. S. P. Spanish*, IV. 238.

[26] V. Ponko, 'N.S.B. Gras and Elizabethan Corn Policy', in *Econ. Hist. Rev.* (2nd series), XVII. 33.

[27] G. Mattingly, *Defeat of the Spanish Armada*, p. 190.

[28] Read, *Burghley*, p. 418.

[29] M. Lewis, *The Spanish Armada*, pp. 101–2.

[30] S. P. Domestic, 212 no. 63.

[31] Dietz, *Exchequer in Elizabeth's Reign*, pp. 100–1.

[32] S. P. Domestic, 212 no. 66.

Conclusion

[1] Best of all in G. Mattingly, *Defeat of the Spanish Armada* (1959). For the actions, armament, etc., M. Lewis, *Spanish Armada*.

[2] *Armada Papers*, II. 259.

Index

427

etc., 43-4, 86, 150, 167, 256, 308; feuds, 139; castles, 162
Bosworth, 27-9, 32, 51, 77
Bothwell, James Hepburn, earl of, 250, 271-4, 276, 382
Boulogne, 11, 19, 124, 168-9, 189, 196, 265; siege (1492), 36; Henry VIII and, 101, 103, 113, 153, 157-61; cost of, 162, 316, 369; Somerset and, 171-2, 174, 176; loss of, 177, 201, 244; League fails at, 399
Bourbon, Charles, cardinal of, 368, 370
Bourbon, constable of, 103-6, 108
Bourbourg, 394
Brabant, 107, 281, 294, 332, 365-7
Brest, 11, 18, 85, 173, 233, 408
Brielle, 318, 371, 395
Bristol, 74-5, 327
Britain, Great, 164, 291, 302, 309; idea of united, 48, 100; Henry VIII and, 152, 163; Somerset and, 167, 172, 180; Elizabeth and, 258, 263, 273
British Isles, 16, 47, 140, 149, 190-91, 206, 235, 241, 249
Brittany, 27, 53, 95, 153, 169; French designs on, 28, 30; Henry VII and, 32-40, 43, 45-6, 48-9, 55, 64, 70; French annex, 11-12, 19, 114
Broughty castle, 171, 176
Bruges, 66-7, 72, 97-8, 282
Brussels, 142, 154, 195, 289-90, 292-4, 313, 330-31, 367
Buchanan, George, 276
Buckhurst, Thomas Sackville, lord, 387
Buckingham, Thomas Stafford, duke of, 35, 80, 83, 100, 109
Burghley, William Cecil, lord, 260, 344; under Edward VI, 195, 199, 201; secretary, 237; baron, 310; lord treasurer, 324; and Elizabeth, 22, 236-8; and trade, 205, 353; and Catholics,

242, 261, 340; and Calais, 244; and Scots, 248-9, 251-3, 255-7, 309, 380, 399; and Queen's marriage, 259, 310-11, 315, 336, 359; and Mary Stuart, 263-4, 269, 274, 276, 382-3; and Condé, 265; and navy, 279, 342, 386, 402; and Netherlands, 292 ff, 315-17, 319-21, 327, 369-71, 376; coalition against, 297-303, 337; and Ridolfi plot, 312-13; and Drake, 351-2; and peace talks, 374-5, 387; on finance (1588), 403-4, 408
Burgundy, 11, 28, 103, 113, 141, 147, 153

CABOT, JOHN, 74-5
Cabot, Sebastian, 75, 204-5
Cadiz, 82, 225, 350, 380, 384-6
Calais, 11, 19, 37, 48, 93, 171, 217, 246, 252, 316; as staple, 41, 68-9, 118; operations from, 85, 97, 103, 157, 160-61, 196; value of, 95, 101, 244-5; meetings at, 96, 124, 126, 130; defences of, 144, 201; Imperial treaty covers, 153, 177; loss of, 208, 232, 239-40; efforts to regain, 265-7, 295; and Armada, 398, 407
Cambrai, 59, 128, 136, 362, 366
Cambridge, 236
Campeggio, cardinal, 93, 98, 119, 120
Campion, Edmund, 338-9, 357, 363
Canterbury, 77, 123, 142, 281, 362
Carberry Hill, 273-4, 277
Carew, Sir Peter, 213-15, 217
Caribbean, 287-9, 349-50, 354, 371-2, 380, 383
Carlos, Don, 212-13, 266, 268-9
Cartagena, 380
Casket Letters, 276
Castile, 53-9, 69, 71, 80

Clark, Bartholomew, 379
Clement VII, pope, 104, 113–28, 130–31
Cleves, 145–8, 154, 379
Cleves, Anne of, 145–7
Clifford, Sir Robert, 40
Clinton, Edward Fiennes, lord, 217, 232, 256, 351
cloth exports: importance, 20, 218; to Antwerp, 37, 54, 118; Henry VII and, 41, 64–71, 75; boom and slump, 185–90, 197; Northumberland and, 202–5; Philip II and, 226; Elizabeth and, 281–5, 345–8; to Hamburg, 300, 302; and war, 388
Cobham, Henry Brooke, lord, 216, 334–5, 375
Cobham, Sir Henry, 308, 311–12
coinage, 162, 179, 184–5, 187, 190, 197, 201–2, 280, 344
Coligny, Gaspard de, admiral, 301, 315, 320–22
Cologne, 129, 141, 283
Como, cardinal of, 339
Condé, Henry, prince of, 326, 358, 397
Condé, Louis, prince of, 264–7, 271, 281, 295, 301–2
Convocation, 87, 90, 134, 147, 200
Cork, 40, 44
corn, 24, 67, 285, 347, 370
Cornwall, 43–4, 47, 87, 91, 175, 177, 181–2, 184, 189
Coruña, 357, 398, 403
council: French, 115, 242, 315; Netherlands, 301, 313, 327, 371, 379, 387, 391–2; Scottish, 154–5, 257, 273; Spanish, 213, 242, 282, 290–91, 301, 312, 365
Council, General, 79, 81, 90, 123–32, 134–5, 180; of Trent, 159, 166, 176, 181, 197, 260–61, 267
council, king's, 41, 80, 82–3, 92, 102, 105, 115, 117–18; in north, 149, 304; in west, 149; regency, 164, 182

Council, Privy, 181, 291, 295, 384; and trade, 21, 204–5, 281, 353, 388; and foreign policy, 22; under Henry VIII, 142, 144, 146; and Somerset, 164–5, 175, 177; Northumberland and, 193–5, 197, 199; Mary and, 209–13, 215, 217, 219–20; Philip and, 223–6, 228, 230–31; Elizabeth's, 236–9, 298; and Scots, 251–3, 256–7; and Pope, 261; and Mary Stuart, 266, 268–70, 274, 276, 308, 314, 381–2; committees, 278; opposition to Cecil in, 297–9, 303; fear Spain, 308, 324; and Alençon, 333, 335–6, 358–9; and musters, 341–2; and Dutch, 369, 375–6, 390; and Armada, 402–3
Courtenay, Edward, 209–12, 214–15, 217
Cranmer, Thomas, archbishop, 125–6, 145, 182, 200
Crichton, William, 339, 363
Croft, Sir James, 213–15, 249–51, 375, 387, 394
Cromwell, Thomas, 105, 132–4, 137, 142, 144–8, 194, 196, 202
customs duties, 62, 68–75, 144, 200, 203, 280–81, 297, 388

DACRE, Leonard, 303–5
Danzig, 64, 73, 346, 348
Darcy, Thomas, lord, 82
Darnley, Henry Stuart, lord, 259, 269–76, 314, 357, 363, 382
Davis, John, 351, 388
Davison, William, 330, 382–3
Dee, Dr John, 205
Denmark, 72–4, 120, 129, 133, 284, 299, 348, 371, 380–81, 387–8
Derby, Edward Stanley, 3rd earl of, 238
Derby, Henry Stanley, 4th earl of, 394

INDEX

Desmond, Gerald Fitzgerald, earl of, 339
Desmond, James Fitzgerald, earl of, 142
Desmond, John Fitzgerald, earl of, 30, 40, 42
Devon, 175, 177, 181–2, 184, 189
diseases, 150, 160, 401; sweating sickness, 16, 99; plague, 16, 119, 267, 282; dysentery, 84; measles, 85; cancer, 260; smallpox, 266; ague, 304; fever, 380
Dorset, Thomas Grey, marquis of, 84–5
Douai, 230, 238
Dover, 14, 18, 95, 144, 292, 307, 313, 318
Dover, Straits of, 103, 153, 244, 315, 395, 399
Drake, Sir Francis, 25, 342; at San Juan, 288; 1571–3 voyages, 349–50; 1577–80 voyage, 351–4, 357, 369; 1581 plans, 360–62; 1585 voyage, 371–2, 380, 383; 1587 voyage, 384–6, 390, 393; and Armada, 18, 395, 401–3, 407
Drake, John, 353
Drury, Sir William, 308–9, 326
Dudley, Guildford, 193, 206, 219
Dudley, Sir Henry, 229–30
Dumbarton, 155, 162, 172–3
Dunkirk, 131, 232, 386, 394–5

EASTLAND, 284–5, 346; Company, 21, 346–8
Edinburgh, 23, 42, 153, 155–7, 170–72, 174, 248, 250, 254, 256, 263–5, 272–4, 279, 317, 326
Edward V, 29–30
Edward VI, 17, 150, 167, 177, 181–2, 195; birth, 137; and Mary Stuart, 152, 155–6, 169, 171–3, 197; accession, 164; Charles V and, 165–6, 168; Northumberland and, 194, 199; finances, 201; death, 206–7;

councillors of, 237, 299
Egmont, count of, 219, 283, 292
Elbing, 346
Elbœuf, marquis of, 250–52, 254–5, 257, 267
Elizabeth I: birth, 126–8; under Henry VIII, 131, 134, 150; under Edward VI, 168, 176, 206; under Mary, 181, 209, 211–12, 214, 219–20, 224, 228–9; accession, 208, 234; character, 234–6, 239, 358, 373; character of policy, 257, 267, 274–5, 311, 324–5; and marriage, 235, 259–62, 310–11, 359; and succession, 259, 264, 297–8, 304; and councillors, 237–8, 253, 274, 298, 336, 382; foreign prospects, 239–43; makes peace, 244–5; rejects Philip II, 245; religious settlement, 246–7, 278, 337–8; and Scots (1559–60), 247–58; and Archduke Charles, 251, 261–2, 293–4, 298; and Mary Stuart (1561–8), 259–77; breaks with Pope, 260–61; French war, 264–7; ill, 266; and military forces, 23, 278–9, 340–42, 399–400; and navy, 279, 342–4, 349, 401–3; and trade, 280–86, 345–8; and oceanic voyages, 286–9, 295, 349–54; Netherlands dispute (1563–4), 282–3; first Spanish quarrel, 290–322; northern revolt, 297–300, 302–5; and Scots (1570–73), 308–9, 326; Anjou and French alliance, 308–12, 315–17; Norfolk and Ridolfi, 312–14; and Netherlands revolt (1572), 317–19; policy there defined, 315–16, 320–21, 330, 376; and 1572 Massacre, 322, 324–7; and Spain, 327–8; and Netherlands (1573–8), 328–36; and Alençon, 334–6, 358–62, 366–7; Catholic plans against, 338–40;

432

John and, 330; execution, 381–2, 387
Mary Tudor, Queen of France, 59–60, 79, 86–9, 114, 206, 259
Mason, Sir John, 196–7, 238
Matthias, archduke, 331, 333, 335, 358
Maximilian I, emperor, 28–42, 45–6, 52–5, 57–60, 66–8, 79–81, 85–8, 91–4
Medina del Campo, 34, 39, 71
Mediterranean Sea, 16, 25, 141; English trade to, 20, 60, 64–5, 71, 74–5, 204, 347–8, 388; Spain and, 39, 119; Antwerp and, 67; galleys, 85, 287; Turks in, 123, 126, 148, 241, 291, 300, 307; Armada ships and stores from, 384
Medway, river, 63, 101, 386, 402
Melville, Sir James, 89, 261, 270
Mendoza, Bernardino de, 332–3, 339, 360, 362–4, 369, 396–8
Merchant Adventurers, 21; Henry VII and, 41, 65, 67–70; ignore Wolsey, 118; complain of cloth, 188; and slump, 190; Northumberland and, 201–3; under Mary, 226–8; move from Antwerp, 283–6, 300, 302; difficulties of, 346–8, 388
merchants: English. See trade; alien, 64–7, 70, 72, 75, 144, 203, 388; Breton, 40; Italian, 66, 185, 245, 283, 346, 374–5; Netherlands, 282–3, 347, 374; Portuguese, 67, 346; Spanish, 70–72, 282, 307, 314, 346
metals, 226; brass, 280–81, 345; copper, 67, 280–81, 345; iron, 345, 348; tin, 64, 347. See also silver
Metz, 191, 206
Mexico, 288–9, 350, 384
Middelburg, 67, 346, 348
Milan, 106, 148, 211, 225, 227; strategic importance, 16, 95; French win, 52–3, 59; lose, 86;

regain, 89, 91–2; Charles V wins, 102, 114–15, 119, 124, 126, 133, 141; negotiations on, 127, 131, 147
military forces: lack of men, 14, 17, 167–8; Henry VII and, 62; Henry VIII and, 79, 144, 159–160; antiquated, 183–4, 252; loyalty suspect, 189; Northumberland and, 198–9, 201–2, 206; mercenaries, 175–6, 184, 199, 202, 232; Mary and, 230–32; Elizabeth and, 251, 278–9, 340–42, 369; trained bands, 23, 345, 355, 399–401, 404; their organization and cost, 341–2, 344, 390; levies against rebels, 31–2, 43–4, 175–6, 216–17, 304–5; expeditions of Henry VII, 35–6, 40–41, 143–4; of Henry VIII, 81–2, 84–6, 102–5, 150, 152, 154, 157–8, 161–2; of Somerset, 170–71, 173–7; Elizabethan, 23, 253, 256–7, 265–7, 326; to Netherlands, 318, 321, 325; Leicester's, 371, 377–9, 383, 386–7, 389–93
minorities, royal, 16, 30, 51, 67, 99–100, 139, 152, 164, 168, 224
Mohacs, 120
monastic lands: sale of, 25, 144, 162, 184, 201; income from, 133; Irish, 149; effects, 180–81, 187, 209, 220–22, 224
monopolies, 70, 75, 203, 205, 225, 280, 284–5, 345, 348, 388
Mons, 319, 321–2
Montague, Anthony Browne, viscount, 255, 300
Montague, Henry Pole, lord, 138, 142–3
Montgomery, count of, 159, 162
Montmorency, Anne de, 228, 264, 266–7
Montreuil, 153–4, 157–8
Moray, James Stewart, earl of, 248, 262, 264, 271–6, 298, 302–4, 306

INDEX

Trinity House, 18, 101
Tunis, 123, 130
Tunstal, Cuthbert, 106, 109
Turkey, 125; trade to, 20, 185–6, 347–8; talk of crusade against, 59, 79, 93–4; in Hungary, 120, 122–3, 141, 148; in Mediterranean, 123, 141, 148, 204; Francis I and, 126–7, 152–3, 159; Philip II and, 241, 254, 287, 291, 300, 307, 316
Turkey Company, 347–9, 384
Tuscany, 313, 347

UNITED PROVINCES, 369–72, 374–9, 383, 386–92, 394–5
Urswick, Christopher, 33
Utrecht, 64, 283, 332, 379, 386, 389, 392; Union of, 365–7

VARGAS, 363
Vassy, 264
Vaughan, Stephen, 129
Venice, 59–60, 64–5, 71, 74–5, 78–81, 85, 89, 347, 355
Venice Company, 347, 349
Vera Cruz, 350
Verde, Cape, Islands, 372, 380
Vienna, 120, 122–3
Vigo, 372, 380
Villalàr, 96, 100
Virginia, 351, 354
Vitelli, Ciapino, 307

WAAD, WILLIAM, 364
Waal, river, 367, 379
Wales, 149, 214–15
Walloons, 292, 330, 332–3
Wallop, Sir John, 154
Walsingham, Sir Francis, 132, 399, 404; French embassy, 310, 315–16, 319–20; secretary, 324–5; and Netherlands, 328, 331, 333–5, 369–70; and Drake, 351, 380; to France, 361; and Armada, 373, 383; peace feelers, 374–5; and Leicester,

376–7, 393; and Babington plot, 381–2
Warbeck, Perkin, 39–49, 68, 86
Warham, William, archbishop, 83, 90–92, 108, 115
Warwick, Edward, earl of, 31, 39, 44, 219. *See also* Northumberland, John Dudley
weather, 96, 152; importance of, 17–18; and Archduke Philip, 56; and 1545 invasion, 160; and Wyatt, 215; and Elbœuf, 252–5; and Le Havre, 267; and Genoese loan, 296; Pacific, 352; and Hawkins (1586), 384; and Armada campaign, 398, 401–3, 407
Western Approaches, 17–18, 84, 174, 214, 403
Westminster, 27, 122, 179, 194, 276
Westmorland, Charles Neville, earl of, 300, 304–5
Weymouth, 56, 215
Wight, Isle of, 144, 153, 160, 229, 278, 402
Wilkes, Thomas, 331–3, 351, 365, 379, 387
Willoughby, Sir Hugh, 205, 227
Willoughby, Peregrine Bertie, lord, 391–2
Wilson, Dr Thomas, 314
Winchcombe, John, 65; son of, 186–7
Winchester, William Paulet, marquis of, 194, 199, 201, 205, 237
wines, 64–6, 70, 74, 84
Wingfield, Sir Richard, 106, 109
Winter, Sir William, 213, 251–5, 257, 279, 342–3, 349, 351
woad, 66, 70
Wolsey, Thomas, cardinal, 22, 83–5, 88–98, 102–9, 113–22, 148, 186, 239
women rulers, 16, 23, 99–100, 164, 209, 237–8, 261, 298
wool, 64–5, 67, 69, 74, 144, 186, 188, 190, 203, 345, 388

446

Wootton, Edward, 371
Wootton, Dr Nicholas, 197, 256
Wyatt, Sir Thomas, 213–20, 230, 238
Wyndham, Thomas, 204–5, 225

YEOMEN OF THE GUARD, 62–3, 79
York, 140, 150, 264–5, 275–6, 298, 304
York, Richard, duke of, 29–30, 40
Yorke, Rowland, 383, 386
Yorkists, 17, 27–32, 34, 38–49, 54–6, 65, 137–8, 183

Yorkshire, 35–6, 43, 87, 91, 136, 175, 303

ZAPOLYA, JOHN, 120, 122, 129
Zeeland, 107, 252; importance of, 19; offered to Elizabeth, 315–16; revolt of, 318–19, 321, 327–8, 335; Gilbert in, 323, 325, 349; and Don John, 329–30, 332; in Utrecht Union, 365–7; and Leicester, 389, 391–3, 395
Zutphen, 379, 383

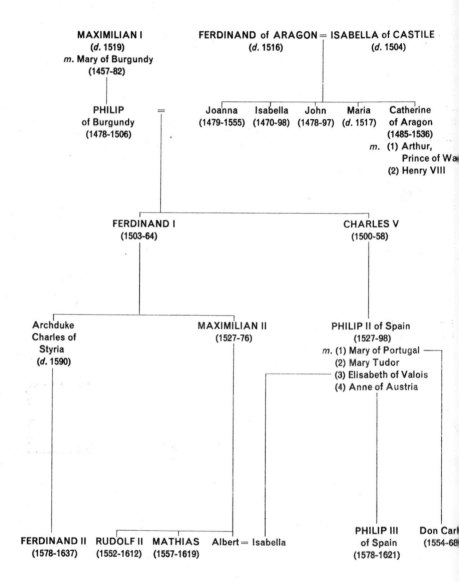

HABSBURGS   SPAIN

MAXIMILIAN I FERDINAND of ARAGON = ISABELLA of CASTILE
(d. 1519)   (d. 1516)   (d. 1504)
m. Mary of Burgundy
(1457-82)

PHILIP = Joanna Isabella John Maria Catherine
of Burgundy (1479-1555) (1470-98) (1478-97) (d. 1517) of Aragon
(1478-1506)   (1485-1536)
             m. (1) Arthur,
               Prince of Wa
             (2) Henry VIII

FERDINAND I   CHARLES V
(1503-64)   (1500-58)

Archduke   MAXIMILIAN II   PHILIP II of Spain
Charles of   (1527-76)   (1527-98)
Styria   m. (1) Mary of Portugal
(d. 1590)   (2) Mary Tudor
           (3) Elisabeth of Valois
           (4) Anne of Austria

FERDINAND II RUDOLF II MATHIAS Albert = Isabella PHILIP III Don Carl
(1578-1637) (1552-1612) (1557-1619)   of Spain (1554-68
               (1578-1621)